The Oprah Phenomenon

THE

oprah

PHENOMENON

Updated Edition

Edited by

Jennifer Harris and Elwood Watson

THE UNIVERSITY PRESS OF KENTUCKY

Publication of this volume was made possible in part by a grant
from the National Endowment for the Humanities.

Editorial and Sales Offices: The University Press of Kentucky
663 South Limestone Street, Lexington, Kentucky 40508-4008
www.kentuckypress.com

13 12 11 10 09   5 4 3 2 1

Library of Congress Cataloging-in-Publication Data

The Oprah phenomenon / edited by Jennifer Harris and Elwood Watson. --
    Updated ed.
      p. cm.
    Includes bibliographical references and index.
    ISBN 978-0-8131-9236-9 (pbk. : alk. paper)
    1. Winfrey, Oprah--Criticism and interpretation. I. Harris, Jennifer, 1971-
II. Watson, Elwood.
    PN1992.4.W56O67 2009
    791.4502'8092--dc22   2009022464

This book is printed on acid-free recycled paper meeting the requirements of the
American National Standard for Permanence in Paper for Printed Library Materials.

Manufactured in the United States of America.

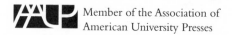   Member of the Association of
                American University Presses

Contents

Part III. Oprah Winfrey on the Page

Foreword

To speak of Oprah Winfrey is to speak in superlatives. She's the richest this, the most powerful that; the first this, the greatest influence on that. What Caesar was to geography, it would seem, Winfrey is to turn-of-the-twenty-first-century culture. Commentators refer to the "Oprahfication" of America much like historians refer to the hellenization of Europe and Asia under Alexander. Winfrey positioned herself at the head of a vast cultural empire and then convinced everybody to confirm that she'd done so. A discussion of Oprah Winfrey nearly always begins with hyperbole.

Oprah Winfrey starts out with one extraordinary gift: the ability to talk to millions of people as though she were directly addressing each of them. Others have had this talent, of course: Arthur Godfrey, Johnny Carson, Fred Rogers, even Walter Cronkite. As these media personalities did, Winfrey uses candor and a virtuoso fluency with the American vernacular to transcend the impersonal nature of electronic media. Television is the perfect medium for her: millions watch it, but they watch one or two at a time, usually in personal domestic spaces. Unlike her TV-savvy predecessors, Winfrey took her ability to be "someone we'd want to invite into our living rooms" and used it as a base camp from which to launch sorties into every nook and cranny of modern communications. With stunning speed, she applied the sophisticated tools of the modern entertainment-industrial complex to become not just a TV star but a lifestyle. It turned out, needless to say, that she was very good at very many things, from acting to publishing.

Long before makeover shows hit prime time, Winfrey realized that a principal theme of the American story is reinvention. From the earliest days of colonial settlement to the mass immigrations of the nineteenth and early twentieth centuries, settlers annihilated their histories, escaped their pasts, and crossed the Atlantic to discover new selves in the new world. In a very real way, the history of the United States is one big makeover show. Oprah Winfrey understood this. Her biography is itself a breathtaking American story of self-creation, and that motif shows up in the earliest iterations of her talk-show persona. Whether through self-awareness, personal resolve, or conscious lifestyle changes, Winfrey's unifying approach to life was one of improvement, actualization, and empowerment, brought about mostly by talking. It worked so well that she extended the franchise, deputizing Dr. Phil to talk away a whole new set of our problems.

Embodied in Oprah Winfrey, and all she has wrought, are all the major themes of contemporary American life: race, gender, and consumerism; celebrity, power, and self-righteousness; optimism, jingoism, and altruism. To approach the subject of Oprah Winfrey is to encounter the possibilities and contradictions of life in the Republic. And it's to encounter them on the exaggerated, super-sized scale of the nation itself.

From the standpoint of the 1950s, the idea that an African American woman would achieve the cultural centrality and power of Oprah Winfrey in just one generation would have seemed highly unlikely. It's a great American story, and like most American stories it's filled with ambiguity and wonder.

Robert Thompson
Syracuse University

Preface to the Updated Edition

Not a day goes by without Oprah Winfrey appearing in the news. Her show topics, guests, charitable endeavors, personal appearances, and reactions to events are all deemed topics in which the general public is or should be interested. Yet, even if a day were to go by where the actions of Winfrey were not deemed newsworthy—if she were to stay home, play with the dogs, and not answer the phone—her name would be inevitably invoked to describe some event, product, or sentiment. The cultural cachet of "Oprah" is such that as a signifier it now bypasses the individual to whom it is attached, instead signaling a whole host of other affiliations.

The cachet of "Oprah" was certainly evident in the days following the November 4, 2008, election of Barack Obama to the U.S. presidency. While networks and newspapers moved to cover the reaction of African American politicians like Jesse Jackson and Colin Powell, it was Oprah Winfrey's enthusiastic response that received the most press coverage: "It feels like something big and bold has happened here . . . like nothing ever in our lifetimes!" proclaimed Winfrey.[1] In an unprecedented move, Winfrey campaigned for Barack Obama, declaring him "my candidate." In endorsing Obama, Winfrey extended her brand to him, encouraging voters to associate him with the same values of personal integrity and social responsibility she promotes on her show. While few voters admitted to being swayed by celebrity endorsements, of those who did, 34 percent of women and 32 percent of men claimed Winfrey influenced their vote, making her the most prominent of all such individuals.[2]

It is a case of how the more things change, the more things stay the same. Winfrey is still the most influential African American woman in the United States; she simply now has the ear of a president—or at least his e-mail: "I'm just hoping the email address doesn't change!" she quipped.[3] She remains wealthy beyond the imaginings of all but a few, making almost \$400 million a year by some estimates. And her media empire shows no sign of slowing down: as her show enters its twenty-fifth year in 2010–2011, Winfrey is poised to launch a cable channel, the Oprah Winfrey Network (OWN), in partnership with Discovery Communications.[4] Her cultural and financial capital remains secure, and while criticisms are ongoing, she continues to weather them. Even as professional scandalmonger Kitty Kelley is publishing an unauthorized biography of Winfrey, she reputedly had difficulty finding enough relevant dirt of the kind that characterizes her previous works.[5] A measure of Oprah Winfrey's iconic status is the likelihood that nothing Kelley exposes will in any way affect her influence or empire.

As the cover of the December 31, 2000, issue of *Newsweek* proclaimed, we are in an "Age of Oprah" and "she is influencing more lives than ever."[6] Winfrey is, in many ways, so pervasive in our culture as to become invisible; we have stopped noticing how extraordinary it is that a single person who does not hold political office can influence our world so remarkably. The essays contained within this volume encourage readers to reflect upon this process, to consider what it means to be an inhabitant, for better or worse, of the "Age of Oprah."

Notes

1. Both Winfrey's response and the extreme journalists went to in obtaining it are covered here: April MacIntyre, "Oprah Talks about Obama," *Monsters and Critics,* November 6, 2008, http://www.monstersandcritics.com/people/news/article_1441328.php/Oprah_talks_about_Obama (accessed November 8, 2008).

2. "Majority of Voters Say Celebrity Endorsements Played No Role in their Decision," *MediaCurves.com,* November 7, 2008, http://www.mediacurves.com/Politics/J7099-CelebsPolitics/Index.cfm (accessed November 8, 2008).

3. "Oprah Talks about Obama"; for an example of her recent influences on sales, see Dan Gallagher, "Amazon Rating Cut on Valuation Despite Sell-Off," *MarketWatch,* November 6, 2008, http://www.marketwatch.com/News/Story/Story.aspx?guid=%7BD174B9BC-E4E5-4912-B633-18DF95AB935B%7D (accessed November 8, 2008).

4. Mike Flaherty, "Oprah Signing Off in 2011?" *Variety,* November 7, 2008, http://www.variety.com/article/VR1117995470.html?categoryid=14&cs=1 (accessed November 8, 2008).

5. Bill Zwecker, "Tell-all Biographer Kitty Kelley Claims Book Won't Be Hatchet Job," *Chicago Sun-Times,* November 14, 2008, http://www.suntimes.com/entertainment/1278988,CST-FTR-zp14.article (accessed November 15, 2008).

6. Janice Peck takes this as the title of her recent book on the subject: *The Age of Oprah: Cultural Icon for the Neoliberal Era* (Boulder, Colo.: Paradigm Publishers, 2008).

Introduction

Oprah Winfrey as Subject and Spectacle

Jennifer Harris and Elwood Watson

For a brief moment in 2002, President George W. Bush faced one of his most savvy media opponents to date: Oprah Winfrey. According to the White House, Winfrey declined to join an official U.S. delegation scheduled to tour the schools of Afghanistan and draw attention to the subordinate role of Afghani women, claiming "she didn't have the time."[1] The news item was quickly disseminated, as befitting anything that tied together so many newsworthy elements: refusing a request of the U.S. president, rebuilding Afghanistan, and Oprah Winfrey herself. The attempt of the White House to draw on Winfrey's cultural currency to galvanize public sentiment is telling; although the mission was ostensibly a gender-based humanitarian one, officials candidly admitted that the "Winfrey strategy" was intended to "dampen images of global violence." Photos of Winfrey extending her ubiquitous open-armed embrace to the citizens of Afghanistan would undoubtedly advance the notion that the Untied States had succeeded in a mission that was really about embracing the people of Afghanistan, welcoming them into the loving fold of democracy and liberty. That an alliance with Winfrey and her audience was primary, and the actual humanitarian mission secondary, was evident from the cancellation of the tour—which was to include Karen Hughes and Condoleezza Rice—after Winfrey declined the invitation.

In some ways, even more interesting than the choice of Winfrey as a revamped Statue of Liberty is the way the White House chose to "leak" this information, and the aftermath of its revelation. Announcing the failure of an event that had never been public knowledge in the first place seems pointless, yet that is exactly what happened. Seemingly a conciliatory gesture to the group of Americans most alienated by "the constant talk of death and brutality in the war on terrorism"—namely, women—the reporting of the failed overture to Winfrey had an unintended result. Instead of advancing the profile of the Bush administration by linking the president's name with the nation's most important media arbiter of female sympathy and liberal humanism, the critique of Winfrey implicit in the announcement—"she didn't have the time"—caused the subject herself to speak out in dissatisfaction, ultimately stating that she "felt extremely used by the Bush administration."[2]

Remarkably, Winfrey chose not to answer the administration's implicit criticism directly; she has remained studiously bipartisan through multiple elections, so an overt counterattack would have been uncharacteristic. Instead, she defeated Bush's accusations through the medium of which she is master (or perhaps mistress)—the networks of women who watch female-centered daytime talk shows. Thus, it was not Winfrey but Star Jones of ABC's highly rated talk show *The View* who answered the implicit charge that Winfrey, known for her philanthropic and caring persona, did not in fact care enough. The *Chicago Tribune* broke the story on Friday, March 29, and the Associated Press immediately picked it up; on Tuesday morning, Jones announced that she had received a call from her friend Winfrey, who had explained that the proposed trip conflicted with other charity commitments. According to Jones, Winfrey was unaware that her inability to participate would result in the trip's cancellation and was displeased with the administration's representation of her as indifferent. By the end of the day, the story had effectively been "killed," and any criticism of Winfrey's refusal effectively muted—not by a published or even firsthand rebuttal, but by the power of women's daytime talk.

"Quiet as it's kept," Toni Morrison writes, a phrase that precedes the telling of some outrageous story or publicly traded gossip.[3] "Quiet as it's kept," Jones's version of Winfrey's words effectively undercut all the more "official" and "serious" media coverage.[4] Moreover, Jones's rebuttal on Winfrey's behalf demonstrates the authority that many female viewers invest in the power of women's friendships as mediated by the talk-show format. It was "enough" to hear Jones's version because both Jones and the viewer are friends of Winfrey—indeed, such friends that her last name is redundant, if not entirely absent, when thinking about her.[5] Jones merely completed the circle of information trading that is common within women's friendships. It is clear that although the Bush administration understood the power of an affiliation with Oprah Winfrey and her legions of fans, it did not anticipate or appreciate the way the relationship between Winfrey and her viewers functions to instigate a counternarrative in which the administration appears manipulative and possibly even boorish.

This momentary underestimation of Winfrey is telling. As many of the contributors to this anthology document, Winfrey has consistently surpassed all expectations in her climb from rural poverty to media dominance. Yet popular discussions of her success often frame it as the result of a "natural" gendered ability to connect emotionally with audiences, eliding the media savvy and business acumen Winfrey has demonstrated in parlaying that capacity to connect into a media empire. This appears to be exactly the trap the Bush administration fell into, attempting to benefit from the cachet of Winfrey without considering her careful control of her own cultural capital. After all, Winfrey does not simply turn viewers into self-designated "friends"; rather, in the process of constructing a relationship with her audience, she transforms them into loyal consumers. Ironically, she is so successful at what she does that many in her audience read her television persona as "real," as unmediated by the very media forces that bring her to them: television, cinema, magazines, and Internet. This imagined relation results in what Louann Haarman identifies as a parasocial relationship, "whereby viewers relate to the media personalities as if they actually know them." Discussing Winfrey, Haarman notes that key to this process is "the construction of the host as 'normal' and accessible, one of us."[6]

Winfrey's biography, as popularly disseminated, enforces this trend of reading her as "normal." Still, it simultaneously asserts her exceptionality in its trajectory. Indeed, Oprah Gail Winfrey's biography reads as an exemplary narrative of triumph in the face of adversity, and it provides the basis of her authority as an advocate of the self-help model of individual improvement. Born to an unwed mother in Kosciusko, Mississippi, in 1954, Winfrey was initially raised by her Baptist grandmother. At the age of six, Winfrey was sent to join her mother in Milwaukee, and for several years she was shuffled between her parents. It was in Milwaukee that she was repeatedly sexually abused. Acting out, she ran away and, at age thirteen, was sent to live permanently with her disciplinarian father in Nashville. At fourteen she gave birth to a premature baby; it died shortly thereafter. However, it was also in Nashville that Winfrey began to improve under the supervision of her father and stepmother, excelling academically and socially.

Winfrey's interest in a media career emerged at this time. After viewing Barbara Walters on the *Today* show, Winfrey decided that journalism was her future. She began working at a local African American radio station, WVOL.[7] Subsequently, while studying on a full scholarship to Tennessee State University, Winfrey was offered a position at a local television station. As the Oprah Web site makes patently clear, this was a breakthrough. Her online biography tellingly begins not with her troubled childhood but with her first career triumph, thus foregrounding its fundamental import: "At the age of 19, she became the youngest person and the first African-American woman to anchor the news at Nashville's WTVF-TV."[8] By 1976, Winfrey was a coanchor in Baltimore, and in 1978 she established herself not just as an on-air figure but as an on-air *personality*, as host of WJZ-TV's *People Are Talking*. In January 1984 Winfrey was poached by WLS-TV as the new host of *AM Chicago*. Her success was evident by the fact that within a year it had been renamed *The Oprah Winfrey Show*.

The significance of Winfrey's achievement cannot be underestimated. Historically, African American women had not been accepted as television hosts by white viewers. Pearl Bailey, Barbara McNair, and Della Reese had all hosted eponymous shows between 1969 and 1971, none of which lasted more than a year.[9] However, the 1980s saw a rise in the number of nonwhite interviewers and hosts, including Bryant Gumbel, Ed Bradley, Arsenio Hall, Sally Jessy Raphael, and Geraldo Rivera. Winfrey was the first African American woman in this cohort to rise to prominence. And not only did she rise; she excelled. What most impressed the Chicago station was Winfrey's ability to go head-to-head in ratings with the era's most popular talk show, *The Phil Donahue Show*, and prevail. Within two months of her arrival in Chicago, she was "garnering 265,000 viewers to Donahue's 147,230." The trend continued as *The Oprah Winfrey Show* went national in 1986 and soon became the top-ranked show in the genre, "Oprah" replacing "Donahue" as a household name.[10]

As the first television talk show to be syndicated (in 1969), *The Phil*

Donahue Show dominated the airwaves throughout the 1970s and early 1980s. It was groundbreaking in its focus on topical social issues and in the host's circulation through the audience to solicit responses and questions.[11] Even the choice of host was innovative; before the arrival of Phil Donahue, talk shows had been the purview of entertainers—Johnny Carson, Mike Douglas, Merv Griffin, Dinah Shore, and the like. As a journalist, Donahue was less interested in entertaining than in educating, soberly sympathizing with guests about what had previously been private issues. Although Donahue pioneered the sympathetic model of talk-show relations, many found his show to be tinged with the paternalism he inevitably invoked. In this way, he was unlike the entertainers-turned-hosts, whose relationship with viewers was far more sociable, premised on shared jokes and humorous anecdotes.

From the first, Winfrey's style differed markedly from Donahue's, drawing on the entertainers' approach of genially engaging the audience. As a host, Winfrey combines her training in journalism with her love of performance, creating the persona of an empathetic and accessible interlocutor. These tactics have proved successful, first garnering ratings and then awards. Furthermore, unlike Donahue, Winfrey opens up to the audience, talking to the camera as one would to a friend—and she does so in her own distinct communicative style that facilitates her relationship with the audience. Notably, Winfrey rhetorically identifies herself with viewers, does not talk down to them, and assumes a shared surprise at new discoveries. In this way, she presents herself not as an informed expert but as an informed witness-participant. Jane M. Shattuc analyzes such practices of verbal identification in a representative episode, observing:

> Winfrey slowly invokes the audience as a larger social collectivity. She directs the debate toward social issues through her selection of questioners and specifically through the rhetorical use of pronouns "you," "I," and "we." To illustrate she says, "I am sure what mothers out there are thinking," or "When I first heard about this, like everybody, I wondered what the big deal is," or (my favorite because it is Winfrey at her most self-aggrandizing), "The question we all have, I am speaking for the audience here and the audience around the world listening."[12]

Although Shattuc finds Winfrey self-aggrandizing in her pronouncements, her viewers appear to identify with the spirit of inclusion she exudes rather than be insulted at being spoken for. One reason they might hesitate to take offense is the accessible vernacular Winfrey often uses to voice such pronouncements. As Andrew Tolson remarks, "she displays a tactile intimacy with her studio audience and has several 'voices' ranging from the formal and serious to the playful black vernacular."[13] The use of an informal vernacular intensifies the intimacy of the show, undercutting the pretense of claiming to speak for all by doing so in speech patterns coded as friendly or even familial.

The parasocial relationship viewers imagine with Winfrey is no doubt assisted by her seeming willingness to collapse the boundaries between the public and the private. This is nowhere more obvious than in her on-air confession in 1986 of being sexually abused, an unprecedented spontaneous revelation by a public figure. In what would come to be recognized as a characteristic move, Winfrey famously transformed this personal trauma into an opportunity for raising public awareness, producing *Scared Silent: Exposing and Ending Child Abuse* (1992), the first documentary to air simultaneously on three networks. Likewise, Winfrey has been remarkably forthcoming about other aspects of her life and her struggles; viewers have not only witnessed her fluctuating body weight but also been privy to her disappointment with various diets, her sense of defeat in the face of aggressive personal trainers, and her inability to resist the comfort foods she loves. Her ongoing confessions of a lack of self-esteem resonate with many viewers and further their sense of commonality and connection.

And yet, we can never forget that Winfrey is also an entertainer. As open as she might be about her insecurities, she is just as reticent to discuss her longtime fiancé Stedman Graham and their life together. Similarly, she does not casually disclose aspects of the lives of her better-known friends. Winfrey's posture of intimacy, then, though seemingly unmediated and natural, is in fact self-consciously constructed—even as her emotional responses might be genuine. As one writer notes of her initial forays in news reporting, "She *really* wanted to be an actress—a person whose job it was to *show* emotion and *live* a story. She never really wanted to be *outside* things that were happening, an observer equipped with cold-blooded objectivity."[14] Beyond her role on *The Oprah Winfrey Show,* Winfrey has realized this dream, appearing as Sofia in Steven Spielberg's cinematic adaptation of Alice Walker's novel *The Color Purple* in 1985 (for which she received an Academy Award nomination). Subsequent roles in *Native Son* (1986) and *The Women of Brewster Place* (1989) proved less critically successful, but Winfrey emerged from the latter as an experienced producer of television movies. Although moviegoers were insufficiently supportive of her attempt to bring Toni Morrison's *Beloved* (1998) to the big screen, her small-screen productions have been particularly popular. Most recently, she has extended her reach to the stage, producing a Broadway adaptation of *The Color Purple*.[15] Notably, her name appears on the marquee over that of the musical and in place of Alice Walker's, suggesting that although Walker may have authored the book, Winfrey authored the performance. What this ongoing investment in drama highlights is Winfrey's conception of herself as a performer. Consequently, emoting is part of her job, and it is the arena in which she has surpassed all her competitors to date.

Even as Winfrey is primarily thought of in terms of her empathetic persona, her position as a media maven is well known. She has a net worth of $1.3 billion, according to *Fortune*.[16] Her tours are sold out; her show draws thirty million viewers a week in the United States alone and is aired in more than a hundred other countries. *O, the Oprah Magazine* boasts a paid circulation of more than two million, and being named as an Oprah's Book Club selection has the power to catapult any work to the top of the *New York Times* best-seller list, including an 838-page novel by a Russian author who has been dead for almost a century.[17] As one journalist noted, "*The Oprah Winfrey Show* rakes in $6 million a week in domestic and international licensing for her Harpo and Viacom-owned K World, which syndicates her show. That works out to more than $300,000,000 per year."[18] Together, these factors lead to Winfrey's presence, even omnipresence, in American culture. As Beretta E. Smith-Shomade notes:

> No other name (except perhaps O. J.) commanded comparable national recognition in the late-twentieth-century pop culture. *Time* magazine lamented the "full Oprahization" of American politics; *Publishers Weekly* claimed an "Oprah Effect" over book sales; the "Oprah Factor" may have impacted the merger between New World Communications and King

World, as well as *Time*'s subsequent buying of the distributor; and Christopher Buckley satirized a fictional conversation between Oprah and Pope John Paul II as "Poprah." Because the name, actuality, and talk show of Oprah Winfrey resonate with people, the mere annunciation "Oprah" conjures the sublime experience of self-help, authority, and release. Depending on the context, the name transforms from subject to verb to adjective.[19]

Given this pervasiveness and influence, it seems logical that the administration of a Texas-bred president would have been more cautious in thwarting such a woman; after all, Winfrey had already taken on the powers of Texas once, and won. As the essay by Jennifer Richardson makes clear, Winfrey is beloved by so many of her viewers that even after seriously injuring the Texas cattle industry with an offhand remark about mad cow disease—"It has just stopped me cold from eating another burger!"—many Texans still enthusiastically embraced her.

As the Texas cattle episode demonstrates, it is not simply that viewers watch *The Oprah Winfrey Show* to be entertained; rather, they value the host's opinions and admit to being influenced by them. Although the power of female consumers and the import of brand loyalty have long been known to advertisers, it was not anticipated that an upstart public figure might command from the public such personal loyalty as to direct their lifestyle choices independent of any outside sponsor. Some see this as an insidious trend, indicative of the worst aspects of modern market capitalism and media influence.

Others worry about the degree to which Winfrey links the need to value oneself with the consumption of goods, as evidenced by the promotion of her favorite products in *O* magazine and on *The Oprah Winfrey Show*. This message of uplift via consumption is one that can be directed only at those classes with the financial ability to realize it. Those who cannot assert their value through the purchase of Winfrey-endorsed goods can look to her spiritual counseling for affirmation, but the underlying message of her biography and show demonstrates one of the fundamental principles of the American Dream: if I am self-actualized and work hard, good things will come to me.[20] And, of course, good things are not simply internal in this construction; they are also external and often very, very pretty. Winfrey's success, then, is evident not only in her position of power, or her exercising of purchasing power, but also in her ability to convince others that mirroring her purchasing habits will bring them closer to her and, by extension, the success she represents.

In this way, Winfrey, a woman of enormous wealth and financial power, participates in the mystification of the marketplace, reconfiguring the buying of good things as an assertion of one's own worth and one's demonstration of that worth through the use of capital in a way that proclaims taste and sentiment. This homespun approach to the exercise of capital—valuing money not for the status it confers but rather for its ability to treat one's hardworking self as it deserves to be treated—is characteristic of her approach to the world of business, which she does not appear to find compelling for its own sake. As an article in *Fortune* observed:

> You'd be hard pressed to find another American chief executive this disarming, this confessional. But it's oh-so-Oprah. Sitting in an overstuffed armchair in her office in Harpo Inc.'s Chicago headquarters, her two cocker spaniels lying at her feet, the chairman swears that if she is a businesswoman, it's in spite of herself. She happily admits that she cannot read a balance sheet. She has no corporate role models. She's kissed Tom Cruise and more than one world leader, but she has never even met Jack Welch or Michael Dell. She's declined invitations from AT&T, Lauren, and Intel to sit on their corporate boards. . . . And she's so wary of investing her own money in the stock market that she once hoarded $50 million in cash, calling it her personal "bag-lady fund."[21]

Obviously, Winfrey is less interested in celebrating corporate knowhow and power than she is in generating and managing its charitable, cultural, and educative counterpart—making money for the pleasure of giving it away. Perhaps this is one reason why it is so easy to buy into the idea that purchasing "Oprah" goods is the equivalent of doing good—the belief that one's dollars will assist in uplifting others, even as one is uplifted by the very process of "Oprah" consumption.

Surprisingly, this public and financial capital has yet to produce a sizable backlash against Winfrey, as it has in the case of Martha Stewart, who also dispenses lifestyle advice in various media. This is not to say that Winfrey has evaded critics. Shortly after the Texas debacle, in an article for the *National Review,* Mark Steyn invoked the language of infection to describe Winfrey's ever-expanding cultural influence:

> In a little more than a decade, Oprah has spread AIDS-like into every nook and cranny of American life. Well, not exactly AIDS-like; she's more the opposite of HIV—whatever she infects grows as plump and bloated as she at her most corpulent. Even the sleepy backwater of American letters: people who hadn't bought a book in ten, twenty years started buying them simply on her say-so. . . . Recently, the publishing industry discovered that, when Oprah recommends a book, not only does that title hit the best-seller charts but so do unrelated books with similar names. . . . If Oprah were to endorse a self-help book called How to Stop Buying Books Just because Your Favorite TV Host Recommends Them, You Pathetic, Craven Loser, it would be an instant best-seller.[22]

Although Steyn's choice of metaphor demonstrates a patent hostility toward Winfrey, paradoxically, he does not criticize her or her choices. Instead, the subjects of his diatribe are the followers of Oprah Winfrey, whom he sees as improperly or insufficiently oriented. As essays in this volume on the Jonathan Franzen book club episode, by Sarah Robbins, and *The Man Show,* by Valerie Palmer-Mehta, demonstrate, such criticisms of Winfrey's sway are often gendered, made by men based on assumptions about her viewers as women.

Notably, when criticisms of Winfrey as an *individual* are voiced, they do not focus on her business practices, her ambition, her means of achieving success, her treatment of employees, her sexuality, or the degree to which her persona is manufactured—all of which are generally evoked when deriding successful women, including Martha Stewart. But whereas Stewart "fell" in the face of federal prosecution, Winfrey, in addition to weathering the White House's not-so-subtle imprecations, has survived the litigation of *Texas Beef v. Oprah Winfrey,* the cultural criticism of Franzen, the online chat room complaints that she is an unqualified "know-it-all," and the accusation that she finds validation in knowingly pandering to an audience composed of predominantly upper-middle-class white women.

Of all the aforementioned charges against Winfrey, both formal and informal, the one that she is a know-it-all is most intriguing, and the one that she privileges a white audience has been most debated. Calling Winfrey a know-it-all is not simply a matter of challenging her knowledge about a number of topics; rather, it involves questioning the basis of her authority, which is generally figured as her experience of psychic pain. This pain might be rooted in the physical—whether it be the effects of poverty, racism, sexual abuse, low self-esteem, or weight—but it is the survival of the psychic legacy and her victory over it that give Winfrey the credibility to speak authoritatively on any number of social issues. Academics have, in their own way, voiced a similar charge, reframing "know-it-all" in terms of Winfrey presenting herself as a self-actualized exemplar via her triumphant biography. In doing so, they argue, she "elides the real-life barriers to success and wealth confronted by the majority of African Americans," thereby "blaming the oppressed for their failures."[23] Moreover, in presenting the self as the locus of change, the show actually serves to "individualize what should be understood as social issues."[24]

Key among the issues Winfrey personalizes is racism, whereby racism in the world of *The Oprah Winfrey Show* becomes "a result of individual opinions, experience, and rights. Ending racism, for the talk show, becomes a matter of healing oneself of prejudice as opposed to collective political change."[25] It is this formulation of the individual as responsible for individual change that makes the show so amenable to white viewers, who are thus absolved of their implication in a larger social structure that disenfranchises nonwhites. Those who see Winfrey as facilitating such white liberal humanism have charged her with enacting the racially loaded persona of the "mammy" for white consumption. As evidence, they point to her on-air behavior: crying with her audience, indoctrinating them into the black vernacular, sharing African American communal knowledge, and—in 1994, following the adoption of a new format designed to facilitate self-improvement—ministering to them. In a 1989 profile of Winfrey for the *New York Times Magazine,* Barbara Grizzuti Harrison wrote:

> In a racist society, the majority needs, and seeks, from time to time, proof that they are loved by the minority whom they

have so long been accustomed to oppress, to fear exaggerat-
edly, or to treat with real or assumed disdain. They need that
love, and they need to love in order to believe that they are
good. Oprah Winfrey—a one-person demilitarized zone—has
served that purpose.[26]

This formulation of Oprah-as-mammy makes some uneasy because it denies Winfrey's individuality while also positing that there
is little if any space for imagined reciprocal relations between a black
female talk-show host and a white female audience. Still, it is undeni-
able that some of those white women (and men, who are often omitted
in discussions of *Oprah* viewers) who imagine a reciprocal relationship
with Winfrey may be aided in this endeavor by what seems to be her
subsuming of racial issues under the rubric of liberal humanism. Nevertheless, we cannot forget that this is the dominant discourse of daytime
talk shows, which are designed, above all, to engage and entertain their
primary audience—not alienate them.

In contrast to those who would condemn Winfrey for her acceptance by white audiences, some critics wonder to what degree popular media figures are ever responsible for the fantasies their audiences
project on them. Another contingent speculates that Winfrey subverts
the expectations of whites so subtly that they are not even aware that
their perceptions are being altered. They point to projects such as the
film version of *Beloved,* which Winfrey produced and starred in, as more
overt manifestations of the rejection of easy formulations of racial harmony. Some have noted that Winfrey's is the most race conscious of
all the daytime talk shows. And yet, although her racial authenticity
is not generally criticized—unlike that of other celebrities and politicians, such as Michael Jackson, Condoleezza Rice, O. J. Simpson, and
Clarence Thomas—she has been accused of not adequately privileging
African Americans over their white peers. Accordingly, commentary on
her racial projects is often guarded. As Shattuc writes:

It would be difficult to describe Oprah—an internationally
syndicated show—as an African-American institution, even
though the host is black, the production company (Harpo
Productions) is owned by a race-conscious black woman, and
its staff dominated by people of color. As Peck argues, the show

neutralizes its racial elements through the leveling effect of individualist ideology. Nevertheless it routinely features black experts who often become the site of political resistance.[27]

Whatever the intent of Winfrey herself, it is clear that statements that might generate uneasy laughter from an audience if uttered by a Chris Rock—such as her comments about obscured black ancestry: "a lot of you all white people in the country is black and didn't know it. And its shaking people up, let me tell you"—are met by her predominantly white studio audience with comfortable laughter.[28] This laughter suggests that they are "in" on the joke. And in a sense, they are: Oprah Winfrey has let them in—to her life, to her studio, and to a community that she promotes on air and in print. The reward for any devoted viewer, regardless of race, is precisely this sense of community and belonging as manufactured by Harpo Productions.

Yet, just as Winfrey is mediated and produced as "Oprah" in part through her audience, this imagined white liberal audience is also in part an imaginary production. Despite any claims to the contrary, "belonging" in the world of Winfrey is patently not the territory of white viewers alone; as Tarshia Stanley's essay asserts, a significant component of her viewers is African American. Further, although some may imagine Winfrey's public persona as oriented primarily toward middle-class white women and white millionaire celebrities such as Tom Hanks, John Travolta, Brad Pitt, and Julia Roberts, Winfrey continually positions herself within a network of black friends, many of whom are coded as family. Viewers know that while Winfrey may be their best friend, Gayle King is hers. Although we frequently see her paired in flirtatious on-screen interviews with white men, Stedman Graham is her fiancé. Patti LaBelle has Winfrey over for dinner; the late Luther Vandross gave her Lalique crystal. Winfrey's show also privileges other African American affiliations, both spiritual and intellectual, most notably her production of African American cinema and her enthusiastic inclusion of Toni Morrison's novels in her original book club—which featured a disproportionate number of books by African American authors overall, when compared to the U.S. population.

That Winfrey manages to position herself within a black cultural context that acknowledges the historical forces of racism (as Morrison's books do, for instance) without alienating her majority white viewers is telling. It speaks to the way Winfrey creates the opportunity for sympathetic identification across a variety of differences, including racial differences. It is this ability that the Bush administration wanted to capitalize on when it invited Winfrey to be the face of an American-led reconstructed Afghanistan. Nothing, it seems, says American values like the image of Oprah Winfrey.

The Phenomenon of Oprah

Nowhere is the complexity of Winfrey's success and the fascination it engenders more obvious than in the diversity of academic attention paid to her and her cultural and media productions. Her book club, her style of communication, her biography, and her relationship with her viewers have all prevailed as academic concerns. This collection includes and expands on those concerns as a means of better understanding the production, circulation, consumption, and reception of the phenomenon that has come to be known as "Oprah." Yet the essays themselves are not unified in opinion; it is appropriate that, given the contested nature of the discourse that surrounds Winfrey as a racial subject, a philanthropist, a nurturing host, and the like, our contributors are divided in their range of responses. Some are critical of the way *The Oprah Winfrey Show* functions to elide matters of race and class, and others see Winfrey as a bridge across racial and class differences; some condemn her promotion of material goods as a way to salvation, and others read her spirituality as empowering. It is not our position as editors to enforce conformity; rather, the dissonance of these essays is indicative of the ambivalence Winfrey invokes in many viewers, as Tarshia Stanley notes in the first essay of this volume. We hope that because these essays both complement and contradict one another, they will serve to dislocate simple endorsements or rejections of Winfrey and facilitate further engaged readings of her iconic presence in American culture.

Despite our desire to create a space of critical dissonance, we have not abandoned order altogether. Part I of this volume considers Winfrey as a racial and gendered subject in three essays considering her reception by black women, white women, and white and black men. Part II shifts to a discussion of the on-stage presentation of Winfrey and the self, approached through a variety of critical perspectives and cultural forms. Finally, part III deals with Winfrey and the medium of print. As many of our contributors suggest, Winfrey is not presented as merely an individual or a cultural force; she is also seen as representing a lifestyle, or a series of strategies, and, importantly, as a way of being.

Oprah Winfrey and Race

For many viewers, crucial to Winfrey's way of being is her relation to race—or, rather, how that relation is perceived. Nowhere is this more evident than in the Winfrey-Hermès brouhaha of 2005. In a much-publicized incident, Winfrey was denied access to the store by both a sales clerk and the store manager as it was closing, even though other shoppers lingered inside. The initial New York Post coverage claimed that Winfrey had been told by a salesperson that the store had been "having a problem with North Africans lately"—a report that both Winfrey and Hermès disclaimed. Regardless, the fact that Winfrey had been refused entry raised questions about race; it was evident to many commentators—Winfrey included—that race had been the impetus for the incident.[29] By the same token, other, less generous commentators accused the star of forgetting that she is black, and they crowed over such a forceful reminder.[30] What these commentators ignored is that Winfrey's race is frequently invoked in attacks on her, perpetrated not in person but certainly in public. For instance, radio host Don Imus has periodically referred to Winfrey using such racially charged phrases as "brown cow." Rather than seeing the Hermès incident in this context, as simply one of many attacks, it was treated as an isolated moment in which Winfrey's celebrity failed to shield her from racial discrimination.

Interestingly, in the United States, the experience of racism is often linked to one's racial authenticity. Yet Winfrey's inability to "buy" her way out of racial attacks via her celebrity or financial clout has not excluded her from criticism about the status of her racial identification. Nor has her philanthropy—including donating millions of dollars to historically black colleges and universities—protected her from charges of racial inauthenticity. Indeed, some of her staunchest critics have gone so far as to declare that she has "abandoned blackness." This criticism has been countered by a number of black publications that consistently acknowledge Winfrey's efforts on behalf of other African Americans. Writes one journalist:

> Oprah, of course, has never left the sisterhood, despite the sniping of player haters who say things like "She's not really Black" or "She treats White people better than Black people." This has always been one of the burdens of Black success: Black resentment.[31]

Winfrey is not oblivious to these criticisms. In an interview with a leading African American publication, she responded to what she saw as her unjust treatment by some African Americans:

> When I first started, everything I did was criticized and talked about particularly by Black people. People would say, "Oh, she's hugging the white people too much," or "She goes to the White people in the audience more" or "she doesn't have enough Black guests on the show." So now when I see these shows where Black people are brought on to be purposely degraded, I wonder where is the outcry now?[32]

In a leading African American women's magazine, she made a similar confession:

> That was the hardest thing for me in the beginning. I used to get criticism all the time. People saying you're not doing enough for other Blacks. I remember going to Sidney Poitier early on and saying, "God, I just can't handle this." It was Maya Angelou who told me, "You alone are enough. You don't have to explain anything else." I finally got it. Just because you're part of my culture doesn't mean you can decide for me. White people don't decide for me. Nobody decides for me. I get to decide for myself. Once I got that, I was free.[33]

As these comments suggest, the most intense criticism of Winfrey—much of it ambivalent—has come from within the African American community. In "The Specter of Oprah Winfrey: Critical Black Female Spectatorship," contributor Tarshia Stanley considers why black women, who recognize Winfrey's achievement and genuine desire to do good, experience ambivalence when watching her show or encountering traces of her public persona in popular culture. According to Stanley, theorists of black visual spectatorship have long identified the spectacular modes of observation practiced by African Americans. Whether black people's engagement with their imagery as represented in film and on television has been acquiescent or resistant, reconstructive or unconscious, black folks are experts at screening themselves and their communities. In the case of Winfrey and her iconographic presence, Stanley suggests, black audiences have either absented themselves from engaging in serious critiques of such a production or been unusually dismissive. According to Stanley, there are no on-screen opportunities for such ambivalence to express itself; thus, it is either internalized or expressed through communal critique.

Stanley's essay posits that key to understanding this interpretive morass is the ambivalence inherent in a viewing relationship that identifies Winfrey as the most successful black businesswoman while combating the ephemeral notion that she is, among other things, a mammy figure for white viewers. Finally, drawing on the theoretical insights of scholars such as Patricia Hill Collins, Stanley explores the semiotic slippage and fracturing that typifies black people looking at black people in the twenty-first century.

If understanding Stanley's analysis is dependent on understanding the concern by African American women that white viewers might "misread" Winfrey or reappropriate her for their own uses, independent of any racial or historical consciousness, then it is useful to consider exactly how this might function. As this apprehension demonstrates, it is not just black people looking at Winfrey through a loaded history of racial representation; it is also white people. Crucial to both readings is the way the stereotypical African American mammy is characterized as naturally wise, jolly, witty, robust, and willing to help others in need, particularly whites. Although some associate these characteristics with Winfrey in a negative way, others do so in a positive way, finding her openness, likability, and compassion refreshing.

In her essay "My Mom and Oprah Winfrey: Her Appeal to White Women," Linda Kay addresses such matters using a personal anecdote as a point of departure. Kay's mother, a widow from New Jersey, encountered Winfrey in an ice cream parlor in downtown Chicago, where they had a nice little chat. According to Kay, this ability to connect and transcend differences is what has made Winfrey so appealing to such a large, ethnically diverse audience. For Kay, it is not that white women align themselves with Winfrey because she negates racial oppression; rather, white female viewers connect with Winfrey because she frees them to talk about their own oppression. In Kay's analysis, viewers align themselves with Winfrey because she speaks the truth about female disempowerment and shame.

Different interpretations of such behaviors and characteristics lead to the possibility of multiple readings of both Winfrey's iconic persona and her motivations, generating the inevitable question: who is Oprah Winfrey? Or, more appropriately, how does one determine who or what Oprah Winfrey is for each of her viewers? In what ways is any individual's imagined relationship to the icon mediated solely by racial identification or experience? How do we weigh these factors in relation to other forms of identification and experience? Can race trump gender for one viewer and not another, while being inseparable to a third?

In contrast to Stanley's ambivalent viewers and Kay's enthusiastic ones, Valerie Palmer-Mehta addresses unambivalent and decidedly hostile responses to Winfrey in her contribution to this anthology, "The 'Oprahization' of America: *The Man Show* and the Redefinition of Black Femininity." On June 16, 1999, the popular Comedy Central series debuted with an episode titled "The Oprahization of America." This was only the beginning of a long-standing series of routines that denigrated Winfrey and in which the hosts declared their intention to "stop her." Palmer-Mehta argues that the hosts invoked and utilized a legacy of psychic violence committed against black women as a way of asserting the patriarchal authority that has been displaced by Winfrey's cultural authority.

In part, Palmer-Mehta suggests, the desire to impose such stereotypes on Winfrey speaks to the way she has been so successful in evading them. Referencing the work of scholar Patricia Hill Collins on the externally defined, controlling images of black women—namely, the mammy, the black matriarch, the welfare mother, the black lady, and the jezebel[34]—Palmer-Mehta argues that Winfrey is successful in outmaneuvering each of these images. Instead, she creates her own self-possessed model of black womanhood that serves as a paragon of empowerment for women of all cultures. Palmer-Mehta furthers asserts that the power of this self-possessed model places white patriarchal supremacist hegemony in jeopardy, which is why Winfrey was targeted by *The Man Show*—a move that simply underscored her overwhelming power and influence.

Oprah Winfrey on the Stage

All these relations and responses to Winfrey are, of course, mediated first and foremost by one's encounter with her on the television screen. It is there that Winfrey has introduced and honed the personable public persona to which viewers respond, whether negatively, positively, or ambivalently.[35] In their essay, "Oprah Winfrey and Women's Autobiography: A Televisual Performance of the Therapeutic Self," Eva Illouz and Nicholas John demonstrate how Winfrey has assumed control of her production though the highly personalized form of the biography. They argue that understanding how Winfrey staged such a biography is key to comprehending the public persona of the television host. According to Illouz and John, rather than being a simple celebrity who is famous for her presence in the media, Winfrey is a biographical icon, famous for the way she staged her entry into the public realm. The authors read this act not only as seminal to Winfrey's fame or her perceived accessibility but also as part of Winfrey's deployment of the private biography to construct public speech. More precisely, they argue that in Winfrey's biography, the "psychic," "personal," or "private" is constituted in the very act of the public telling of her life story. In short, the authors demonstrate how the commodification of biography is central in explaining how the private becomes public and how—by extension—the public Winfrey becomes a private friend.[36]

In her contribution, "From Fasting toward Self-Acceptance: Oprah Winfrey and Weight Loss in American Culture," Ella Howard explores one exceptionally well-known aspect of Winfrey's public biography. Winfrey has approached weight loss the same way she has approached other sensitive issues—by speaking publicly about what had previously been a private issue. Audience members have been privy to every development in Winfrey's diet and exercise regimen because Winfrey has staged each step for their consumption. On November 15, 1988, Winfrey announced that she had lost sixty-seven pounds on the Optifast diet plan and punctuated that announcement by wheeling out a wagonload of the same amount of animal fat and proudly showing off her size ten jeans. Liquid diets, a fad from the 1970s, experienced a major revival following that broadcast. When the diet did not prove to have long-term success, Winfrey shared this fact, too, openly discussing her weight gain and her search for new nutritional alternatives.[37] In the mid-1990s Winfrey and her favorite chef, Rosie Daley, published a cookbook featuring recipes that were low in fat, sugar, and salt—a trend Winfrey called "clean eating."[38] In October 1998 she appeared on the cover of *Vogue* magazine in a dazzling black dress and newly svelte figure—achieved at the insistence of *Vogue* editors.

Howard argues that Winfrey's candor about her own dieting experiences helped break down barriers of silence and shame surrounding obesity, as well as the complex reasons fueling the tendency to overeat among many Americans, especially women. Further, Howard illustrates how the media controls women's perceptions and demonstrates that Winfrey is not immune to such pressures. Ironically, Howard also shows how Winfrey's fluctuating weight has become an industry in and of itself, complete with endorsements, book tie-ins, and magazine columns, as well as launching the careers of Rosie Daley and personal trainer Bob Greene. By locating Winfrey's actions in and impact on the American health and fitness industry, Howard affirms Winfrey's power as a cultural force.

Whereas Howard sees Winfrey's discussion of her weight as being liberating for her audience, two other contributors address how Winfrey's discussion of spirituality has been received as enlightening or as creating the potential to affirm alternative spiritual values or practices. It has been posited that Winfrey's message of New Age spirituality began in 1994, when she took stock of her then eight-year-old program. In a bold move of self-evaluation, Winfrey invited a panel of television critics to debate the question, "Are Talk Shows Bad?" At the end of two days of critical review, Winfrey asked panelist Vicki Abt, a Penn State sociologist and author of a book denouncing television talk shows, for suggestions on how to redirect her program. Abt proposed a shift in focus to great books and art. Another guest, television critic Tom Shales, opined, "I would like to see more smart people on TV. Fewer ordinary people, more extraordinary people."[39] Initially, Winfrey did not take either the "extraordinary people" or the "great books" route. Rather, she decided to rebuild her show with the rhetoric and principles of a loosely bound spiritual movement typically referred to as the New Age. Guests such as Marianne Williamson and other New Age gurus of the mid- to late 1990s discussing and promoting their books became commonplace.[40]

It is this transformation and its practical implementation that Maria McGrath addresses in "Spiritual Talk: *The Oprah Winfrey Show* and the Popularization of the New Age." McGrath discusses how Winfrey and the majority of her viewers became tired of the daily televised display of human misery and the "unseemly" goings-on in the lower classes—displays that highlighted a world lacking in consensus and cultural standards. In locating the individual as the center of life and asserting a need for individual connection and empowerment, Winfrey provided a model for self-empowerment that reproduced the rhetoric of New Age spirituality and also kept the chaos at bay. McGrath demonstrates that in choosing this path, Winfrey emerged as an influential disseminator of New Age discourse. Notably, by adopting a New Age philosophy, Winfrey also found a solid ethical framework for purposeful living. Although she acknowledges the inspirational and transformative potential of such philosophies, McGrath also draws attention to their failings. In privileging the need to get one's own house—the self—in order before one can assist others, this discourse elides the real social forces that often impede individuals or the networks or communities in which they are embedded (critiques also made in this anthology in different ways by Malin Pereira and Marjorie Jolles). Moreover, McGrath highlights the reality that, however rewarding it might be as a philosophy, the narrative of self that the New Age promotes is incapable of containing certain traumas.

Denise Martin is less concerned with the effect of Winfrey's spirituality on others and more interested in evaluating its practice, integrity, and composition. In "Oprah Winfrey and Spirituality," Martin considers the body of Winfrey's work holistically and locates it within multiple spiritual traditions, whether indigenous, traditional, contemporary, or some combination. In particular, she demonstrates that the spiritual themes found in the many forms of cultural expression and production in which Winfrey is personally and professionally involved are rich and complex. In this way, Martin dislocates the emphasis of previous contributors on the production and dissemination of Winfrey's projects and considers instead the work they are overtly intended to do. Notably, Martin reads many of Winfrey's enterprises not as attempts to generate capital—either cultural or economic—but as efforts to honor the ancestors, such as Winfrey's efforts to bring Toni Morrison's novel *Beloved* to the big screen. For Martin, any analysis of Winfrey's cultural production is inextricable from her production of a public and cultural spirituality. This spirituality is presented as rooted in the wisdom and experiences of the past, engaged with contemporary reality, and proactive in creating a space where people can actualize their potential.

That critics tend to read Winfrey's promotion of spirituality as genuine, even if they criticize its composition or dissemination, is noteworthy. Although many celebrities have been taken to task for their promotion of seemingly simplistic and perhaps eccentric or ungrounded spiritual philosophies, Winfrey's sincerity has not been called into question. It is this same sincerity that served her so well in a much more secular sphere—namely, her trial in Texas. Although the move from spiritual to secular may seem abrupt, we contend that Winfrey's emphasis on transparency and honesty characterizes both her spiritual praxis and her conduct during the intense media scrutiny of her trial. Therefore, part II closes with an essay by Jennifer Richardson, "Phenomenon on Trial: Reading Rhetoric at *Texas Beef v. Oprah Winfrey.*" In this instance, it is notable that the battle emerges not from Winfrey's issues of self-esteem but rather from externally imposed forces. And it is remarkable that this is one of the few public fights—like the Franzen episode or the declined trip to Afghanistan—in which Winfrey has been embroiled. As such, her reception during the trial is key in establishing her cultural power. On December 29, 1997, a group of cattle producers, including Cactus Feeders Inc. owner Paul Engler, filed a lawsuit against Winfrey, her production company Harpo, and *Oprah Winfrey Show* guest Howard Lyman for false disparagement of public foods, business disparagement, defamation, and negligence.[41] What is interesting here is that, in theory, Winfrey should have had a limited ability to control the rhetoric of the trial beyond her defense. Yet, as Richardson makes clear, the rhetorical work that Winfrey undertook in establishing her media personality inescapably shaped her reception during the trial.

In affirming the rhetorical role of Winfrey's celebrity, Richardson explores what she refers to as "televisual rhetoric on trial," arguing that events such as *Texas Beef v. Oprah Winfrey* highlight the mass media's role in shaping and steering the stories Americans consume. Richardson ultimately posits that the coverage of the trial and its rhetorical patterns exemplify how institutions of civil society serve the interests of the dominant ruling class, governmental agencies, and corporate financiers, who regulate not only what Americans put into their mouths but also what they can say about it. In this way, she suggests, Winfrey simply proved herself to be a more powerful institution than those her opponents represented.

Oprah Winfrey on the Page

If Winfrey's win in a Texas court was a surprise, it pales in comparison to her most unanticipated triumph in an equally unexpected realm. Before Winfrey, no one had considered the degree to which a talk-show host might become a publishing powerhouse. Yet this is exactly what Winfrey has accomplished, not only through her own book publications and magazine but also through the enthusiastic endorsement of literary works by others. Introduced in 1996, Oprah's Book Club was an instant success, transforming a bevy of writers—ranging from well-established authors such as Toni Morrison to previously obscure ones such as Janet Fitch—into cultural and financial success stories. From October 1996 to March 2002, forty-seven books were selected by Winfrey, each becoming a best seller. Then, on April 4, 2002, Winfrey announced on-air that she was discontinuing the book club. Her stated reason for doing so became famous within literary circles: "The truth is, it has become harder and harder for me to find books on a monthly basis that I am really passionate about."

Winfrey's emphasis on personal courage and individual potential was reflected in the initial book club selections. As Malin Pereira notes in "Oprah's Book Club and the American Dream," many of the book club selections are stories of women who triumph over adversity and achieve success through the process of self-actualization—a biographical trajectory that not only mirrors Winfrey's but also affirms the model she disseminates to her viewers, something that Dana Cloud refers to as a rhetoric of tokenism.[42] Yet Pereira argues that rather than reifying the narrative of the American Dream, the show and its host struggled to maintain a consensus about both its desirability and its attainability, particularly for African Americans and the lower classes. Moreover, Pereira argues that the act of privileging reading practices that foreground personal experience opened the door to dissent. As a result, texts that invited criticism of American mythologies of progress—in particular, Wally

Lamb's *She's Come Undone; Breath, Eyes, Memory* by Edwidge Danticat; and *We Were the Mulvaneys* by Joyce Carol Oates[43]—provided a space to disrupt the individualistic discourse of *The Oprah Winfrey Show.* Pereira demonstrates that a nascent awareness that the dream is illusory and potentially corrupt erupts into the show's discourse through silences, broken snatches of arguments, crying, and even public disagreement between the authors and the show's host.

Perhaps because the attempt to repress such eruptions had previously been read uncritically, and because the novels themselves were interpreted as uniformly uncritical of American life because of Winfrey's interpretive framework, cultural critics initially argued that book club discussions were superficial—a criticism contested by Kathleen Rooney and Celia Konchar Farr.[44] In two recent books, both authors challenge the supposition that the practices engaged in by Winfrey and her audience produced less complex readings. Likewise, in their contribution to this anthology, Roberta Hammett and Audrey Dentith affirm that a more complex reading is produced by viewers. However, these authors do so by demonstrating that it is not simply a matter of what readers "get" from the books; rather, they examine how Oprah's Book Club invoked particular pedagogical practices that influenced how readers ascribed meaning. In "Some Lessons before Dying: Gender, Morality, and the Missing Critical Discourse in Oprah's Book Club," Hammett and Dentith examine the literary strategies employed by *The Oprah Winfrey Show* in its televised and online discussions. Locating such reading practices historically, the authors suggest that the book club privileged critical discourses that facilitated conservative readings, ones that do not open up the books' political possibilities. Like Pereira, these authors criticize Winfrey for shutting down these other possibilities and asserting her own interpretive authority. Nevertheless, they suggest that the book club was a worthwhile endeavor with the potential to disrupt the status quo and improve basic literacy skills, even if it did not advance cultural or critical reading skills.

Cultural critics, however, did not even acknowledge the value of improving literacy skills. This elitist dismissal of Oprah's Book Club selections by some supposedly highbrow circles culminated when she chose Jonathan Franzen's novel *The Corrections.*[45] Until this moment, Winfrey had been able to ignore or sidestep any real criticism of the book club, focusing instead on the formation of reading communities, the enthusiasm of publishers and fans alike, and praise from organizations such as the American Library Association. When Winfrey selected Franzen's novel, however, she set in motion a series of arguments about the content and method of her book club choices. The highbrow and lowbrow debate reached its climax, and it did so in terms of gender.

Given the highly publicized nature of the Franzen debacle, it was inevitable that one of our contributors would consider its origins and operations and what it reveals about our contemporary cultural preoccupations and assumptions. In "Making Corrections to Oprah's Book Club: Reclaiming Literary Power for Gendered Literacy Management," Sarah Robbins explores the conflict from several perspectives: the agenda to get more Americans reading on a regular basis, the gender- and class-based interpretations that were inferred—or imposed—by the mainstream media, and how the reincarnated version of the book club functions as its own form of corrective. In particular, Robbins argues that in reconstituting her book club to focus on the classics, Winfrey moved from the realm of the popular, coded as feminine, to the realm of the academic, coded as intellectual. In doing so, Winfrey managed to mediate the gender-based conflict over reading that had erupted during the Franzen episode—a conflict that threatened her position as a figure of cultural authority as well as her influence on book sales. Finally, following Judith Fetterley's assertions that women's interpretive practices have significant cultural value,[46] Robbins demonstrates that Winfrey uses not simply reading but also modes of reading gendered as female as a means of empowerment for both herself and her viewers.

The pedagogy and practices assigned to reading in the book club inevitably spill over to the other main organ of literacy in the Winfrey media empire, *O, the Oprah Magazine,* launched in May 2000. It promotes messages in common with the book club, including tie-ins, and it features names and faces familiar to viewers, but as a magazine patently engaged with discourses of self-help and self-improvement, it also insists that there is a value in active reading, rereading, and mediating the self through such a process. In both ways, then, it promotes the Winfrey message through the Winfrey medium—mediated by Winfrey's own interpretive lens and, indeed, by the icon herself, who is foregrounded throughout the magazine.

Importantly, O magazine has been seen as defying the general trend in American women's magazines. It has become the most successful female-oriented magazine in American history: in 2002, at the end of its second year of publication, National Magazine Publishers of America listed O, with a total paid circulation of 2.3 million readers, in the thirty-first spot on its list of top one hundred magazines. Headed by Gayle King, Winfrey's best friend, O has become one of the few magazines in which black women exercise such a large, nationwide influence. Only *Essence,* founded in 1970 and targeting African American women, can make a similar claim. The difference is that O addresses issues that concern women of all races and economic classes. As Patricia Williams observes:

> If the world were a different place, I suppose I might join those who have sneered that O is just another yearning-for-a-middle-class lifestyle magazine like *Martha Stewart Living.* But however obvious the similarities may be, for me the distinguishing feature of O is its visualization of a mixed society as "normal." I don't mean it's colorblind. Rather, it purposefully arranges people like bouquets of wildflowers. People with differing looks, opinions, tastes, and ages are put side by side to ruminate about random things—marriage, money, books etc. … It's equalizing in a very quiet sense, this pictorial impression that the soap opera of life's little mission touches everyone.[47]

The message is clear: black women can be the material of which successful crossover magazines are made. Likewise, racial inclusivity is not only desirable but also chic.

Clearly, O aims to inspire through its visual representations of women who do not embody the physical ideal promoted by Western society. In stressing their nonconformity, it likewise promotes a message of unity in such diversity. This unity in diversity is evident not only in the visual landscape of the magazine but in its rhetorical landscape as well. As Marjorie Jolles discusses in "Knowing for Sure: Epistemologies of the Autonomous Self in O, *the Oprah Magazine,*" besides promoting a visual politics of nonconformity, the magazine also promotes a philosophical one that privileges the idea of the self-actualized individual who is independent of controlling social and market forces. Yet Jolles points out that there are fundamental contradictions inherent in such a message, and not simply because it comes from a magazine that advertises particular goods for purchase. Notably, Jolles argues that al-though Winfrey makes a valiant effort to emphasize the importance of women viewing themselves through their own unique individuality, this is more likely to assist middle- and upper-class women who have the means to access the rhetoric of Emersonian self-reliance. In this way, Jolles's argument is tied to Pereira's critique of the operation of the American Dream in Oprah's Book Club. The difference is that whereas the books cannot adequately contain or elide eruptions of critique, the magazine can and does. It is left to Jolles, then, to point out that the un-critical promotion of a rhetoric of self-reliance places Winfrey at odds with various feminist critics, particularly feminists of color, who have often argued against individualism and in favor of community as the primary grounding of identity.

Damiana Gibbons's essay, "Oprah Winfrey's Branding of Personal Empowerment," builds on Jolles's argument. Whereas Jolles identifies the operation of a discourse in *O*, Gibbons considers how it is rein-scribed and enforced via the magazine. According to Gibbons, *O* not only sets a standard for women to aspire to but also sets in place the mechanisms to ensure that the standard is enforced. Invoking Foucault's notion of the Panopticon, Gibbons uses *O* magazine to ground an analysis of what she calls Oprah's Panopticon. In this way, she is in alignment with those critics who read *O* as simply another shrewdly calculated attempt by Harpo Productions to enlarge its already con-siderable empire. These individuals argue that it is not the person-al empowerment of women that *O* magazine promotes, but rather the increasing empowerment of Winfrey. Gibbons also considers the related criticism that Winfrey's efforts to encourage her viewers to constantly move forward, to conspicuously consume, to subscribe to the "Oprah" program—her books, her gurus, her favorite things—as a means of creating and sustaining their new and improved identities is merely a form of sophisticated capitalism.

Conclusion

The boundary between the Oprah Winfrey fan as both friend and con-sumer is indistinct. In part, this is rooted in what Winfrey represents as a social contract: although she acknowledges that she is obligated to her audience, she also sees that obligation as a public responsibility or trust. In return, she "does good"—by suggesting an uplifting philosophy, book, or even bra. This public accountability is key to her media persona, and her audience expects her to uphold her end of the bargain in a way that does not apply to most other media personalities. It is for this reason that Winfrey's denunciation of James Frey, author of *A Million Little Pieces,* an Oprah's Book Club selection, is so important. When it was revealed that Frey had fabricated significant parts of what was purported to be a memoir, Winfrey initially stood by him, citing the book's emotional resonance and message of redemption as its own kind of truth. But as the revelations became more convoluted and more morally reprehensible—including charges that he had lied about his role in the death of a childhood acquaintance to enhance his own tragic persona—Winfrey withdrew her support. In an interview that aired January 26, 2006, she charged Frey with dishonesty and apologized to her audience for her earlier defense, stating, "I left the impression that the truth does not matter and I am deeply sorry about that. But that is not what I believe. And to everyone who has challenged me on the issue of truth, you are absolutely right."

Winfrey's language was telling. In her repeated use throughout the show of the pronoun "I," she asserted her anger, her sense of betrayal, and, above all, her displeasure at the position Frey had placed her in. For Winfrey, trust and truth are key to her brand; to be placed in a position that caused her—however inadvertently—to let her audience be duped is to undermine the basis of her relationship with her viewers, a relationship of which she is fiercely protective. Clearly, as evidenced by the anecdote related at the beginning of this introduction, Winfrey dislikes being used, and she is equally displeased by the possibility of being seen as endorsing something to which she has not knowingly agreed. In a strange way, both the Bush and Frey incidents represent the degree of Winfrey's cultural authority: whereas the Bush administration did not dare respond, Frey could hardly afford not to.

This cultural authority is what our anthology hopes to unpack from a variety of perspectives: How does Winfrey function, circulate, even come to define celebrity authority? How has one individual come to define a series of cultural practices, becoming a noun, a verb, an adjective, and an adverb? And what are the implications? If this anthology can, through a range of critical arguments and perspectives, begin to answer some of these questions, to render the assumption of cultural

Chicago Public Library
Blackstone
4/23/2011   2:10:51 PM
-Patron Receipt-

ITEMS BORROWED:

1:
Title: The Oprah phenomenon /
Item #: R0424628743
Due Date: 5/14/2011

-Please retain for your records-

RROSS

authority and imagined reciprocal relations less natural, to draw attention to the way media discourses and relations are formed and disseminated, then we have, as academics, done our own kind of Winfreyesque "good."

Notes

1. "Oprah Declines Bush Afghan Invite," Associated Press, March 29, 2002.

2. Michael Starr and Adam Buckman, "Oprah Complains to Pals on *The View:* White House Set Me Up," *New York Post,* April 3, 2002, 70.

3. Toni Morrison, *Beloved* (New York: Knopf, 1987).

4. Winfrey confirmed to media sources that Jones's words accurately reflected her feelings on the matter. See http://extratv.warnerbros.com/dailynews/extra/04_02/04_03a.html (accessed January 1, 2006).

5. Beretta E. Smith-Shomade, *Shaded Lives: African American Women and Television* (New Brunswick, N.J.: Rutgers University Press, 2002), 152.

6. Louann Haarman, "Performing Talk," in *Television Talk Shows: Discourse, Performance, Spectacle,* ed. Andrew Tolson (Mahwah, N.J.: Lawrence Erlbaum Associates, 2001), 33, 46.

7. Bernard M. Timberg, *Television Talk: A History of the TV Talk Show* (Austin: University of Texas Press, 2002), 135.

8. See http://www.oprah.com/about/press/about_press_bio.jhtml.

9. Donald Bogle, *Primetime Blues: African Americans on Primetime Television* (New York: Farrar, Straus and Giroux, 2002), 357–59.

10. Timberg, *Television Talk,* 137.

11. Ibid., 7.

12. Jane M. Shattuc, *The Talking Cure: TV Talk Shows and Women* (New York: Routledge 1996), 95–96.

13. Andrew Tolson, "Talking about Talk," in *Television Talk Shows: Discourse, Performance, Spectacle,* ed. Andrew Tolson (Mahwah, N.J.: Lawrence Erlbaum Associates, 2001), 136.

14. Timberg, *Television Talk,* 136.

15. Edward Wyatt, "Oprah Winfrey to Back 'Purple.'" *New York Times,* September 26, 2005.

16. Patricia Sellers, "The Business of Being Oprah," *Fortune,* April 2002, 50–64.

17. Leo Tolstoy, *Anna Karenina* (New York: Modern Library, 2000).

18. Sellers, "The Business of Being Oprah," 50–64.

19. Smith-Shomade, *Shaded Lives,* 149.

20. See Debbie Epstein and Deborah Lynn Steinberg, "American Dreamin':

Discoursing Liberally on *The Oprah Winfrey Show*," *Women's Studies International Forum* 21, no. 1 (1998): 77–94.

21. Sellers, "The Business of Being Oprah," 50–52.

22. Mark Steyn, "The Republic of Oprah," *National Review,* March 23, 1998, 30–33.

23. Smith-Shomade, *Shaded Lives,* 153, 158.

24. Shattuc, *The Talking Cure,* 98.

25. Ibid.

26. Barbara Grizzuti Harrison, "The Importance of Being Oprah," *New York Times Magazine,* June 11, 1989, 6.

27. Shattuc, *The Talking Cure,* 101.

28. Corinne Squire, "Who's White? Television Talk Shows and Representations of Whiteness," in *Off White: Readings on Race, Power, and Society,* ed. Michelle Fine (New York: Routledge, 1997), 242.

29. Robin Givhan, "Oprah and the View from Outside Hermès' Paris Door," *Washington Post,* June 24, 2005, C01.

30. See, for instance, any number of blogs, including http://journals.aol. ca/enteditorca/PoppedCulture/entries/833 and http://lifegoesoff.blogspot. com/2005_06_01_lifegoesoff_archive.html (accessed January 30, 2006). See also responses to James Hill, "Oprah Caught 'Shopping While Black,'" http:// www.bet.com/Entertainment/oprahhermes.htm?wbc_purpose=Basic&WB CMODE=PresentationUnpublished&mb=1 (accessed January 1, 2006).

31. Audrey Edwards, "The O Factor," *Essence Magazine,* October 2003, 180.

32. Laura Randolph, "Oprah! The Most Powerful Woman in Entertainment Talks about Her Fame, Her Father and Her Future in TV," *Ebony Magazine,* July 1995, 23.

33. Edwards, "The O Factor," 180.

34. Patricia Hill Collins, *Black Feminist Thought: Knowledge, Consciousness and the Politics of Empowerment* (New York: Routledge, 2000).

35. See Sherryl Wilson, *Oprah, Celebrity and Formations of Self* (New York: Palgrave Macmillan, 2003).

36. See also Eva Illouz, *Oprah Winfrey and the Glamour of Misery* (New York: Columbia University Press, 2003).

37. Gloria-Jean Masciarotte, "C'mon Girl: Oprah Winfrey and the Discourse of Feminine Talk," *Genders* 11 (Fall 1991): 93.

38. Rosie Daley, *In The Kitchen with Rosie: Oprah's Favorite Recipes* (New York: Knopf, 1994).

39. Tom Shales as quoted in "Are Talk Shows Bad? Part II," *The Oprah Winfrey Show,* September 13, 1994 (Burrelle's transcript), 23.

40. Marianne Williamson, *Illuminated Prayers* (New York: Simon and

Schuster, 1997); Marianne Williamson, *Woman's Worth* (New York: Ballantine Books, 1994).

41. *Texas Beef Group v. Oprah Winfrey,* U.S. District. Court, N.D. Texas, 2:96-CV-208-J, 11 F.Supp.2d 858, decided February 26, 1998, LEXIS 3559, https://web.lexis-nexis.com/universe (accessed April 20, 2001).

42. Dana Cloud, "Hegemony or Concordance? The Rhetoric of Tokenism in 'Oprah' Winfrey's Rags-to-Riches Biography," *Critical Studies in Mass Communication* 13, no. 2 (1996): 115–37.

43. Wally Lamb, *She's Come Undone* (New York: Random House, 1994); Edwidge Danticat, *Breath, Eyes, Memory* (New York: Farrar, Straus, Giroux, 1994); Joyce Carol Oates, *We Were the Mulvaneys.* (New York: Wheeler Publishers, 2001).

44. Kathleen Rooney, *Reading with Oprah: The Book Club that Changed America* (Fayetteville: University of Arkansas Press, 2005); Celia Konchar Farr, *Reading Oprah: How Oprah's Book Club Changed the Way America Reads* (Albany, N.Y.: SUNY Press, 2005).

45. Jonathan Franzen, *The Corrections* (New York: Farrar, Straus and Giroux, 2001).

46. Judith Fetterley, *The Resisting Reader: A Feminist Approach to American Fiction* (Bloomington: Indiana University Press, 1978).

47. Patricia Williams, "Anatomy of a Fairy Tale Princess," in *When Race Becomes Real: Black and White Writers Confront Their Personal Histories,* ed. Bernestine Singley (Chicago: Lawrence Hill Books, 2002), 174–75.

Part I

Oprah Winfrey
and Race

The Specter of Oprah Winfrey

Critical Black Female Spectatorship

Tarshia L. Stanley

Theorists of black visual spectatorship have long considered the spectacular modes of observation practiced by African Americans with regard to popular representations of themselves. Whether black people's engagement with their imagery has been acquiescent or resistant, reconstructive or revisionary, critics agree that black people are experts at looking for themselves and at themselves in visual media. In the case of Oprah Winfrey—talk-show host, actress, producer, bibliophile, and businesswoman—critical black spectators have either absented themselves from serious critiques of her iconographic presence and function or dismissed her presence as one constructed for white audiences. This essay examines the provocative position from which critical black female spectators *see* the icon of Oprah Winfrey and is informed by the theories of bell hooks and Deborah Willis. It explores the ambivalence inherent in a "looking relationship" that identifies Winfrey as the most successful black businesswoman while combating a peripheral suspicion that she may be, among other things, fodder for a white cultural imagination adept at swilling the physical and visual bodies of black women.[1] Key to this consideration is the way the iconography of Oprah Winfrey intersects with historically powerful and racially laden controlling images—most notably, those that relate to black maternity and mothering and the emotional labor of black women.

In *Reel to Real: Race, Sex, and Class at the Movies,* cultural critic extraordinaire bell hooks contends that black women in particular have had to engage in complex self-reflective looking relationships. She describes the historical looking relationships that black women developed with regard to the racist and sexist images presented to them in Hollywood race films. As hooks notes, although most black women were (and are) aware of the racist constructions inherent in screen imagery, that awareness did not translate into active engagement in a critique positioned beyond race and encompassing issues of sex, sexuality, or class. Yet there are many black women whose spectatorial analyses are quite complex, even if they do not couch them in academic language.

In fact, hooks explains that many black women engage in looking relationships so complex that "alternative texts" are formed on screen. She writes, "We do more than resist . . . black women participate in a broad range of looking relations, contest, resist, revision, interrogate, and invent on multiple levels."[2] Consequently, critical black female spectatorship often comprehends the historical, patriarchal, cultural, commercial, racial, sexual, and gendered reproductions of their own imagery. What is fascinating about hooks's critique is that her multipositioning of the black woman's sight can be perceived as a strength rather than a fragmentation. Critical black female spectatorship is a conscious creativity that can be co-opted as a weapon of both deconstruction and revision and allows a black woman to read well beyond the composition on the screen.

This ability to read (see) the presentation of the body she occupied was one of the survival skills passed on from black woman to black woman in this society. African American women had to be adept at perceiving how others viewed them and their surroundings in lightning-quick montages. For many years, the black woman's existence and safety in certain situations were dependent on her ability to know how she would be interpreted—that is, as wife, mother, sister, maid, bitch, or whore. Although some of the categories made her less available within a tradition of coercion and rape, some made her more so. Yet, no matter how sophisticated her interpretive skills, a black woman in this society was unsafe.

In the Beginning Was the Image

Since the inception of mass media, black female imagery has been used to maintain the status quo and fuel the capitalist machine. Deborah

Willis writes in *Picturing Us: African American Identity in Photography* that the first images of black women in mass distribution were of black female bodies either naked or at work. The images of black women at work often showed them caring for white children or reprimanding their own. Willis highlights a set of lantern slides called "Trouble Ahead, Trouble Behind." These slides, which were circulated in the 1880s, depict a black woman dressed in what looks to be faded calico; the trappings of ultrapoor working-class blackness surround her. There are two children: one asleep, the other drawing on the wall. The boy has written the word "mamy" as a title for his picture. In the next slide the mother spanks the child, and we understand the caption "Trouble Behind" in its full context. Willis reports that these images, called "Black Americana . . . were produced for the amusement of a white audience" and "now exist as frozen racial metaphors from a time when images of African Americans were rarely produced by or for African Americans."[3]

Although it is understood that such imagery—a black mother whipping her child and the child's depiction of his mother as a mammy—is fraught with derisive assumptions about black life, it is important to note that what hooks deems "black looks" could both resist and reconstruct this imagery. Intellectuals such as Ida B. Wells-Barnett wrote extensively about the ways that this kind of imagery reinforced stereotypes for both the white viewer and the uncritical black viewer. At the 1893 Columbia Exposition in Chicago, she passed out a tract that she had authored, titled "The Reason Why the Colored American Is Not in the World's Columbia Exposition."[4] It is significant that while Wells-Barnett was fashioning a public discourse about representations of black people, the Davis Milling Company was inculcating the American psyche with the image of Aunt Jemima. The company paid a black cook named Nancy Green to be the living embodiment of its new pancake mix. Wholesalers were so intrigued by Green's demonstration at the exposition that more than "50,000 merchant orders" were placed.[5]

Even as Wells-Barnett was practicing resistance to popular iconography, W. E. B. DuBois's looking relationships were focused on reconstructing black imagery, as exemplified by the American Negro Exhibit, a collage of photos depicting black life that he assembled for display at the Paris Exposition of 1900.[6] DuBois conceived of the exhibit as way to directly combat the negative images of black people prevalent at the turn of the twentieth century. Thus there is a long history of black people developing intricate looking relationships that range from participation in to resistance of such pernicious imagery. This history, which includes black women's ability to reconfigure presentations of themselves, has never been simple and uncomplicated. And regardless of how practiced the critical black female spectator was, the ability to negotiate manifestations of her imagery became increasingly convoluted in the last decades of the twentieth century.

In the late twentieth century, the advent of multiple cable channels, the capacity to record television programs and rent videos, the ability to access the Internet, and the production of music television represented significant possibilities for black women's looking relationships. Images that were previously inaccessible to the average viewing audience became more easily available. Yet, as history demonstrates, an increase in media genres or productions does not necessarily translate into an improvement in the representation of African Americans. Purposeful strides made during the 1950s and 1960s to create multidimensional, if distinctly middle-class, media images of black women gave way first to caricatures of the blaxploitation era and then to the almost complete erasure of black female imagery in film and television in the mid- to late 1970s (with the exception of a few television situation comedies). The response by African Americans to the creation of *The Cosby Show* in the early 1980s was further evidence of how concerned black people were with combating stereotypical depictions of themselves on screen.

When *The Oprah Winfrey Show* became nationally syndicated in 1986, black female iconography entered a decidedly new stage. In the ensuing two decades, Oprah Winfrey has become a billion-dollar corporation. From Oprah's Book Club, which is credited with increasing recreational reading in America, to co-ownership in the Oxygen Network and the creation of *O* magazine, Winfrey demonstrates her multimedia power. It would seem that the multidimensional representation of black womanhood that countless nameless black women had been waiting for had finally arrived in the body and enterprises of Oprah Winfrey. Yet, for the critical black female spectator adept in self-assessment—or, rather, at assessing the self that has often been re-created for her by others—there is tension when looking at Oprah Winfrey.

The question that asserts itself is: To what degree is Winfrey understood as African American by a white viewing audience? And to what degree is she representative for a black one? In the essay "Black Bodies/

American Commodities," Robyn Wiegman notes that the presentations of the black mother and daughter in the first of the *Lethal Weapon*
films (1987) were not liberating or indicative of a society ready to embrace African American women as equals; rather, they were dangerously
dismissive of black women's history by foregrounding the patriarchal,
racist, sexist society that routinely shut them out. Citing the use of the
mother as a space for heterosexual masculinity to rework itself, and the
virgin daughter (who, coincidentally, has a crush on the white hero) as
a site of nonsexual, noncompetitive interaction between the black male
and white male protagonists, Wiegman points out the film's reinforce-
ment of and aspiration to a bourgeois ideal for the black family that
ignores connotative associations with blackness. She writes:

> The black woman's homogenization into categories tradition-
> ally occupied by the white woman is part of a broader pro-
> gram of hegemonic recuperation, a program that has as its
> main focus the reconstruction of white masculine power in
> the face of feminist and civil rights discourses of the 1960s.
> So strong was this recuperation in the Reagan era that even
> affirmative action programs were challenged for "depriving"
> white men of their civil right.[7]

Wiegman's argument is useful for looking at Oprah Winfrey. For Wiegman, simply replacing what would have traditionally been white female characters with black female characters is problematic. In this way,
Wiegman calls into question any paradigm that would ignore the racism and sexism simultaneously ingrained in the history and experience
of black women. By ignoring these markers, which have shaped the
way black women live their lives, the film is guilty of a "program of
hegemonic recuperation . . . that has as its main focus the reconstruction
of white masculine power."[8]

    We might think of Winfrey's rise to iconic and economic power in
the midst of the Reagan era as another way of negating challenges to a
racist, sexist power structure. Certainly it has been suggested that part
of Winfrey's success is rooted firmly in a system of hegemonic recovery
that, in the end, takes the teeth out of critiques of what hooks calls a
patriarchal, white supremacist, capitalist power structure. After all, there
was never a better example of the American Dream realized—minus

the spouse and the 2.5 children—than Winfrey. Winfrey's humble beginnings, her establishment of a media empire, and her penchant for
philanthropy seemingly offer resolute proof of the Horatio Alger ethos.
It is worth noting that Winfrey established her empire at the commencement of the information age, just as Alger's literature launched
the rhetoric of bootstraps and self-determination at the dawn of the
Industrial Revolution.

Chained Memories

Oprah Winfrey is our mammy, according to Laurie L. Haag.[9] The mammy is one of the oldest archetypal images of African American women.
Part of the mammy icon's usefulness to antebellum society was that she
conveyed a black mothering that privileged its relationship with white
children while negating the black mother's love and commitment to
her own children. This iconic figure was not meant to accurately reflect
the black woman's feelings about mothering; rather, it was generated
out of a white desire for affirmation, as well as slave owners' practical
need to create surrogate mother-nurturers, both real and ideological,
for their legal and out-of-wedlock children. These black women were
expected and encouraged to care for their white charges not only at
the expense of their own families but also at the expense of their individuality. According to Trudier Harris, the black serving woman's role
became more important than the woman herself; "she should cook,
clean, take care of the children—and be invisible or self-effacing."[10] The
mammy figure retains cultural currency because she represented, and
continues to represent, the eradication of black maternal competency
and black female autonomy, as well as the lasting effect of the exploitation of black female labor.

In addition to being a supernurturer, the mammy was best known
for being disconnected from her community. Historically, mothering
in the black community has been under siege. From children being
taken away from their mothers and sold under slavery, to the Moynihan
report in the 1960s, to the highly publicized welfare queens and crack
babies of the 1980s, it seems that black women are most frequently represented as failures at mothering their own. The mammy is the quintessential example of this. In her critique of such dominant forms in
American literature Harris writes, "Features inherent in the job made

it necessary for the black mammy to deny her own family in order to rear generation after generation of whites who would, ironically, grow up to oppress blacks yet further."[11] This denigration of herself, her family, and her community is inherently painful for critical black readers of mammy figures. Popular literature and film have always portrayed the mammy from the dominant society's perspective. Seen from that viewpoint, it was good and even desirable to spend one's life in service to another's family and another's community without compensation or acknowledgment. However, from the viewpoint of the mammy's natural children, the iconography further denigrated black family and community.

The language associated with the mammy serving the needs of a dominant white society resonates in the public commentary that surrounds Winfrey. And it does so in ways that black female spectators find troubling. As recently as 2003, a sociological study of audience responses to talk shows titled "Viewer Aggression and Attraction to Television Talk Shows" praised *The Oprah Winfrey Show* as genuine and sincere. According to the investigators—who identified Winfrey's viewership as still largely female and middle class—"They felt comfortable with Oprah Winfrey as they would a friend and found her to be a natural, down-to-earth person."[12] For the black female spectator already harboring ambivalent feelings about Winfrey, the words "natural" and "down-to-earth" set off alarms, because this is the same language used to describe the mammy in literature, advertising, and visual media since the mid-nineteenth century. In fact, since *The Oprah Winfrey Show*'s inception, the fan base has described its relationship to Winfrey much as white society did to the mammy. Winfrey's audiences saw her, at least initially, as their friend and confidant, but usually in the most one-sided terms. Winfrey's shows were cited as informative, but they rarely made viewers feel as if they were being forced to think about inequities in society. Instead, shows were about finding oneself and one's dream job, decorating one's home, throwing wonderful parties, getting good recipes, and raising great kids. Winfrey created a media space for women's talk that had not previously existed; however, when her shows presented topics that may have been deemed controversial, the audience at home and in the studio could resolve any problem with tears and Winfrey's assurance that everything would be all right.

The most frequent comments made about Winfrey as a host concern her ability to interact positively with her audience—both studio and television. Haag attributes Winfrey's success to her ability to utilize "girl talk." She cites Winfrey's "self-disclosure" as one of the reasons audiences are drawn to the talk show. Yet, after spending the majority of the essay extolling Winfrey's ability to communicate in a female fashion, Haag concludes, "She is our mammy, our therapist, our cheerleader, our moral conscience, our role model, and our harshest critic when it is appropriate."[13]

The critical black female spectator—perhaps any critical spectator—would find this kind of assessment disturbing. Given the history of pain and psychological damage that the mammy figure represents for Americans of African descent, it is careless not to critique the use of the icon and its relationship to categories such as cheerleader, role model, and moral conscience. The scholarship on the imagery of the mammy, particularly scholarship generated by black women, is tainted not only with disdain but also with pain. When writers such as Trudier Harris, Patricia Hill Collins, and bell hooks engage the mammy, she is not a historical concept but a contemporary enemy. For them, the mammy is not only alive but doing exceptionally well. The mammy image is still as powerful in the twenty-first century as it was at the turn of the twentieth century because the dominant society continues to prefer interacting with her.

In many ways, this is what *The Oprah Winfrey Show* does for its mainstream audience: allows a guilt-free space where history and current manifestations of capitalism, racism, and sexism rooted in that history do not matter. In this way, Winfrey's audience exists in a multicultural space where the only concern is what one looks like on the inside (unless one is overweight). Audiences can approach every show without guilt or apprehension because they are "remembering their spirits," and these quests for spirit and interpretations of spirit do not usually include profound critiques of society.[14]

The Specter of Mammy

"Often aunt jemimas are toms blessed with religion or mammies who wedge themselves into the dominant white culture. Generally they are sweet, jolly, and good-tempered."[15] In his interpretive history of blacks in Hollywood film, Donald Bogle fractures the mammy figure into the mammy and the Aunt Jemima, describing the former as always being cantankerous and the latter as good-natured. What they have in common is their physical size and appearance: each is most often represented as rotund. This physical characteristic, understood as excess, renders them nonthreatening to the white spectator, who links such physical excesses to the excesses of maternity. Although Winfrey seems to have moved beyond the struggle with her weight, for many years, it was a critical factor. In an essay on black female appetite and its implications, Doris Witt quotes from a review of a book on mass-marketing strategies by Jean-Christophe Agnew: "What are we now to make of a figure like Aunt Jemima, whose 100-year old kerchief was finally removed from her head during her most recent makeover last July? Now she is said to look like Oprah Winfrey."[16] It is telling that Agnew likens the image of Aunt Jemima to Winfrey, and not vice versa. Although traditional renditions of the mammy–Aunt Jemima iconography gave her an abnormally large or fat body, Agnew made this comment after Winfrey's first significant weight loss; she was slim at the time.[17] Interestingly, Aunt Jemima had also undergone a makeover; her hair was straightened and her face was made significantly slimmer, perhaps indicating that she, too, had lost weight. Although Agnew does not specify who said that Aunt Jemima looks like Winfrey, it is safe to assume that, at least in part, he was referring to the people who, after a century, still bought Aunt Jemima pancake mix and who watched *The Oprah Winfrey Show*.

Agnew backed away from any further critique of the Aunt Jemima makeover in relationship to Winfrey. Thus, the reader is left to wonder whether the Quaker Oats Company commissioned a makeover intentionally hoping to reinvigorate its icon by associating her with Winfrey, or whether subconscious ideologies of black female imageries were at work. Whatever the reasoning, a reciprocal meaning is evoked: Aunt Jemima is like Oprah, and Oprah is like Aunt Jemima.

The physical size of the mammy–Aunt Jemima icon was important historically because the other prevailing icon of black female imagery was the jezebel, who was wildly promiscuous and overtly sexual. The mammy was thus relieved of the burden of sexuality, making her close proximity to antebellum planter-class families safe and bearable. The plantation mistress did not have to compete with mammy sexually because the latter was usually cast as an asexual compilation. Her size removed her from the category of sexual temptation, and her round to rotund image—an ancient and perhaps universal symbol of maternity—solidified her ability to mother.

Winfrey's size and her battle with her weight were said to make her more human to her audiences. In fact, Winfrey devoted several shows to audience members, usually women, who disliked her after her weight losses. Although it would have been possible to delve more deeply into her audience's investment in her size, the shows usually ended with the audience members simply admitting jealousy and promising to work harder on their own problems. Winfrey's up-and-down weight through the years may speak to her subconscious understanding of the acceptable black female body. Because society's history with the black female body is so tenuous and fraught with history, the asexual mammy body is one that dominant society accepts and seems to enjoy. It may be that Winfrey was submitting to dominant ideology rather than resisting it.[18]

For critical black spectators who want to support Winfrey, viewing *The Oprah Winfrey Show* can be like hooks's watching of old race films. The kind of revisionary spectatorship that hooks describes often has to be invoked. For instance, although Winfrey is the star and a black woman, her shows are rarely about issues specific to black women. It is uncommon for the expert psychiatrists, life coaches, and panelists to be black women. Although Winfrey is probably responsible for launching the short-lived television career of Iyanla Vanzant, Vanzant did not receive the kind of sustainable acceptance from Winfrey's audience that Phil McGraw did.[19] In a *Newsweek* article, a broadcaster and Winfrey fan was quoted as saying, "I don't think [Vanzant] could ever be as big because she's not as universal."[20] It appears that Vanzant, known for being an Afrocentric motivational speaker, was too ethnic for Winfrey's viewers. Although, in theory, she was "just like them," Vanzant is also a mother, a grandmother, and a wife, which distances her from the sexless, childless, manless mammy that historical and contemporary members of the dominant society find acceptable. The critical black audience is aware that Winfrey is not a mother and is only scripted as a mothering presence to her audience; her advice and philanthropy are legendary. Winfrey has maintained for years that her work prevents her from having children of her own. Instead, she has opted to educate children from all over the world. Although I am not implying that mothering is a necessary part of womanhood, the fact that Winfrey is not a mother and has never married is significant in thinking about her cultural iconography. Winfrey has not traditionally been cast as a sexual figure, thus making her less threatening and more palatable to an audience (one that is typically white, middle class, and female) that would benefit from not having to deal with a sexualized black female body on screen.

Multiple Ways of Seeing

The traditional, iconic mammy nurtured dominant society. She suckled children, gave sage advice, fixed wonderful meals, exhibited exceptional loyalty, and, as a result, was often the family confidant—all at the expense of her own needs or those of her family or community. The mammy is now more difficult to articulate than she was in her younger days. She has metastasized and mutated; she has become so sophisticated that traditional analyses are tempted to break apart in the face of this. It is difficult for critical spectators to call attention to the ways in which Winfrey's relationship with her audience is reminiscent of the role the mammy played in dominant society.

In *Black Sexual Politics,* Patricia Hill Collins writes, "A good deal of Winfrey's success lies in her ability to market herself within the familiar realm of the mammy, not violate the tenets of being a Black lady, yet reap the benefits of her performance for herself."[21] Collins clearly articulates what many critical black female spectators inherently know. Rather than a revolutionary act, Winfrey's acceptance by mainstream America and the world is predicated on the historical role of the mammy in relation to her charges and to the white family. Winfrey's success is indicative of the way dominant society is prepared and trained to engage black female iconography. The black woman has to be serving in some capacity, no matter how much she benefits financially from the relationship.

Winfrey, via her show, provides spiritual nourishment for her audience. In fact, for several years the major theme of her show was "remembering your spirit." Thus, Winfrey became the point of contact for an affluent dominant society to get in touch with itself. The show has also provided physical nourishment, in the form of cooking segments, recipes, and diet advice. The difference between the mammy and Winfrey is that the latter has been paid handsomely for her "milk" and was clever enough to realize that she should be the distributor of her product as well—in the old days, it would have been impossible for mammy to profit from the service she provided. The question then becomes whether the same critique can be applied to the iconography of Oprah Winfrey. Can a mammy be a mammy if she profits from her services? Can a mammy be a mammy if she builds girls' schools in Africa?

This is the anxiety that critical spectators feel when they engage Winfrey's imagery. Many of these spectators want to applaud Winfrey and congratulate her for breaking down barriers and in some ways rectifying the negative imagery of African American women. Winfrey represents the best of black female agency, energy, and intellect; however, critical spectators also fear that she represents something else. Many critical black spectators are uncomfortable with *The Oprah Winfrey Show* because they detect the same kind of erasure Wiegman identifies in *Lethal Weapon*. Tales of Winfrey's meteoric rise to power and fame always begin with a prelude of humble beginnings. Her story is told in a way that insists she was different from other black children, called out and set apart from an early age. For those of us who remember integration and affirmative action, it may be difficult to witness this particular bootstrap story without crying out for the prequel.

In addition to the reinscription of the mammy figure, Winfrey's relationship with the dominant society—and, I believe, her continued participation in the reciprocal capitalist relationship—is also reliant on the Alger ideology. Collins continues her critique by pointing out Winfrey's

> individualistic ideology of social change that counsels her audiences to rely solely on themselves. . . . Yet Winfrey's message stops far short of linking such individual changes to the actual resources and opportunities that are needed to escape from poverty, stop an abusive spouse from battering, or avoid job discrimination. . . . The organizational group politics that helped create the very opportunities that Winfrey herself enjoys are minimized in favor of personal responsibility that resonates with the theme of "personal responsibility," used by elites to roll back social welfare programs.[22]

Collins articulates my own personal difficulty with Winfrey. The self-help diatribe, though popular, is useless if it is not paired with a realistic methodology and real resources. Winfrey owes her success at least in part to the collective efforts and real suffering of other individuals and groups. There could not be an *Oprah Winfrey Show* and the huge success of its host if not for the efforts of structured protest and the passage of antidiscrimination laws. In her passion to push rugged individualism, Winfrey does not seem to acknowledge that marginalized individuals have always had to marshal themselves in groups to subvert a system designed to keep them marginalized. Although it is true that we are all responsible for ourselves, it is also true that there are real and inherent hurdles in society that effectively work to thwart the efforts and undo the bootstraps of certain individuals as they attempt to struggle upward.

There is another way in which the looking relationship with Winfrey is laden with tension for critical black female spectators; it has to do with the way Winfrey becomes yet one more purveyor of the market system. Often disguised as advice or suggestion or discovery or one of "Oprah's favorite things," Winfrey sells herself—in part as the buying of self. In 2006 Winfrey's magazine was advertising the "Live Your Best Life Tour." According to the O magazine Web site, the tickets cost $185 to attend the lecture and luncheon, and the "Live Your Best Life Online Workshop" cost $24.95 for those who could not attend in person.[23] The lecture and workshop promised to provide Winfrey's "personal insights and life moments." Winfrey's dietary strategies, her exercise routine, her clothes, her memories, and her "spirit" are all for sale. Thus, it is possible to purchase Winfrey's life experiences, personal triumphs and tragedies, and life lessons in lieu of having those experiences oneself. Winfrey's body becomes the surrogate body, reminiscent of the bodies of slave women that were used to produce milk, food, labor, and more workers. She has made millions of dollars selling the idea of buying "Oprah" as one method of being fulfilled. Once again, it is the body of a black woman that acts as feed and seed for the ideological body of the dominant society.

In addition, a number of careers and businesses have been launched, and a number of books have been sold, because Winfrey promoted them on her show. This affirmation of consumerism is by no means unique to Winfrey and is, of course, the ultimate goal of capitalism. Yet Winfrey bills herself as the champion of the weak and the promoter of charity. She does many good deeds for the weak with one hand and cycles the system that would make them weaker with the other. Winfrey is the ultimate corporation.

Although critical black female spectators may be glad that Oprah Winfrey is where she is and are aware that she reached that echelon because of her tenacity, intellect, and market savvy, we also long for an acknowledgment and critique of a world system designed to keep the majority of marginalized people marginalized. We long for the queen of talk to talk about the fact that magnificent and impressive achievement does not always have to be defined as money, and remembering a spirit does not necessitate reaching into one's wallet and purchasing it from Oprah Winfrey. Although we are immensely proud, we sense an erasure of the black woman, both historically and culturally, in Winfrey's relationship with her mainstream audience. We wish her even more success, but we cannot help but wonder why it feels as if Winfrey has distanced herself from everyday black people and why allusions to the American black community on the show sound performatory.

It is not popular to challenge the foundation of Winfrey's wealth—her ability to sell her advice, her nurturing, and herself to white America. Because she has sold it well, and because she has become rich, there is a tendency not to question her methods. Money wins out in the end as the qualitative signifier in a society bent on a bourgeois ideology of achievement. Yet, for the critical black female spectator, it is hard to watch Winfrey because we see much more than we care to and much less than we want to. At the back of the audience, straining to get to the microphone and hoping to touch Winfrey's hand, is the specter of the mammy and how she has economically and psychically driven a society. Outside the audience, critical black female spectators are hoping that we will finally be able to watch the show and see Oprah Winfrey—not recycled ideologies and iconographies disguised in a Valentino dress.

Notes

1. I will be using critical theories that range from film and photography to cultural criticism as a way to explore black women's looking relationships with Oprah Winfrey as an icon.

2. bell hooks, *Reel to Real: Race, Sex, and Class at the Movies* (New York: Routledge, 1996), 210.

3. Deborah Willis, *Picturing Us: African American Identity in Photography* (New York: New Press, 1994).

4. Patricia A. Turner, *Ceramic Uncles and Celluloid Mammies: Black Images and Their Influence on Culture* (Charlottesville: University of Virginia Press, 1994), 49.

5. Ibid.

6. See Deborah Willis and David Levering Lewis, *A Small Nation of People: W. E. B. DuBois and African American Portraits of Progress* (New York: Amistad Press, 2003).

7. Robyn Wiegman, "Black Bodies/American Commodities: Gender, Race, and the Bourgeois Ideal in Contemporary Film," in *Unspeakable Images: Ethnicity, and the American Cinema,* ed. Lester D. Friedman (Urbana: University of Illinois Press, 1991), 320.

8. Ibid.

9. Laurie L. Haag, "Oprah Winfrey: The Construction of Intimacy in the Talk Show Setting," *Journal of Popular Culture* 26 (1993): 115–21.

10. Trudier Harris, *From Mammies to Militants: Domestics in Black American Literature* (Philadelphia: Temple University Press, 1982), 11–12.

11. Ibid., 35.

12. Alan M. Rubin, Paul M. Haridakis, and Keren Eyal, "Viewer Aggression and Attraction to Television Talk Shows," *Media Psychology* 5, no. 4 (2003): 331.

13. Haag, "Oprah Winfrey," 112.

14. For several seasons, the focus of *The Oprah Winfrey Show* was helping audience members and television viewers connect or reconnect with their spirits.

15. Donald Bogle, *Toms, Coons, Mulattoes, Mammies and Bucks: An Interpretive History of Blacks in American Films* (New York: Continuum, 1994), 9.

16. Doris Witt, "What (N)ever Happened to Aunt Jemima: Eating Disorders, Fetal Rights, and Black Female Appetite in Contemporary American Culture," in *Skin Deep, Spirit Strong: The Black Female Body in American Culture,* ed. Kimberly Wallace Sanders (Ann Arbor: University of Michigan Press, 2002), 240.

17. It was 1988 when Winfrey appeared on her show in size ten Calvin Klein jeans after having used a liquid diet to lose weight.

18. For a further discussion of black female appetite and the dominant society's relationship to it, see Witt, "What (N)ever Happened to Aunt Jemima."

19. I do not want to imply that there is an authentic or monolithic presentation of blackness, but I believe that the critical black female spectators' view of Winfrey has to be considered.

20. Julie Scelfo, "The Contender: An Oprah Disciple Gets Her Own Show," *Newsweek,* January 8, 2001, 48.

21. Patricia Hill Collins, *Black Sexual Politics: African Americans, Gender and the New Racism* (New York: Routledge, 2004), 142.

22. Ibid., 143.

23. *O* magazine Web site: http://www.oprah.com/presents/2003/lybl/pres_2003_lybl_main.jhtml?promocode=800.

My Mom and Oprah Winfrey

Her Appeal to White Women

Linda Kay

In the mid–1980s I was a single white female (SWF) working as a sports-writer for the *Chicago Tribune*. I lived in a condominium in downtown Chicago with a view of Lake Michigan. I did not own a car, walked everywhere, and reveled in my status as a city girl. My mother, who had raised three kids in a New Jersey suburb and was recently widowed, vis-ited Chicago regularly. On the days I went to work, she passed the time at Water Tower Place, an impressive mall and condominium complex that stretches seventy-four floors above Michigan Avenue. The main entrance to the mall featured a waterfall cascading between a pair of escalators. Flagship department stores, boutiques, and bookstores radi-ated out from a central eight-story atrium sliced vertically by three glass elevators. My mom would often head to the mall to catch a movie.

One day after seeing a film she stopped by an ice cream parlor just outside the cinema. The place was virtually empty. As my mother finished up her treat, in walked the best-known resident of the Water Tower condominium complex, Oprah Winfrey, wearing a knit cardigan and white pants and accompanied by a small boy. Her newly syndicated talk show was gaining her fame outside Chicago, as was her Academy Award nomination for *The Color Purple*. "I watch your show every day and I think you're great," Mom said, as Winfrey stood at the counter wait-ing to place a take-out order. Winfrey turned around and smiled, then introduced the little boy as her nephew. She and my mother continued to chitchat, and then she ordered an ice cream for the boy and a choco-late malted for herself. "Don't tell anyone," she told my mom conspira-torially. Meanwhile, a waiter, excited by the celebrity's presence, was trying unsuccessfully to locate a blank piece of paper for an autograph. He grabbed my mother's check from the table and asked if he could use it to collect Winfrey's signature. My mother agreed. Winfrey signed her name on the back of the check and then looked at my mother and cracked, "Don't think this means I'm paying the bill."

My mother's encounter with Oprah Winfrey speaks volumes about the talk-show host, who has the ability to connect with perfect strang-ers as if she has known them all her life. Early on in her fame, she was comfortable chatting with anyone and everyone—older white ladies included. In return, white women were comfortable with her. They found her approachable. They viewed her as a friend. They connected with her—and they still do.

Connections are the subject of this essay, or, more precisely, how Oprah Winfrey "makes the connection" with white women (to use a variation on the title of the fitness book she coauthored with trainer Bob Greene). But before I go further, I must reveal an unexpected con-nection I discovered during my research: to my surprise, I realized that my mother and Oprah Winfrey were born on the same day—January 29. These two women with the same birthday, born precisely twenty-seven years apart, seemingly had little in common when they met in the ice cream parlor that day. But scratch the surface, and the com-monalities emerge and extend beyond a shared horoscope. My mother, a retired bookkeeper, connected with Winfrey for the same reasons that millions of other white women have connected with her in the past and continue to do so today. Their shared birthday became for me a serendipitous connection, a talisman of sorts, and a departure point for other more potent links.

Back to the Beginning

By the time *The Oprah Winfrey Show* wraps up in 2011, after twenty-five years on the air, the host will have touched three generations of white women—my mother's, my own, and my daughter's. Winfrey's show is rated top among women aged eighteen to thirty-four,[1] and a ratings spike among young adults reportedly caused her to reconsider two previously announced retirement dates in 2006 and 2008.[2] Her goal is to reach another generation of women.

In 2001 the audience for *The Oprah Winfrey Show* consisted of 72 percent women, a figure that has remained fairly consistent since the show started in syndication in 1986. According to Nielsen Media Research, the show's average daily audience consisted of 5,022,000 women aged eighteen and over in the period between October 2000 and September 2001. Of those 5 million-plus women, 4,112,000 identified themselves as white; 1,856,000 of these white viewers were between the ages of eighteen and forty-nine, and 2,256,000 were fifty or older.

First, let's consider why white women over fifty—Winfrey's core audience and my mother's contemporaries—connected so strongly with a young black woman. To do that, we have to go back to the show's beginnings. What is now *The Oprah Winfrey Show* started in 1984 when Winfrey took over as the host of *AM Chicago*. Within a month, the morning show was more popular than *Donahue,* a nationally syndicated talk show that was likewise based in Chicago. Something was brewing.

I asked my mother's opinion, and she said that she had never liked Phil Donahue. She felt that he was an actor and was condescending. It bothered her that in 1975 he had divorced his first wife, with whom he had five children. Mom never watched *Donahue* after *The Oprah Winfrey Show* came on the air. She was drawn to Winfrey, but she was also turning her back on Donahue.

Interestingly enough, ratings for *Donahue* increased after *The Oprah Winfrey Show* arrived. According to Ed Papazian, president of the New York–based Media Dynamics, which publishes the annual statistical bible on the television industry called *TV Dimensions,* Winfrey "recatalyzed" the entire realm of daytime talk shows. Her high ratings in the coveted 4:00 to 5:00 P.M. time slot, between soap operas and the early local news, actually convinced stations to give *Donahue* and other talks shows a more advantageous niche.[3] Previously, *Donahue* had never made it onto the top-ten list of nationally syndicated programs, but it did in February 1987, just months after the debut of *The Oprah Winfrey Show.* In that 1987 survey, *The Oprah Winfrey Show* placed fourth on the top-ten list, and *Donahue* ranked tenth; *Donahue* aired on 181 stations that year, compared with 143 for *The Oprah Winfrey Show.* The following year, *The Oprah Winfrey Show* was carried by nearly fifty more stations, and *Donahue* by two more; *Oprah* moved up to third on the top-ten list, and *Donahue* moved to eighth. In 1989 *The Oprah Winfrey Show* dropped to fourth and *Donahue* rose to sixth, but that rise was temporary. *Donahue* dropped off the list in 1990, resurfaced at number ten in 1991, and failed to make the list again.[4] Phil Donahue ended his show in the spring of 1996. Ratings were on the decline in several major markets, and even his affiliate station in New York, where the talk show was then based, had dropped the show from its schedule.

Phil Donahue is widely credited with introducing an issue-oriented platform to daytime talk television. *The Phil Donahue Show* first aired in 1967; it was syndicated two years later and became simply *Donahue* in 1974. When Oprah Winfrey entered the national scene almost two decades after Donahue, she adopted his platform of issue-oriented talk but diverged from his style as a communicator. Clearly, *The Oprah Winfrey Show* gave viewers like my mother an alternative that they found refreshing and empowering.

Analyzing the rhetoric of *Donahue* in an article written in 1984, two years before the advent of *The Oprah Winfrey Show,* Frank Tomasulo makes a forceful case that reinforces Mom's belief that Donahue condescended to his audience. Rather than seeing him as a champion of women's issues, Tomasulo argues that Donahue actually undermined female authority by establishing himself as a "surrogate, symbolic Father," an authoritarian figure who controlled the discussion. Tomasulo cites the way that the show often opened—with the studio audience literally in the dark, suggesting that they, along with the viewers at home, did "not really know enough about the issues under discussion." Other techniques were employed to establish a paradigm that placed Donahue as the rational "owner of debate, Talk, the Law and language" and cast the predominantly female audience as "emotional, unenlightened and intolerant." Donahue, according to Tomasulo, also used his patriarchal power as a way to keep the discussion within bounds, using certain expressions ("Not much time," "We're running out of time," "Don't make a speech") to prod the audience "to encapsulate arguments into catch phrases and ensure that there is no time for reflection."[5]

A scholar who appeared on both *Donahue* and *The Oprah Winfrey Show* captured perhaps the essential difference between the two hosts. Deborah Tannen, a professor of linguistics at Georgetown University, witnessed the different communication styles of Donahue and Winfrey when she was a guest on both shows to discuss her book *You*

Just Don't Understand: Women and Men in Conversation. In a profile of Winfrey written for *Time* in 1998, when Winfrey made the magazine's list of the hundred most influential people in the twentieth century, Tannen noted that Donahue's show featured mostly what she labeled "report-talk"—talk that placed an overt focus on information and expert commentary. Winfrey, in contrast, took "report-talk" and transformed it into "rapport talk," which Tannen defined as a back-and-forth conversational style that is the "basis of female friendship, with its emphasis on self-revealing intimacies." According to Tannen, Winfrey directed the focus of her program away from experts and toward ordinary people talking about personal issues. "Winfrey related my book to her own life," Tannen wrote. "She began by saying she had read the book and 'saw myself over and over' in it. She then told one of my examples, adding, 'I've done that a thousand times'—and illustrated it by describing herself and Stedman [Graham]." According to Tannen, "with Winfrey, the talk show became more immediate, more confessional, more personal." In summing up Winfrey's influence on and importance to the world of entertainment, Tannen cited her ability to understand that although television conveys information, it also acts like a family member and "sits down to meals with us and talks to us in the lonely afternoons." Tannen continued, "Oprah exhorts viewers to improve their lives and the world. She makes people care because she cares. That is Oprah Winfrey's genius and will be her legacy."[6]

Time for Girl Talk

Not too long ago, I conducted an admittedly unscientific survey at my mom's assisted-living residence. I passed around an imaginary microphone to residents and staff—a group of white women of various ages—and asked them why they liked Oprah Winfrey. Replies differed, depending on the respondent's age. Older viewers who had watched *The Oprah Winfrey Show* from its earliest days identified two reasons why they connected with the host: first, her determination to make something out of her life despite considerable obstacles ("She had such a hard childhood," said a woman in her eighties), and second, her willingness to share her life frankly with her audience. Middle-aged women largely connected with Winfrey's quest for personal growth—an exploration of self that requires a frank and open character ("She's sincere," said a woman in her fifties). Younger women were more likely to see Winfrey as an inspirational figure performing good works ("She's a role model," said a woman in her early forties).

For my mother, now in her late seventies, Winfrey's humble start provided a strong point of connection. My mother did not come from Mississippi, did not grow up impoverished, and is obviously not black. But my mother is a first-generation American whose own mother was smuggled out of Russia as a teenager to escape persecution; my grandmother traveled alone by ship to the United States with only the clothes on her back. My mother's father also fled Russia as a youth and never saw his parents again. Witnessing the immigrant experience marked my mother. She watched her parents learn to read and write English. She watched them try to better themselves as they provided for five children. My mother could certainly connect to Winfrey's Horatio Alger story of raising herself above modest circumstances and making something out of almost nothing. But what she and other white women could not do was openly discuss their difficulties. White women like my mom did not believe in airing their dirty linen in public. In that sense, Winfrey broke new ground for these women. In turn, they bonded with her more powerfully. When she revealed her foibles, admitted her weaknesses, owned up to mistakes, and, quite importantly, related her shame, she was speaking for millions of women who had been socialized to keep such experiences to themselves. Gloria-Jean Masciarotte contends that *The Oprah Winfrey Show* made a significant contribution simply by "displaying the space" for female stories, particularly stories dealing with painful subjects or ill-defined struggles.[7] Tannen writes that Winfrey's power comes from telling her own secrets—"divulging that she once ate a package of hot dog buns drenched in maple syrup, that she had smoked cocaine, even that she had been raped as a child."[8]

In examining Winfrey's ability to connect with her viewers, Laurie L. Haag cites her success in constructing intimacy in a talk-show setting. Haag contends that she did it with "girl talk" and the characteristics associated with it: most importantly, self-disclosure, but also supportive listening behaviors that include sustained eye contact and nonverbal gestures, such as touching an arm or a shoulder. Winfrey also builds intimacy, according to Haag, by spontaneously reacting to what happens on the program—hooting, howling, laughing, or crying as the situation dictates, allowing the viewer at home to do the same. Haag credits a number of female talk-show hosts from the 1960s and 1970s with paving the way for Winfrey by employing similar girl-talk strategies. "In the 1960s, Dinah Shore invited us each morning to *Dinah's Place,* complete with living room and kitchenette. . . . Virginia Graham invited us over for *Girltalk,* a slightly more gossipy form of chat than [that] offered by Shore, and Joan Rivers had her own 'can-we-talk' format in 1969." These shows and others "established a recognizable place for women's talk and the female voice on television."[9]

Winfrey, however, took girl talk a good deal further, and her popularity grew as she divulged more intimate details of her life. As Haag notes, self-disclosure is a unique aspect of female friendships. In same-sex friendships women tend to disclose more than they do in male-female relationships, and the messages they disclose to each other are more emotional and profound. Significantly, self-disclosure tends to encourage more self-disclosure, thus generating a greater sense of intimacy. Many of the details of Winfrey's life, particularly the sexual abuse she suffered as a child, did not become public until after the release of *The Color Purple.* Accordingly, Haag posits that the "evolution of the legend of Oprah" really began after the film. That legend includes her earliest years living with her grandmother in Mississippi, her tumultuous pre-adolescence and early teenage years with her mother in Milwaukee, her move to Nashville and a far more disciplined existence with her father, and the chain of successes and failures with men, jobs, self-esteem, and her weight. As Haag astutely points out, Winfrey's contemporaries in the talk-show world lack such legends, and it is the legend that is largely responsible for Winfrey's success with white women. "The legend, as it has evolved, is a vital part of our relationship with Winfrey and a vital part of her incredible success, serving to let us feel intimate with her as well as making both her obvious ethnicity and her amazing success acceptable to a . . . largely white audience."[10]

The legend that enables white woman to feel an intimacy with Winfrey transcends economic and social strata. Tipper Gore, wife of the former vice president, appeared on the show in 1999 to reveal that she had battled clinical depression. She told the talk-show host, "I couldn't will myself out of it, pray myself out of it or pull myself up out of it." Replied Winfrey, "It takes a lot of courage to come on and say 'this happened to me.'" As she praised her guest, we in the audience grasped that Winfrey's courage to disclose is what allowed people like Gore to do the same. It is her fearless ability to self-disclose that most distinguishes Winfrey from her peers.

Her extraordinary use of girl talk to create intimacy is obvious even to her detractors, who often find her unexpectedly disarming. During the fall of 1991, Vicki Abt, a professor of sociology and American studies at Pennsylvania State University, carried out a content analysis of talk shows that resulted in an article (written with Mel Seesholtz) called "The Shameless World of Phil, Sally, and Oprah: Television Talk Shows and the Deconstructing of Society."[11] Even before Abt's findings were published, they engendered controversy and media attention and led to a two-day appearance on *The Oprah Winfrey Show* at the start of the 1994–95 season. In a lengthy footnote in a 1997 book coauthored by Abt, the professor mulls over her appearance on the show and admits having conflicted feelings about the host. Abt acknowledges that her experience on the show "adds credence to Oprah's abilities to put people at ease before and during the show." As Abt describes it (in the third person), Winfrey's first question, off camera, was, How do you like my shoes?—referring to her new, very fashionable footwear. "It was as if they were old friends, and Abt's fashion opinion counted for something," the footnote recounts. "During the course of the show, Oprah continually referred to Dr. Abt as 'Vicki,' and, even when the audience was furious at Abt for attacking talk shows and especially their icon, Oprah Winfrey, Oprah acted as if she would protect her guest. . . . Through it all, Oprah's charisma was overwhelming. It was difficult not to believe in her sincerity and good will. She would make the perfect government diplomat."[12]

The Legend Continues

Winfrey's notable ability to construct intimacy, whether with her studio guests or with a live audience, is clearly illustrated in a commencement address she gave at Wellesley College in May 1997, when the daughter of her longtime partner, Stedman Graham, was one of the graduating class of some six hundred women.[13] That speech was an amalgam of the approaches and philosophies that make Winfrey so appealing to white women, be they senior citizens, baby boomers, or the young, largely white group of Wellesley graduates she was addressing. In it, she shares her painful experiences and embarrassing moments. She also lets the graduates enter her personal realm right away, mentioning her partner almost immediately ("Stedman is my beau, my fiancé, don't ask me when we're going to get married"). She says that when she was young, she wanted very much to attend Wellesley herself but was unable to obtain a scholarship to do so. She admits to living vicariously for the past four years through Wendy, Graham's daughter, a poignant statement coming from one of the most famous women in the world.

The rest of the speech reproduces the tone of her recent shows, which emphasize transformation, both physical and emotional, and encourage viewers to reach for their dreams. She weaves the philosophical and the personal into her address by detailing five lessons she has learned that helped make her life better. Before delivering the medicine, she jokes that the graduates should be happy there are only five and not ten lessons. Winfrey then deftly proceeds to interlace her personal struggle with ideas that are meant to be motivational, instructional, and inspirational.

First lesson: Every experience teaches you more fully who you really are. For a long time, Winfrey tells the students, she wanted to be someone else. She talks about trying to have thighs like Diana Ross; about undergoing a makeover at the behest of a news director and "allowing them to put a French perm on my Black hair and having the perm burn through my cerebral cortex . . . and not having the courage to say 'this is burning me' and coming out a week later bald." She recounts making glaring pronunciation mistakes while anchoring the news in Baltimore and one day laughing out loud when she erred: "This is when I broke out of my Barbara (Walters) shell. . . . I decided then to pursue the idea of being myself."

Second lesson: When people show you who they are, believe them the first time. Winfrey relates that she and Wendy have had many discussions about this concept. "When it comes to men situations . . . when he doesn't call back the first time, when you are mistreated the first time, when you see someone who shows you a lack of integrity or dishonesty the first time, know that that will be followed by many, many, many other times." She does not elaborate, but the precision of the message makes you understand that she speaks from personal experience.

Third lesson: Turn wounds into wisdom. Winfrey tells the audience that she was removed from her news anchor position in Baltimore because she would sometimes cry when covering a sad story. "It wasn't until I was demoted as an on-air anchor woman and thrown into the talk show arena to get rid of me that I allowed my own truth to come through." Her talk-show debut "felt like breathing, which is what your true passion should feel like."

Fourth lesson: Be grateful. "I believe that if you can learn to focus on what you have," Winfrey says, "you will always see that the universe is abundant and you will have more." She suggests that the graduates keep journals and list five things for which they are thankful every night. "You all are all over my journal tonight," she tells them.

Fifth lesson: Create the grandest vision for your life, because you become what you believe. Every life, Winfrey asserts, speaks to the power of what can be done. "When I was a little girl in Mississippi, growing up on the farm, only Buckwheat as a role model, watching my grandmother boil clothes in a big iron pot, I realized somehow inside myself, in the spirit of myself, that my life could be bigger, greater than what I saw." And with that, Winfrey closes her speech by reciting Maya Angelou's poem "Phenomenal Woman."

It is a highly personal speech, trademark Oprah Winfrey, ostensibly directed at the young women who are just starting out on life's journey. However, Winfrey's speech also targets the parents and grandparents in the audience. It manages to convey life lessons that are relevant to everyone, no matter their age, along with an acknowledgment of personal struggle, a recognition that is appealing to an older generation. As Winfrey relays one maxim after another, it is easy to envision the grandparents and parents of these young women nodding their heads in agreement. As she does on her show, Winfrey uses the opportunity to connect multiple generations, using her own experience as the bridge.

Girls Like Me

Although middle-aged white woman like myself—Winfrey's contemporaries—do not have the same connection to her that our mothers do, she has touched many of us just the same. We have watched her make mistakes, admit them, and learn from them. We have watched her struggle to grow and change and evolve. We connect because we have experienced the same struggles.

I first started watching *The Oprah Winfrey Show* because I was intrigued by the host's public battle with her weight. Living in Chicago,

I had seen Winfrey around town. At a wedding to which we were both invited, I admired her gutsy choice of a fuchsia dress and matching wide-brimmed hat—not exactly an outfit for a wallflower, and certainly not an outfit one would associate with a woman who was self-conscious about her size. To me, it seemed that Winfrey had made peace with being overweight. Not so, as I was to learn in the coming years.

In 1988, when Winfrey announced that she was losing weight on the Optifast diet, so many people called for information about the diet that no one could get through. The wild reaction was an early testament to Winfrey's unwitting (at the time) marketing power and a precursor to her staggering influence when it comes to almost any venture, whether it be Rosie Daley's 1994 cookbook *In the Kitchen with Rosie* (which I gave friends for Christmas); her magazine, O (named 2001 Start-up of the Year by *Adweek*); her support of Dr. Phil McGraw (who now has the second-highest-rated talk show next to Winfrey's); or an enormously popular book club that has made her the fairy godmother of the publishing industry. (Her endorsement of the classic *Anna Karenina* provides a perfect example of Winfrey's disarming brand of self-disclosure. "This book was on my must-read list for years," she admits, "but I was scared of it. Let's not be scared of it. I'm going to team up with all of you and we'll read it together.")

The Optifast program, of course, was only the beginning of Winfrey's public battle of the bulge. As she ruefully writes in an article for O magazine, she starved herself for four months on Optifast, got down to 145 pounds, and stayed there for precisely one day before the regaining began.[14] As Winfrey struggled with her food problem, I was in the audience watching; having been there and done that myself, I had learned, blessedly, that no diet program would cure the emotional triggers in one's head. Along with an audience of millions, I watched as Winfrey gained, lost, and regained.

In Chicago, rumors circulated that she had been spotted at various restaurants eating mashed potatoes (her personal weakness) when she was supposed to be dieting. Some found it comical, but I did not. The public spectacle continued to play out every day on television. Winfrey lost weight while working out with exercise maven Bob Greene. She ran a marathon and lost more. But after the Texas beef trial and disappointment over the tepid box-office response to her movie *Beloved*, she ate her way up to two hundred pounds. In August 2001 she walked into her doctor's office suffering from heart palpitations and elevated blood pressure. At that point, according to her own account, she finally accepted that no diet would do the trick when you have "used food to relieve stress, for comfort, and to momentarily stand in for joy." She accepted that there are "no shortcuts or secrets, no magic patches or pills." Her words resonated with white female baby boomers because they went far beyond weight. There are no shortcuts or magic pills to help us succeed in life, in work, in marriage, or as parents.

It is as a parent that I have reengaged with Winfrey, using her show to teach my own daughter about the value, importance, and joy of giving. When Winfrey linked up with Heifer International in an effort to convince folks to buy a cow, chicken, or goat in the belief that the purchase of a gift animal could drastically improve the lives of the less fortunate, I hit on a good way to interest my animal-crazy teenager in a discussion about giving instead of receiving. However tentative, it is a connection that now links my daughter to the queen of talk.

A Final Word

January 29, 2004: my mother's birthday, and Oprah Winfrey's birthday too. Unfortunately, my mom was in the hospital, but she watched Winfrey's party from her hospital bed—never making the connection that they were born on the same day. "Oprah's 50th Birthday Bash" drew the show's highest ratings in eight years. More than 14 million viewers tuned in—66 percent more than on an average day, and the highest viewership of a single-day episode since November 1993.

As my mother put it, the birthday party was an extravaganza. "Everybody knew about it," she remembers, "and everybody and his uncle was there." It started on television with a "surprise" party and continued all weekend long with a dinner in Chicago as well as a celebration at Winfrey's home in Santa Barbara. The television studio, placed off-limits to the talk-show host while party preparations were under way, held ten thousand flowers, a four hundred–pound cake, and a cast of luminaries that included John Travolta, Stevie Wonder, and Tina Turner. Jay Leno flew in from the West Coast to join the fun and then jetted back for *The Tonight Show*. Winfrey, Graham, and her best friend, Gayle King, participated in the singing and dancing on the set. Travolta made a champagne toast ("You are a citizen of the world and you are a hero to mankind"), and Wolfgang Puck catered a birthday meal featuring crayfish and jumbo shrimp from Louisiana, lobster from Maine, and catfish from Alabama. Sugar cookies hand-painted with an O were dispensed, as were raw silk handbags filled with favors that included custom flannel pajamas.

Mom still watches the show after all these years—not as faithfully as she did at one point, but several times a week. I asked why she is still drawn to Winfrey, and her response echoed the reasons that made her connect with her from the start: "She has such ambition and drive. She educated herself, and she didn't let all those bad things in her life stop her from making her life better. That's a very important part of why I still like her and admire her. She opens up new worlds to people. Her message is you can shine if you apply yourself."

The notion of rising above circumstance against the odds and, not insignificantly, the notion of transformation as a limitless process form the bedrock of the "Oprah" legend and are the source of her appeal. The sense of infinite possibility that Winfrey presents so compellingly is encapsulated in Phoebe Gilman's captivating children's book *Something from Nothing,* adapted from a Jewish folktale.[15] The book tells the story of Joseph, whose grandfather, a tailor, makes him a blanket when he is a baby. As he gets bigger, the boy does not want to give up the blanket, even though it is torn and worn. He takes it to his grandfather, who turns the blanket into a jacket. Later, when the jacket is too small, Grandpa cuts, snips, and sews, turning the jacket into a vest. The process of transformation continues for years as the indomitable Joseph and the skilled and resourceful Grandpa team up to make something from nothing, time after time. Meanwhile, a family of mice residing in the basement steadily gathers all the scraps to enhance a parallel and ever-changing universe in their own underground home.

The something-from-nothing legend that surrounds Oprah Winfrey resonates for white women in much the same way. For first-generation Americans whose families came to the United States fleeing oppression or hunger or war, Winfrey transcended the color line. She pulled herself up by the bootstraps, faced the obstacles, and, importantly, made something from nothing. She is perceived as being fashioned by grit, determination, hard work, and desire. Winfrey's experience, though different in the details, reflects the life stories of women regardless of color and age. Winfrey's story reverberates because it comprises large doses of both struggle and transformation. Winfrey's story captures the boundless possibilities that life holds, despite the hurdles, an idea that resonates for us, our daughters, our sisters, and our mothers—for every woman.

Notes

1. Paige Albiniak, "Syndies Won't Stop Seeking Youth," *Broadcasting and Cable,* October 27, 2003.

2. Josh Grossberg, "Oprah Keeps her Day Job," *E! Online News*, May 20, 2003, http://www.eonline.com/News/Items/Pf/0,1527,11833,00.html.

3. Telephone interview with Ed Papazian, July 19, 2004.

4. *TV Dimensions* (New York: Media Dynamics, 2002).

5. Frank Tomasulo, "The Spectator-in-the-Tube: The Rhetoric of Donahue," *Journal of Film and Video* 36, no. 2 (1984): 6–9.

6. *Time,* June 8, 1998, 197–98. http://www.allperson.com/allperson/legend/0000000932.asp.

7. Gloria-Jean Masciarotte, "C'mon Girl: Oprah Winfrey and the Discourse of Feminine Talk," *Genders* 11 (Fall 1991): 89, 82.

8. *Time,* June 8, 1988, 197–98.

9. Laurie L. Haag, "Oprah Winfrey: The Construction of Intimacy in the Talk Show Setting," *Journal of Popular Culture* 26 (1993): 116–19.

10. Ibid., 118.

11. Vicki Abt and Mel Seesholtz, "The Shameless World of Phil, Sally, and Oprah: Television Talk Shows and the Deconstructing of Society," *Journal of Popular Culture* 28 (1994):171–91.

12. Vicki Abt and Leonard Mustazza, *Coming after Oprah: Cultural Fallout in the Age of the TV Talk Show* (Bowling Green, Ohio: Bowling Green State University Popular Press, 1997).

13. Oprah Winfrey, Commencement Address, Wellesley College, May 30, 1997, http://www.wellesley.edu/PublicAffairs/Pahomepage/winfey.html.

14. Oprah Winfrey, "Oprah's New Shape," *O, the Oprah Magazine,* January 2003, http://www.oprah.com/health/omag_200301_fit_story.jhtml.

15. Phoebe Gilman, *Something from Nothing* (New York: Scholastic Press, 1992).

The "Oprahization" of America

The Man Show *and the Redefinition of Black Femininity*

Valerie Palmer-Mehta

The hit Comedy Central series *The Man Show* debuted on June 16, 1999, to ratings that broke all records for the channel. The introductory program was titled "The Oprahization of America," and original hosts Jimmy Kimmel and Adam Carolla had this to say about talk-show host Oprah Winfrey and contemporary social relationships in the United States:

> KIMMEL: We're here because we have a serious problem in America and her name is Oprah. Millions and millions of women are under Oprah's spell. This woman has half of America brainwashed.
>
> CAROLLA: She tells them what to read, what to eat, what to think, what to do. . . .
>
> KIMMEL: We're the ones that are supposed to be telling them what to do, right? Enough is enough. The Oprahization of America must be stopped.
>
> CAROLLA: This Oprah needs to do a little less brainwashing and a little more sock washing.
>
> KIMMEL: We are here today to reclaim the airwaves, to take back the medium we invented. Hey, who invented the television, a man or a woman?

AUDIENCE: A man!

CAROLLA: That's right. And he didn't invent it for Oprah or Rosie. . . . He invented it for Charlie and his Angels and Hogan and his Heroes. . . . Those were shows men could enjoy.

KIMMEL: We want to return to that era and that is what this show will be—a joyous celebration of chauvinism.

When Carolla states that Oprah Winfrey should be doing "a little more sock washing," the camera pans to the loudly cheering studio audience. The only black man in the audience is shown with both arms raised high above his head, cheering enthusiastically in solidarity with (and, in fact, more strenuously than) his white brothers (this act of solidarity is confounded later in the series when Kimmel engages in minstrelsy in a regular segment that disparages basketball player Karl Malone). The camera also focuses on two Asian men and one Asian woman who are applauding and smiling (an act of solidarity that is confounded on the August 27, 2000, episode, "Myths and Facts about College," when Carolla places a bespectacled Chinese youth on the checkout counter and tells young college men that they don't need to do homework because they can get their "very own Chinese kid" to do it for them). At various points during Kimmel and Carolla's proclamation about Winfrey, the camera shows black and white "Juggy Girls," sparsely clothed young women whose function is to dance provocatively for the studio and home-viewing audiences and to reinforce the misogynistic rhetoric of the hosts by smiling, nodding, and clapping (obviously, this relationship is confounded from the start). The rest of the audience is composed of white, presumably heterosexual men who are cheering the hosts' proclamation. By focusing the camera on diverse audience members who seemingly approve of the hosts' message (though one would be naïve to think that this is anything other than manufactured), Kimmel and Carolla attempt to make this an issue of gender, not of race—a case of men's united attempt to consolidate their power over women.

Although the misogyny in this excerpt warrants its own study, more perplexing and provoking is the hosts' frequent declaration of their disdain for Oprah Winfrey and their desire to "stop her." Of all the women disparaged on the program during the original hosts' four-season tenure, Winfrey's name came up more frequently than any other.[1] It is difficult to understand how anyone could have such contempt for

Winfrey, considering the many obstacles she has overcome in her pursuit of success and the extent to which she has shared her success with others.

Despite extremely humble beginnings in Mississippi, being shuffled around among her grandparents and her estranged mother and father, and enduring sexual abuse, Winfrey secured a scholarship to Tennessee State University. During her sophomore year, she became the first black and the first woman anchor of Nashville's WTVF-TV. Now, three decades later, "when Winfrey talks, her viewers—an estimated 14 million daily in the U.S. and millions more in 132 other countries—listen."[2] Deborah Tannen explains that viewers trust Winfrey's perspective and actively participate in any endeavor she initiates:

> Any book she chooses for her on-air book club becomes an instant best seller. When she established the "world's largest piggy bank," people all over the country contributed spare change to raise more than $1 million (matched by Oprah) to send disadvantaged kids to college. When she blurted that hearing about the threat of mad-cow disease "just stopped me cold from eating another burger," the perceived threat to the beef industry was enough to trigger a multimillion dollar lawsuit (which she won).[3]

Although Winfrey's influence over her television audience—and the entertainment industry in general—is impressive, she has also managed to affect national policy. In 1991 she initiated the National Child Protection Act, which later became known as the "Oprah bill." When President Bill Clinton signed it into law in 1993, a national database of convicted child abusers was established. This advocacy is in keeping with Winfrey's other efforts to create change through major philanthropic efforts. The Oprah Winfrey Foundation supports hundreds of organizations that seek to empower and educate women, children, and families in the United States and abroad. Clearly, Winfrey's reach has been enormous and, in concrete ways, enormously positive.

Why would a woman who has engaged in such roundly positive efforts rouse such ire from *The Man Show?* As the polemical opening of the debut program suggests, the changing state of power relationships in the United States has been the subject of increasing debate since the early 1970s. Although these debates have taken many forms, from men's movements to self-help books to polemical treatises such as Lionel Tiger's *The Decline of Males,* a recurring claim has been that white American masculinity is in "crisis." As John Beynon explains, the causes identified as key to such a crisis "remain vague."[4] However, the crisis is often linked to the social movements of the 1960s and 1970s that spurred new rights and opportunities for women, minorities, and gays while questioning and presumably disrupting white male power and privilege. This struggle has been reflected in the media in many forms, but one of the most acute responses was *The Man Show,* which its original hosts called "a place where men can come together, a Shangri-la if you will," to talk about contemporary life as heterosexual American men in the midst of feminism, political correctness, the Oprahization of America, and, of course, their (perceived) loss of power. Sharon Willis suggests that the content of popular culture is not "imposed from without on a passive public" but is "responsive to certain collective demands or desires" at large in society. Popular culture "responds to, reads, and maps collective fantasies, utopian and anxious," as well as "social configurations of power and desire, pleasure and violence."[5] What does a production like *The Man Show* suggest about collective white male fears and fantasies and the configurations of power in U.S. society? And what does this have to do with Oprah Winfrey?

In her landmark book *Black Feminist Thought,* Patricia Hill Collins states, "Because the authority to define societal values is a major instrument of power, elite groups, in exercising power, manipulate ideas about Black womanhood. They do so by exploiting already existing symbols or creating new ones."[6] The white supremacist capitalist patriarchy, a phrase bell hooks uses to refer to the existing power structure in the United States, has long sustained itself and its values by controlling images of black femininity and painting black women as distant, alternatively exotic and dismal or pitiable Others. In so doing, elites have attempted not only to control how the larger society perceives black women but also to tinker with black women's subjectivity. Because the powerful are loath to relinquish dominance, such images are often prefigured to ensure the status quo: "Maintaining images of U.S. Black women as Other provides ideological justification for race, gender and class oppression."[7] Those who seemingly do not fit that image, such as Oprah Winfrey, often evoke intense public scrutiny and dialogue.

Undoubtedly the power to define oneself and one's cultural group is significant and is one of the most meaningful routes to political, social, and psychological empowerment. It is not surprising, then, that efforts in this direction continue to be the site of struggle and that the representation of Winfrey is of interest to so many.

Collins presents several prevailing stereotypes that have contributed to the continued oppression of African American women in the United States: mammy, black matriarch, welfare mother, black lady, and jezebel. It is my contention that Winfrey is too fluid to be boxed into these categories; rather, she traverses and outmaneuvers the controlling images of black womanhood that Collins outlines, carving a new niche for black women, and women in general, in her presentation of self. The power of this image places white patriarchal hegemony in jeopardy, making Winfrey an ideal target for criticism. *The Man Show* assails Winfrey in the hope of regaining white male hegemony by attempting to repossess and redefine her image of black femininity according to its terms and thus weakening the productiveness of her image.

In this essay, I provide an explication of Collins's conception of controlling images of black women and the way Collins and others conceive of Winfrey's influence. Next, I outline how *The Man Show* represents Winfrey and the attempts to attack her image. Finally, I analyze the reasons behind the hosts' contempt for Winfrey and what this suggests about contemporary social relationships.

The Struggle for Self-Definition: Controlling Images of Black Women

Collins maps out five predominant controlling images that have functioned to objectify and oppress African American women. She presents these images as "a starting point for examining new forms of control that emerge in a transnational context, one where selling images has increased in importance in the global marketplace." The first stereotypical image, which has functioned to legitimize and support the institution of slavery and the enduring economic exploitation of domestic workers, is the mammy, "the faithful, obedient domestic servant." In this role, the African American woman is expected to provide love, "nurturing and caring for her White children and 'family'" at the expense of her own, thus "symbolizing the dominant group's perceptions of the ideal Black female relationship to elite White male power." Although the mammy "may wield considerable authority in her White 'family,' the mammy still knows her 'place' as obedient servant." The image of the mammy has been "muted" today because black women have gained jobs with more prestige and power, but "the basic economic exploitation where U.S. Black women either make less for the same work or work twice as hard for the same pay persists."[8]

The second image is that of the black matriarch, who is a black mother in a black home. Whereas the mammy "represents the 'good' Black mother [in a white home], the matriarch symbolizes the 'bad' Black mother [in a black home]." This stereotype depicts African American women as unfeminine, aggressive, and too strong, and it blames the emasculation of black men and their incapacity to assume social power on black women's "inability to model appropriate gender behavior." This rhetorical maneuvering has functioned to blame black women, rather than slavery and institutionalized racism, for black poverty. It has also sabotaged black women's assertiveness and power and undermined the alternative family power structure that female-headed households represent. Collins suggests that it is no coincidence that "the public depiction of U.S. Black women as unfeminine matriarchs came at precisely the same moment that the women's movement advanced its critique of U.S. patriarchy" and "in the midst of considerable Black activism."[9]

The third image, that of the welfare mother, depicts black women as lazy and "content to sit around and collect welfare, shunning work" and passing on a poor work ethic to a multitude of economically unproductive children. This image justifies the state's involvement in black women's reproductive business. The welfare mother stereotype emerged in the United States after black women fought for and gained political power and then struggled to acquire equal access to state services, such as antidiscrimination legislation and social welfare programs. The image stigmatizes the welfare mother "as the cause of her own poverty and that of African American communities," and once again, it functions to shift the "angle of vision away from structural sources of poverty." Finally, Collins asserts that "typically portrayed as an unwed mother, she violates one cardinal tenet of White, male dominated ideology: she is a woman alone." Consequently, the treatment of the welfare mother "reinforces the dominant gender ideology positing that a woman's true worth and financial security should occur through heterosexual marriage."[10]

The image of the black lady, which is a modern version of the mammy, consists of "the hardworking Black woman professional who works twice as hard as everyone else" to achieve the status she has earned. As a direct result of her accomplishments, she is construed as less feminine because she has had to compete with men in the workplace. Further, she has no man in her life; either she has no time for one because of her job, or she has simply forgotten how to treat a man. Despite her success, her work is sometimes considered questionable because of affirmative action, which has been criticized for being reverse racism and for taking away "jobs that should go to more worthy Whites, especially U.S. White men."[11]

Finally, Collins presents the image of the historic jezebel, a figure that emerged during slavery to justify the sexual exploitation of female slaves by positing them as sexually aggressive; this image has reemerged in contemporary culture in the form of the hoochie. These images dovetail and reinforce one another, as each "represent[s] a deviant Black female sexuality." Such representations also stand in contrast to white female sexuality, which is seen as passive. "Normal female heterosexuality is expressed via the cult of true White womanhood, whereas deviant female heterosexuality is typified by the 'hot mommas' of Black womanhood." Collins argues that the hoochie is framed as having "materialistic ambitions where she sells sex for money"; she may also participate in "so-called deviant sexual practices such as sleeping with other women," as well as "'freaky' sexual practices such as engaging in oral and anal sex." Collins laments that the contemporary hoochie has permeated not only popular culture in general but also the black community in particular, with little protest. Drawing on the lyrics of "Hoochie Mama" by 2 Live Crew, Collins expresses concern that the black community has accepted these images of "woman bashing," forgetting the historical legacy of this imagery. "Not only does such acceptance mask how such images provide financial benefits to both 2 Live Crew and White controlled media, such tacit acceptance validates this message."[12]

Interestingly, Collins herself argues that Winfrey has functioned to reinforce the stereotypical images of the mammy and the black lady. In *Black Sexual Politics,* Collins acknowledges Winfrey's influence in the following statements: "Oprah Winfrey has had a far greater impact within American culture than any other living African American woman," "her corporate power is impressive," "she instructs and raises general consciousness on a list of important social issues ranging from child abuse to wife battering to rape," and "Winfrey's immense success provides a stamp of endorsement to any philosophy that she might endorse that goes far beyond any expertise she might possess on any given topic." Collins then expresses concern that "a good deal of Winfrey's success lies in her ability to market herself within the familiar realm of the mammy, not violate the tenets of being a Black lady, yet reap the benefits of her performance for herself."[13] Collins continues:

> Following the footsteps of Hattie McDaniel, Winfrey's career seemingly echoes McDaniel's reply to those who criticized her acceptance of stereotypical roles. McDaniel once said, "Why should I complain about making seven thousand dollars a week playing a maid? If I didn't, I'd be making seven dollars a week actually being one!" Winfrey constitutes the penultimate successful modern mammy whom African American and, more amazingly, White women should emulate.[14]

Although it might be a stretch to compare Oprah Winfrey to Hattie McDaniel, it suggests the degree of concern Collins has regarding the image Winfrey portrays, even as she recognizes Winfrey's influence.

Collins suggests that Winfrey's tendency to focus on promoting personal change precludes more powerful and comprehensive discussions of social and structural inequities in U.S. society that have functioned historically to oppress the black community: "Winfrey reinforces an individualistic ideology of social change that counsels her audiences to rely solely on themselves. Change yourself and your personal problems will disappear." Collins continues:

> Yet Winfrey's message stops far short of linking such individual changes to the actual resources and opportunities that are needed to escape from poverty, stop an abusive spouse from battering, or avoid job discrimination. The organizational group politics that helped create the very opportunities that Winfrey herself enjoys are minimized in favor of a message of personal responsibility that resonates with the theme of "personal responsibility" used by elites to roll back social welfare programs.[15]

By focusing on personal, individual change, Winfrey veers away from political discussions that might spark her audience to think more meaningfully about changing the societal structures that enable poverty, crime, drug abuse, spousal abuse, and the like. By favoring the individual over the social, Winfrey is not only acquiescing to the status quo but also promoting it. Thus, she appears to symbolize "the dominant group's perceptions of the ideal Black female relationship to elite White male power."[16]

Dana Cloud and Corinne Squire have made similar observations regarding Winfrey's negotiation of power relationships and social structures but have drawn different conclusions about the purpose or effect of this negotiation. Cloud argues:

> "Oprah" is caught in the double-bind of having to continue to stress empathy, emotion, and identification with women on her show while endorsing a therapeutic discourse that blames individuals, extracted from their social context, for their problems. She can never admit the need for systematic structural change and collective political activity.[17]

Cloud examines biographical narratives written about Winfrey for traces of liberal ideology that use her success to promulgate the notion that the United States is a meritocracy that rewards individual effort and is not plagued by issues such as racism, sexism, and class warfare. Cloud contends that many of the biographies function to create "a token 'Oprah' persona whose life story . . . reinforces the ideology of the American Dream, implying the accessibility of this dream to Black Americans despite the structural economic and political barriers posed in a racist society to achievement and survival." Cloud does not criticize Winfrey herself but only the way popular culture tends to whitewash Winfrey and hold her up as a testament to the truism that this is a land of equal opportunity, without questioning why "the success myth is continually belied by the realities of class, race and gender stratification in capitalistic society."[18]

Cloud also invokes the mammy image in relation to Winfrey when she recounts *America's All Star Tribute* to Winfrey, in honor of her receipt of the America's Hope Award in 1990. Cloud argues that Winfrey was framed by this event as a "liberal hero" and that her persona was inextricably tied to children by the "Help Our Children" theme of the program, which was reinforced by a song of the same title performed by M. C. Hammer and by the "continual emphasis on 'Oprah's' philanthropic projects such as literacy campaigns and big-sister programs." Because of this, Cloud contends, "Here 'Oprah' is constituted as mother-figure to the children of the world, and more specifically as the mammy, benevolent Black guardian of White children everywhere (and on her talk show, of the women in her audience)."[19]

Squire's analysis contains a comparable observation regarding Winfrey's focus on the self and self-help: "It could be argued that Oprah's psychologism sometimes drowns out its, at times, more complicated representations of power relationships." Squire's concern about *The Oprah Winfrey Show* tends to mirror Cloud's concern about the biographical narratives: "The show's persistent focus on self-esteem ties into an implicit liberal democratic politics of rights, responsibilities and choice."[20] However, Squire provides a different perspective on the reasons behind and the benefits of Winfrey's tendency to focus on the self rather than on structural obstacles or issues: "Oprah's optimism about psychological improvement is associated with beliefs in religious redemption and in social progress, for which redemption is itself a metaphor." Squire states that a reading of *The Oprah Winfrey Show* can be related to readings of the film *The Color Purple:*

> Andrea Stuart . . . has suggested that Black women watching *The Color Purple* read its happy ending not within the film narrative, where it seems inconsistent and sentimental, but within broader religious, social and historical narratives where it offers an important antidote to hopelessness. Perhaps Oprah's daily psychological resolutions of dramatic suffering support a similar reading.[21]

Although Winfrey's tendency to focus on the self might preclude a deeper analysis of structural inequities, it might also provide temporary psychological relief and support in a society plagued with such inequities. Yet ultimately, the structural obstacles that cause this hopelessness and stress are not dealt with in a way that might alleviate the problems.

Following Cloud and Collins, I agree that iconic figures such as Winfrey are often appropriated and used strategically as symbols of individual success that function to place the blame for problems such as poverty and crime on individual failings, often at the complete exclusion of long-standing structural and cultural inequities. I also concur that, given her status and power, Winfrey could use her influence to make these inequities more apparent to her audience in an effort to promote broad-based social change and to disrupt this appropriation. Interestingly, on *The Man Show,* Winfrey is not appropriated as a symbol of the efficacy of the American Dream or as representing the "ideal" relationship to white male power. Rather, she can be read as symbolizing white men's decreasing power in a post-1960s society and their attempt to roll back this shift in power.

I contend that Winfrey is too fluid to be contained by Collins's categories. She engenders a new image of black womanhood, and womanhood in general, that serves as a paragon for all women, despite their marked differences. The influence of this image is perceived as so disconcertingly powerful that Winfrey has become the target of a variety of critics who attempt to disrupt and redefine this portrayal of self that Winfrey provides. *The Man Show* represents one such attempt.

The Man Show Attacks Winfrey

A core tenet of Winfrey's ethos has been her capacity to communicate empathy and care for others on her television program and in her public interactions. Because she engages in self-disclosure about her personal life, Winfrey generates feelings of closeness and immediacy among many of her viewers. This element of her persona has frequently been cited as the reason she is able to connect with the American people, leading to her unparalleled success. Additionally, by bringing personal issues to the forefront of the media culture, Winfrey has popularized the radical feminist principle of valuing and expressing the personal in the public sphere. Squire reports, "Winfrey touches audience members a lot, cries and laughs, and they touch, laugh and cry back. These exchanges signify an empathy that is traditionally [stereotypically] feminine, but also feminist in its insistence on the 'personal.'"[22] Perhaps it is not surprising, then, that the hosts of *The Man Show* chose to attack the source of her strength and popularity: her empathetic public persona.

As indicated by the dialogue quoted earlier, mockery of Oprah Winfrey was a central aspect of the debut program. Winfrey was also the focus of the first installment of *The Man Show* book club, which debuted on June 30, 1999. Hosts Kimmel and Carolla state, "While we make fun of women's shows, there are some things we can learn from them . . . like the book club." As Collins reports, "almost single-handedly, Winfrey got America to read, an impressive accomplishment in a mass-media-saturated society that balks at funding libraries and public education."[23] Ignoring this aspect of Winfrey's endeavor, Kimmel and Carolla present their first book selection, the front cover of which features a picture of Winfrey with two large bags of cash. The hosts then announce the title of the book, "Oprah Is a Big, Fake, Money-Grubbing Pig." Carolla exclaims, "I wouldn't read that book if the vowels made my penis grow." To undermine Winfrey's credibility, the hosts suggest that she does not care about her audience or the issues that are raised on her program. Rather, they indicate that she fakes emotion to generate goodwill and, ultimately, as a means of making money.

Similarly, Kimmel engages in minstrelsy and drag when he dresses up in a fat suit in a segment called "Oprah Jimfrey." Although some of these segments did not make it onto the air, they are available as bonus features on *The Man Show* DVD collection (season 1, volume 2). This particular segment features Jimfrey on the toilet giving advice; in her bedroom with a tied-up Stedman Graham (Winfrey's longtime partner), whom she abuses as she discusses coping with pain; and in her living room trying to connect with her inner angel, who tells her, "there's pie left in the fridge." These images function to demean Winfrey, to undermine her credibility as a caring person in the private sphere, and to make light of her struggle with her weight.

A bonus feature on the DVD that features a caricature of Graham is particularly telling. As Oprah Jimfrey, Jimmy Kimmel states, "We all live with pain and although I have not personally experienced it for years, many people suffer quietly every day. For example, my man-friend Stedman. Stedman here lives with a great, great deal of pain, isn't that right, Stedman?" The camera pans to the man playing Graham, who is tied up bondage style, hanging upside down with his arms handcuffed and his mouth gagged. Oprah Jimfrey takes the gag off his mouth and he frantically cries, "Let me go, you crazy bitch!" Jimfrey replaces the gag over Stedman's mouth and continues: "As the philosopher Bertrand Russell once wrote, 'part of life should be an unbearable pity for the suffering of mankind.' Isn't that right, Stedman?" As Jimfrey speaks, she whips Stedman, proclaiming, "Learn to live with pain, learn to love with pain. Until next time, I'm Oprah Jimfrey." Again in this feature, Kimmel attempts to undermine Winfrey's credibility by suggesting that the way she lives her private life is much different from that suggested by her public persona. Behind closed doors, Winfrey is depicted as a control freak who abuses her lover while hypocritically teaching others about coping with pain. Part of the humor is the contrast in images: it is suggested that Winfrey is a sexually aggressive dominatrix, or a hoochie, but this notion is undermined by her clothes, which are extremely modest, covering her entire body. The image also evokes the black matriarch, which suggests that black women are too aggressive and, as a result, emasculate their men. Further, Kimmel indicates that Winfrey no longer understands pain now that she has encountered wealth and success, a move that works to divorce Winfrey from her experiences as a girl and render them useless as a basis for her displays of empathy.

Regardless of one's opinion about Oprah Winfrey, there is little dispute that she wields great influence, even on the hosts of *The Man Show*. In addition to attacking Winfrey's empathetic public persona, Kimmel and Carolla speak frequently about her cultural power. For example, as quoted earlier, Kimmel states that Winfrey "has half of America brainwashed." In the following excerpt from the episode "Sperm Bank," which aired on July 1, 2001, Kimmel disparagingly states that Winfrey's influence has infiltrated even his own home. Kimmel complains about Winfrey's sway over his wife as he and Carolla discuss the debut of her new magazine, *O*:

KIMMEL: Something terrible happened during our hiatus last June . . . you may have read about it in the newspaper.
CAROLLA: Oprah put out a magazine!
AUDIENCE: Boo!
CAROLLA: She felt that the TV, movies, books, Internet and all that crap just wasn't getting her message out to enough people.
KIMMEL: My wife has a 'scription to this friggin' thing; subscription actually. It is filled with all kinds of uplifting, new age self-improvement and—uh—hard liquor ads, by the way. . . . Because positive thinking is a lot easier when you have a buzz going.

CAROLLA: What can you do? Unfortunately women are reading
now-a-days.

Kimmel replies, "Yes, they are. They're reading stuff like this." Kimmel
points to the headlines on the front cover of the magazine as he reads
them aloud: "Oprah talks to her hero, Nelson Mandela." Kimmel then
pulls out some stickers and says, "I have these stickers that I think really
might help unbrainwash my wife. You just affix them right here." He
places a sticker on the magazine and reads the new *The Man Show*–
approved headlines: "And now, '*The View's* Star Jones: Now She's Fat . . .
Lawn Mowing: It's Not Just for Men . . . The Oral Sex Diet . . . How I
Lost Fifty Pounds.'" The audience cheers loudly in response.

In this clip, Kimmel relates a personal reason for his contempt for
Winfrey: he is frustrated by the influence Winfrey, her program, and her
publications have over his wife and, presumably, their relationship and
household. In contrast to the image of the mammy—a black female
who has considerable authority yet knows her place—Kimmel's perception of Winfrey indicates that she is violating boundaries and wield-
ing authority that is not contained or controlled by white men—or, at
least, not by this particular white man. Indeed, in Kimmel's eyes, Winfrey is controlling him through his wife. Consequently, it would not be
a stretch to say that this fails to be "the ideal Black female relationship
to elite White male power."[24]

The Man Show highlighted Winfrey's influence yet again in its
"Powerful Women" episode, which aired on July 9, 2000, demonstrating that Winfrey's authority is not only unconstrained by white male
hegemony but also challenging it. The hosts begin by explaining that
Bill Gates and Bill Clinton are among the most powerful men in the
country. They contemplate who the most powerful women are and
decide to ask women that question in their "natural habitat—the mall."
The women that Kimmel interviews cite Winfrey more than any other woman, with Hillary Clinton coming in second. One interviewee
has difficulty remembering the name of the individual she wants to
identify and describes her choice to Kimmel. When he offers Winfrey's
name and the woman answers affirmatively, Kimmel says, "It's funny
that you'd forget a name like that. . . . Cuz I gotta tell you, that name
runs through my head *constantly*." The sequence then turns to Carolla
and Kimmel in their La-Z-Boy chairs. Kimmel states, "It is not like

we really edited that up. There's a lot of stupid women at the mall on Wednesday." Then he pauses and states, "*We gotta stop that Oprah.*" Carolla responds, "We sure do." To the Juggy Girls, dressed in superhero costumes, he commands, "Wonder Juggies, activate," and they smile approvingly and dance on cue.

Kimmel's negative comment about the women at the mall is offensive but predictable. However, his comment about Winfrey is curious. Whereas the most powerful men in the country are not insulted at all, Winfrey has been insulted on previous programs and on this show Kimmel indicates that, for some reason, she must be stopped. The decision to deride Winfrey rather than Hillary Clinton may be a result of the amount of vilification Clinton already receives in the mass media, while Winfrey continues to enjoy predominantly positive press.

Additionally, the fact that Winfrey enjoys immense popularity and influence in the public realm without the benefit of white men, marriage, family, or the sexualization of her body challenges crucial tenets of hegemonic masculinity. Specifically, in contrast to the image of the black lady, Winfrey's strong *and* feminine persona is a central aspect of her program, and she uses these characteristics to tap into the predominantly female, multiethnic viewing audience. Rather than being a cause of poverty, as indicated in the stereotype of the black matriarch, Winfrey's strength has been fundamental to her business success and her subsequent status and wealth. Further, Winfrey is not "a woman alone," because she has long enjoyed the company of Stedman Graham, a successful professional, even though she has consciously chosen to remain unmarried.[25] Indeed, when Sharon Stone stated, somewhat sheepishly, during an interview on *The Oprah Winfrey Show* that she was not inclined toward marriage, Winfrey nodded approvingly and said, "You're speaking to the choir leader," while laughing. The success and status of both Winfrey and her companion, as well as Winfrey's longtime commitment to helping women improve their lives (even if the focus is primarily psychological), work to undo the ideological work of these racialized images and to undermine, to a certain extent, the dominant gender ideology.

The Man Show's criticisms of Winfrey typically focus on her empathy or her influence. A more perfidious spirit marks the final attacks on Winfrey mentioned here, underscoring the depths to which the hosts desire to control Winfrey's influence and the lows to which they will go to accomplish that end. A regular part of the program is a segment entitled "Man-o-vations," in which inventions "made by men for men" to improve the quality of their lives are featured. On the episode "Jobs," which aired on November 3, 1999, Kimmel presents the game "Hungry, Hungry Oprahs: The Frantic Burger Munching Game," a parody of the game Hungry, Hungry Hippos. The front of the box shows four hippos with hair like Winfrey's. Carolla, holding a miniature hamburger, states, "Whoever's Oprah gobbles up the most hamburgers wins." Then Carolla and Kimmel proceed to play the game, which features a combination of Winfrey's features and those of a hippopotamus. This attempt to discipline Winfrey through her embodiment is a familiar strategy in U.S. society. Historically, men's bodies have received marginal scrutiny, but the public eye continually polices the female body, and white male hegemony attempts to humiliate those who do not conform to white standards of beauty. As Naomi Wolf argues, "The cultural fixation on female thinness is not an obsession about female beauty but an obsession about female obedience."[26] Such policing serves to accustom women to having the minutiae of their personal, everyday lives scrutinized and managed, thus making it easier to influence and control other facets of their public lives. Additionally, encouraging a dysfunctional obsession with their bodies distracts women from more meaningful pursuits, such as striving to achieve social, economic, and political power or effectuating social change. Cecilia Hartley contends, "Women who do not maintain rigid control over the boundaries of their bodies, allowing them to grow, to become large and 'unfeminine' are treated with derision in our society, and that derision is tied inextricably to the personal freedom of women."[27] Winfrey's highly public struggle with her weight, combined with attempts to deride her efforts and her embodiment, underscores the insidiousness and pervasiveness of the pressure women face to conform to a particular standard, regardless of their status or influence. It also suggests that no one is immune from such attacks, even someone as powerful as Winfrey.

On a subsequent program, Kimmel and Carolla offer Winfrey's disembodied head on a rope—a simulation of soap on a rope. Carolla remarks that he would really like to clean his posterior with the Oprah Winfrey soap. Rather than undermining her credibility, this attack attempts to demean Winfrey outright by reducing her to an object one uses to clean the dirtiest parts of one's body. Further, her disembodied head on a rope invokes images of lynching, an inappropriate gesture by any stretch of the imagination. This seems to be a desperate attempt to grasp power by reminding Winfrey of a time not so long ago when "uppity" black women would be punished not with words but with violence. This represents *The Man Show*'s most pathetic play for power, but also the seriousness of its hosts' desire for control.

Reflections

The destabilization of the straight white male's normativeness has created a crisis in masculinity that erupts in social, political, and personal contexts in contemporary U.S. culture. *The Man Show* is a response to this crisis manifesting in the mass media. Since the emergence of the social movements of the 1960s and 1970s, the hegemonic male has been compelled to respond to the breakdown of white male normativeness and, in some instances, to create new strategies in the struggle for dominance. The representation of Winfrey on *The Man Show* is one aspect of a complex range of representations in contemporary mass media dealing with the struggle to regain white male hegemony.

The hosts employ humor to broach topics publicly that would normally receive voice only in private conversations because of their sensitive nature, such as the fears, concerns, and frustrations felt by the hegemonic male as a result of the increasing presence and power of women and minorities. By creating their own "Shangri-la," where the white male is once again the unquestioned center of power, the hosts are able to speak "kindly words of comfort to the intimidated ego" of the straight white male.[28] Although the hosts deny an external reality in which minorities and women are attaining greater power and voice in the public sphere, they appropriate the images of these groups to generate humorous content for the program and to minimize their potency. One need only look to the representations of Winfrey to recognize how such groups' social concerns are at once denied and appropriated. At first glance, this maneuvering might be dismissed as harmless parody, but it is precisely because it is framed as humor that it is acceptable in the public sphere. The humorous frame makes it appear that there is no ideological work being conducted, and it can be all the more persuasive for its subtlety. When the attacks are examined in their entirety, and not as single moments of humor, a pattern emerges that suggests the primary fear of straight white men: the prospect of sharing power as a result of the emerging influence of women and minorities, as symbolized by Oprah Winfrey. The hosts of *The Man Show* struggle to regain hegemony in a society where they are becoming increasingly marginalized; they do so by ridiculing Winfrey and her accomplishments as they attempt to repossess, redefine, and thus disrupt the influence of her image of black femininity.

Although the hosts of *The Man Show* went to great lengths to ridicule Winfrey and attempt to marginalize the image of black womanhood she presents (suggesting her level of influence), few would argue that Winfrey is radical or revolutionary in her approach. This points to Winfrey's contradictory nature. That is, her presence destabilizes the stereotypes defined by Collins and disturbs white male hegemony, yet she also functions to support the status quo. By focusing on self–help and providing a psychological model for individual change, Winfrey tends to avoid meaningful discussions of cultural and structural inequities and the possibility of effectuating broad–based social and political transformation. Of course, the fact that we expect so much from Winfrey indicates the dearth of women and minorities in the public sphere advancing progressive causes. Additionally, the hosts' decision to attack someone as politically neutral as Winfrey suggests that empowered elites are loath to relinquish their dominance; instead, they attempt to limit productive images of black femininity. Ultimately, such efforts underscore the need for more insistent and radical approaches to social change, for if someone as neutral as Winfrey comes under attack, the state of progressive political strategy and action is clearly languishing.

Notes

1. The program ran with its original hosts for four seasons, ending in July 2003, when Jimmy Kimmel was offered a position as a late–night talk–show host on ABC. Hoping to maintain the popularity and profitability of the program, the network hired two new hosts, Joe Rogan and Doug Stanhope, who debuted on August 17, 2003. When the new hosts took over, the polemical opening statements that functioned to galvanize the viewing audience were dropped, and the attacks on Winfrey ceased as well. Initially, the public seemed eager for *The Man Show* to continue, as indicated by the 1.7 million viewers who tuned in to watch "The New Guys," but the ratings fell, and the show was canceled in June 2004. Because Rogan and Stanhope did not target Winfrey

for criticism, I do not analyze their programming. For the purpose of this study, I focus predominantly on the first two seasons of *The Man Show,* although the attacks on Winfrey continued throughout the first four seasons. The examples noted here are representative of the overall content and tone of the criticisms lobbed at Winfrey.

2. Deborah Tannen, "Oprah Winfrey," *Time 100: The Most Important People of the 20th Century,* http://www.time.com/time100/artists/profile/winfrey3.html.

3. Ibid.

4. John Beynon, *Masculinities and Culture* (Buckingham, England: Open University Press, 2002).

5. Sharon Willis, "Disputed Territories: Masculinity and Social Space," *Camera Obscura* 19 (1989): 8.

6. Patricia Hill Collins, *Black Feminist Thought: Knowledge, Consciousness and the Politics of Empowerment* (New York: Routledge, 2000), 69.

7. Ibid., 70.

8. Ibid., 72–74.

9. Ibid., 75–76.

10. Ibid., 78–80.

11. Ibid., 81.

12. Ibid., 81–84.

13. Patricia Hill Collins, *Black Sexual Politics: African Americans, Gender and the New Racism* (New York: Routledge, 2004), 142–43. Collins also recognizes Winfrey's influence briefly in her book *Black Feminist Thought,* where she states, "Black women's access to the media remains unprecedented, as talk show hostess Oprah Winfrey's long-running television show and forays into film production suggest" (41).

14. Collins, *Black Sexual Politics,* 142.

15. Ibid., 143.

16. Collins, *Black Feminist Thought,* 72.

17. Dana L. Cloud, "Hegemony or Concordance? The Rhetoric of Tokenism in 'Oprah' Winfrey's Rags-to-Riches Biography," *Critical Studies in Mass Communication* 13 (1996): 129.

18. Ibid., 116.

19. Ibid., 125.

20. Corinne Squire, "Empowering Women? *The Oprah Winfrey Show,"* in *Feminist Television Criticism,* ed. Charlotte Brunsdon, Julie D'Acci, and Lynn Spigel (New York: Clarendon Press, 1997), 107, 108.

21. Ibid., 108.

22. Ibid., 101. I added the word *stereotypically* to draw attention to the fact that women are not naturally more empathic than men but are encouraged

through socialization in a white, patriarchal society to demonstrate this quality, whereas men are discouraged from demonstrating it. In a traditional patriarchal society, binary oppositions are encouraged (such as the distinctions between rational-emotional, strong-weak, and feminine-masculine), often at the expense of the self. I do not believe that people are either this or that; rather, I believe that there is a fluid relationship between attributes that are often cast as binaries. That is, people are both rational and emotional, are both strong and weak, and have both feminine and masculine traits.

23. Collins, *Black Sexual Politics,* 143.

24. Collins, *Black Feminist Thought,* 72.

25. Ibid., 79.

26. As quoted in Cecilia Hartley, "Letting Ourselves Go: Making Room for the Fat Body in Feminist Scholarship," in *Bodies Out of Bounds: Fatness and Transgression,* ed. Jana Evans Braziel and Kathleen LeBesco (Berkeley: University of California Press, 2001), 62.

27. Ibid., 65.

28. Sigmund Freud, "Traditional Theories of Laughter and Humor: Sigmund Freud," in *The Philosophy of Laughter and Humor,* ed. J. Morreale (Albany, N.Y.: SUNY Press, 1997), 116.

Part II

Oprah Winfrey
on the Stage

Oprah Winfrey and Women's Autobiography

*A Televisual Performance of
the Therapeutic Self*

Eva Illouz and Nicholas John

It has become somewhat commonplace to suggest that the genre of talk shows has blurred the private and public spheres by exposing to public view secrets hitherto confined to the bedroom (or whispered into the ear of a professional). However, the process by which the private is made public is still largely unclear. To become a public form of speech, a private utterance must undergo a transformation, that is, be recoded as a public performance. In this essay, we suggest that Oprah Winfrey's construction of her biography on television is exemplary of the kind of cultural transformation that the private must undergo in order to become public. Winfrey's performance of her private self is paradigmatic of the mechanism by which the private is recoded for public consumption as a spectacle.

Because of the importance of autobiographical speech in making the private self into a public site, we focus on women's traditional relationship with autobiographical discourse, examining the conditions under which autobiography passes from private to public. First, we introduce the field of autobiographical studies and present four issues that have been raised by the feminist critique in that discipline. We then show how Winfrey's own autobiography reverberates with these four characteristics of feminist autobiography.

Autobiography:
Background and the Feminist Critique

As a genre, autobiography inherently problematizes the relationship between private and public selves and involves the issue of which elements
of the former should be selected to produce a coherent picture of the
latter. How is the distinction between private and public selves articulated in the case of Oprah Winfrey? To what extent does such an articulation point to a singularly feminine way of authoring autobiography
or, more generally, a feminine approach to the public sphere? How do
women navigate the passage from private to public self, and how does
it differ from purportedly masculine ways of authoring autobiography
and dealing with the public-private distinction? An interesting subfield
of feminist writing has developed around these questions, challenging
mainstream assumptions about the life worth documenting and how
one should write one's own history. With an approach similar to that of
feminist historians, feminists in this field have critiqued "malestream"
research for ignoring women's autobiographies, disvaluing the issues
women write about, and rejecting stylistic innovations in the structure
of the autobiographical text. In particular, they have highlighted four
distinct characteristics of women's autobiography: its content, the fluid
and disjunctive nature of the self and its narrative, its interdependence,
and the extent to which the story is still evolving. Given these characteristics, which we expand on presently, does Oprah Winfrey conform
to the genre of women's autobiography? And how does she manipulate
the private-public distinction?

The first critique of mainstream research concerns content. The
genre of autobiography was long dominated by men; it was seen as the
description of a great man's trajectory to his position of public prominence and importance. It is the "systematic account of a whole existence"—one that is worth accounting for.[1] In Georg Misch's seminal
work, for instance, because they are written by the very men who shape
it, autobiographies are seen as a way of understanding the Zeitgeist.[2] In
this sense, autobiography is a record of public achievement. According
to such a model, there is room in an autobiography for the story of
one's education and career milestones, but much less so for descriptions
of personal relationships with one's parents, siblings, spouse, and other
private matters. This helps explain women's relative marginality in the

field, in terms of both the number of famous women autobiographers and the research interest in women who wrote autobiographies—at least until the 1980s and the advent of the subgenre of women's autobiographical studies.

Women's relative confinement to the domestic sphere, especially prior to the twentieth century, and the concurrent devaluation of that sphere meant that women's lives were deemed inherently less interesting and valuable than those of most men. If what made an autobiography interesting was how a great man reached his position of greatness, it is obvious why women's autobiographies were on the sideline for so long. It was widely felt that autobiographies need not go into "certain personal details. . . . These include one's domestic life, minor illnesses, and other matters considered trivial and mundane."[3] There was also a perception that "instead of adventures and vocations, of existential angst and alienation, women write about the sphere of domesticity and the affective curve in the plot of love."[4] In other words, women did not have experiences deemed worthy of autobiographical documentation (namely, a rich public life).

In addition to differing in content, theorists claim that women's autobiographies are less chronologically strict and more anecdotal than men's are. As a reflection of their experiences, women tend to write "disjunctive narratives and discontinuous forms [that] are more adequate for mirroring the fragmentation and multidimensionality of women's lives."[5] In other words, there is a fluidity, or a lack of linear teleology, in women's autobiography.

Third, the feminist literature argues that women place a stronger emphasis on interdependence and community in their autobiographies, at the expense of stressing individual integrity and separateness. This observation follows the writings of feminist psychoanalysts such as Nancy Chodorow, who argues that women and men have a different experience of *I* and that women are less straightforwardly individualistic and logocentric and more "plural, continuous and interdependent."[6]

Finally, and in contrast to the autobiographical model in which the self is presented as a finished object, women tend not to write "mythic" tales (in terms of "how I overcame obstacles to reach the summit"). Rather, they see themselves as being "unfinished" or involved in a "constructive *process* [of] becoming a self-affirmed human being."[7]

Feminist critique is thus directed both at the canon, claiming that it excludes women's works, and at the accepted way of writing autobiographies and determining what is deemed worthy of inclusion. Indeed, a central characteristic of women's autobiographies is that they turn the public and private inside out, placing the domestic in full public view. In this sense, it is a compromised genre from the outset, to which the autobiographical speech of talk shows might be a direct heir. Here, we must distinguish between two different meanings of *public*. One meaning is simply "that which is seen by many people," such as when we talk about being in the public eye. Another meaning, however, refers to the use of collective norms that are perceived as being appropriate ways to conduct affairs of state, resolve social conflict, and contribute to the general good of society. What is perhaps new and unprecedented in talk shows is that they activate both meanings of *public* in reference to the private sphere.

It is clear that the stories Winfrey tells about herself on her show and elsewhere fall within the affective and private spheres, be they about her weight or the sexual assaults she was subjected to in childhood. Through these examples, and the way they are related and represented on television, Winfrey continues, accentuates, and radicalizes elements of women's autobiography.

Oprah Winfrey and Feminist Autobiography

Winfrey is not only the famous host of a famous show; she is also a public persona with a notorious life story. One of the central differences between Winfrey and other stars is that whereas most media celebrities are visual icons of beauty and youth, Winfrey is first and foremost a *biographical icon*. She is someone that we know not for her beauty or her acting talent but for the way she has staged her own personal life. Her life story is of particular interest for two reasons: First, it was one of the central factors that made *The Oprah Winfrey Show* so different from other talk shows—it abolished the distance between a presumably distant host and an overexposed guest. Second, through the public exposition of her most private secrets, Winfrey constructed a persona who has no precedent in American culture at large.

One is struck by the remarkable fit between the way researchers define women's autobiography and the way Winfrey has constructed herself through television (as well as the way she helps her guests construct themselves). We can see this through a number of categories that overlap the four types of critique discussed in the previous section: the types of revelations Winfrey makes on her show (content), their order of telling (fluidity and juxtaposition), the style of their telling (interdependence), and Winfrey as a work in progress—a biography in the making (evolution). However, in addition to these shared features, there are three main qualities of Winfrey's public autobiographical narratives that suggest something new and different: (1) she recounts her failures, or, more precisely, stories of the wounds inflicted on her psyche and her body; (2) she performs this blatant, almost parodic display of failure against the background of her awesome success and glamour; and (3) the more negative symbolic capital Winfrey expresses on television, the more positive symbolic and economic capital she accrues. We return to these points later and locate them within the therapeutic ethos, but first we return to the feminist critique and how it is demonstrated by Winfrey's biography and also subverted by her in an original way.

Content

What is perhaps most distinctive about Winfrey's biography is how well known some of its fragments are. Winfrey's life has been recounted as a story of wounds and failures, yet her persona seems to have emerged not in spite of these hardships but because of them. This is how her biography is typically written:

> At 9, she was raped by a teenage cousin who was babysitting. He took her to the zoo and bought her ice cream so she wouldn't tell. That year, in the playground, a schoolmate told her how babies were made, and she says the worst horror of the rape was going through the entire fifth grade believing she was pregnant. . . . Throughout the next five years she was repeatedly abused by three other men, trusted family friends. Growing up in Milwaukee, she lied, broke curfew, stole from her mother's purse, ran away from home and tried to date everything "with pants on." . . . At home she is one of those anxious women who cleans before the housekeeper arrives, just to make sure the housekeeper doesn't get a bad impression.[8]

If her life story has captured the American imagination, it is because she is a feminine response to the characters created by Horatio Alger and offers a feminine parody of the masculine myth of self-help. She has regularly revealed secrets that have one thing in common: they bear the mark of a failed psyche and unsuccessful relationships. To a great extent, Winfrey's celebrity derives from the fact that she has made public the various acts of violence that were perpetrated against her body. Although she grew up in a physical state of utter poverty and deprivation, Winfrey has incessantly stressed that the psychological obstacles she faced were more significant, and in that respect, her biography of success differs significantly from that of the great (male) success stories we are familiar with. Far from boasting of some ineffable power or talent, Winfrey casts herself as the condensed version of the problems that plague ordinary women—lack of self-esteem, sexual abuse, obesity, failed romantic relationships. These attributes with which Winfrey has constructed her persona de-fetishize the plastic icons of stardom. She became famous not *in spite of* having been abused but *because* she was abused and, furthermore, because she publicized that abuse. The revelations Winfrey makes are within the realm of the personal and domestic.

Winfrey actively develops the theme of the psychic wound as she constructs her biography, as evidenced by the way she packages her life story.

> She [Winfrey] also confesses her own personal tragedies. In the past, she has recounted her failed relationships, a childhood episode of sexual abuse, and her constant battle to lose weight. These insights have endeared her to America, making her one of the most sought after speakers in the country. . . . Oprah Winfrey says she still has trouble thinking of herself as a celebrity. . . . As successful as she is at present, Oprah admits that the going has not always been smooth, particularly in her personal life. In her less confident days, she says that she relinquished her self-respect to men. "The relationships I had were totally detrimental," she says. "I was a doormat. But the thing about it is, you realize that there is a doormat overload out there because everybody's been one. Now, I say, 'I will never give up my power to another person.'"[9]

In conformity with the genre of the success story, Winfrey's autobiography stresses the hurdles that blocked her path to fame. But one element characterizes these obstacles: they are all related to a failed psyche or failed relationships. In other words, Winfrey always defines her hurdles as psychological rather than material ones, despite the fact of difficult material conditions as well. Furthermore, Winfrey's career has been punctuated by the construction of what can be called "psychic events." For example, Winfrey had long been promising a book about her life, but one day she dropped a journalistic bombshell by announcing that the book would not be written after all. Because of the way she constructed it, what was ultimately a nonevent (the nonwriting of a book) became worthy of press attention and was actually transformed into an event with biographical significance:

> Emerging from the buzz, the banter, the brouhaha caused by Oprah Winfrey's bombshell announcement that she would not release her eagerly awaited book this fall missed the real story [sic]. This book—unfinished, unpublished, unseen by the public—this book changed her life. . . . Writing her life story forced her to confront all her demons, to, as she puts it, "stand and look at myself naked." What she saw staring back at her stunned her. And then it freed her. "As I peeled away the layers of my life, I realized that all my craziness, all my pain and difficulties, stemmed from me not valuing myself," she says. "And what I now know is that every single bit of pain I have experienced in my life was a result of me worrying about what another person was going to think of me." What other people were going to think of her if she stopped The Book almost made Oprah go through with it even though for months, her inner voice had been telling her it was not the story she wanted to release.[10]

A few elements are important here. First, what made the nonwriting of a book so newsworthy was its transformation into a psychic event—namely, Winfrey's discovery of a part of her inner self, an act that crosses the boundary between the public sphere and the realm of psychic privacy. Second, this nonevent was translated into a narrative of psychic suffering—that is, a narrative in which the obstacles are psychic in nature. Third, what is unique about psychic obstructions is that they can continue to be obstacles even when one is at the peak of one's fame and glamour. Contrary to material obstacles, which are, by definition, overcome once and for all by stardom, psychic obstacles can be produced almost endlessly and are not incompatible with celebrity. In fact, because psychological narratives of selfhood are impervious to either logic or empirical evidence, they can actually thrive on success (for instance, if one is afraid of success or feels unworthy of success). Finally, as suggested by the previous excerpt, this narrative of psychic suffering can easily be converted into a narrative of self-change and, ultimately, success. This is structurally embedded in the narrative itself, for in the very act of revealing her fear of being judged by others, Winfrey overcomes it. Indeed, many of Winfrey's autobiographical confessions are highly performative, in the sense that at the moment of their utterance they elicit a change.

Thus, psychic narratives of the self can be capitalized on twice: once as the confession of a psychic secret, which can be recycled as a story ready for consumption, and once again as the story is turned into a tale of liberation. The telling of the story in public becomes one more episode in Winfrey's biography that brings psychic closure, thus turning the media into active participants in her own autobiography. After all, it is through her confession in the newspaper or on television that inner freedom, inner peace, liberation, or new resolve—all phrases used by Winfrey herself—can be attained.

But what is the cultural mechanism that enables Winfrey to convert these autobiographical narratives of psychic wounds and failure into a form of public communication? Winfrey's failings and failures can become a public story because she casts them in the cultural code of what we call a *therapeutic biography*. Like all narratives, the therapeutic biography is structured around the tension between a goal and the impediments to its attainment. In the therapeutic narrative, the goal is psychic well-being or health, and the obstacles to that well-being constitute what narratologists call a complication—something that gets the action going. In the therapeutic narrative, complications can be either traumatic events or wounds inflicted by other people or self-defeating beliefs and behavior.

Several features of the therapeutic biography allow its ready conversion into a media commodity for public consumption. It demands very little economic investment, requiring only that someone let us peek into the dark corners of his or her psyche. It also enables the mo-bilization of a number of professionals—therapists, psychiatrists, doctors, and a wide variety of personal consultants—who are eager to appear on television to promote their name and expertise. In other words, the therapeutic biography relies on and sustains a large group of profession-als who use television to transform their expertise into a market com-modity. The therapeutic biography is highly recyclable by the media industries and is a good source of stories for journalists; the fact that these stories narrow the gap between stars and ordinary people makes them intrinsically newsworthy. Finally, through the ideology of self-help and self-change, the therapeutic biography bestows unprecedented legitimacy and power on the media, as the very act of relating such a narrative helps bring about the desired change.

Fluidity and Disjunction

Whereas male autobiographies usually have a strong sense of purpose and are told in a unidirectional fashion, Winfrey's revelations about her life are not necessarily made in chronological order, which is another similarity between the way she constructs her biography on television and the way women tend to write autobiographies. The organization of her on-screen biography is thematic rather than chronological, associa-tive rather than preplanned and linear. In this way, her autobiography differs from the canonical autobiography, in which the writer's life is presented as heading directly and almost inevitably toward a certain end point. In addition to a disjunctive narrative, Winfrey's biography displays a striking juxtaposition between glamour and the quotidian: on the one hand, we are all aware of Winfrey's Hollywood lifestyle and her fêted appearance on the cover of *Vogue* magazine; on the other hand, she publicly confesses to gruesome past events and dull and familiar ongo-ing problems such as weight control.

The form of one's biography is not detached from its content, just as the fluid retelling of one's life story might be said to mimic daily life. Whereas the canonical male autobiography imposes a form on the shapeless, chaotic, and continuous flow of events in day-to-day life, the associative and (at least seemingly) spontaneous nature of Winfrey's au-tobiographical speech more readily espouses the disjunctive character of everyday goings-on.

Interdependence

The nature of the arena in which Winfrey and her guests make their revelations and tell their stories determines that they will be told in a dialogical fashion. In other words, Winfrey's autobiography is not constructed privately and individually but rather through interaction with other people. This is especially true of the stories told by her guests, but also of Winfrey herself. She does not relate episodes of her life in the style of a lecture; instead, she does so through interaction with her guests and the audience, with whom she has a symbiotic relationship.[11] Her words elicit responses, and those responses feed back into Winfrey's stories. The strength of the audience becomes apparent if one tries to imagine the show without the audience there. It is not just that the audience stands in for the viewers at home, making them feel as if they are there and bringing them closer to the action. Instead, there is a feeling that Winfrey really talks with the studio audience and that it becomes part of the story as she unfolds it.

For instance, Winfrey mixes her own story in with those of other people. To give an example, while interviewing Tipper Gore, the wife of former vice president Al Gore, Winfrey subtly transforms herself into the one delivering the information:

> WINFREY: What about the rap about him [Vice President Gore]—being boring . . . I have to say this because when I first got—Stedman . . .
> GORE: Yeah.
> WINFREY: . . . and I have been together now so many years, but anyway, when I first . . .
> GORE: It's not boring, is it?
> WINFREY: No. No. But I was just gonna say this . . .
> GORE: Right.
> WINFREY: . . . when I was first introduced to him . . . somebody said to me "Oh, Stedman, he is so boring" and what they meant was he has integrity . . .
> GORE: Right.
> WINFREY: . . . he's gonna be monogamous, he has character, he stands up for what he believes in.[12]

Winfrey frequently uses this technique of interjecting episodes and emotions from her own life. At times, it becomes unclear who the real interviewee is or whether the only aim of Winfrey's confessions is to provoke more intimate revelations from her guests. It is quite clear, then, that rather than reflecting the model of the isolated man alone at his writing desk, Winfrey instantiates a much more social and interdependent style of creativity. Again, this style of self-disclosure—revealing herself while interacting with others—blurs the distinction between private (dialogue) and public (eye).

An Evolving Story

Winfrey's on-screen biography is presented not as a finished product but as an evolving spectacle. Indeed, no one does this quite as well as Winfrey does. Let us offer a famous example: In 1984, at the beginning of her career, a *Newsweek* article described Winfrey in a way reminiscent of the black mammy: "nearly 200 pounds of Mississippi-bred black womanhood, brassy, earthy, streetsmart and soulful."[13] Five years later she was described in a *New York Times* article as "slim and awfully glamorous."[14] Clearly, this was a spectacular transformation, made all the more so by its relentless documentation by television and the popular press. Winfrey's weight loss was vividly brought to life when, in November 1988, she brought out on stage a little wagon containing sixty-seven pounds of beef fat—the exact amount she had managed to shed. Displaying her new slim body in her new Calvin Klein jeans, she made the show a personal platform for her self-transformation.

But in 1989 the story took a new turn: Winfrey confessed that she had gained back seventeen pounds, thus bringing a new twist to the narrative plot of her weight loss. As she said, "the battle only begins with losing the weight . . . keeping it off is really the true challenge."[15] This story took another stunning narrative turn, again witnessed by the whole nation, when in 1998 Winfrey appeared on the cover of *Vogue,* a position coveted by the most glamorous Hollywood stars. The story of Winfrey's struggle with her weight offers a *narrative spectacle,* that is, a story evolving within the real time of real life. And indeed, the story continues.

What is even more interesting is that after her on-screen revelations, Winfrey's life really did change as she grew thinner and more successful, glamorous, and self-confident. She thus became her own ideal guest, showing that television can and does change lives. What is so peculiar about Winfrey's biography is that it enacts the self-proclaimed vocation of her show to change lives. What is unprecedented is that Winfrey offers us the spectacle of a biography in the making; she displays a biographical narrative that unfolds in real time and encompasses the changes experienced by her body and psyche.

Taken together, all the different stories, revelations, and surprises throughout the years mean that we have not yet seen the final chapter on Oprah Winfrey. In addition to her weight, other ongoing issues include her nonmarriage to Stedman Graham, her decision in the mid-1990s to make the program "higher brow," revelations about her sexual abuse and her subsequent feelings, and any number of other ruminations and decisions. All these elements give the impression of someone who is "becoming," not someone who is reflecting on how she reached a final state.

Conclusion

Women's autobiography is beset by issues of representation. Certain strands of the feminist critique argue that writing itself is a male project and that autobiographical writing is conducted within the framework of the liberal individual—a distinct and overwhelmingly public self. If the very form of autobiographical writing is male biased, women will have a difficult time representing themselves through it.[16] The fact that Winfrey does not represent herself through a written autobiography (and in fact has repeatedly postponed the publication of an autobiography) points to a novel way of overcoming this problem of self-representation—namely, through the medium of television.

The enactment of Winfrey's on-screen biography through her talk show closely fits the way feminist critics have discussed women's autobiographies. To some extent, she even takes the points made in that literature to their logical extreme. This can be seen in two ways. First, Winfrey bypasses the problematics of *écriture feminine*—that is, of how to write as a woman in a style and genre so heavily dominated by men and perceived as inherently masculine—by *not writing*. Instead, she talks—not to herself or directly into a camera in an isolated studio, but rather in front of and together with a live audience. Second, she turns her autobiography into a real-time piece of work. She need not try to convey a sense of unfinishedness through the written word—she actually performs it live and in real time.

Notes

1. Wayne Shumaker, *English Autobiography: Its Emergence, Materials, and Form* (Berkeley: University of California Press, 1954), 8.

2. Georg Misch, *A History of Autobiography in Antiquity* (1907; reprint, London: Routledge and Paul, 1950).

3. Estelle C. Jelinek, *The Tradition of Women's Autobiography from Antiquity to the Present* (Boston: Twayne, 1986), 5.

4. Sidonie Smith, *A Poetics of Women's Autobiography: Marginality and the Fictions of Self-Representation* (Bloomington: Indiana University Press, 1987), 17.

5. Jelinek, *Tradition of Women's Autobiography,* 188.

6. Smith, *Poetics of Women's Autobiography,* 13; Sidonie Smith and Julia Watson, "Introduction: Situating Subjectivity in Women's Autobiographical Practices," in *Women, Autobiography, Theory: A Reader,* ed. Sidonie Smith and Julia Watson (Madison: University of Wisconsin Press, 1998), 16–18.

7. Jelinek, *Tradition of Women's Autobiography,* 187; emphasis in original.

8. Alan Richman, "Oprah," *People Weekly,* January 12, 1987, 48.

9. Charles Whitaker, "The Most Talked-about TV Talk Show Host," *Ebony,* March 1987, 38–44.

10. Laura Randolph, "Oprah Opens up about Her Weight, Her Wedding and Why She Withheld the Book," *Ebony,* October 1993, 130.

11. For more about the cultural sources and resources of the improvisational and dialogical nature of her talk show, see Eva Illouz, *Oprah Winfrey and the Glamour of Misery: An Essay on Popular Culture* (New York: Columbia University Press, 2003), chap. 7.

12. "Tipper Gore on Depression," *The Oprah Winfrey Show,* June 2, 1999.

13. Harry F. Waters and Patricia King, "Chicago's Grand New Oprah," *Newsweek,* December 31, 1984, 51.

14. Barbara Grizzuti Harrison, "The Importance of Being Oprah," *New York Times,* June 11, 1989, 54.

15. Anne Saidman, *Oprah Winfrey: Media Success Story* (Minneapolis: Lerner Publications, 1990).

16. See Smith and Watson, "Introduction."

From Fasting toward Self-Acceptance

Oprah Winfrey and Weight Loss in American Culture

Ella Howard

In 2002 Oprah Winfrey stated, "I did a head-to-toe assessment, and though there was plenty of room for improvement, I no longer hated any part of myself, including the cellulite. I thought, This is the body you've been given—love what you've got."[1] The story of Winfrey's dramatic rise to stardom is widely known. An African American woman born into rural poverty, shuttled from one relative to another, and the victim of prolonged sexual abuse, Winfrey prevailed over nearly every imaginable disadvantage to pursue a career in broadcasting. Proving her critics shortsighted, she created a revolutionary new approach to talk television that has spawned many imitations but no equals. Twenty years after her debut on *AM Chicago,* she controls one of the world's largest media empires. Her colleague, Dr. Phil McGraw, describes Winfrey's caricature in the popular imagination: "We might imagine that in every moment of her life, she's somehow bursting onto a stage, hugely confident and in control, arms outstretched in that familiar wave as music washes over the whole scene."[2]

Yet Winfrey inspires more complex emotions than simple admiration for her remarkable achievements. During the late 1980s, when *The Oprah Winfrey Show* became a nationwide phenomenon, Winfrey was framed in cultural discourse as the counterpoint to rival talk-show host Phil Donahue. Donahue might have embodied the quintessential sensitive New Age man, but Winfrey was not afraid to cry with her guests,

101

embrace them, and speak about her own life traumas. The personal connection many audience members and viewers felt with Winfrey played a major factor in her own success. Her predominantly female fans have kept her show strong in the ratings, made her book club selections into best sellers, subscribed to *O, the Oprah Magazine,* read and posted on the message boards and in the "O Groups" on her Web site (Oprah.com), and purchased every available ticket for public appearances such as her "Hi, Gorgeous! A Celebration of You" tour in 2004.[3] Ultimately, Winfrey has transcended the boundaries of the television medium, entering viewers' homes as an approachable friend, wise woman, and witty confidant. Her charismatic revelations of her own insecurities, weaknesses, and moments of self-doubt have endeared her to millions.

Winfrey welcomed her audience into her struggles with weight loss and body image as well. Approaching weight loss as she has other sensitive issues, she has often spoken publicly about what had previously been a largely private topic. Her repeated efforts to attain and maintain a lower body weight have served as a magnet for attention, criticism, and judgment. Carrying on this struggle in the scrutiny of the public eye has posed specific challenges for Winfrey. On a 2004 broadcast, she remarked, "Think of how you feel in your own personal life when you have to go to a wedding or you have to show up at something in public. Imagine what that would be magnified a million times over, as I have lived it, when you are struggling in the public."[4]

Yet the desire for weight loss is also widely shared. Some viewers tune in to Winfrey's various weight-loss episodes to acquire specific information and tips, others to find more general support and encouragement, to hear inspiring success stories, or merely to affirm the difficulty of the process. As she has spoken of her fluctuations in body size, experiences with various diets and exercise regimens, and subsequent feelings ranging from triumph to inadequacy, Winfrey has appeared not as a distant, wealthy celebrity but as a vulnerable person to whom her audience can relate.

Winfrey has been central to the development of the self-help industry, her television show providing an unprecedented platform for authors to disseminate their ideas and promote their books. Most self-help manuals navigate a complex path between self-acceptance and self-improvement. Readers are often encouraged to accept and love themselves as they are and to stop habits of relentless self-criticism. Yet most of these books also focus on a specific theme of self-improvement and are marketed to those who love others too much, cower in fear in social situations, or suffer from any one of hundreds of other afflictions. This tension between therapeutic self-acceptance and active self-improvement complicates much of Winfrey's discourse around weight loss and body image. She has presented herself, at various moments, as a "successful" and a "failed" dieter; a champion of low-fat, "clean" eating; a recovering "food addict"; an "emotional eater"; an exercise enthusiast; and a seeker of a healthier body. An eclectic mix of approaches, Winfrey's struggle with body weight and body image parallels the major trends in nutrition and fitness in the United States since the 1960s.

The controversial relationships between feminist ideals and the self-help and weight-loss industries add another layer to this narrative. Feminists have both applauded and criticized the self-help movement's tactics and goals, appreciating its efforts to put women in touch with their feelings, but recoiling from its insistent push for improvement of the individual rather than reform of society. Similar feminist criticism has blasted the diet industry for contributing to a culture of fat phobia in the United States instead of promoting greater acceptance of a variety of body types. Winfrey's public stance on weight issues has subjected her to scrutiny and criticism on both fronts.

This essay traces Winfrey's journey from liquid dieting to strenuous exercise to "getting real" with Dr. Phil. Through a consideration of Winfrey's experiences, I analyze the shifting standards of female health, fitness, and body type in recent history. Examining Winfrey's actions and the discourse around them reveals some of the inherent tensions and contradictions between the push for self-acceptance and self-improvement in the self-help movement of the postfeminist era.

Understanding Postfeminist Diet Talk

The Oprah Winfrey Show has often been characterized as a female space, one where women gather to watch other women discuss topics that many men would consider either too personal or too frivolous to pursue publicly. In that sense, it resembles the consciousness-raising groups of the 1960s that formed the basis of the women's movement. As women came together and shared their experiences, they discovered the common ground on which they stood and developed new perceptions of both their personal and political situations.

As part of the self-help movement, daytime talk shows rest on a commitment to the therapeutic process of discussing past experiences and current concerns, acknowledging one's emotional responses, and working toward personal growth and development. Historians have traced the American fascination with therapeutic self-improvement to the late-nineteenth-century birth of corporate culture, consumerism, and modern advertising.[5] Scholars of the post-1960s era have characterized related phenomena as emblematic of a narcissistic focus on the self, with little regard for social change or even for society.[6]

Observers remain divided on the question of whether women's interests are served or hindered by either daytime talk shows or the self-help movement more broadly. Some emphasize the inherent connections between therapy and consciousness-raising, noting that second-wave feminists actively drew on therapeutic theories and practices in developing their strategies.[7] Others note that what might initially appear to be pointless narcissistic reflection can have deeper meaning for women. They argue that since women have been (and remain) an oppressed group taught to ignore their own needs in favor of others', encouraging them to pay attention to their feelings and desires can be beneficial.[8] The quest for happiness and fulfillment is itself a legacy of feminism, some remind us, noting that the success of the women's movement allowed women to ask for more than they had historically been granted.[9] In that sense, the spirit of female empowerment infuses the entire self-help movement, as women seek to change situations that previous generations would have merely accepted.

Critics of the self-help movement mount equally compelling arguments. Self-help discourse does nothing to further the causes of social justice, they point out, as it often equates individual suffering across lines of ethnicity, race, class, gender, and sexual orientation. Thus, we are asked to empathize with racists, rapists, abusers, and molesters who suffered difficult childhoods.[10] In this regard, the movement is criticized for failing to encourage political action or even to facilitate the development of political consciousness. As Wendy Kaminer wryly observes, "Feminism is women talking, but it is not women only talking and not women talking only about themselves."[11] Echoing the theories of French philosopher and historian Michel Foucault, cultural critics have also questioned the logic of the search for the "authentic self" that the self-help movement inspires. Following standardized exercises mandated by mass-produced workbooks, we may be chasing phantoms, not uncovering more honest identities but creating new, equally socially constructed, albeit more socially acceptable ones. Our search for personal liberation may be leading us into a form of voluntarily self-inflicted social control.[12]

These varied interpretations, though contradictory, are all viable, and at specific times and in certain situations, each is undoubtedly true. It is within this contested terrain that Winfrey has waged a search for her ideal physique, setting out to re-create her body by regulating her activities and disciplining her desires. At times, she has expressed feelings of victory and celebrated her achievement of the physical ideal, crediting therapeutic strategies with helping to liberate her from troubled relationships with food, exercise, and physical appearance. At other times, she has represented herself as a failure in her quest, expressing frustration and despair. But throughout her struggles she continues to rely on the self-help model, employing new or familiar therapeutic strategies in pursuit of her goals.

Winfrey's foregrounding of the role of personal healing, growth, and empowerment in her quest for weight loss effectively preempts a "traditional" feminist critique of her situation. She has stated adamantly that her efforts to lose weight have been undertaken not to render her more appealing to longtime fiancé Stedman Graham, but rather solely to please herself.[13] More significantly, although a second-wave feminist critique might argue that placing so much emphasis on altering one's physical body represents simple capitulation to rigid, patriarchal standards of beauty, such an analysis falls short when attempting to address the situation of a woman who wishes to heal the emotional scars she carries from childhood sexual abuse and thus free herself from a negative body image. The connection that Winfrey has repeatedly drawn between these themes of self-acceptance and self-improvement through weight loss have also left little room for a critique of society's refusal to accept women's diverse body types, the negative effects of the crushing pressure on young women to be thin, or other concerns.

Freedom from Food: Starving in Recovery

On *The Oprah Winfrey Show,* guests frequently bare all about a variety of potentially sensitive topics, including their weight. It is not unusual for such guests to be celebrities; on a broadcast following her highly publicized arrest for drunk driving, country singer Wynonna Judd launched an effort to lose weight, declaring, "I'm desperate, you know? I'm in the public eye. I'm so successful, but personally, you know, I suck. I don't have it together."[14] Other episodes have featured noncelebrities who lost dramatic amounts of weight, such as forty-four-year-old Reverend Ray Thomas, who shed more than three hundred pounds. Thomas held up his "before" pants, crediting his success in part to the therapeutic effect of addressing his repressed emotional pain over childhood neglect, a bad marriage, and the deaths of his grandmother and brother.[15] Such revelations and stories are framed as inspirational motivators for viewers struggling with their own weight.

But the primary dieter on the show remains, of course, Winfrey herself. She staged one of the most famous moments in television history on the November 15, 1988, episode called "Diet Dreams Come True." Winfrey announced that on her latest diet she had lost sixty-seven pounds, and to dramatize the achievement, she came out on stage pulling a child's red wagon filled with an equivalent amount of animal fat. Clad in size ten Calvin Klein jeans, a slim-fitting sweater, and stylish high-heeled boots, Winfrey showed off her new, lean body with pride.[16]

She earned that victorious trip across the stage by practicing strict self-denial. On the Optifast plan, Winfrey had consumed no solid food, subsisting on a scant four hundred to eight hundred calories per day in the form of five glasses of water mixed with nutrient packets. Optifast is not cheap; it is available only to those with $2,000 to $3,000 to spend on the program. It is recommended only for those seeking to lose more than fifty pounds and should be administered under medical supervision. Along with rival products, such as Medifast, such programs are collectively referred to in the medical community as very low calorie diets (VLCDs). On VLCDs, weight loss can be extremely rapid, averaging two to five pounds per week. Dieters are warned to expect side effects, including fatigue, constipation, hair loss, anxiety, and nausea.[17]

Winfrey had long described her relationship to food using the language of the recovery movement. Recalling a day when she had eaten maple syrup–covered hot dog buns, Winfrey remarked, "Now, looking back, I see no difference between myself and a junkie, scrambling for a needle and whatever dope might be around. Food was my dope."[18]

She announced that she was ready to stop the cycle of excess food consumption: "I was addicted to food just as people are addicted to alcohol or drugs, but I knew this time I was ready to break that addiction because I didn't need the crutch anymore."[19] Winfrey's plan to maintain her new body weight required vigilant monitoring of her caloric intake and swift, vigorous action on the heels of any indulgences. In her words, "I eat all kinds of food now, but in moderation. I eat just enough to appease my hunger, sometimes only a spoonful of this and a forkful of that, and if I eat a big meal or a rich dessert, I'll fast the next day or run an extra mile or two. I know I have to work consciously the rest of my life to keep it off, but that's what control is about. If I can control my eating, everything else falls into place."[20]

For a woman whose career was progressing so dramatically (her show had gone national three years earlier), Winfrey devoted a great deal of personal energy to her weight. Her success, in part, fueled her preoccupation; as her celebrity status grew, so did the pressures to conform to normative standards of size. The publicity generated by her dramatic weight loss added even more pressure. As Winfrey remarked, "I'm not going to gain it back because of fear of tabloids and everything that would be printed if I gained one pound."[21] Terrified of losing control of her eating, as well as other aspects of her life, Winfrey was obsessed with weight loss and body image. In that regard, she echoed the concerns of many individuals suffering from disordered eating. The level of desperation Winfrey experienced was reflected in the extremity of the weight-loss plan she chose.

But VLCDs, which are really a modified form of fasting, are only one of the more extreme forms of dieting pursued by those seeking ideal bodies. Since the late 1960s, a variety of diets have achieved popularity through media promotion, mass marketing, and publication in inexpensive paperback editions. The trend began with *The Doctor's Quick Weight Loss Diet* in 1967.[22] Dr. Irwin Stillman informed hopeful readers that they could lose up to five, ten, fifteen, or more pounds per week on the diet by eating "all-protein" foods such as meat, fish, eggs, cottage cheese, and clear soups without vegetables. Within its first five years on the market, the book had sold seven million copies worldwide. Clearly, consumers longed for rules, plans, and regimens to follow. Following the success of Stillman's book, Dr. Robert Atkins launched the Atkins diet.[23] That program (which recently enjoyed a dramatic revival) also focused on low- and no–carbohydrate consumption. Adherents of the Atkins diet are guided to determine their personal critical carbohydrate levels—the amount of carbohydrates allowed each day.

Other restrictive diet plans followed, including the popular Scarsdale Diet.[24] Proffering the possibility of losing an average of one pound per day, the low-fat, low-calorie, low-carbohydrate diet must be followed precisely, with no substitutions. Breakfast each day is a standardized and sobering affair: one-half grapefruit, one slice of toasted protein bread with no butter or jam, and plain coffee or tea without sugar, cream, or milk. When at parties or bars, dieters are encouraged to request the "Scarsdale Special Highball"—soda water over ice, with a citrus wedge.

Liquid diets, too, enjoyed popularity in the 1970s, with sometimes tragic outcomes. Dr. Robert Linn published *The Last Chance Diet* in 1976.[25] Promising quick results, the book soon sold 2.5 million copies. This plan encouraged followers to drink liquid protein supplements while eating no solid food. The predigested animal protein was fabricated from by-products (hides and tendons) and did not contain the nutrients essential to survival. The Food and Drug Administration (FDA) and the Centers for Disease Control attributed seventeen deaths to the diet, which had devastating effects on the hearts of its adherents.[26] Likewise, the Cambridge diet, named after inventor Dr. Alan Howard's position at Cambridge University, was a modified version of the liquid protein diet, also with substantial health risks. Howard's program met the U.S. recommended daily allowance for vitamins and minerals but totaled only 330 calories per day. By late 1982, the FDA reported 132 complaints of illness and six deaths resulting from the Cambridge plan.[27]

The Optifast plan that Winfrey followed was just one in a series of radical diets that swept the nation. For those unable or unwilling to stop eating solid foods entirely, Slim-Fast now offers a low-priced, higher-calorie, over-the-counter version of a liquid diet. Much like products such as Metrecal of the 1960s, Slim-Fast boasts that "a shake for breakfast, a shake for lunch, and a sensible dinner" allows dieters to lose weight safely.[28]

It is no coincidence that this diet craze followed on the heels of the feminist movement. Naomi Wolf has described "the beauty myth" as "the last one remaining of the old feminine ideologies that still has the power to control those women whom second-wave feminism would have otherwise made relatively uncontrollable: it has grown stronger to take over the work of social coercion that myths about mother-hood, domesticity, chastity, and passivity no longer can manage."[29] In-deed, the advertising industry often couched appeals to women's vanity, their longing for eternal youth, and their desire for the slim bodies of preadolescent girls in the very language of liberation employed by the women's movement. By 1984, as Nancy Reagan stood guard against communism in her size four suits, there were three hundred diet books in print in the United States alone.[30]

With the national obsession with a svelte physique so prevalent in the 1980s, Winfrey's struggle to lose weight resonated with many viewers, who emulated her use of the liquid diet with untold devastat-ing results. Sales of Optifast skyrocketed, and related products such as Slim-Fast enjoyed increased media exposure by association. Many of Winfrey's fans resented her promotion of such a dangerous diet plan and felt betrayed by her decisions. Others wondered how such a strong and powerful woman could be reduced to starving herself publicly in pursuit of an elusive body size.

Winfrey could not maintain her low body weight after she com-pleted the diet. Once she resumed eating solid foods, she immediately began to gain weight. By her own account, she weighed 142 pounds on the day she wheeled the wagon of fat onstage and 168 pounds one year later. She recorded in her journal that day, "I'm thoroughly disgusted with myself. I couldn't even get thin for the anniversary show. Where is my resolve? Every day I awaken with good intentions and then I fail."[31] Two years after her dramatic weight loss, she wrote:

> I cried in my office after someone mentioned my clothes and the way I've been dressing: wrong colors, wrong style. Cried because I know that means lots of people have been discussing it. No one says anything. But I feel them avoiding the subject. I cried for my poor miserable self having gotten to this state. Scale said 203 pounds this morning. Controlled—just con-trolled by it. Every day waking up with a plan. By the end of the day, not following through, feeling diminished, less of a person, guilty, ugly, you name it. Trying to gain control know-ing that God says I already have it. Where is it, God? Dancing on the M. C. Hammer show with the fattest behind I've ever

seen. I saw that tape and can't deny it anymore. I really am fat
again.[32]

Winfrey was later informed that the crash diet had depleted her body's
muscle tissue and lowered her metabolism to such an extent that regaining the weight was nearly inevitable. Nevertheless, at the time, she
interpreted the events in the way the media encouraged dieters to see
such results—not as a failure of the diet but as a failure of the self.

Dieting through Strenuous Exercise

In 1991 Winfrey appeared on the cover of *People,* saying, "I'll never
diet again."[33] Although disenchanted with diet regimens, she remained
dissatisfied with her personal appearance. Nominated for a Daytime
Emmy Award in 1992, she became distraught over the thought of attending the ceremony. She later recalled hoping to lose: "Yes, God, let
Phil [Donahue] win. So I won't have to get up and pull my skirt down
and waddle my way up to the stage with the nation watching my huge
behind."[34] Although she won that night, Winfrey wrote, "I felt so much
like a loser, like I'd lost control of my life. And the weight was symbolic
of how out-of-control I was. I was the fattest woman in the room."[35]
Amidst a crowd of arguably the thinnest people in the country, Winfrey
felt out of place; in nearly any other setting, she would not have been
considered significantly overweight.

By this time, Winfrey had been on a diet of low-fat foods prepared
by her chef, Rosie Daley, for several years. Winfrey would later arrange
for the publication of the cookbook *In the Kitchen with Rosie* and appear
on its cover. *In the Kitchen with Rosie* became the fastest-selling book
in history, at six million copies. In her brief introduction to the book,
Winfrey framed her development of a taste for low-fat dishes in the
context of her evolving understanding of the psychological importance
of food in her life. Discussing her southern childhood, she wrote, "Back
then, food meant security and comfort. Food meant love."[36] Learning
to enjoy modified versions of her favorite foods, explore new flavors,
and separate meals from some of their emotional connotations helped
Winfrey maintain a stable body weight, but she remained dissatisfied,
carrying 237 pounds on her five foot seven inch frame.

At a Colorado health spa, Winfrey teamed up with Bob Greene, who would soon become her personal trainer. With Greene's assistance, Winfrey began a rigorous running program. As a novice, she jogged and walked at a seventeen-minute-mile pace, but by November 1993, she was running a five-mile loop at an eight-minute-mile pace. Fitting the workouts into Winfrey's hectic schedule was difficult; she began running four miles each morning at 5 A.M., followed by a second session in the late afternoon. By midsummer 1994, Winfrey was logging up to fifty miles per week. She ran that year's Marine Corps Marathon, waving to cheering fans flanked by Greene and reporters from the *National Enquirer*.[37] Winfrey's strenuous running program allowed her to lose weight. By late 1993, her weight had dropped to 148 pounds again. Her accomplishment sparked popular interest in her running program. In 1995 she was featured on the covers of both *Fitness* magazine and *Runner's World,* her photo emblazoned with headlines such as "Oprah Did It, So Can You: How She Lost 70 Pounds and Finished the Marathon."[38] In 1996 Greene and Winfrey capitalized on the public fascination with her fitness program, writing *Make the Connection: Ten Steps to a Better Body—and a Better Life.* The book contained Greene's nutrition advice, preaching the benefits of a balanced, low-fat diet consumed in small portions and accompanied by plenty of water. Significantly, he encouraged readers to exercise nearly every day to achieve rapid results, rather than the three times per week that had long been advised by experts.

This advice was interwoven with Winfrey's narrative of her lifelong struggle with weight loss. Some of the anecdotes were painful memories of meals eaten in secret and shame, while others were humorously uncharacteristic of the persona she portrayed on television. For example, while running with Greene in Italy, he had mocked her for feeling the effects of too much wine consumed the previous evening, and she recalled raising her middle finger in reply.[39] Greene's occasionally smug attitude may have triggered a similar response from Winfrey's fans. In a series of articles he wrote for *Good Housekeeping,* detailing her training program, Greene described Winfrey's failure to keep up the rigorous schedule of diet and exercise during the holiday season: "For the first time in ten months she called to cancel a training session with me. The occasion was her fortieth birthday in January. Suddenly I realized she was using her birthday as an excuse not to exercise, just as she used Thanksgiving, the company party, and all the other events as a reason to overeat or eat the wrong foods."[40] Greene's zealous approach to diet and exercise surely alienated or intimidated some readers.

But many Americans seemed to be searching for a health program just like Greene's. Running, previously an activity reserved for serious athletes, had become increasingly popular with average Americans in the 1970s. By 1983, more than four hundred marathons were held annually in the United States to accommodate 157,000 participants.[41] Along with running, other forms of vigorous aerobic activity took hold in the 1980s. During the first half of the decade, approximately twenty-five million Americans tried aerobics classes in more than fifty thousand aerobics studios nationwide.[42] No longer was the moderate exercise advised by the medical community for decades enough to satisfy the average exerciser. People now devoted their time and energy to extremely strenuous activities.

Ostensibly, a search for improved health and fitness prompted this trend toward low-fat eating and vigorous exercise. American popular culture was permeated with the notion that overweight people, defined as those weighing more than advised by the height and weight charts used by doctors and insurance companies, were by definition unhealthy and were destined for early graves due to heart disease, diabetes, and myriad other health problems.

Feminist critics had interrogated these presumed links between weight and health for years. In the early 1980s, Kim Chernin cited medical research questioning such claims, noting that, for people without hypertension (high blood pressure), a somewhat higher body weight did not pose serious health risks.[43] Especially for women, the connection between slenderness and health exacerbated existing body issues. A 1984 study revealed that far more women described themselves as "too fat" than any objective standard could substantiate.[44] Poor judges of their own body size, women were misdiagnosing themselves as dangerously overweight and embarking on fitness programs that may have been unnecessarily extreme.

But the primary motivation for the fitness craze remained the desire to cultivate an attractive physical appearance. In the United States during the late 1980s and 1990s, the physical ideal for both women and men became a fit body—one with visible muscles. Buns, thighs, abs, arms, and legs of steel were an elusive goal pursued by millions who purchased videotapes and weight sets for home use or joined gyms. A woman who might have been considered physically perfect in 1960 was, by 1990, "full-figured," "flabby," and undesirable by the standards of the mainstream media.[45]

Critics have termed this fitness craze a "wellness epidemic," subverting the rhetoric of the "obesity epidemic" constantly invoked in the media.[46] Not surprisingly, Winfrey, too, has been accused of becoming a "model of obsession" with her conversion to long-distance running.[47] Exercising as a form of weight control, rather than as a purist pursuit of improved cardiovascular health, appropriate blood pressure levels, and other mundane fitness goals, is criticized by some observers as little improvement over crash dieting. Laura Fraser wrote, "For many people who struggle with their weight, exercise is like a diet. They figure if Oprah can do it, they can do it. . . . We came to admire the exercise-obsessed rather than to wonder whether they should get a life."[48]

Winfrey credits much of the success of her running program with the fact that she has come to terms with painful events in her past. The "connection" that she and Greene urged readers to make was the one between psychologically traumatic events, repressed feelings and desires, and other abstract reasons and the consumption of inappropriate types or amounts of food, termed "emotional eating." While working on an autobiography planned for release in 1993 (which Winfrey later canceled), she reflected on the sexual abuse she had suffered as a child and made the connection between those events and her issues with body weight. Winfrey said, "It's important, I think, for people to make the connection that (weight) is an emotional problem that manifests itself physically."[49] This mix of psychological and physiological explanations of weight gain and loss is characteristic of Winfrey's therapeutic approach to problem solving.

However, remarks Winfrey made at the *Make the Connection* book launch revealed a persistent contradiction. While nodding toward self-acceptance, she continued to emphasize the pursuit of an extremely ambitious fitness goal: "I love this book because for so many years I struggled and wanted to be Diana Ross. Then I realized that I just have to settle into what is the best body for me. I'm about a size ten now. And I'm going to work out this summer to try to get back to eights, because my closet is full of eights. . . . So I'm going to work out really hard."[50]

After running the marathon, Winfrey continued her low-fat diet and exercise program, maintaining a relatively stable body weight for four years. In 1998, after completing the film adaptation of Toni Morrison's novel *Beloved,* Winfrey was asked to pose for the cover of *Vogue* magazine, on the condition that she lose twenty pounds. Though inciting some feminist criticism, Winfrey agreed and appeared on the magazine's cover in the traditional pose of a fashion model. Clad in a cashmere Ralph Lauren dress and sapphire and diamond jewelry designed by Fred Leighton, Winfrey had attained one of society's most coveted positions, that of a cover model.[51] However, in the years following the Vogue appearance, Winfrey again gained weight, citing disappointing ticket sales for *Beloved* and the highly publicized Texas cattle trial for triggering a return to inappropriate eating and exercise habits. But the trial that would inadvertently contribute to her weight gain also brought her into contact with Phil McGraw, who would soon become her most outspoken ally in her continued campaign for weight loss.

"Getting Real" and the Turn toward Tougher Talk

Impressed by McGraw's direct communication style and pragmatic approach to problem solving as a trial coach, Winfrey invited him to be a guest on her television program. The appearance soon led to the recurring "Tuesdays with Dr. Phil" and, ultimately, McGraw's own daily program, *Dr. Phil.* In many ways, McGraw's style is the opposite of Winfrey's, providing a counterpoint to her gentle yet direct style of interviewing. Whereas Winfrey can ask probing questions with a warm tone and a demeanor conveying sincere interest in the response, the same queries from McGraw come across as a thinly veiled challenge to (in his trademark phrase) "get real about fat" or "get real fat." Winfrey calls McGraw's advice "the cold, hard truth, but exactly what our overweight guests needed to hear."[52] Like Winfrey, McGraw invokes his personal experience with body weight, but his purpose is not to convey empathy with guests. Instead, he highlights the superiority of his own life choices, pointing out that if he were not health conscious and athletic, he too would be genetically predisposed to being significantly overweight.[53]

Following his success on *The Oprah Winfrey Show,* McGraw published several best-selling books, including a companion set on weight loss: *The Ultimate Weight Solution: The 7 Keys to Weight Loss Freedom, The Ultimate Weight Solution Food Guide,* and *The Ultimate Weight Solution*

Cookbook: Recipes for Weight Loss Freedom.[54] His advice largely echoes that of Greene and many other authors: perform a combination of cardiovascular activities and strength training several times per week; eat a low-fat diet composed of fruits, vegetables, and other nutritious foods; and drink plenty of water. Like his viewers, McGraw's readers are drawn in by his characteristically blunt language, such as his insistence that we determine our "get-real weight." McGraw also emphasizes the importance of therapeutic approaches in his program. Readers are encouraged to focus on "right thinking," defined as a ban on negative, self-defeating thoughts, and the healing of old psychological wounds that prompt emotional eating.[55] This commonsensical advice, innocuous enough in print form, assumes a different dimension on television in the context of McGraw's insistence that individuals take personal responsibility not only for their actions but also for their environments.

McGraw's attitudes toward body weight and body image foster a judgmental, confrontational atmosphere on the episodes of *Dr. Phil* that address the subject. The two-part episode "My Big Fat Attitude" underscores the tendency of both McGraw and Winfrey to focus on self-improvement rather than social change. Whereas Winfrey's charisma and personal investment in the topic of body image complicate the messages sent by her broadcasts, McGraw's position is starkly clear, as are its political ramifications. For instance, on an earlier episode focusing on lawsuits relating to body weight, McGraw acknowledged the validity of the position of a man suing an airline for seating him next to an overweight passenger, while dismissing the notion of a class-action lawsuit against the fast-food industry by parents of overweight children as "a load of crap!" In McGraw's words, "I don't know how many grams of fat are in a Big Mac, but I'd have to be a moron to not know that it's fattening."[56] The topic sparked enough interest for McGraw and his producers to arrange a follow-up program featuring guests with starkly differing viewpoints on issues surrounding body weight. Two guests, Sally and Maryanne, requested to appear on the show to air their disagreements with McGraw's weight-loss advice and to raise public awareness of alternative views on the subject. The positions adopted by his guests were couched in far from subtle terms; viewers were informed through captions that Sally "Says Society Should Accommodate Fat People," while another guest, Cindy, "Says Fat People Disgust Her."

Early in the broadcast, McGraw clarified that he was interested in offering weight-loss advice to people who wanted it, not in harassing those who were content with their current body size. Maryanne replied thoughtfully, "But the problem is, you may be saying that, but society is telling us, 'You have to change. You're not OK the way you are.'" McGraw quipped, "Well, go see society. Don't come see me." More than simply avoiding the question of his own power as a cultural force, McGraw's reply highlighted his relentless focus on individual solutions to social problems. McGraw continued to list five misconceptions commonly held about people of size, assuring viewers that such people were not unaware of their weight, lazy and slow, all overeaters, always hungry, or always unhappy with their size. McGraw then screened a videotape of Cindy's crassly antagonistic views toward overweight people:

> I've been grossed out by fat people whether they're eating or not. I think that they've got really no one else to blame other than themselves. No one sat there and forced them to eat three chickens at a time. Fat might be fine for some people, but in today's society, if you're not tall and thin, you're nothing. . . . When my husband and I go out shopping I'll pick a woman in the store that's got the biggest butt that I can find, and I'll joke with him and I'll point to her and I'll say, "Honey, I'm gonna do that for you," you know, as in "pork myself out," and he looks at me and goes, "If you do, you're gone."[57]

McGraw correctly labeled Cindy rude, judgmental, arrogant, and condescending. However, beginning the show by pointing out the fallacy of commonly accepted ideas about body weight and then presenting an example of extreme prejudice ensured that McGraw's positions would appear moderate in comparison. McGraw then went on to recite a litany of health complications associated with obesity, including an increased risk of diabetes, heart disease, cardiovascular problems, and autoimmune deficiency.[58]

As the episode progressed, Sally continually reframed McGraw's questions, calling for deeper consideration of the logic behind the social pressure to be thin. When McGraw asked her whether she would be interested in losing a significant amount of weight, she employed a metaphor of racial identity to dramatize the question: "Would you—I mean if—if an African-American person could take a magic pill and become white, would they? Well, it's easier to live in this society if you're not a minority group. You know, would it be easier for me to live if I was thin? Oh, yeah."[59] McGraw disputed each argument Sally presented, insisting that responsibility belonged at the individual level.

Sally attempted to refocus the discussion more broadly, drawing connections between the social stigma attached to obesity and the forces of capitalism: "perhaps we need to look at it as a different paradigm. Who said that—what the ideal body shape is? I mean, I think that people need to understand that, you know, all of the stigma against fat people, all of the barriers are because there's this Madison Avenue, there's a $33 billion a year diet industry in this country that sells us on the idea that fat people don't deserve a place in this world." McGraw replied, "Hey, I agree 100 percent. . . . Really, I do. I mean, I don't care what you look like if you like what you look like. . . . But what I don't want you to do is say, 'I like how I look when I really don't just because it's sour grapes, and I don't think I can get to the other side.'"[60] By acknowledging the validity of Sally's position and then reframing the issue as one of personal responsibility, McGraw blocked her efforts at each turn.

Here, then, was the core of McGraw's therapeutic philosophy. Regardless of the topic, he urged guests to "take responsibility" for their lives and situations. Although more confrontational than many of his colleagues, McGraw's insistent emphasis on each person's role echoed that of the self-help industry at large. Such logic encouraged individual rather than collective solutions and sidestepped efforts to bring about social reform.

Another guest on the show, Marilyn, weighed more than four hundred pounds. After a lifetime of dieting, she had decided that, upon turning forty, "The roller coaster was over, the dieting was over, the bingeing was over. I made a conscious decision that I was gonna take full responsibility for my happiness."[61] Determined not to be imprisoned by embarrassment or fear of people's reactions, Marilyn had overcome her uneasiness about wearing a swimsuit in public and taken up swimming at a local university pool. Marilyn spoke of the health benefits as well as the personal pleasure she found in swimming. Although McGraw pushed Marilyn to consider losing weight to improve her health, he did not assail her claims of self-acceptance, as he had Sally's. He asked the audience whether they thought Marilyn was truly happy with herself, and many felt that she was. In the words of one audience member, "It's the whole attitude; that—the way she speaks, the way she does things. She took initiative to go and swim, regardless of what other people think. She feels that she has a right to do everything and anything that everybody else—where it feels like the other lady is more judgmental, and she attacks a lot of people for, I think, a lot of—of her own inside issues that she has."[62] Marilyn was framed as a model of self-acceptance, adjustment, and "happiness," while Sally's questioning of social standards earned her a description as unhappy, angry, and "attacking people."

Clearly, the self-help orientation of both Winfrey's and McGraw's programs left little room for the criticism of social ills. Whether Winfrey was crying with a guest or McGraw was reprimanding one, both consistently returned the discussion to the role of the individual rather than that of society, short-circuiting meaningful discussion of strategies for social change. Personal adaptation was often promoted at the expense of agitation or protest. Although some people undoubtedly strengthened their personal resolve through self-help practices and went on to work toward social reform, countless others merely internalized the notion that they were flawed, maladjusted, nonconformist individuals.

In her widely read, scathing article on Winfrey, Barbara Grizzuti Harrison astutely observed, "This is a problem intrinsic to the medium; that an engaging Oprah Winfrey is part of a process that engenders passivity is our problem, not hers."[63] Indeed, the problematic nature of the conflicting messages embedded in the diet and self-help advice circulating through the popular media extends far beyond a critique of any single individual. Although Winfrey's shifting stance on weight loss and body image offers a useful lens through which to analyze a variety of topics, her personal decisions remain, in the end, less important than the broader social values that shape the meaning of her actions.

Toward Health and Self-Acceptance

In 2001 Winfrey was frightened by heart palpitations that her doctor attributed partially to her recent weight gain. Suffering from high blood pressure, she was advised to lose weight for health reasons. Unlike her previous fitness efforts, which had stemmed from her desire to "fit into a size eight," Winfrey wrote, her new immediate concern was "trying not to die." Working with Greene, she developed a new fitness program that involved strength training to preserve muscle and thirty minutes of aerobic activity each day, a more moderate and balanced approach than she had advocated in the past. In a 2003 article in O magazine, she unveiled her workout, emphasizing the importance of health factors over those of physical appearance. She wrote, "You've got to love yourself and do the work it takes to sustain your most powerful engine: good health. Without it nothing else matters." Winfrey mentioned the program's effect on her body weight but buried it at the end of the article: "I've gotten a clean bill of health from my doctors—no cardio problems—but I'm still striving every day toward a healthier me. The side effect: I've now lost thirty-three pounds. I'm on no particular diet—I just eat smaller portions, and I still watch the refined carbohydrates. I favor fish, chicken, fruit, vegetables, and lots of soups. . . . I feel great. I'm sleeping well. I'm loving myself."[64]

The photographs accompanying the article featured Winfrey doing challenging strength training exercises. On the full-page lead photo, she was shown performing a "standing fly," smiling happily, looking strong, fearless, and grounded. One is tempted to contrast that image to the one on the cover of Vogue five years earlier, where Winfrey was shown reclining passively and awkwardly on a chair, her body contorted into one of the traditional poses of the cover model. But such a comparison would not do Winfrey justice, for even the controversial Vogue article was a bold act: she appeared with her African American Beloved costars in gowns evocative of nineteenth-century dress, saying that she wanted to "have us all dress the way we would've dressed had we not been slaves and had some money."[65] In the interviews for the accompanying article, she also foregrounded the traditional lack of ethnic diversity in the magazine. Asked whether appearing in Vogue had been one of her childhood ambitions, she told the interviewer and the magazine's readers, "Dreamed to be in Vogue? I'm a black woman from Mississippi. Why would I be thinking I was gonna be in Vogue? I would never have even thought of it as a possibility. That's why it's so extraordinary. . . . Vogue is the big house! Didn't think I'd be sitting at that table!"[66]

Due in part to her own actions, Winfrey will forever be associated with the topic of weight loss and body image. The theme emerges in many journalistic accounts of her life and career and permeates discussions of her accomplishments. Her various efforts at weight loss have attracted unprecedented media attention, as have her reflections on the psychological factors in her struggle. On a personal level, Winfrey's work in this regard has undoubtedly inspired some women to improve their own self-image and achieve new goals. Others have found her words and deeds hurtful, feeling alienated by her efforts to achieve slenderness at all costs. Because of her work to bring elements of the private realm into the public eye and her consistent modeling of self-help practices, Winfrey's life and work are nearly inextricable.

More significantly, the type of discourse that Winfrey's program and the self-help industry have fostered around weight loss has proved to be hostile to campaigns for acceptance of a variety of body types. Winfrey's remains an extremely powerful voice in the contemporary media. As this essay has shown, though, her talk would fall on deaf ears if she were not saying something people wanted to hear.

Notes

This essay was inspired by conversations with Tanya Koukeyan and benefited from feedback from Jon Beasley-Murray, Maria Rosales, Lisa Schweitzer, Susan Hacker, and Bruce Schulman.

1. Oprah Winfrey, "This Is the Body You've Been Given—Love What You've Got," *O, the Oprah Magazine,* August 2002, 196.

2. Phil McGraw, *Life Strategies: Doing What Works, Doing What Matters* (New York: Hyperion, 1999), 4; B. Kimberly Taylor and David Oblender, "Oprah Winfrey," in *Contemporary Black Biography: Profiles from the International Black Community,* vol. 15, ed. Shirelle Phelps (New York: Gale Research, 1997), 230–34.

3. James A. Fussell, "High on Oprah," *Kansas City Star,* May 2, 2004.

4. "Wynonna Judd: Fighting for Her Life," *The Oprah Winfrey Show,* February 11, 2004 (Harpo Productions transcript), 2.

5. T. J. Jackson Lears, "From Salvation to Self-Realization: Advertising and the Therapeutic Roots of the Consumer Culture, 1880–1930," in *The Culture of Consumption: Critical Essays in American History, 1880–1980,* ed. Richard Wightman Fox and T. J. Jackson Lears (New York: Pantheon Books, 1983), 5.

6. The best known work on this theme is Christopher Lasch, *The Culture of Narcissism: American Life in an Age of Diminishing Expectations* (New York: Norton, 1978); see also Jane M. Shattuc, *The Talking Cure: TV Talk Shows and Women* (New York: Routledge, 1996), 120.

7. Franny Nudelman, "Beyond the Talking Cure: Listening to Female Testimony on *The Oprah Winfrey Show,*" in *Inventing the Psychological: Toward a Cultural History of Emotional Life in America,* ed. Joel Pfister and Nancy Schnog (New Haven, Conn.: Yale University Press, 1997), 300.

8. Shattuc, *The Talking Cure,* 121.

9. Elayne Rapping, *The Culture of Recovery: Making Sense of the Self-Help Movement in Women's Lives* (Boston: Beacon Press, 1996), 5.

10. Wendy Kaminer, *I'm Dysfunctional, You're Dysfunctional: The Recovery Movement and Other Self-Help Fashions* (New York: Vintage Books, 1993), 155–56.

11. Ibid., 31.

12. Ibid., 164–65; Shattuc, *The Talking Cure,* 111–36.

13. "Oprah Winfrey: Says She Shed 67 Pounds for Herself, Not for Love," *Jet,* December 19, 1988, 28–31.

14. "Wynonna Judd," 1.

15. "Emotional Eating," *The Oprah Winfrey Show,* January 3, 2002 (Harpo Productions transcript), 18–19.

16. Bob Greene and Oprah Winfrey, *Make the Connection: Ten Steps to a Better Body—and a Better Life* (New York: Hyperion, 1999), 11–13.

17. George L. Blackburn, "A New Look at Liquid Diets," *Prevention,* April 1989, 100–102; Laura Jack, "Are Liquid Diets All Wet?" *Mademoiselle,* April 1989, 154–55; Andrea Fine, "Liquid Diets Make You Thinner but May Pose Big Fat Health Risks" (interview with Dr. Thomas Wadden), *People Weekly,* April 23, 1990, 105–6.

18. Greene and Winfrey, *Make the Connection,* 7–9.

19. Oprah Winfrey, "Wind Beneath My Wings," *Essence,* June 1989, 46.

20. Ibid., 102.

21. "Oprah Winfrey: Says She Shed 67 Pounds," 31.

22. As cited in Dr. Irwin Maxwell Stillman and Samm Sinclair Baker, *The Doctor's Quick Weight Loss Diet Cookbook* (New York: D. McKay, 1972).

23. Fran Gare and Helen Monica, *Dr. Atkins' Diet Cookbook,* under the supervision of and with an introduction by Robert C. Atkins (New York: Crown Publishers, 1974).

24. Herman Tarnower and Samm Sinclair Baker, *The Complete Scarsdale Medical Diet Plus Dr. Tarnower's Lifetime Keep-Slim Program* (New York: Rawson, Wade Publishers, 1978).

25. Dr. Robert Linn with Sandra Lee Stuart, *The Last Chance Diet—When Everything Else Has Failed: Dr. Linn's Protein-Sparing Fast Program* (Secaucus, N.J.: L. Stuart, 1976).

26. Pamela G. Hollie, "Liquid Protein: Turmoil Intensifies," *New York Times,* January 27, 1978; Jane E. Brody, "Personal Health; Examining the Safety of the Cambridge Diet, a Four-Week Plan to Lose Weight Quickly," *New York Times,* November 16, 1983.

27. Brody, "Personal Health"; "Medical Researchers Urge Caution in Use of Cambridge Diet," *New York Times,* November 25, 1983.

28. Blackburn, "A New Look at Liquid Diets," 102; Harvey Levenstein,

Paradox of Plenty: A Social History of Eating in Modern America (New York: Oxford University Press, 1993), 242.

29. Naomi Wolf, *The Beauty Myth: How Images of Beauty Are Used against Women* (New York: William Morrow, 1991), 10–11.

30. Susan Douglas, *Where the Girls Are: Growing up Female with the Mass Media* (New York: Times Books, 1995), 246; Levenstein, *Paradox of Plenty,* 237, 244.

31. Winfrey, journal entry, November 14, 1989, in Greene and Winfrey, *Make the Connection,* 15.

32. Winfrey, journal entry, August 15, 1990, in Greene and Winfrey, *Make the Connection,* 16–17.

33. "Big Gain, No Pain," *People Weekly,* January 14, 1991, 82–85.

34. Greene and Winfrey, *Make the Connection,* 1.

35. Ibid., 2.

36. Oprah Winfrey, introduction to *In the Kitchen with Rosie: Oprah's Favorite Recipes,* by Rosie Daley (New York: Knopf, 1994), xi.

37. Greene and Winfrey, *Make the Connection,* 31; "The Oprah Winfrey Plan," *Runner's World,* March 1995, 64–66.

38. Greene and Winfrey, *Make the Connection,* 100–101.

39. Ibid., 187–89.

40. Bob Greene, "Fitness Connection," *Good Housekeeping,* December 1996, 74.

41. Roberta Pollack Seid, *Never Too Thin: Why Women Are at War with Their Bodies* (New York: Prentice-Hall, 1989), 238.

42. Ibid., 236.

43. Kim Chernin, *The Obsession: Reflections on the Tyranny of Slenderness* (New York: Harper and Row, 1981), 31–33.

44. Susan Bordo, *Unbearable Weight: Feminism, Western Culture, and the Body* (Berkeley: University of California Press, 2003), 55–56.

45. Ibid., 57.

46. Seid, *Never Too Thin,* 240.

47. Laura Fraser, *Losing It: America's Obsession with Weight and the Industry that Feeds on It* (New York: Penguin, 1997), 45.

48. Ibid., 271.

49. Marjorie Rosen, "Oprah Overcomes," *People Weekly,* January 10, 1994, 45.

50. Joanna Powell, "I Was Trying to Fill Something Deeper," *Good Housekeeping,* October 1996, 81.

51. Steven Meisel, "Oprah's Moment," *Vogue,* October 1998, 322–30, 392–93.

52. "Dr. Phil's Weight Loss Advice," *The Oprah Winfrey Show,* January 30, 2001 (Harpo Productions transcript), 1.

53. Ibid., 10.

54. Phil McGraw, *The Ultimate Weight Solution: The 7 Keys to Weight Loss Freedom* (New York: Free Press, 2003); *The Ultimate Weight Solution Food Guide* (New York: Pocket Books, 2003); and *The Ultimate Weight Solution Cookbook: Recipes for Weight Loss Freedom* (New York: Free Press, 2004).

55. McGraw, *The Ultimate Weight Solution Food Guide,* 8, 25–26.

56. "Fight over Fat," *Dr. Phil,* September 26, 2002 (Harpo Productions transcript), 1.

57. "My Big Fat Attitude," *Dr. Phil,* November 27, 2002 (Harpo Productions transcript), 3, 4–5, 7.

58. Ibid., 9.

59. Ibid., 11.

60. "My Big Fat Attitude: Part II," *Dr. Phil,* January 28, 2003 (Harpo Productions transcript), 10.

61. "My Big Fat Attitude," 12.

62. "My Big Fat Attitude: Part II," 15–16.

63. Barbara Grizzuti Harrison, "The Importance of Being Oprah," *New York Times Magazine,* July 11, 1989, 134.

64. Oprah Winfrey, "Oprah's New Shape: How She Got It," *O, the Oprah Magazine,* January 2003, 53–56.

65. Meisel, "Oprah's Moment," 329.

66. Ibid.

Spiritual Talk

The Oprah Winfrey Show *and* *the Popularization of the New Age*

Maria McGrath

Nineteen ninety-four was an important year for Oprah Winfrey. In anticipation of her upcoming fortieth birthday, she began a radical program of self-transformation. To gain control over her lifelong battle with weight, she decided to abandon all fad diets for a more consistent plan of healthy eating and a strict daily running schedule. In a *Ladies' Home Journal* interview in November 1994, Winfrey reflected on her commitment to her new exercise regime:

> Running is the greatest metaphor for life, because you get out of it what you put into it. . . . This is the hardest thing there is for me. Nothing is harder—work, accomplishments, achievements—than the actual mental and physical discipline that it takes to do this. But this is what I have to do to get the kind of mental and physical sharpness that I want.[1]

This kind of vigilance, and a closely controlled diet, took the talk-show maven from a size twenty-four to a size eight between 1993 and 1994.[2]

After putting her personal house in order, Winfrey turned to the long-brewing discontent among her staff. In response to a near mutiny against the tyrannical reign of executive producer Debra DiMaio, Winfrey encouraged DiMaio to bow out. The vacancy was filled by the promotion of less dictatorial senior producer Dianne Atkinson Hudson.

And in the vacuum created by the absence of DiMaio's micromanagement, Winfrey stepped in and assumed a more prominent role in the daily production of her show.[3]

It is unclear whether the personal milestone of turning forty or the new makeup of her staff inspired Winfrey and her cohorts to reinvent her show. Either way, in 1994 Winfrey took stock of her then eight-year-old program. Assessing the past and future of her talk show in a September 1994 *Entertainment Weekly* interview, Winfrey recalled an especially unsavory moment during an earlier program:

> The day I felt clearly the worst I've ever felt on television was sometime in '89 when we were still live and we had the wife, the girlfriend, and the husband, and on the air, the husband [unexpectedly] announced to the wife the girlfriend is pregnant. And the expression on her face—it pains me to think of it—I looked at her and felt horrible for myself and for her. So I turned to her and said, "I'm really sorry you had to be put in this position and you had to hear this on television. This never should have happened." That's when I said, "We cannot do this anymore." I can't say we never did another show with conflict, but that's when I first thought about it.[4]

At the time, Winfrey admitted that she thought the confessional format had educational value. Real people confessing their troubles could raise the country's awareness about issues traditionally kept secret at great cost to their victims, such as sexual abuse, infidelity, and sexual identity crises. But as she reached that milestone birthday in 1994, Winfrey found herself getting impatient with her guests' whining about the unfairness of their lives. She explained her newfound desire to motivate change and not simply wallow in pity: "I have to move on. We're not gonna book a show where someone is talking about their victimization. . . . The last time I did a show on women being stalked, they said how hard it is, and I recognize it is. But five years ago I would have been more sensitive to it. Last year I said [to the stalked women], 'So move. So move!'"[5]

Searching for a new focus for her program, Winfrey turned to the insights of the New Age movement. A spiritual seeker herself, Winfrey harvested the complex of New Age practices and beliefs to halt her show's descent into talk television's fetishization of human cruelty and psychological dysfunction. She abandoned the shock format and made spiritual uplift, individual will, personal responsibility, and grand cosmic design the guiding principles of her shows. Initially, Winfrey may not have comprehended the degree to which these choices would attach her show to the New Age movement. She may have been unaware of the countercultural origins of post-1960s "seeker" mentality or the history of post-1960s American religiosity; yet, by making psychologically framed spirituality (with Christian inflections) the core of each show, at the end of the twentieth century, Winfrey transformed herself into the television queen of New Age awareness.

From Counterculture to New Age: Spirituality and Religion in Post-1960s America

Religious scholar Robert Wuthnow notes that, according to 1996 Gallup poll figures, Americans remained religiously active throughout the second half of the twentieth century, with a majority professing "faith in God [and] claiming to pray often to that God."[6] Although 62 percent of Americans claimed to belong to a church or synagogue, Robert Fuller argues that based on various polls taken in the 1990s, close to 40 percent of Americans had no denominational affiliation yet still defined themselves as spiritual. These statistics confirm that at the turn of the twenty-first century, the United States was the most actively religious nation in the West.[7]

For religious scholars, what is most fascinating and instructive about modern American religiosity is not the quantity of citizens partaking but the quality of their spiritual routines. Fuller, Wuthnow, and others suggest that since the 1960s, American spirituality definitively shifted from theological obedience and denominational identification to the radical individualism of spiritual seeking and self-realization. Religious scholars describe this as Americans' transmutation from "churched" to "seeker" spirituality, with seekers "rejecting a religious identity but affirming a spiritual one."[8] Thus, whereas the 1950s saw a church- and synagogue-related religious revival, since the 1960s, worshipful Americans, especially baby boomers swayed by countercultural anti-establishmentarianism and New Left political iconoclasm, have defined their spirituality as fundamentally significant to their lives but rarely dependent on orthodox religious doctrine or institutions. From the perspective of countercultural rebels in the 1960s and baby boom seekers thereafter, the United States' religious establishments interfered with (rather than assisted) cosmic communion and individual enlightenment.

In their search for alternative methods and venues for spiritual expression, 1960s cultural rebels abandoned Christianity and Judaism for explorations of Buddhism, Hinduism, Taoism, Native American religions, Greek mythology, and various other philosophical schools. Given the counterculture's privileging of intuition and emotion over scientific rationality, the self-discovery method of Eastern religions (especially the esoteric sects of Zen Buddhism, Sufism, and Taoism) and the multiperspective polytheism of Greek and Native American mythology made them compelling spiritual counters to monotheistic traditions.

A considerable segment of these cultural rebels pursued spiritual study at places such as Esalen, a retreat established in 1961 in Big Sur, California. Yet for a significant number of counterculturalists, the psychological search for self-realization—with its immediate, worldly satisfactions—proved more compelling than the long-term project of spiritual development through meditation and prayer. As Esalen lecturer Carl Rogers wrote in *On Becoming Human* (1961), "Neither the Bible nor the prophets—neither Freud nor research, neither the revelations of God nor man can take precedence over my own direct experience."[9] Like Rogers, many nonconformists of the 1960s pursued self-actualization as a heroic resistance to the superficiality of modern American culture.

For many seekers, the pursuit of authentic existence did not end with the demise of the counterculture; rather, it was transformed. As Wuthnow argues, by the 1980s and 1990s, spirituality became more evident in these "non-religious . . . therapeutic discussions of the self," with the self "reconceptualized to offer personal power and to serve as the key to spiritual wisdom."[10] Post-1960s spiritualists also distinguished themselves from their counterculture predecessors by their strong belief in the coming of a new spiritual age.

Marilyn Ferguson first announced this millennialist vision in *The Aquarian Conspiracy: Personal and Social Transformation in the 1980s.*[11] Described by Richard Kyle as the "Bible of the New Age," Ferguson's *Aquarian Conspiracy* argued that the counterculture, with its searcher mentality, communalism, and experiments in altered consciousness, had effectively destabilized the Protestant consensus. As a consequence, the United States (and other Western cultures) was free to break into new spiritual territory.[12] In this New Age, the soul—a concept that many 1960s cultural critics had discarded with Judeo-Christianity—reemerged. The goal of the New Age seeker would not be the heightened awareness or "peak experiences" pursued by the counterculture but rather a sense of unity with some cosmic power, be it the earth goddess Gaia, Hindu Karma, Sioux deity Wakan Tanka, or even Jesus Christ.

Determined to rectify the grand spiritual-moral breakdown, the New Age believers created alternative institutions to forward global enlightenment. Emphasizing the power of the mind-body connection to facilitate healing and employing gently acting "natural" herbal prescriptions and noninvasive methodologies, the New Age health movement was created as a counter to "regular" medicine. As an alternative to institutional religion, a panoply of occult, metaphysical, and psychospiritual practices found a place under the New Age umbrella.

Although critics of the New Age recognize that this movement has reinvigorated American religious consciousness, they wonder whether certain narcissistic tendencies make it more politically regressive rather than culturally progressive, as advocates argue. The New Age's hyperindividualist construal of spirituality is particularly troublesome to religious scholar Paul Heelas. From Heelas's perspective, the New Age movement seems to be fixated most tenaciously on the 1960s ideal of "unmediated individualism," not the social structural critique that originally inspired the religious revolution of the period.[13] New Age devotees, Heelas argues, believe that self-realization can occur only "by moving beyond the socialized self"; thus they deny "values or meaning systems having their origin outside of the individual."[14] In the end, the individual is culpable for his or her own torment. For these reasons, Heelas and others remain skeptical of the liberatory radicalism of the New Age movement.

It is hardly surprising that the late-twentieth-century baby-boom elite, who value both the iconoclasm of the 1960s and the tried-and-true American ideal of rugged individualism, would be attracted to this spiritual movement. However, it is a little unexpected that Oprah Winfrey, who won her fervently loyal audience by sympathetically exploring the difficulties of modern existence—particularly the social-psychological dilemmas of the underclass—would embrace a spiritual philosophy that tends toward victim blaming. Yet from roughly 1995 to 2002, Winfrey turned her show into a televised medium for "un-churched" spiritual education and reflection. After 2002, her show's spiritual thumping softened, with entertainment, relationship advice, and celebrity interviews coming to the forefront; thereafter, more ex-plicitly spiritual material appeared in her magazine and in her Web page chat rooms and bulletin boards. At the turn of the twenty-first century, with a newfound mission "to empower people and . . . be a catalyst for people beginning to think more insightfully about themselves," Win-frey emerged as an influential force in the post-1960s New Age spiri-tual movement.[15]

The Making of the New Age Oprah

Due to her growing discomfort with the shock-talk format, on Sep-tember 12 and 13, 1994, Oprah Winfrey invited a panel of television critics to participate in a two-part show entitled "Are Talk Shows Bad?" The specific impetus for what Winfrey called a "self-examination" of her afternoon talk show was Penn State sociologist Vicki Abt's screed in the *Journal of Popular Culture* called "The Shameless World of Phil, Sally, and Oprah: Television Talk Shows and the Deconstructing of So-ciety."[16] As the title implies, Abt's article blamed television talk shows for the demise of social standards in the nation. Because these shows flaunted sexual deviants, miscreants, criminals, and ne'er-do-wells, they legitimated abnormality and, as Abt wrote in a later book devoted to the subject, "rapidly eroded the boundaries that we have established to control behavior and to make sense of our life."[17] Already leaning away from the confrontation-trash style, Winfrey offered her stage as a debate forum for such criticisms.

At the end of the second episode, Winfrey asked for suggestions to set television talk shows in a fresh direction. Abt advised a shift to the high culture of great books and great art. Another guest, TV critic Tom Shales, volunteered his vision for improvement, stating, "I'd like to see more smart people on TV. Fewer ordinary people and more ex-traordinary people. . . . In the '50s NBC did a series called 'Wisdom.' And they would interview Bertrand Russell and Frank Lloyd Wright and Carl Sandburg. . . . The very median level of the talk show, this one perhaps notwithstanding, has sunk very, very low. And I think it's got to be brought up somehow."[18] Although Winfrey did not take the elitist, "extraordinary people" route suggested by Shales and Abt, she did determine to break her association with the genre that these respected pundits and academics (and her own inner censor) considered the seeds of civilization's destruction—or, at best, the "dumbing down" of America. As she confessed to an interviewer, "I've been guilty of doing trash TV and not even thinking it was trash. I don't want to do it anymore."[19]

After this nationally broadcast exercise in self-analysis, Winfrey (and her staff) made sure that her program looked different, sounded different, and was decidedly different in content from its first nine years. More experts appeared; gradually, audience participation became more limited and staged. This regulation of the show bestowed greater authority on Winfrey and her guests and afforded them more time to drive home the moral-spiritual lesson of the day. In 1996 she began her eleventh season with a new theme song, entitled "Get with the Program," and created a book club with monthly, televised meetings. She added new features to her daily program, such as "Remember Your Spirit" and the "Angel Network," and she established her Web site with chat rooms and message boards.[20] And in 2000 she expanded her imprint on American culture with the advent of a monthly publication, O, the Oprah Magazine.[21] The titles of episodes of The Oprah Winfrey Show also changed. Topics that had appeared prior to 1994, such as "My Husband Raped Me" (June 15, 1992), disappeared and were replaced by regular features such as "Lifestyle Makeovers" or a show entitled "Go to Your Destiny" (December 8, 2000). Although themes of personal uplift and self-realization had certainly been present in the earlier format, they had generally acted as moralizing sound bites offered by Winfrey or an expert psychologist at the end of a televised hour of lively audience debate and confessing guests—a format still followed by other talk shows.[22]

The very things that associated Winfrey with the spiritual New Age were (and are) missing on The Montel Williams Show, Sally Jessy Raphael, Ricki Lake, The Jerry Springer Show, and various other Johnny-come-latelies of talk television. On a typical day, September 23, 2002, shows entitled "Battlin' Babes" on The Jerry Springer Show and "Moms Addicted to Meth" on The Montel Williams Show obviously lacked any connection to spiritual doctrine or self-improvement. Certainly, other talk shows were not untouched by the post-1960s spiritual revival, but in general they skimmed from the occult pool of the New Age. Appealing to a popular fascination with the afterlife, before her show ended in 2002, Sally Jessy Raphael regularly showcased psychic Char Margolis and medium George Anderson, author of *We Are Not Forgotten: George Anderson's Messages of Love and Hope from the Other Side* (1994). Psychic Sylvia Browne could be seen regularly on *The Montel Williams Show* in the early 2000s. Although this attention to the afterlife indicated a certain investment in things beyond the superficial and the material—a goal of all New Age thinking—the occult seemed to have no other purpose than to offer contact with the dead and predictions of the future. It did not place the direction of one's life and spirituality in the hands of the individual but simply assuaged anxiety about the unknown. Winfrey's spiritual dogma, as it emerged daily in the late 1990s and early 2000s, was more activist, less enthralled with the magic of cosmic forces than with the use of spiritual wisdom gained through reading, seminars, therapy, and the like as a springboard for self-actualization.

This was the fundamental difference between Winfrey's revamped show and those of her competitors. All talk shows are a product of what social critic Philip Rieff describes as "the triumph of the therapeutic" in post–World War II American culture.[23] They all, including *Oprah,* offer popular psychology and self-help strategies to solve their guests' problems, and they all assume that talk—the very essence of psychoanalysis—can unravel personal crises. Yet Winfrey alone insistently and consistently placed the therapeutic within a spiritual framework. Although cultural critics Jane M. Shattuc and Gloria-Jean Masciarotte[24] celebrated Winfrey's older style because it exposed the arbitrariness of entrenched social norms—holding no particular ethic or lifestyle as holy or natural, especially sexual and gender standards—Winfrey rejected this immersion in moral relativity when she revamped her show over the 1994–1995 season. In so doing, she traded in the tangled complexities and dark ironies that had emerged spontaneously in her earlier audience-centered format for the pat certainties and rosy optimism of the New Age.

This choice might have resulted in failure; Winfrey's audience, accustomed to the rather spicy and tumultuous style of her previous show, might have balked at this pedantic turn, but it did not. In fact, even though *The Oprah Winfrey Show* did experience a slight drop in ratings, it remained number one among talk shows every season and, as of September 2002, consistently drew an average twenty-one million viewers a week.[25] And although the subject matter climbed up the cultural ladder, the audience remained on the lower end socioeconomically. As described by the *Chicago Tribune,* Winfrey's faithful are "80% female and more likely to be black, less educated (though more educated than daytime TV viewers generally) and of lower income."[26] It seems that Winfrey's audience stayed tuned because her show articulated a compelling critique of late-modern America and offered emotional and spiritual guidance that was lacking elsewhere on television. As Marcia Z. Nelson argues, Winfrey's spiritual talk succeeds because, even though she shows suffering, unlike her talk-show compatriots, "she also shows reasons for it and responses to it, just as religions offer."[27]

What I refer to as *The Oprah Winfrey Show*'s New Age design evolved slowly. Initially, her expert guests were pop psychologists or motivational speakers. In 1999 John Gray, the author of *How to Get What You Want and Want What You Have* (2000) and *Men Are from Mars and Women Are from Venus* (1992), was a recurring expert guest; so was a motivational speaker named Iyanla Vanzant. Over time, guests who more clearly conveyed a spiritual worldview replaced these quick-fix inspirational experts. This move away from self-help further separated Winfrey's show from the "trash talk" shows that made a regular habit of inviting inspirational orators. With the presence of Gary Zukav, the author of *Dancing Wu Li Masters* (1986) and the *Seat of the Soul* (1990), as her own personal New Age guru, Winfrey pulled her show more fully into the New Age. Simultaneously, she disassociated herself from the popularized paranormal sects of the New Age. The line between herself and shock-talk television was tenuous, but the more she glommed on to what Ted Peters describes as three of the central concepts of the New Age—holism, the higher self, and potentiality—the more she made her program a roundtable for the contemplation of spiritual values.[28]

Holism and Potentiality—Oprah Style

The first of these core New Age concepts, holism, became the nucleus of Winfrey's new look. According to 1960s counterculture critics, the fractious dualisms of Western thinking—mind and body, reason and emotion, East and West, heaven and earth—stood in the way of global unity and an individual's spiritual development and physical wellness. As far as 1960s cultural rebels could tell, everything was connected. One could not expect to have bodily health if one's mind was sick. And one could not live a fully spiritual life if one acted religiously only within the confines of the church. Post-1960s spiritual seekers turned to Eastern religions and various mystic philosophies because they did not separate the sacred and the profane. Thus, they seemed to offer a more unified and holistic view of being. Following these schools of thought, spiritual seekers did not have to wait for the afterlife to come in contact with the metaphysical. If they practiced mindfulness, empathy, and sensitivity to family, friends, and community, sparks of divinity would alight in their here and now.

To convincingly reach her vast audience and broadcast a spiritual message through the very profane medium of television, the revised *Oprah Winfrey Show*'s guiding spiritual belief would have to be open, flexible, and integrative. Holism satisfied all these requirements. This theoretical malleability opened up Winfrey's New Age program to those who had no religious affiliation or who had rejected the church of their childhood. At the same time, holism set a high standard for her viewers, weighting every action and decision with cosmic consequence.

Evidence of *The Oprah Winfrey Show*'s adoption of holism can be seen in its "Lifestyle Makeover" segments, which promised to help viewers "make over your life, mind, body and spirit."[29] It is also apparent in two of the show's regular guests, Dr. Christiane Northrup and Dr. Andrew Weil, both of whom preached the benefits of holistic healing. On January 27, 1999, Northrup explained the importance of holistic thinking in the maintenance of health: "Mind and body are a seamless web, and every thought we have changes our biochemistry. . . . The vast majority of your thoughts and emotions are either creating healthy tissue or destroying healthy tissue." On the Web page devoted to Northrup's appearance, Winfrey's own interpretation of holism was outlined:

Several times during the show Oprah reminded us that Dr. Northrup's views weren't "one-shot" exercises, but part of an entire way of living that includes caring for yourself, paying attention to the people, places and things that bring you joy, and eliminating negativity from your life. If you're one of those people who feel you just don't have the time for it, remember this advice from Oprah: "*Caring for yourself is not self-indulgence. It's self-preservation.*"[30]

The suggestion that each individual controls not only the direction of his or her life but also his or her physical health through the mind-body connection appeared with such frequency that it could be considered a cardinal rule of Winfrey's spiritual-moral credo. Additionally, the belief that authentic well-being can be achieved only through total (or whole) life renovation became a view unique to *The Oprah Winfrey Show*. Other talk shows made recommendations about how to solve specific personal problems—a cheating husband, a teen pregnancy—but were less interested in such thoroughgoing life renovations.

Convinced that she could raise the nation's moral profile, Winfrey set the bar higher. Her show's bootstraps spirituality appealed to many late-twentieth-century Americans looking for a sense of certainty in an unruly modern world. With the power of transformation squarely in their hands—not in some outside, uncontrollable entity such as the government, the church, or society—they could, ostensibly, gain mastery over their lives. Yet the New Age's certitude was achieved by papering cheery psychospiritual platitudes, such as holism, over human anguish and social inequality.

The Higher Self and Authentic Selfhood

According to New Age holistic theory, an unhealthful emotional and psychological self can block actualization of the higher self or *authentic self*. *Oprah* regular Gary Zukav detailed the path to authentic selfhood in *The Seat of the Soul* (1990), a book that Winfrey characterized as supremely inspired. Her Web page notes that aside from the Bible, it is "the most powerful book she has ever read." Winfrey exudes, "If there was just one book on the planet that I could recommend it would be this book."[31] In his books and on Winfrey's show, Zukav offered practical, real strategies for the attainment of authentic selfhood "through humility, forgiveness, clarity and love."[32] He also suggested that an individual life is merely one part of a longer transmigration of the soul from one body to the next. A person can either follow or break away from his or her soul path, but breaking away always leads to dissatisfaction and deep longing for reunification with the soul "mothership."[33]

On Zukav's August 4, 2000, appearance, he explained the role of human will in spiritual transformation: "You are worthy. You are not on this earth by accident. You have a reason to be here. . . . You are here to create an authentically empowered life. There is no guarantee you will do it. It's up to you."[34] On another episode, he stated:

> There's no simple formula. Your life is unique. It's suited for the healing and expression of your soul. Your path won't be like any other. I'm suggesting be aware of what you're feeling because your feelings are the force field of your soul. Experience everything you are feeling. Feel despair, pain, jealousy. . . . Where it is going to go is some place that's more powerful and more deeper than could have been pre-planned. It's the same with your life. Let it go but use your will consciously. When you feel depressed or jealous or sad or angry, understand that these are the things that you must heal in order to go where your wholeness is calling you to.[35]

This belief in the cosmic intention of pain and the importance of emotional and psychological consciousness in the face of grief became an essential part of Winfrey's spiritual-moral dogma. The resolution of mortal desolation on other talk shows was far less inspiring and final. On *The Jerry Springer Show*, guests emoted, they yelled at one another, and the audience judged them. At the end of the show, Springer opined about the source of his guests' tragedies but ultimately wagged a teacherly finger at the messes they had created. How to prevent such catastrophes was made far less clear, and how to make sense of unwarranted misfortune and tragedy in the world was not a goal of his show.

Oprah's New Age world answered the question of suffering. Individuals would experience varying degrees of pain based on their karma and their intentions in the face of accumulated karma (a concept that Zukav employed frequently on the show from 1998 to 2001). Consciousness and one's desire to be free from patterns of unthinking action determined one's experience of life. For Zukav and Winfrey, the potentiality to realize authentic selfhood made life abundantly hopeful. Peters explains the five parts of potentiality as follows: (1) there is great potential in each of us, (2) education and experimentation awaken our potential, (3) self-transformation is possible, (4) self-fulfillment and transformation are proper goals in life, and (5) we must stretch beyond our five senses to reach our fullest consciousness. From Peters's perspective, living by these simple rules facilitates greater awakening.[36]

These components of potentiality encapsulate the spiritual philosophy forwarded by Winfrey's renovated show. The books in her book club tended to focus on these five principles. The questions on her book club Web page, her synopsis of each work, and the televised discussions revolved around these spiritual guidelines. Not only the book club but also most shows during her New Age apex were devoted to one of these five ethics, as their titles suggest: "Finding Your Authentic Self" (October 13, 1998), "Personal Success with John Gray" (December 8, 1999), "Get Your Power Back with Gary Zukav" (September 13, 2000), "Lifestyle Makeover: Living with Integrity" (September 25, 2000), "Understanding Your Emotional Style" (January 25, 2001), "Calmness in Simplicity: Life Lessons from a Simple Journey" (April 13, 2001), "Letting Go of the Past with Dr. Phil" (May 15, 2001). Even when a celebrity appeared as the major guest (which they frequently did), the discussion centered on that celebrity's struggle to reach his or her genuine potentiality. In March 2002, teen idol Brandy appeared on *Oprah* to discuss her absence from the media spotlight in the past few years. Describing what she believed to be the lessons learned from her recent nervous breakdown, the young singer offered a rather convoluted spiritual analysis:

> I dreamt a lot. I saw things I've never seen before. This was my time to ask God, "Who are you? Show me who you are." And everything was just shown to me. Everybody was the same, everybody is love. Everything is everything. That was all in my dreams. I just woke up feeling like a brand new person. I woke up feeling like, okay, I want to do everything in love. That was just a great feeling.[37]

Brandy's self-evaluation was typical of the post-1994 *Oprah Winfrey Show* narrative that tied up all the frayed ends that appeared when average Americans tried to reach their potentiality or discover their higher selves.

Confronting Evil: September 11 and the Soft Underbelly of the New Age

Occasionally, the danger and complexity of modernity intruded on the upbeat tone and individualist emphasis of Winfrey's New Age spirituality. Yet the manner in which the program dealt with life's dangers further delineated Winfrey's style of talk television from her older format and that of her lowbrow competitors. As she repeatedly stated in interviews in 1994, she was no longer interested in the motivation of criminals and other threatening social outcasts. Therefore, she would never again invite a rapist onto her stage to apologize to his victim. In fact, from 1994 forward, *The Oprah Winfrey Show* framed the evil and pathological as pervasive but subterranean forces that should be controlled by law and avoided through self-protection. This approach to danger indicated a heightened social paranoia, as demonstrated by show titles such as "What's Happening Inside Your Child's School?" (December 10, 1999), "Protect Yourself from Holiday Crime" (December 13, 1999), and "Drugs in Your School" (December 22, 1999). Ulrich Beck suggests that this persistent anxiety is innate to the "risk society" of the late-modern period. The systemic transformations brought on by modern globalization shake "the fundamental belief in the conventional social order" and bring on the "return to uncertainty."[38]

Prior to 1994, *The Oprah Winfrey Show* was willing to risk face-to-face confrontations with social disorder and the lower classes. In Winfrey's 1994 "self-examination" show, Vicki Abt lamented the presence of talk-show guests that she "didn't want next to" her. Explaining her study, Abt petulantly quipped, "I, by the way, had watched hundreds of hours and was amazed at my absorption into these antics of people that I wouldn't want to spend five minutes with in real life, and I don't want them as next door neighbors." Winfrey insightfully responded, "But they are next to you. You're in the world with them. You're in the world."[39] By 1995, this commitment to be in this world, to seriously consider the unseemly side of America not just in a defensive law-and-order framework but as part and parcel of modern life, was outshone by the bright light of New Age spirituality.

Nevertheless, Winfrey's repeated attempts to push malice underground were undermined by the fragility of a philosophy based almost entirely on individual perception and consciousness. A program featuring Winfrey's favorite "life strategist," Dr. Phil McGraw, demonstrates this point. Appearing on the show entitled "Letting Go of Your Past" were two anguished guests—a man who had accidentally shot his best friend when he was a child and a 911 operator who could not get over an emergency call she had received from a ten-year-old boy who had been mortally stabbed in a public bathroom.

McGraw convincingly released the man from his long-term anguish because the death of his friend had been accidental. He had not meant to kill him and was deeply sorry. McGraw seemed to make sense of the man's despair and expiate his guilt through a psychodrama of forgiveness. The other case was murkier. The malicious murder of an innocent child made no sense, cosmic or otherwise. It was not an accident—it was an act of evil. Could Winfrey's spiritual credo reconcile this inexplicable wrongdoing? If Gary Zukav had been the expert, he might have suggested karma as a cause, but that would have been a hard pill for the audience to swallow. McGraw suggested that there was no sense to be made of the killing, but the 911 operator should interpret this event as an opportunity to learn something about the dangers of the world. This solution rang a bit hollow, and the woman seemed neither relieved nor transformed. The avoidance of malevolence, the suggestion that everything is a matter of apprehension and self-direction, is the soft underbelly of the New Age and of Winfrey's spiritual-moral credo.

The events of September 11, 2001, took Winfrey's New Age self-actualization exuberance even further to task. The attacks on the United States—acts clearly perpetuated for political purposes and motivated by a complex of social, cultural, and historical forces—jolted *The Oprah Winfrey Show* out of its inward gaze. Like the rest of the nation, Winfrey fixated on the why of September 11 and sometimes even engaged in political analysis. This was short-lived, however, and programs in the early aftermath such as "Is War the Only Answer?" and "Islam 101" were quickly outnumbered by the well-worn discourse of self-protection, analysis, and uplift and schmaltzy media events such as "Music to Heal Our Hearts" (September 21, 2001) and "Salute to Great Teachers" (October 22, 2001). A show entitled "Dr. Phil on Deciding What's Important Now" (October 9, 2001) concluded that relationships and self-knowledge were most important. And in another episode, lifestyle management guru McGraw advised viewers "How to Control Your Fears" (October 18, 2002).

It is not surprising that *The Oprah Winfrey Show* quickly reverted to familiar and comforting territory when faced with the profound challenge of September 11. Nor did any other talk show approach these events from a more international perspective or with greater critical acuity. In the aftermath of the World Trade Center tragedy, *The Jerry Springer Show, The Montel Williams Show,* and others either fell into reactionary patriotism or rapidly resumed their regular formats. *The Oprah Winfrey Show's* quick retreat highlights the inability of Winfrey's spiritual framework, and the New Age philosophy from which it was constructed, to contend with the social structural and global political powers that, in addition to family, relationships, self-protection, and spirituality, shape Americans' lives.

During the weeks following 9/11, Winfrey turned to house therapist McGraw to provide direction in this newly frightening and unfamiliar world. On the September 19 show, "Dr. Phil Helps Grieving Americans," McGraw provided three steps to begin healing:

1. Give yourself permission to own your feelings. Feel whatever you're feeling, and be where you are.
2. Manage those feelings. You always have a choice: you can withdraw from life, or you can face your feelings and work with them. If you decide to withdraw, you'll miss out on the vibrancy of life.
3. Find meaning in the process of healing.[40]

Similar advice had been given to troubled guests before 9/11 and would be given long after. According to the New Age therapy provided by McGraw, self-perception is the source of individual authority, for as number six of his ten "life laws" states: "There is no reality, only perception."[41] One can decide what to make of an event, be it personal or geopolitical. Thus, even September 11, with its worldwide reach and implications, could be sorted out within a feeling and healing framework.

In the previously mentioned show from May 2001 entitled "Letting Go of Your Past," such advice about healing and self-consciousness had been offered to the 911 operator who had witnessed (over the telephone) a child's grisly killing. McGraw suggested that her "internal dialogue" had frozen her emotionally. She needed to change her thinking, because the world was not going to change. Yet, even if the frightened woman could reassure herself that she would be more careful and cautious, the bottom of her world had fallen out.

In some ways, lowbrow talk shows, with their moral ambiguity, more genuinely address the dilemma of modern survival. They recognize that people do bad things and that they should be made responsible through public condemnation. But they do not hold out hope that a confession will transform the confessor forever; some people are just bad, beyond repair. The intent of these shows is less didactic, more playful and cynical about their ability to change the world (more so *The Jerry Springer Show* than *Sally Jessy Raphael* and *The Montel Williams Show*, whose hosts tend to take themselves more seriously). Their mocking parade of evildoers, rather than Winfrey's perpetually bubbly stories of spiritual success, implies that this situation is not amenable to change, that there is no euphoric end in sight.

Shock talk's acknowledgment of the ironies of life mirrors some of the fundamental precepts of the esoteric Eastern religions pursued by counterculturalists in the 1960s and quilted into New Age spirituality. A cyclical conception of the nature of existence is central to certain schools of Buddhism and Hinduism. There is no end point; rather, birth and rebirth lead, in some cases, to individual enlightenment but not to the transformation of the human society as a whole. This is why worldly renunciation is such a crucial first step on the path to enlightenment, for attachment to the world is equated with attachment to ego and a hope for social progress and evolution.

From 1995 to late 2002, *The Oprah Winfrey Show*'s spirituality stood between talk television's everything-goes resignation and reveling in the problematic immanent world and the otherworldliness of Eastern mysticism. As an alternative to shock television and the general moral slipperiness of postmodern America, New Age thinkers such as Gary Zukav, Andrew Weil, and even down-to-earth Phil McGraw helped Winfrey build an ethical framework for purposeful life out of spiritual therapy. Although it seemed to falter in the face of the most perplexing questions of existence—sorrow and evil—Winfrey's unchurched spirituality satisfied her audience's quest for stability in a "risk society" that highbrow mysticism and lowbrow trash television dodged.[42]

Epilogue: Another Oprah for a New America

Whether by coincidence or simply as another stage in its constant evolution, after September 11, 2001, *The Oprah Winfrey Show* gradually dropped the spiritualist framework inaugurated in 1995. New Age thinkers such as Zukav disappeared from the program, and regular "Remembering Your Spirit" and "Lifestyle Makeovers" features ended. In 2002 Winfrey terminated her book club, which had generally featured novels from the women's psychospiritual journey genre, and reintroduced a new version of it in June 2003. Inaugurating the new club with John Steinbeck's *East of Eden,* Winfrey committed to select only "great reads that have stood the test of time."[43] Finally, in the fall of 2002, the last of Winfrey's psychospiritual advisers left to create his own daily program, *Dr. Phil.* Winfrey's show still dealt with relationship issues and personal development, and uplift remained a theme, albeit in less strictly spiritual language, with cheerleading, can-do episodes such as "Life Lessons from Funny People" (November 17, 2002), "More Extraordinary Families" (March 10, 2003), and "Oprah's 'Chutzpah' Awards"(April 20, 2004).

Perhaps the tragedy of September 11 so shook Winfrey's faith in the coming New Age of spiritual illumination that she felt she had to abandon this vision. Or perhaps Winfrey had so successfully transmitted her spiritual message into popular culture that she felt it was no longer under her control. Perhaps with her good friend Dr. Phil McGraw covering self-actualization and spiritual growth on his show, she did not want their programs to overlap. Or perhaps, approaching her fiftieth birthday, she once again wanted to renovate her show, but this time with a lighter, less erudite tenor—more celebrities, more celebration, more helpful topics, and more plain old fun and inspiration minus the difficult obligations of karma and enlightenment.

Yet, for a few years at the turn of the third millennium, Oprah Winfrey and her sizable audience dove deeply into spiritual philosophy. Her message boards and chat rooms were (and sometimes still are) filled with lively debate over issues such as the relationship between Christianity and karma, the existence of evil, and intention versus social constraints, demonstrating her audience's active engagement in the spiritual questions raised on the program. In one such Internet exchange, a viewer identifying herself as "One Is All" praised *The Oprah Winfrey Show* for its important spiritual work:

Thank you Edward Peterson [another message board participant] for so graciously, eloquently, and sensitively recognizing

the gift we all have received from people with courage and
a message like Gary, Oprah, and Phil. I find choices and intentions easier to make now when I remember the idea and
reality that we really are One in God or the Universe. Each
of us planted with a special seed which will bear fruit or not
depending on our choice.[44]

Another viewer, "BLACKWOMAN33," expressed her gratitude for Winfrey's New Age focus:

Dear Oprah, God Bless you for everything that you have done
to help people get in touch with their spirits. With the help
of Gary Zocov [sic] Today, you have inspire me yet another day
to keep on striving for complete peace with myself, Thank you
for everything. I do believe you are an angel sent from heaven.
I have watched your show since it has first began, and through
my teachings from you and your guests, I have overcome my
former, constant thoughts of suicide. Thank you for always giving me reasons to keep going. God Bless you Ms. Winfrey.[45]

In these chat rooms, viewers struggled with the internal incongruities
of New Age spirituality and tried to reconcile the movement with their
Christian educations, their political orientations, and their own moral
codes. Although many viewers grappled with a sense of inadequacy in the
face of such a rigorously individualist spiritual doctrine, millions of them
eagerly turned to her program to learn more about holism, potentiality,
the higher self, the soul, and other standards of the spiritual New Age.

Notes

1. Melina Gerosa, "What Makes Oprah Run?" *Ladies' Home Journal,* November 1994, 202.

2. In the pursuit of this form, Winfrey went so far as to end her summer
vacation in Paris. She explained to interviewers Luchina Fisher, Steve Dale, and
Savrina McGarland, "You order a salad in France and it comes in a cream sauce.
. . . I came home early because I didn't like the food." See "In Full Stride,"
People Magazine, September 1994, 84.

3. Dana Kennedy, "Oprah Act Two," *Entertainment Weekly,* September
1994, 20.

4. Ibid., 24–25.

5. Ibid., 25.

6. Robert Wuthnow, *After Heaven: Spirituality in America since the 1950s* (Berkeley: University of California Press, 1998), 1.

7. Robert Fuller, *Spiritual but Not Religious: Understanding Unchurched America* (Oxford: Oxford University Press, 2001), 1.

8. Wade Clark Roof, *Spiritual Marketplace: Baby Boomers and the Remaking of American Religion* (Princeton, N.J.: Princeton University Press, 1999), 3.

9. Rogers quoted in Wuthnow, *After Heaven,* 49.

10. Ibid., 157.

11. Marilyn Ferguson, *The Aquarian Conspiracy: Personal and Social Transformation in the 1980s* (Los Angeles: J. P. Archer, 1980).

12. Richard G. Kyle, *The New Age Movement in American Culture* (Lanham, Md.: University Press of America, 1995), 67.

13. Paul Heelas, *The New Age Movement: The Celebration of the Self and the Sacralization of Modernity* (Oxford: Blackwell Press, 1996), 19.

14. Ibid., 21.

15. Winfrey quoted in J. Randy Taraborrelli, "The Change that Has Made Oprah so Happy," *Redbook,* May 1997, 5, http://ehostvgow11.epnet.

16. Vicki Abt and Mel Seesholtz, "The Shameless World of Phil, Sally, and Oprah: Television Talk Shows and the Deconstructing of Society," *Journal of Popular Culture* 28 (1994): 171–191.

17. Vicki Abt and Leonard Mustanzza, *Coming after Oprah: Cultural Fallout in the Age of the TV Talk Show* (Bowling Green, Ohio: Bowling Green State University Press, 1997), 8.

18. Tom Shales quoted in "Are Talk Shows Bad? Part II," *The Oprah Winfrey Show,* September 13, 1994 (Burrelle's transcript), 22.

19. Kennedy, "Oprah Act Two," 24.

20. As of September 2002, this Web page averaged thirty million page views and two million users per month and received twelve million e-mails each week. "Oprah.com Facts," www.Oprah.com (accessed August 28, 2004).

21. *O* magazine's first issue sold out, and it continues to have more than 2.5 million readers each month. It rose to number seventeen in 2003, up from twenty-five in 2002, according to "*Adweek* Magazine's Special Media Report: Hot List 2004," www.mediaweek.com/mediaweek/top_titles.jsp.

22. Jerry Springer usually closes his show with a trite lecture. Montel Williams takes this a step further, acting as a wise patriarch throughout the show, dishing out moral edicts and fatherly judgments to his guests.

23. Philip Rieff, *The Triumph of the Therapeutic: Uses of Faith after Freud* (Chicago: University of Chicago, 1966).

24. Jane M. Shattuc, *The Talking Cure: TV Talk Shows and Women* (New

York: Routledge, 1996); Gloria-Jean Masciarotte, "C'mon Girl: Oprah Winfrey and the Discourse of Feminine Talk," *Genders* 11 (Fall 1991): 81–110.

25. "History," www.Oprah.com (accessed August 28, 2004).

26. Will Lester, "Bush, Gore Hope Oprah Will Be the Way to Gain Crucial Female Votes," *Chicago Tribune,* September 8, 2000.

27. Marcia Z. Nelson, *The Gospel According to Oprah* (Louisville, Ky.: Westminster John Knox Press, 2005), 7.

28. Ted Peters, *The Cosmic Self: A Penetrating Look at Today's New Age Movements* (San Francisco: Harpers, 1991), 59–71.

29. "Lifestyle Makeovers," *The Oprah Winfrey Show,* May 13, 2001, www.Oprah.com.

30. "Northrup on Holistic Healing," *The Oprah Winfrey Show,* January 27, 1999, www.Oprah.com.

31. "Gary Zukav," *The Oprah Winfrey Show,* April 23, 1999, www.Oprah.com.

32. Ibid.

33. Ibid.

34. "Gary Zukav," *The Oprah Winfrey Show,* August 4, 2000, www.Oprah.com.

35. "Gary Zukav," *The Oprah Winfrey Show,* February 10, 2004, www.Oprah.com.

36. Peters, *The Cosmic Self,* 4.

37. "The High Cost of Fame for Singer/Actress Brandy," *The Oprah Winfrey Show,* March 18, 2002, www.Oprah.com.

38. Ulrich Beck, "The Reinvention of Politics: Towards a Theory of Reflexive Modernization," in *Reflexive Modernization: Politics, Tradition, and Aesthetics in the Modern Social Order* (Stanford, Calif.: Stanford University Press, 1994), 6–8.

39. "Are Talk Shows Bad? Part I" *The Oprah Winfrey Show,* September 14, 1994 (Burrelle's transcript), 22.

40. "Dr. Phil Helps Grieving Americans," *The Oprah Winfrey Show,* September 19, 2001, www.Oprah.com.

41. "Dr. Phil Helps Feuding In-Laws," *The Oprah Winfrey Show,* September 26, 2000, www.Oprah.com.

42. I am indebted to Eva Illouz for my understanding of the dilemma of suffering in the late modern era, especially her articulation of theodicy as fundamental to modern liberal democratic culture.

43. "June 2003 Book Club Relaunch," *The Oprah Winfrey Show,* August 8, 2004, www.Oprah.com.

44. One Is All, message boards, www.Oprah.com, 4:27 P.M., March 31, 2000.

45. BLACKWOMAN33, message boards, www.Oprah.com, 11:52 P.M., March 21, 2000.

Oprah Winfrey
and Spirituality

Denise Martin

The public persona of Oprah Winfrey is a richly textured and complex mosaic composed of artist, philanthropist, television host, actress, author, publisher, producer, advocate, filmmaker, teacher, businesswoman, and media-pop icon. Many critical works that address Winfrey consider her performance of these roles within the context of gender studies, media studies, or both. Although such readings are certainly accurate, they tend to neglect the equally rich and compelling spiritual and religious themes found in Winfrey's collective body of work. These themes can be interpreted according to the rubric of the New Age movement; however, an alternative examination of Winfrey's cultural production reveals a blend of African, African American, Eastern, and metaphysical philosophical and religious traditions. The fusing of such seemingly disparate elements functions to create a unique public and cultural spirituality that is rooted in the wisdom and experiences of the past, engaged with contemporary reality, and committed to providing information that helps people lead more empowered lives.

There are five core concepts that form the basis of this exploration into the spiritual themes in Winfrey's cultural production: faith, African spirituality, African humanism, Eastern spirituality, and metaphysical studies. Like the five elements and energies of Chinese cosmology, the five pillars of Islam, the five components of Kenyan scholar John S. Mbiti's African ontology, the Dogon concept of five as the synthesis of creator and creation, and the five powers of Buddhism, these five core concepts provide a succinct yet comprehensive basis for this discussion.

This essay considers Winfrey's five religious and spiritual themes across a diverse sampling of her professional and personal work, including the film *Beloved, O* magazine, *The Oprah Winfrey Show,* Oprah.com, and her philanthropic endeavors.

Religion and Spirituality

Winfrey says, "I have church with myself: I have church walking down the street. I believe in the God force that lives inside all of us, and once you tap into that, you can do anything."[1] Central to this discussion of Winfrey's public and cultural spirituality are contemporary definitions of *religion* and *spirituality*. Though both have their origin in Latin—*religion* from *religare,* "to bind," and *spirituality* from *spiritus,* invoking breath, courage, vigor, the soul, and life—each has distinct characteristics, depending on the beliefs held by followers of a specific tradition. Religion and spirituality are ultimately *experienced* as personal phenomena, though each is *perceived* on cultural, historical, social, and national levels. Therefore, there is a disconnect between what scholars, theologians, ministers, priests, and other practitioners may espouse as religion or spirituality and the actual view held by an individual. The two main academic definitions of religion are substantive and functionalist, with the first stressing the belief content and the second dealing more with the role religion plays in society.[2] The substantive approach also presupposes that the belief content must deal exclusively with God, the supernatural, the transcendental, and the unexplainable. The functionalist approach echoes this sentiment, in that the role religion plays in society is distinguished by the fact that it is concerned with the "ultimate"—that is, the transcendent issues that governmental or social programs cannot address, let alone resolve.

The problem with these definitions is that they are not always applicable when viewed outside of the religious context of a Western model of Christianity. What about cultures that see everything as being in some way related to the ultimate and do not even have a word or concept that equates with Western *religion?* According to Ghanaian philosopher Kwame Gyekye, traditional African culture presents such a situation:

> In African life and thought, the religious is not distinguished from the nonreligious, the sacred from the secular, the spiritual

from the material. In all undertakings—whether it be cultivating, sowing, harvesting, eating, traveling—religion is at work. To be born into the African society is to be born into a culture that is intensely and pervasively religious and that means, and requires, participating in the religious beliefs and rituals of the community. One cannot detach oneself from the religion of the community.[3]

It is through this rubric—the legacy of African retentions—that we might best situate the philosophy espoused by Oprah Winfrey. Her public discourse clearly echoes an African concept of blending the material and spiritual, as epitomized by the mission statement for the April 2005 issue of O, the Oprah Magazine:

> The ultimate in being healthy is to operate at full throttle—physically, emotionally, and spiritually. It's being alert, feeling alive and connected to life and the Source of all Being. If you look at your life as a circle and all its aspects (family, finance, relationships, work, etc.) as sections of it, you'll see that if one part is malfunctioning, it will affect the whole.[4]

John S. Mbiti refers to this interconnectedness of sacred and secular, material and spiritual, as an African religious ontology, where everything is perceived and experienced in a religious or spiritual context.[5] According to Dona Richards, it is this spiritual ontology that not only survived the Middle Passage and enslavement but is in fact the key element of African culture that responded to Western culture, thus producing the uniqueness of African American culture.[6] In espousing such tenets, Winfrey, then, is demonstrating her inheritance of this spiritual tradition, albeit as mediated by New World experiences.

So what approach to religion takes into account diverse cultural understandings of belief, purpose, function, action, and meaning? Beverley Clack and Brian Clack propose a model whereby religious systems are defined as "frames of orientation"; these "may express deep-felt emotions about the human condition; or they may be systems for self reflection and assessment rather than theoretical explanations of this world and the human life within it."[7] This model provides space to explore "ultimates" and how those ultimates are negotiated. This model likewise invokes the idea of experience and perception: if the experience of religion is primarily about understanding and negotiating a relationship with the ultimate, whatever that ultimate is, then the perception is how that understanding and negotiation are made visible.

Yet despite this reconfiguration of religion outside of a Western context, we are more likely to associate Oprah Winfrey with spirituality than with religion. Spirituality is perhaps harder to define than religion because it is much less structured, yet it overlaps with ideas traditionally associated with religion. In fact, the *HarperCollins Dictionary of Religion,* published by the American Academy of Religion, does not have an entry for *spirituality.*[8] Nonetheless, the word has become more visible in the United States in recent years and has even been linked to the U.S. Army.[9] In a recent article on the subject, spirituality is defined according to several traits with which viewers of *The Oprah Winfrey Show* would be familiar: a sense of profound inner peace, overwhelming love, unity with earth and living things, complete joy and ecstasy, meeting with or listening to a spiritual teacher or master, a sense of God's energy or presence, seeing a spiritual figure, witnessing or experiencing a healing of body or mind, a miracle, communicating with someone who has died, and near-death or life-after-death experience.[10]

Of all these, it is the experiential nature of spirituality that Winfrey most profoundly affirms. Namely, spirituality is experiential: it is not based on what a person believes or states in a creed, but rather what a person experiences. As a result, in spirituality, individuals choose what and how to incorporate a concept into their spiritual practice. In this way, spirituality is fundamentally self-defined. Robert Fuller refers to this phenomenon as being unchurched—that is, not identified with the formal structure of religion but nevertheless an assertion of the need to lead a spiritual life.[11] In this way, spirituality can be thought of as a "lived" religion or a "harmonic" religion rather than a received religion. Appropriately, the fluidity of such practices reproduces the idea of the spirit itself. Spirit, according to Richards, is "especially important for an appreciation of the African-American experience. Spirit is of course, not a rationalistic concept. It cannot be quantified, measured, explained by or reduced to neat, rational, conceptual categories as western thought demands. Spirit is ethereal. It is neither touched, moved, seen and felt in the way that physical entities are touched moved seen and felt."[12] Religion is like water; it is fluid, tangible, identifiable by sight and sound, seeks its own level, and takes the shape of its container. Spirituality, like its Latin root implies, is vapor in air; it is religion that has undergone intense heat. It has no distinct shape and is not bound by gravity. It is still tactile, but in a subtle way. Religion and spirituality are thus in essence the same thing, but they have different ways of manifesting. The paradox of Oprah Winfrey is that in disseminating the spiritual to others, she has in many ways become the priestess of the unchurched, defining the spiritual in a way that borders on the religious.

Faith

About faith, Winfrey says, "Faith sustains me, though. Faith that, no matter what, no matter how difficult life becomes, I'll be okay."[13] Winfrey was raised in the Baptist tradition while growing up in Mississippi, Milwaukee, and later Nashville. By age six, faith in her destiny was activated with the help of her grandmother and Paul's Letter to the Romans (15:1), which affirms: "We then that are strong ought to bear the infirmities of the weak, and not to please ourselves." According to Winfrey, "Despite my age, I somehow grasped the concept. I knew I was going to help people, that I had a higher calling so to speak." Before she could manifest that calling, Winfrey had to deal with experiences that tested her faith not just in her destiny but also in her sense of self: "There's only one way I've been able to survive being raped, molested, whipped, rejected . . . only one way to cope with fears of pregnancy, my mother on welfare, my being fat and unpopular. As corny as this sounds, my faith in God got me through."[14]

Faith is commonly described as belief that has been tested by fire. As Winfrey conveys it, faith is an operational concept, not just something one possesses but something one implements, something on which to build personal, professional, and creative expression. As she constructs it, faith allowed her to acquire her own studio and take control of her own show; faith created a space for her intuition to flourish. Of particular relevance to this narrative is the certainty of her faith, which inspired Winfrey to undertake the ten-year project of bringing Toni Morrison's novel *Beloved* to the screen because she felt that the message was vital to African Americans.[15] As Winfrey saw it, the project was a tribute to the strength of her ancestors.

African Spirituality

Winfrey acknowledges her heritage when she says, "I awakened early and did my daily prayer to the ancestors."[16] In traditional and even Christianized and Islamized Africa, the place of the ancestors is one of prominence and power. The ancestors have the primary responsibility of looking after the physical, emotional, mental, and spiritual well-being of their living descendants. In turn, it is the responsibility of the living to look after the ancestors. The cultures of the Yoruba, the Igbo, the Dahomey, and others all included rituals that attested to the prominence of the ancestors, and appropriately, the concept of honoring ancestors appears among their African descendants throughout the diaspora; for example, this is evident in the Santeria faith, where it is said that the "ancestors come before the saints." Once in the Americas, African peoples from disparate ethnic and religious groups began a cultural metamorphosis, drawing on what they knew, remembered, and experienced. Out of this metamorphosis came a new sense of ancestors and identity, one forever tainted by the horrors of enslavement and its inherent dispossession, degradation, and fragmentation of place, culture, and self. This new sense was characterized by a collective identity. Because many enslaved Africans were denied access to their specific family history or place of origin, Africa as a whole assumed additional meaning as a point of spiritual and cultural reference. African Americans embraced the totality of the African experience: the shattered lives that resulted from being snatched and sold, the death and misery of the Middle Passage, and the sufferings both told and untold. Familial, kin, and clan ties were no longer a primary factor in determining one's ancestral relationship. Lacking the specific knowledge of who one's ancestors were and the specific rituals to engage them, the collective and historical Africa became an important reality in the African American religious experience.[17]

But what are the broader implications when a once vibrant and dynamic interaction between the living and the deceased endures such a tremendous geographic, temporal, spiritual, cultural, and communal rupture? What does it mean for African American agency, identity, community, history, and spirituality? Morrison's novel *Beloved* explores the consequences of a corrupted relationship among individual, spirit, and community. Morrison's presentation of these consequences also provided an intense opportunity for Winfrey to personally and artistically engage a painful aspect of the African American experience within a spiritual context. Winfrey observed:

> I felt in some way it was my own remembering, I knew it, I knew Sethe, when I encountered her I felt that she was in some way a part of myself. I didn't know how and wasn't able to explain who this woman was and why it felt so much like myself. But I felt I knew her or had known her or was in some way connected to her. And the more I read, the deeper that feeling became, and I was overcome with the idea of bringing her to life.[18]

Morrison turns her pen unflinchingly on the meta-dialogue and subconscious of the African American experience. This can be uncomfortable. The story is of Sethe, an escaped slave who, facing capture by her former owner, kills her daughter rather than allow her to endure the slow death and suffering of enslavement. Her daughter stays in her life both as a true spirit and later as an embodied spirit who struggles to understand her mother's actions. Based on the true story of Margaret Garner of Kentucky, *Beloved* explores a dark and all-too-real aspect of slavery. At the level of pure reiteration, the story is defined by its shock value. Yet *Beloved* is an affirming story if only because those who experienced the brutality of slavery are given a voice through the novel. Enslaved Africans had little or no control over their lives, but even more poignantly, they had little or no control over their physical bodies. Basic bodily expressions such as movement, rest, reproduction, and adornment were controlled by their owners. *Beloved* is the story of an enslaved woman who seeks control for herself and her child. In insisting on representing Sethe's choices on the page and on-screen, Morrison and Winfrey insist that we recognize ancestors as more than just slaves or "ancestors in chains." They have names, thoughts, feelings, and agency, if only for the brief twenty-eight days that Sethe is free. And they had to make choices that were often heart wrenching and unfathomable.

Considering the story in an African spiritual context highlights Sethe's choice and the consequences of her actions as a means of exposing the deep cosmological issues at the core of the novel. *Beloved* illustrates the very thing that so many West African traditional religious practices are designed to prevent: the circular and chain-reaction break-down between earthly and spiritual communities when disharmony manifests. The disharmony is obviously fundamental to the institution of slavery in general but is personified by "Schoolteacher"; it is also evident in the operations of the black community in Cincinnati, which does not warn Sethe that Schoolteacher is coming. Such disharmony is also, of course, evident in Sethe herself. Each feels the rippling effects of their actions, but since the novel deals with African spiritual sensibilities, the murdered child, Beloved, has agency and becomes a prominent character. This enlarges the dialogue beyond a two-dimensional moral discourse about right and wrong to show the real consequences of this horrendous epoch of the human experience. The enslaved in North America were not only pushed to their emotional, physical, and psychological edge but also forced to dwell there. For African Americans to understand where their centers are today, they need to be aware of the edge. Winfrey says, "My original intention in making *Beloved* was the same as Toni Morrison's in writing the book: I wanted people to be able to feel deeply on a very personal level what it meant to be a slave, what slavery did to a people, and also to be liberated by that knowledge."[19]

By invoking the ancestors and their tremendous power while working on *Beloved,* Winfrey participated in a key aspect of African spirituality. She recalls reading names from a list of ownership papers in her collection of slave memorabilia: "I would call out the names—Joe and Bess and Sara and Emily and Sue and Dara—from that list every morning. I lit a candle, spoke their names, and attempted to honor their spirits."[20] This ritual is intended to evoke the ancestors, the mediators in the spirit world positioned to guide, advise, and even punish those who neglect their presence. Winfrey's connection with the ancestors is unmistakable: "Every person that has come before you existed for this moment that you're in now. You're part of your past, and the past lives with you. . . . You carry the strength and power and courage of the Ancestors with you every day. And that's what every one of their lives was for so that your existence might be possible."[21] This is almost an exact restating of a portion of the Zulu declaration of self:

> For I am a cluster
> I am Father-Mother
> I am the cluster of phenomena which constitute me

I am Father-Mother-Child
I am the past, the present and the future[22]

Winfrey's commitment to making *Beloved* exemplifies the Akan concept of *sankofa*, which is composed of *san* (return), *ko* (go), and *fa* (look, seek, take) and literally means "to return and get it." In Akan culture, there is a mythical bird that flies forward with its head turned backward, reflecting the Akan belief that the past serves as a guide for planning the future. The bird symbolizes a people and their heritage. The proverb that accompanies this image is this: there is nothing wrong with learning from hindsight.[23] *Beloved* provides a rare opportunity for this collective reflection.

African Humanism

In the Western tradition, humanism—with its emphasis on the literature of antiquity and themes of nature—is said to have begun with Dante. Since then, humanism has expanded to include modern, religious, secular, literary, Christian, and Judaic themes, to name just a few. Nevertheless, the core philosophy remains that the value, measure, and responsibility of actions and experience rest with the individual. Winfrey, for example, says, "I act as if everything depends on me and pray as if everything depends on God."[24] Yet the way in which this value is contextualized can reflect a political, religious, secular, agnostic, or atheist orientation.

Humanism has an even longer tradition on the African continent. One of the earliest manifestations of a humanistic concept was the ancient Egyptian idea of *maat:* the balance, order, justice, reciprocity, and harmony that are inherent in the universe and that all ancient Egyptians, regardless or social standing, were charged with upholding. The result of living *maat* was depicted as one's heart being lighter than a feather during judgment in the afterlife, but the moral and social order it provided for Egyptian society was essential for its day-to-day functioning.[25] Other African concepts that reflect a humanistic approach to life are *muntu*, or human beingness, a Bantu belief meaning a "vital force endowed with intelligence and will,"[26] and *èniyàn*, the Yoruba word for human, which translates as "people in the world chosen to do good." The Zulu declaration of self states that it is the purpose of human beings to do good despite the challenges that come from being human.[27] The place assigned to human beings in an African ontology is explained by Mbiti, who says that the African universe is comprised of five parts: God, spirits, humans, plants and animals, and phenomena.[28] At the center of the universe are humans. Humans are the priests of the universe charged with taking care of creation and one another. This system maintains that there is a simultaneous secular and sacred role to human activity, an idea common to many early African American spiritual practices.

African humanism most definitely resonates within the context of slavery, the setting of Morrison's *Beloved* and therefore the site to which Winfrey returns. Enslaved Africans were instructed in a version of Christianity that stressed adherence to an abstract set of standards that contradicted their daily reality. Enslaved Africans understood this situation very well: "Dey allus done tell us it am wrong to lie and steal but why did de white foks steal my mammy and her mammy?"[29] Moreover, Christianity promised life everlasting for believers, but how were African Americans supposed to deal with the afflictions they were suffering in the here and now? They reacted by forming humanistic organizations. The Free African Societies of Boston and Philadelphia, which served as mutual aid societies to both free and enslaved Africans, were among the earliest documented efforts. More covertly, enslaved Africans used hush harbors, prayer meetings, and night sings not only for prayer but also to exchange food, information, and support. The humanistic functions of the institution that would later be called the black church grew out of such activities. Later, the formation of simultaneously religious and nationalistic groups such as the Moorish Science Temple and the Nation of Islam critiqued the perceived passiveness proselytized to African Americans about their spiritual, social, economic, and political condition.

Other groups sought to focus solely on the human condition by rejecting religion in favor of the communist, atheistic, or agnostic position during the middle twentieth century.[30] Liberation theology, which emerged in the 1960s, addressed the plight of African Americans within a Christian context.[31] The powerful Black Panther Party developed a free breakfast program as one of its signature community initiatives. More explicitly spiritual, the African-derived Rastafarians' "livity," Alice Walker's womanism, and Katie Cannon's womanist ethics are different reflections of African humanism.[32] Livity sees no distinction between being, knowing, and doing. Womanism is "committed to survival and wholeness of entire people, male and female," and loves love, music, dance, the moon, spirit, food, and roundness.[33] All such practices express a humanist ethos while at the same time demonstrating. that African or African American humanism is not categorically religious, atheistic, or agnostic but is a reflection of the complexities of the African American experience.

The philanthropy of Oprah Winfrey can be read within this tradition of African American humanism, but there are also major paradoxical distinctions. Winfrey has chosen to exercise her philanthropy outside of organized religion, and her humanistic endeavors are not specifically directed toward African Americans. Likewise, although there are spiritual elements in Winfrey's humanistic activities as demonstrated on *The Oprah Winfrey Show,* on Oprah.com, and in *O* magazine, these media are heavily dominated by commercial interests. Notably, Winfrey's philanthropy does not make spreading or embracing a particular religious view a focal point. In fact, it could be argued that Winfrey's philanthropy is distinctly nonreligious, focusing instead on education, arts, and empowerment. Winfrey's Angel Network (the public charity she founded in 1997 that allows people to get actively involved in organizations featured on the show and on Oprah.com) includes organizations devoted to such subjects as arts, celebrity, computers and technology, human rights, literacy, pets, sports, and travel. Amnesty International, the Culture Project, Special Olympics, and Heritage Expeditions are all part of the network, and none of them identifies a religious affiliation in their descriptive statements. Although African Americans have particularly benefited from Winfrey's philanthropy, they have not been identified as the targeted group.

This variation from African American tradition—some see it as the "selling out" of tradition—is indicative of a long-standing quandary African Americans have faced: how to engage and address the unique concerns of African Americans that have developed in the historically hostile atmosphere of oppression yet not let that atmosphere define and limit their individual activities. W. E. B. DuBois captured this tension nicely with his idea of double consciousness: two warring ideals in one dark body, two souls, two thoughts, two unreconciled strivings.[34]

For Winfrey, it appears that one of the primary conflicts is how to affirm a humanistic approach using media that are dominated by the values of commerce. This becomes particularly difficult when creating a forum to discuss human experience is seen as synonymous with exploiting that experience—particularly when it is traumatic.[35] Likewise, how does one reconcile enjoying material objects and asserting the primacy of the spiritual? For instance, the October 2005 issue of O magazine includes both an inspirational message from Winfrey about aging and her articulated preference for a particular $465 handbag. In an African context, there is no distinction between sacred and secular; therefore, there is no conflict in Winfrey's desire to share aspects of each that she enjoys. Interestingly, both examples speak to a worldview in which experience is shared, whether it be suffering or pleasure.

Eastern Spiritual Philosophies

Eastern spiritual philosophies are the most subtle and indirect themes in Winfrey's works. She frequently draws on them, particularly Buddhist-inspired messages, featuring Eckhart Tolle's *The Power of Now* as one of Oprah's Favorite Things 2002 and Gary Zukav's *The Seat of the Soul* on her show. Notably, in Buddhism, the path to enlightenment begins with an understanding of the nature of suffering; therefore, Buddha's Four Noble Truths deal explicitly with suffering: suffering, the origin of suffering, the cessation of suffering, and the path leading to the cessation of suffering.[36]

Winfrey has engaged these principles in her own way. For example, she has been frank about her own experience of suffering, relating the trauma of her sexual abuse and the distorted sense of self she experienced well into her adult years. Thematically, suffering also dominated the discourse of the early years of *The Oprah Winfrey Show*, as guests confessed their various traumas on air and allowed the audience to voyeuristically endure and overcome such experiences. Yet Winfrey abandoned this approach in 1994, moving the show's focus from reiterating the trauma to providing strategies to cope with it—in other words, moving beyond suffering and exploring the other three truths. To do this, Winfrey enlisted the help of trained therapists such as medical doctor and metaphysician Deepak Chopra, financial adviser Suze Orman, writer Gary Zukav, relationship expert John Gray, and women's holistic health physician Christiane Northrup. This collection of specialists distinguished themselves by their holistic approaches to problem solving.

As this new approach proved successful, it was incorporated into O magazine. Similar to other women's magazines, in that it addresses material and domestic concerns, its monthly mission statements, daily affirmations, and inspirational tone also acknowledge difficult situations but direct the reader away from suffering. Feature articles might focus on self-diagnosis, researching one's family history, healthy eating, managing money, and relationships. Regular columns include "What I Know for Sure," an inspirational message from Winfrey; "Breathing Space," a collection of beautiful pictures to view and share; and columns from Phil McGraw, Suze Orman, Martha Beck, and other self-help holistic practitioners. O magazine takes readers through the four truths. For example, the focus of the October 2005 issue is aging. One article asks readers what scares them about getting older. Answers address appearance, health, financial, and other familiar concerns. Another article features prominent older women who share stories about how they cope; others suggest ways to change how to think about aging, plan financially for old age, and have an enriching experience caring for aging parents. Collectively, the articles identify the source of suffering, which is aging; the origins of suffering, which are one's fears and attitudes about aging; the cessation of suffering, which means that aging does not have to be unpleasant; and finally, how to stop the suffering by making the necessary changes.

This awareness, or mindfulness (*smirti*), does not deny the experiences of the past but instead takes the approach that whatever happened is over; you are here in the present, and you can decide how you are going to react to the memory and consequences of the past event. Like *sankofa,* it involves an active engagement of the past in the present in order to create future present moments. As for mindfulness, there must be an awareness of causal relationships, which in turn leads to a growth in *dharma* (the proper course of conduct).[37] This awareness manifests in Winfrey's understanding of intention: "I believe that intention rules the world. I always ask myself (and others I work with) 'What is my (and your) intention? And is the intention pure enough to carry you through the difficult times so that you never waver?'"[38]

Though articulated here as brief phrases, the concepts of the Four Truths and mindfulness are complex. This interpretation does not imply a similar level of engagement in Winfrey's work. After all, Buddha was after *nirvana,* the extinction of all notions. Winfrey's slogan of spirituality, "Live Your Best Life," found on the opening page of her Web site and as the title of her interactive online workshop, does not propose such a depth, scope, or austerity of vision.

The Metaphysical

The slogan "Live Your Best Life" is a point of departure for the metaphysical because it embodies the theme of personal transformation often found in metaphysical teachings. The key to this category is the emphasis on esoteric principles that regulate activity in the universe. As Winfrey says, "Whether you're aware of that or not, physical laws exist; but beneath the surface of every physical law there is also the metaphysical."[39] Many Abrahamic religions have esoteric or mystical teachings and practices, such as the Kabbalah in Judaism and Sufism in Islam, but they do not constitute the mainstream of their traditions. Therefore, although the metaphysical reflects ideas found in religion, it prefers underlying principles over beliefs and dogma. What distinguishes this metaphysical category from a psychological self-help perspective is the idea that the transformation has to be holistic—that is, involving the entire person on spiritual, mental, and material planes.

When *The Oprah Winfrey Show* shifted in the mid-1990s and began to feature psychological and spiritual experts to help address guests' problems, the spiritual experts chosen (such as Chopra, Zukav, Marianne Williamson, and Sharon Salzberg) represented teachings outside the traditional borders of religion. Winfrey herself would remain nondenominational as well, using terms such as *Spirit* and *Omnipotent Force* as opposed to *God.*[40] In the process, Winfrey crafted a unique intersection of New Age philosophy and mainstream America, using her media profile to present authors with alternative views who may have been unknown to many in her audience. Her deliberately "unchurched" presentation of spirituality presented a space for those alienated by organized religion or the new revivalism typically presented by the media, as evidenced by twenty-four-hour religious cable programming, books such as *The Da Vinci Code,* the Left Behind book and movie series, and Mel Gibson's popular movie *The Passion of the Christ.* When considered in light of apocalyptic interpretations of political and geological events, such media disseminations of religion seemed severe and proscriptive when compared to the self-actualized model of spiritual hybridity proposed and practiced by Winfrey. Her incorporation of multiple spiritual messages to provide a model of an individually centered practice that affirms one's worth as well as one's worth to others via humanistic philanthropy, awareness, and engagement is compelling in its assertion of human value, not failure.

Conclusion

In examining the cultural production of Oprah Winfrey, there is evidence of mindful engagement and avoidance of numerous religious and spiritual themes, most notably her self-professed faith in God and herself. Beyond the common expression of gratitude to God, as articulated by other highly visible and successful media or entertainment personalities, Winfrey has embraced the suffering of her enslaved African ancestors and used that legacy as a catalyst to first connect with her own experience and then project that experience throughout her media empire and disseminate the idea that it is possible to transcend suffering. She might be considered an African humanist because she chooses when to engage the sacred or secular in expressing her concern for fellow human beings—but not quite, because her humanism extends beyond the African experience. She might be considered just a humanist, because of her philanthropy and message of empowerment—but it stands in conflict with the commercial values and objectives of her mass-media dominance. She might be considered religious for promoting metaphysical teachers who emphasize spirit—but not quite, because she artfully avoids religious dogma as a recurring theme. Winfrey's reluctance to stay neatly in a category while earning financial and popular success will continue to be touted, analyzed, and criticized, but perhaps Winfrey's more subtle legacy will be her creation of and commitment to a public spirituality that blends the historical, secular, and commercial dimensions.

Notes

1. Janet Lowe, *Oprah Winfrey Speaks: Insights from the World's Most Influential Voice* (New York: John Wiley and Sons, 1998), 122.

2. Beverley Clack and Brian R. Clack, *The Philosophy of Religion: A Critical Introduction* (Cambridge: Polity Press, 1998), 2.

3. Kwame Gyekye, *African Cultural Values: An Introduction* (Philadelphia: Sankofa Publishing, 1996), 4.

4. See http://www2.oprah.com/omagazine/200504/omag_200504_mission.jhtml.

5. John S. Mbiti, *African Religions and Philosophy,* 2nd ed. (Oxford: Heinemann, 1990).

6. Dona Richards, "The Implications of African American Spirituality," in *African Culture: The Rhythms of Unity,* ed. Molefi Asante and Kariamu Welsh Asante (Trenton, N.J.: Africa World Press, 1993), 207–32.

7. Clack and Clack, *The Philosophy of Religion,* 5.

8. Jonathan Z. Smith, ed., *The HarperCollins Dictionary of Religion* (San Francisco: HarperCollins, 1995).

9. L. D. Palmer, "Spirituality Becomes 'Resilience' and Joins the U.S. Army," *Spirituality and Health* (December 2003): 52–59.

10. Karen Herrick, "Learning the Language of Spirituality," *Journal of Religion and Psychical Research* 28 (2005): 25–34.

11. Robert G. Fuller, *Spiritual but Not Religious: Understanding Unchurched America* (New York: Oxford University Press, 2001).

12. Richards, "The Implications of African American Spirituality," 208.

13. Bill Adler, ed., *The Uncommon Wisdom of Oprah Winfrey: A Portrait in Her Own Words* (Secaucus, N.J.: Birch Lane Press, 1997), 23.

14. Lowe, *Oprah Winfrey Speaks,* 122, 120.

15. Oprah Winfrey, *Journey to Beloved* (New York: Hyperion, 1998), 18.

16. Ibid., 45.

17. Charles Long, "Perspectives for a Study of African American Religion," in *Down by the Riverside: Readings in African American Religion,* ed. Larry Murphy (New York: New York University Press, 2000), 9–19.

18. Winfrey, *Journey to Beloved,* 13.

19. Ibid., 28.

20. Ibid., 25.

21. Ibid., 24.

22. Molefi K. Asante, and Abu S. Abarry, *African Intellectual Heritage: A Book of Sources* (Philadelphia: Temple University Press, 1996), 376.

23. G. F. Kojo Arthur, *Cloth as Metaphor (Re)Reading the Adinkra Cloth Symbols of the Akan of Ghana* (Legon, Ghana: Cefiks, 2001), 181.

24. Lowe, *Oprah Winfrey Speaks,* 128.

25. Maulana Karenga, *Maat: The Moral Idea in Ancient Egypt* (New York: Routledge, 2004).

26. Didier Njirayamanda Kaphagawani, "African Conceptions of Person:

A Critical Survey," in *A Companion to African Philosophy*, ed. Kwasi Wiredu (Malden, Mass.: Oxford, 2004), 332.

27. Asante and Abarry, *African Intellectual Heritage*, 371.

28. Mbiti, *African Religions and Philosophy*, 15.

29. Albert J. Raboteau, *Slave Religion: The Invisible Institution in the Antebellum South* (New York: Oxford University Press, 2004), 295.

30. Anthony B. Pinn, "African Americans and Humanism," in *Down by the Riverside: Readings in African American Religion*, ed. Larry Murphy (New York: New York University Press, 2000), 273–86.

31. James H. Cone, "Black Theology as Liberation Theology," in *Down by the Riverside: Readings in African American Religion*, ed. Larry Murphy (New York: New York University Press, 2000), 389–413.

32. Adrian Anthony McFarlane, "The Epistemological Significance of 'I-an-I' as a Response to Quashie and Anancyism in Jamaican Culture," in *Chanting Down Babylon: A Rastafari Reader*, ed. N. S. Murrell (Philadelphia: Temple University Press, 1998), 107–21; Alice Walker, *In Search of Our Mother's Gardens: Womanist Prose* (New York: Harcourt Brace, 1983); Katie Geneva Cannon, *Katie's Canon: Womanism and the Soul of the Black Community* (New York: Continuum, 1996).

33. Cannon, *Katie's Canon*, 22.

34. W. E. B. DuBois, *The Souls of Black Folk* (New York: Dover, 1994).

35. Eva Illouz, *Oprah Winfrey and the Glamour of Misery* (New York: Columbia University Press, 2003).

36. Thich Nhat Hanh, *The Heart of the Buddha's Teaching: Transforming Suffering into Peace, Joy and Liberation. The Four Noble Truths, The Noble Eightfold Path and Other Basic Buddhist Teachings* (Berkeley, Calif.: Parallax Press, 1998).

37. Edward Conze, *Buddhist Meditation* (London: George Allen and Unwin, 1959), 62.

38. Winfrey, *Journey to Beloved*, 29.

39. Ibid., 28.

40. Kelly Willis Mendiola, "The Hand of a Woman: Four Holiness-Pentecostal Evangelists and American Culture, 1840–1930 (Ph.D. diss., University of Texas at Austin, 2002).

Phenomenon on Trial

Reading Rhetoric *at* Texas Beef v. Oprah Winfrey

Jennifer Richardson

In January 1998 a conglomerate of cattle producers from Texas sued talk-show host Oprah Winfrey for comments she made on her show about the safety of the U.S. beef supply. Like many good stories, this one could begin with, "In the beginning was the Word."[1] At every turn, the trial lends itself to a rhetorical critique: it was an event born of, centered on, and sustained by the word. It began with what Winfrey said, to whom, and where, and it insists on being about what people can say, to whom, and where. It never would have happened if not for Winfrey's phenomenal power to move audiences with a single sentence. "'If Jerry Springer had said something about mad cow,' said Jeff Borden of *Crain's Chicago Business,* 'it would be zero impact. Rosie, Geraldo, limited impact. Oprah said it, it had big impact.'"[2] It was literally a rhetorical trial about the persuasive power of ethos, logos, and pathos. Indeed, in their initial comments, Winfrey's lawyers explicitly relied on rhetoric as a concept and an argument (as well as a means to persuade) to publicly make their case against the cattlemen suing her, contending that the remarks she had made on her show were "opinion, hyperbole, or rhetoric, not statements of fact."[3] Looking at how the mainstream press covered the event and the issues it involved becomes an exploration of American public rhetoric about rhetoric.

Texas Beef v. Oprah Winfrey involved an episode of *The Oprah Winfrey Show* titled "Dangerous Foods" that aired in April 1996, one segment of which focused on mad cow disease. The official transcript of this particular episode is unavailable.[4] However, according to numerous print and Internet sources, at one point in the conversation, Winfrey remarked that the possible link between dangerous practices on U.S. feedlots and mad cow disease "has just stopped me cold from eating another burger!"[5] Within an hour of this now infamous declaration, "cattle futures prices . . . dropped below the 'limit down'—the price that determines when trading will be suspended for the day."[6] Over the next several weeks this downtrend continued, and the cattle-feeding industry lost an estimated $87.6 million in what quickly became known as the "Oprah Crash."[7]

Despite the appearance of a cause-and-effect relationship, there is no way to prove definitively that the "Dangerous Foods" show caused the depression in the cattle markets. In fact, prices for cattle futures had been in decline for several weeks before the *Oprah* broadcast because of widespread drought, rising feed costs, an excess of available cattle, and the global mad cow scare that originally prompted the show.[8] Nonetheless, many American cattle producers blamed the comments made on *Oprah* for their financial woes. Representatives from the cattle industry complained publicly that the show had been unfairly edited and made them look bad. In retaliation, they pulled "$600,000 in advertising from Oprah's network" and threatened to pursue legal action against the talk-show host.[9]

On December 29, 1997, a group of cattle producers, including Paul Engler, filed a lawsuit against Oprah Winfrey, her production company Harpo, and *Oprah* guest Howard Lyman for false disparagement of perishable foods, business disparagement, defamation, and negligence.[10] Engler is president and co-owner of Cactus Feeders Inc., a cattle-feeding business with custom lots in five Texas towns. He has served on the board of directors and the executive committee of both the National Cattlemen's Beef Association (NCBA) and the Texas Cattle Feeders Association (TCFA), and he has been honored for his work in the cattle industry with numerous awards. In 2000 Engler "retired from service as a U.S. Department of Agriculture appointed member of the Cattlemen's Beef Board."[11] According to one description, Engler is "a smart, innovative and tough self-made millionaire who's known throughout the cattle feeding industry as one who often shoots first—from the hip as well as the lip—and asks questions later."[12] Engler represented an interesting gap in the mainstream media's coverage of the Winfrey lawsuit, particularly after the actual trial began. Although Winfrey's testimony, courtroom comings and goings, and other routine activities were reported in detail by the national popular press, Engler was all but ignored. In the shadow of Winfrey's hyperethos, Engler was generally overlooked despite his long-standing local presence and his considerable influence in the business and politics of the cattle industry.

Texas Beef v. Oprah Winfrey was the first case in the country to be tried using the controversial food disparagement laws adopted by thirteen states during the 1990s.[13] The debate over the laws involves their constitutionality with regard to the First Amendment's protection of free speech: "Many civil libertarians are convinced that the food-defamation statutes—often 'banana bills' and 'veggie libel' laws—stifle free speech and press."[14] Supporters of the laws argue that "if activists stand up and say 'cauliflower causes breast cancer,' they've got to prove that . . . to the degree that the mere presence of these laws has caused activists to think twice, then these laws have already accomplished what we set out to do."[15]

Notably, the laws in each state are "based on a model law drafted by the Animal Industry Foundation (AIF), a nonprofit trade group funded by Purina, Cargill, assorted chemical and pesticide companies, and various agriculture associations (Paul Engler's Cactus Feeders is listed as an AIF 'Silver Supporter' in the group's newsletter)."[16] In other words, the likely beneficiaries of the food disparagement laws—large agricultural corporations involved in food production and distribution—are members and sponsors of the group directly responsible for writing and instituting them. Engler's interests are implicated here at every turn: his company funded the association that wrote the law, and he was a high-ranking member of at least one of the associations that lobbied for passage of the law in his state.[17] As long as they remain in place, the "veggie libel laws" serve to silence the advocates of consumers in cases such as *Texas Beef v. Oprah Winfrey* by making public declarations of debatable information and opinion punishable in a court of law. Significantly, in the mainstream media, the food safety issues raised on the "Dangerous Foods" episode of *Oprah* were left behind in the wake of the controversy whether it was legal to even raise them.

The Winfrey trial was to take place in Amarillo, Texas, "the heart of Texas beef country, where 25 percent of the nation's grain-fed cattle is produced, where the city's largest employer is a slaughterhouse, and where the courthouse has a mural of cattle above the elevators."[18] Early on, public sentiment in Amarillo clearly favored the cattle producers. "Ban Oprah" buttons and bumper stickers reading "The Only Mad Cow in America Is Oprah" appeared throughout the community.[19] Interestingly, public opinion visibly shifted in Winfrey's favor after her arrival in Amarillo and her decision to tape episodes of her show there. According to reports, "many Amarillo residents were infatuated with their famous guest. . . . Curiosity seekers waited in long lines to hear her testify," and "tapings of her show . . . were the hottest ticket in town."[20] New bumper stickers reading "Amarillo Loves Oprah" began to appear.

Instead of offering support for the cattle producers, the people of Amarillo surprised trial participants and pundits by publicly favoring the talk-show host. As one Amarillo attorney put it, "Engler thought he was walking into a hometown court and putting a foreigner on trial. To these cattlemen, Oprah—a successful black woman from Chicago—seems like a foreigner. But the real comeuppance is that Engler is a lot more foreign to people here than Oprah. People in Amarillo watch *Oprah* every day."[21] The extensive publicity caused by the superstar defendant prompted the judge to issue a gag order that prevented the litigants from speaking publicly about the trial. As soon as the order was issued, and for the duration of the trial, Winfrey's lawyers tried unsuccessfully to have the gag order lifted and the trial venue changed.

The jury selection process also generated media attention. One article reported that the judge "asked the 57 potential jurors if they had any bias in the case. Thirteen were eliminated on that basis in the morning and early afternoon sessions before the final 12 jurors were selected from a remaining pool of 44. Based on their own statements, at least five members of the panel have past ties to the agriculture industry. The jury includes no blacks."[22] Although the racial makeup of the jury was not widely discussed in the mainstream press during the trial, it became a more prominent issue after the verdict. The jury of eight women and four men was seated on January 20, 1998, and opening statements began the following day.

For four weeks, the Texas Beef group presented its case against Winfrey and her codefendants. Instead of beginning counterarguments after the plaintiffs rested, Winfrey's legal team filed a motion to have the entire lawsuit thrown out. After hearing arguments from both sides on this motion, Judge Robinson dismissed all the charges except for the accusation of business disparagement, based on "insufficient proof that Winfrey knowingly disseminated false information" and on the determination that "the food disparagement statute does not apply to cattle, because they are not perishable foods."[23] Notably, Robinson's decision meant that the controversial veggie libel laws that the trial was expected to test were no longer a factor. The setting aside of the food disparagement charges marked a turning point in the case. Along with the controversial statutes, the case's potential impact on the First Amendment and the rules governing free speech in the United States was removed. The court continued to hear arguments regarding the business disparagement claim for another week; both sides rested on February 25. The next day, the jury found in favor of Winfrey.

The national press picked up on what would become the "Oprah trial" as soon as the "Dangerous Foods" episode aired on April 16, 1996. In what became a rhetorical pattern of omission, the overwhelming majority of reports about the trial centered on issues of free speech and freedom of the press, but not on the controversial issues that those rights permit the press to explore. In connection with these First Amendment issues, media coverage focused largely on Winfrey and her phenomenal celebrity and on the mood of Amarillo and the town's reaction to the popular talk-show host. As the trial progressed, the media coverage of the trial actually became a topic of interest that was repeatedly discussed in the media's commentary on the trial.

Although there has been a significant increase in Americans' use of the Internet as a news source recently, in 1996 a Time/CNN poll reported that 59 percent of people in the United States received most of their news from television.[24] Indeed, as a popular marketing slogan for the American Broadcasting Companies asserts, "More Americans get their news from ABC than from any other news source." A 1997 study conducted at Ohio University confirmed that most adults across the country got their news and information from television first (67 to 70 percent) and newspapers second (58 percent).[25]

Early reports about the lawsuit and trial focused on free speech issues rather than the health issues concerning mad cow disease and the possibility of its occurring in the United States. The First Amendment's free speech provision remains one of the most celebrated and controversial features of American democracy. It is also one of the most explicitly rhetorical. In the most general sense, free speech is about who can say what, to whom, and when. More specifically, it has commonly been used as an argument for persuading audiences and for forwarding particular agendas. Another interesting rhetorical implication lies in the way speech as a concept has been conceived and interpreted with regard to the First Amendment—not strictly as linguistic texts that are written or spoken, but as symbolic communication of any form. In the United States, "First Amendment protection is not limited to 'pure speech'—books, newspapers, leaflets, and rallies. It also protects 'symbolic speech'—nonverbal expression whose purpose is to communicate ideas."[26]

Although debate continues over the specifics, most Americans support the notion that people should be free to publicly express whatever opinions and positions they hold. Rodney Smolla, a professor at the University of Richmond Law School, agrees "that in a sense both deep and wide, 'freedom of speech' is a value that has become powerfully internalized by the American polity. Freedom of speech is a core American belief, almost a kind of secular religious tenet, an article of constitutional faith."[27] According to the American Freedom Foundation's State of the First Amendment report for 1997, around the time of the trial, only 1 percent of respondents said that "the right to speak freely about whatever you want" was not important; 27 percent of respondents believed that it was important; and the significant majority, 72 percent of respondents, believed that it was essential.[28] These attitudes have changed since September 11, 2001. According to the State of the First Amendment 2002, "for the first time in our polling, almost half of those surveyed said that the First Amendment goes too far in the rights it guarantees. About 49% said that the First Amendment gives us too much freedom, up from 39% last year and 22% in 2000. The least popular First Amendment right is Freedom of the Press."[29]

During the trial, the ideologies of the First Amendment and the terms associated with it, such as *freedom, democracy,* and *American,* were used as a rhetorical defense for Winfrey and her case, both in court and in the popular press. This emphasis on the democratic principles of freedom of speech for individuals and freedom of the press for the media, both of which Winfrey identifies with, formulates an appeal that relies on the American public's belief in the theories and principles outlined in the U.S. Constitution. Historical uses of this kind of rhetoric have been largely successful. Even in cases in which the expression being protected is distasteful or disagreeable to mainstream ideology and politics, the First Amendment right to that expression has generally been upheld. For instance, Supreme Court cases dealing with the freedom of expression "have sided with *Hustler* magazine, Playboy's television network and a white supremacist group."[30]

One early report on the trial, which aired on the *NBC Nightly News* on June 5, explained that "Winfrey declined an interview, but her lawyer's saying she stands behind the right to produce shows that inform and enlighten the public. And many libel experts say the food laws plainly limit free speech." The report concluded by noting, "ranchers think they have a strong case with the Texas food law, but legal scholars say they face two big challenges, Oprah Winfrey and the Constitution."[31] The final words here imply that the talk-show host and the Bill of Rights hold equal sway in contemporary American society, a provocative suggestion that alludes to the cultural capital of celebrity ethos.

As the trial date approached, television coverage centered around the First Amendment and the constitutionality of the lawsuit. On January 5, 1998, an entire episode of *CNN Crossfire* was devoted to hosts Bill Press and Pat Buchanan, consumer advocate Ralph Nader, and former assistant secretary of agriculture John Bode debating the legality of the Oprah Winfrey case. During the program, Nader claimed that lawsuits based on the veggie libel statutes are "designed to stifle free speech" and "are unconstitutional. Their only purpose is to keep people from expressing their opinion and expressing their mind, whether it's reporters or editors or ordinary people or citizens or consumer groups." Bode argued that lawsuits such as this would not impact a necessary and welcome "aggressive discussion of food safety."[32] The coverage of Winfrey's trial contradicted Bode's comment, as the popular press neglected to discuss the food safety issues in any real detail. The mainstream media may have been fixated on the potential threat to their collective First Amendment rights, but they failed to exercise that right because they neglected to investigate both the constitutional validity of the food disparagement laws and the governmental and corporate systems that put them on the books in the first place.

Interestingly, primarily news reports that occurred either before or after the actual trial considered these issues the most, if at all. During the trial, and especially after Winfrey arrived on the scene, the coverage clearly changed in tone and style. Following her arrival in Amarillo, the mainstream media became obsessed with the talk-show host. This shift in focus reflects the rhetorical currency of celebrity in the American popular press. News reports that feature the hyperpopular Winfrey doing *anything* are clearly more appealing to Americans who watch the *Nightly News* than those featuring law experts or consumer advocates arguing the constitutionality of the case. It also represents a rhetoric aimed at entertaining its various audiences rather than educating or informing them about the issues at hand. The mainstream media's emphasis on the superstar marginalized the ways in which the case affected the "free" speech of the average citizen.

By the time the trial began, coverage had saturated the popular press, and the number of texts focusing on the case grew dramatically. On January 20, 1997, the day the jury was seated, the story was featured on the ABC, CBS, and NBC morning news shows, as well as on the ABC and NBC nightly news programs.[33] CNN had a reporter on the scene offering live updates during *CNN Early Edition* and *CNN The World Today* and devoted an episode of *Burden of Proof,* its legal analysis program, to the topic. Fox's *Hannity & Colmes* also aired an episode devoted to the case. The trial was the cover story in *USA Today,* and there were Associated Press wire updates throughout the day. The principal focus of the national coverage was on Winfrey's ethos and the impact she had on Amarillo, which was no great surprise.

Winfrey's ethos goes beyond what she says in certain situations; it consists of the total package that "Oprah" has come to signify in American popular culture. Aristotle's conception of ethos refers to character, especially moral character, and it is "regarded as an attribute of a person, not of speech."[34] Unlike deliberative appeals, ethos is similar to artistic appeals, in the sense that the character and personality of an individual, not just what an individual says or writes, are evaluated. Aristotle establishes that a positive or appealing ethos is formed through practical wisdom (*phronesis*), virtue (*arete*), and goodwill (*eunoia*).[35] In his notes on Aristotle's ideas about ethos, George A. Kennedy defines the Greek word *ethos* to mean "'moral character' as reflected in deliberate choice of actions and as developed into a habit of mind."[36] However, it can also mean "qualities, such as the innate sense of justice or a quickness of temper, with which individuals may be naturally endowed and which dispose them to certain kinds of action" or the "trustworthy character of a speaker as artistically created in a speech."[37] It is in all these senses, and not just in what she explicitly states, that Winfrey's ethos is conceived and perceived.

Saying that Oprah Winfrey is a superstar only suggests her phenomenal popularity as a cultural icon, a symbol of women, African Americans, and Americans somehow simultaneously. A *USA Today* story that ran at the beginning of the trial included a passage called "Anatomy of Power" that cataloged the details of the talk-show host's popularity: "Forbes has declared her the world's highest paid entertainer. Disney has a multipicture movie deal with her. She was given the People's Choice Award for 'Favorite Television Performer' a week ago. But it is her influence that made *Life* magazine put her on its cover in September as 'America's most powerful woman.'"[38] In the midst of the trial, a poll posted on "the *Amarillo (Texas) Globe News'* Web site shows 4,035 of 4,685 people believe Oprah Winfrey will win a whopping victory over the Texas cattle ranchers."[39] Her fame and status are preeminent in this country, and she maintains her power and prominence to the current day.

Recently, Winfrey's celebrity has also been a topic of scholarly discussion by academics.[40] In his 1994 book *Claims to Fame: Celebrity in Contemporary America,* Joshua Gamson offers an exploration of the motives of what he calls "identification-driven audiences"; he includes interviews of Winfrey's fans, who explain that the talk-show host seems like someone to whom they can relate.[41] The notion that Winfrey appeals to her audiences through their identifications with her is articulated in detail by P. David Marshall, who focuses on Winfrey as a case study of "the phenomenon of the emergence of celebrity within the institution of television."[42] In effect, Marshall argues that Winfrey's fame is based on rhetorical identification between interlocutor and audience, that her ethos is essential to her successful pathetic appeals, and that it is this important rhetorical relationship that has made her a star. Various audiences' close identification with the talk-show host remained an element of the trial coverage right up to the verdict.

Winfrey's ethos was not just the reason that the trial was covered so widely; it was a main topic of that coverage. Her "Oprahness" was as an important issue. As an article in the *Chicago Tribune* explained, "Winfrey is not your typical celebrity endorser. . . . A $500 million industry with her own fiercely loyal audience, Winfrey commands a combination of celebrity status, credibility, and results." One oft-cited example of Winfrey's persuasive prowess is the fact that when she "holds up a book or a CD on her show, it becomes an instant best seller. One of the novels she featured on her televised book club had a title similar to another book in release—and that book even hit the charts, because of all the Oprah fans who bought it by mistake."[43] The day jury selection began, a live report from Amarillo on *CNN The World Today* pointed out that instead of focusing on the legal proceedings inside, "the focus was more outside the federal courthouse, with squeals of excitement at the talk show host's court comings and goings."[44]

The rhetorical role of Winfrey's celebrity remained a prevailing feature in the coverage of the trial. When she moved tapings of her show to Amarillo, it was headline news on the Associated Press wires.[45] Which guests were scheduled to appear on the talk show and the ensuing clamor to get tickets became news stories. It is no accident that the topics and guests for the shows taped in Amarillo highlighted the local community and featured Texans and Texas-themed shows. During the first episode taped in the Lone Star State, Winfrey "two-stepped with Patrick Swayze, was serenaded by Clint Black, and tried on a 13-carat diamond ring supplied by a genuine millionaire oilman."[46] Winfrey aligned herself with other well-known and well-loved celebrities who, not coincidentally, appealed to those audiences most likely to offer their support to Engler and the cattlemen.

These reports offer insight into some of Winfrey's own sophisticated and savvy rhetorical tactics. Winfrey is a rhetorician, and a successful one, not only for her in-studio audiences but also for her national audience of millions. According to a *Good Morning America* report near the end of the trial, "since moving her show to Texas, her ratings are up 7 percent."[47] Indeed, during "her first week on location—coinciding with the February ratings sweeps—Winfrey drew her highest national Nielsen numbers of the 1997–98 season."[48]

By moving her show to Amarillo, Winfrey capitalized on her status as a television celebrity who "embodies the characteristics of familiarity and mass acceptability."[49] Her personal participation in the trial not only signified her commitment to the case but also served to bridge the distance between viewers at home and the star, intensifying the sense of camaraderie and support that many people already had. Her proximity to trial observers and to the people of Amarillo, and her willingness to embrace the local population and the unique elements of their culture, clearly appealed to audiences in Texas and elsewhere in the region. *The Oprah Winfrey Show—Texas Style,* as the show was temporarily retitled, not only appealed to the show's regular viewers but also had the potential to generate new viewers interested in the novelty of the case, tuning in to see what Winfrey did and said during the highly publicized trial. These appeals encouraged and maintained multiple audiences' identification with the talk-show host.

The extent to which the focus remained on the talk-show host to the neglect of other relevant and important legal and civil issues reinforces the notion that ethos goes beyond what one says; all the actions of the celebrity become "text." One oft-repeated theme was to report on the mood of Amarillo and the ways in which "everyday folks are abuzz about the talk show queen's visit to answer a cattlemen's lawsuit and tape Texas-flavored episodes for her show."[50] *People Weekly* declared that Amarillo "has unofficially been Oprahville since Winfrey touched down in her private Gulfstream jet on Jan. 19."[51] Indeed, according to an article in the *Atlanta Journal-Constitution,* the town's affection for the celebrity was "mirrored by local TV stations that often tailor their news just for Winfrey: one morning anchor implored Winfrey during a newscast to come on the show; another station offers Winfrey daily sightseeing advice; another gives the Chicago weather and sports scores."[52]

The daily details of Winfrey's stay in Amarillo drew intense attention, and many reports centered on the celebrity's personal life. The *Amarillo Globe-News* ran a daily column during the trial called "Eye on Oprah" that offered regular reports on the talk-show host's exercise routine, eating habits, and activities around town. One report divulged how "Roasters Coffee & Tea Co., located close to the ALT [Amarillo Little Theater], has busily filled cups with mochas, lattes and other highfalutin coffee drinks for Oprah's production people."[53] Another disclosed that some locals "have seen her running a route through Quail Creek and around Medical Park about 5 A.M.," but it warned readers not to "think about getting too close. Jogging along with her are six good-sized security guards."[54] Importantly, even though "people think and feel that they know her, and they like her," there remains a clear distance between the celebrity and the general public.[55] It is not Winfrey who visits the coffee shop but her staff, and when she is out in public, she is protected from personal interaction by bodyguards. The rhetorical intimacy created between the fans and the star on the set of the show and during the coverage of the trial does not reflect the reality of the social separations between the two. Despite the rhetorical appearance of accessibility, Winfrey remains cloistered.

When the talk-show host began to testify at the trial, the coverage became even more Winfrey-centric. Although there was media coverage when the prosecution's witnesses and experts testified, it was not reported live or with the same depth and detail as Winfrey's time on the stand. According to *CBS This Morning,* Winfrey's appearance on the witness stand "has no doubt been the highlight of this trial so far."[56] Here status as a talk-show host was a major element in the way she was perceived and constructed by her audiences, both inside and outside the courtroom. The media's intensified focus on what was happening inside the courtroom offered additional insight into the rhetorical situation of the trial proceedings.

The *Today* show emphasized how "the Texas standoff between the talk show host and cattle ranchers in Amarillo took a star turn yesterday when Oprah Winfrey took the stand" and described how "Winfrey looked at jurors, and at times, had the whole courtroom laughing as she compared her ratings to that of talk-show rival Jerry Springer."[57] One reporter in the courtroom noted that Winfrey "came off as soft" on the witness stand and that the spectators were "very attentive. The jury was looking straight at her, and the audience was jam packed to capacity."[58] These descriptions capture the interplay of tropes, appeals, and identifications inherent in moments when the rhetorical situation and its elements are dramatized and enacted.

Here, the ethos of the defendant on the witness stand and the pathos of the judge, jury, reporters, and observers overshadow the logos of the actual questions and answers contained in the testimony. The Associated Press remarked that, "on the witness stand, Ms. Winfrey has exhibited the skill in front of a microphone that has helped her create a top-rated, Emmy Award–winning show."[59] A legal analyst on *CNN Today* confirmed that "the woman is dominating the courtroom just by sheer force of sincerity and personality," explaining, "she's been trained for this practically her whole life. She's been ready for this role for years and years, adapting to a different circumstance, communicating with people, overcoming obstacles. This is what she's about. This is a great test for her, and she is clearly passing it."[60] In other words, Winfrey's experience with the recurring rhetorical situation on her talk show, which essentially requires her to navigate specific rhetorical situations as they relate to larger ones, intersected with and influenced her experience with the rhetorical situation of the courtroom—to her advantage.

As her testimony continued, reporters observed that Winfrey looked tired and acted annoyed as she answered questions under oath. A *CBS This Morning* segment asserted that "Oprah may be getting tired of answering, instead of asking, the questions" as she "is clearly becoming irritated. We are seeing on the stand not simply a witness, but we are seeing the full force of the personality of Oprah Winfrey, the star."[61] Again, Winfrey's ethos and her rhetorical strategies were central to and even defined what was reported about her and her testimony. During these trial reports, Winfrey was shown transcending and transforming the rhetorical situation of the trial and her role as a defendant in it. On the witness stand, she adopted the kinds of rhetorical postures she had practiced, proved, and improved during the rhetorical situations that make up *The Oprah Winfrey Show*.

Indeed, according to one report, Winfrey "tried to pour on the charm for the jury as if it were, well, a studio audience." The article went on: "With energetic eyes and quick little head turns that made her glossy hair bounce—a trademark of hers that gives the impression everything in life is a surprise—the 44-year-old Ms. Winfrey looked directly at jurors the way she does her studio audiences while saying she didn't have an anti-beef agenda on an April 1996 show on mad cow disease." [62] Based on these descriptions, the boundaries between the kinds of rhetorical situations and strategies in effect during trial testimony and those in effect during talk television had been blurred. In these moments, the Winfrey trial evidenced some slippage between the forensic and the popular, between the rhetoric of the courtroom and the rhetoric of the culture that contains it.

Winfrey's testimony referred to the First Amendment in general and to her personal connection to and representation of it as a national talk-show host. She stressed that her show "is not a news magazine. It's not the evening news," and she noted that her audiences recognize the difference between these television genres.[63] In another oft-quoted bit of testimony, she explained, "I feel in my heart I have never done a malicious thing to any human being. To have these charges brought against me, it is the most painful thing I have ever experienced."[64] Here, Winfrey's rhetorical construction of herself emphasizes her personal ethos and integrity and alludes to her reputation as an honest and respectable public figure. It reminds the audience that she has used the public platform of her show for altruistic purposes, promoting literacy, education, and other social causes through programs such as her Angel Network and book club. Winfrey's comments also stress her own private ethics and emotions, personalizing the issues at hand. These kinds of intimate, emotional appeals work to further connect and identify Winfrey with her audience, which she praises as intelligent and discerning.

Interestingly, many of these same reports referred to the way the gag order regulated speech about the trial. A *CBS This Morning* report ended with the point that "none of the participants can talk about this case until it's over. But once it is, Oprah says she'll have plenty to say. Don't be surprised if her first words come on a certain talk show."[65] Such comments stressed the way the trial controlled the speech of the participants and brought to mind the larger freedom-of-speech issues involved in the lawsuit. Several articles about the trial proceedings included Winfrey's responses to questions from journalists outside the courtroom. When asked about details of the case, Winfrey replied variously: "I wish I could say more,"[66] "I can't—oh, I can't say anything about this,"[67] and "Not a word, not a word . . . I wish I could."[68]

The importance and significance of words and the freedom to speak one's mind are central to Winfrey's comments. The fact that they were reported confirms the notion that when Oprah Winfrey speaks, people listen, even if all she says is that she cannot say anything. Her remarks to reporters reiterated her desire to speak and reminded her audiences that they were hearing an abridged version of the trial. And they reflected on the larger constitutional issues already in the forefront of the trial and its coverage, reinforcing the notion that the case was fundamentally about the right to free expression. The gag order and Winfrey's response to it suggested what was at stake in the case and the possible repercussions of the verdict and its impact on the First Amendment. Winfrey's articulations of her forced silence constituted a rhetorical defense against such rhetorical restraints.

How the mainstream press portrayed the trial became part of the event itself and a feature of its coverage, so that production and consumption were intertwined as the spectacle of the spectacle became newsworthy in and of itself. One *New York Times* article pointed out that "even before the start of the trial there were circus elements here,"[69] and a live report on *CNN The World Today* described the mood outside the courtroom as having a "carnival atmosphere."[70]

An article in the *Atlanta Journal-Constitution* devoted considerable attention to this topic, pointing out that the trial "transformed this Panhandle outpost of 160,000 people into a kind of ground zero for the Media Age. The tidy square in front of the three-story Marvin Jones Federal building is lined with a dozen satellite trucks—with names such as Skylink and Starcam—from Lubbock, Dallas, Houston, and Oklahoma City. TV reporters camped in tents represent all the major networks, CNN and even the British Broadcasting Corp."[71] Toward the end of the trial, a broadcast on National Public Radio's *Morning Edition* led with the observation that the trial "has been an entertaining spectacle for the town of Amarillo and the panhandle of Texas."[72] Indeed, as the intense national coverage by major news outlets verified, *Texas Beef v. Oprah Winfrey* was an entertaining spectacle for the entire country. Despite other equally exciting and important events that occurred contemporaneously, the trial galvanized the attention of the American press. According to one Associated Press article, even the "heavily hyped presidential sex questions failed to curtail news media interest in the Winfrey case, as TV and newspaper reporters stood in line for courtroom seats."[73]

The *Amarillo Globe-News* devoted several reports to the national media's enthusiastic interest in the trial. The publisher of Amarillo's newspapers, Garet von Netzer, confirmed that Winfrey's visit was "clearly the biggest media event in the city's history,"[74] and the *Globe-News*'s editorial page editor agreed, remarking that "there may be nobody alive today who will see a bigger media circus than this."[75] The impact of the trial and its celebrity participants on the small Texas town, amplified by and through the mainstream media, increased attention to the trial on a national level. The weekend after the verdict, a report on *NBC Nightly News* described how "some of the citizens of Amarillo, Texas, are suffering from a rare condition that may be called post-Oprah syndrome" and noted that "even though some prominent citizens were on the losing end of the lawsuit against Oprah, the trial took a back seat to the spectacle of Oprah and the celebrities."[76]

The fact that the trial generated such widespread interest, to the extent that the media's attention to the event became a feature of the story, was due in large part to its superstar defendant. It demonstrates the power of ethos to shape what is featured as news and how that news is reported. It reflects aspects of Theodor Adorno and Max Horkheimer's ideas about the culture industry, as described in *The Dialectic of Enlightenment,* and its enduring connection with the capitalist economy within which it operates, confirming the rhetorical appeal of well-known personalities and how that appeal translates into larger audiences, higher ratings, and increased business. Headlines featuring Winfrey contain, create, and circulate cultural and economic capital in ways that headlines featuring mad cow disease or Paul Engler simply do not. News reports focused on Winfrey also incite less reaction from those in positions of power, from governmental bureaucracies and agricultural corporations, than do those about mad cow disease or the safety of the U.S. beef supply. Not only does the spectacle of the spectacle sell well; it is also safe.

In the end, the public conversation about the Oprah trial, widely circulated in the mainstream press, remained focused on rhetoric, on the word in theory but not the words in question. Interestingly, in television, print, and Internet sources *not* considered mainstream, and in the conversations of activists or special-interest groups on the periphery of the mass media, these issues were widely discussed and debated. According to the National Council against Health Fraud (NCAHF), "the Mad Cow Disease story would be a non-story in the USA if it were not for the propaganda efforts of vegetarian groups. EarthSave, PETA, PCRM, and the Seventh-day Adventist website have seized upon the opportunity to frighten people into behaving in ways they find ideologically delightful."[77] What the NCAHF, a conservative watchdog organization, clearly derides are the counterhegemonic efforts of health and food safety advocates who fear that the food disparagement laws will continue to make nonstories out of the issues they support.

Public-relations watchers, vegetarians and vegans, animal rights activists, and other advocacy groups all used the event of Winfrey's trial to promote their own particular causes. Two days after the "Dangerous Foods" show aired, members of People for Ethical Treatment of Animals (PETA) visited Harpo studios in Chicago dressed as barnyard animals in support of Winfrey.[78] In a February 1998 press release, the vegetarian group EarthSave International publicly announced its support for Oprah Winfrey and codefendant Howard Lyman, a board member of the organization.[79] Notably, Winfrey did not become an advocate for any of the causes related to the trial; she neither endorsed nor encouraged any single ideology or politics save the one that protected her own fiscal and professional interests: the First Amendment and its protection of speech on her talk show. During her posttrial press conference, Winfrey insisted that her opinions about beef had not changed, that she was still "off burgers," and that she would not censor herself during on-air discussions, despite the influence her comments have on her audiences and their potentially widespread repercussions.[80]

Importantly, the celebrity status and economic privilege that enabled Winfrey to express and defend her comments in the first place remained intact at the end of the trial. In contrast, ordinary citizens who lack the resources to plan, finance, and carry out the kind of defense Winfrey had were faced with the ordinary, real consequences of the trial. Winfrey does not have to think twice before saying, "I'll never eat another burger," knowing how influential her opinions are, but the majority of Americans who are not Oprah Winfrey *do* need to consider what they say.

Winfrey may have ended up as the symbolic champion of every American's right to voice his or her own opinion, but she is not "Every-American." Forward and backward, Winfrey is a corporation. Not many people have the ability to wage a legal battle like the one Winfrey won in Amarillo, with a team of high-priced lawyers and advisers, yet her victory was construed as a victory for the democracy and freedom of all Americans. Rarely mentioned is the fact that the lawsuit was essentially one megacorporation suing another megacorporation, a war between corporate business giants each attempting to protect their financial bottom lines. The verdict ultimately vindicates the power of the word, but it does not add to the discourse about anyone's right to use or not use it.

Noticing what is omitted or ignored in the overall rhetorical fabric of an event like the Oprah trial allows for a more complete understanding and complex analysis of general rhetorical instances and occasions. It points to the ways in which speech—who can speak where and about what—is regulated by laws that explicitly censor conversation and by the political and economic bureaucracies that more subtly but no less severely limit the boundaries of free speech. And it highlights the mass media's role in shaping and steering the stories that Americans consume. In the end, the media coverage of the trial and its rhetorical patterns exemplify how institutions of civil society serve the interests of the dominant ruling class, governmental agencies, and corporate financiers who regulate not only what Americans put into their mouths but also what they can say about it.

Notes

1. In *A Rhetoric of Motives* (Berkeley: University of California Press, 1950), 192, Kenneth Burke points out that "Man is essentially a 'rational' (that is, symbol-using) animal (as stated in the opening words of St. John, '*In the beginning* was the Word')." Richard M. Weaver, "The Cultural Role of Rhetoric," in *Language Is Sermonic: Richard M. Weaver on the Nature of Rhetoric,* ed. Richard L. Johannesen, Rennard Strickland, and Ralph T. Eubanks (Baton Rouge: Louisiana State University Press, 1970), 34, also considers "the word" in its biblical contexts, including the Gospel of John.

2. Quoted in Jeff Flock, "Oprah's Power over Influence," *CNN Chicago,* January 22, 1998, http://www.cnn.com/CNN/bureaus/chicago/stories/9801/oprah/index8.htm (accessed October 27, 2002).

3. Aaron Epstein, "Where's the Beef? For Oprah, It's in Court—Due to Angry Ranchers," *Chicago Tribune,* January 4, 1998, http://pqasb.pqarchiver.com/chicagotribune/doc/25157128.html (accessed October 15, 2002).

4. Burrelle's Information Services, the official source of transcripts of *The Oprah Winfrey Show,* reports that the "Dangerous Foods" transcript is unavailable because it has been "removed at Harpo's request . . . due to legal or copyright reasons."

5. One such source is "Mad Cow and Oprah," *Earth Island Journal* 11, no. 3 (1996), http://www.earthisland.org/eijournal/new_articles.cfm?articleID=435&journalID=58.

6. "Appeals Court Upholds Win in 'Mad Cow' Lawsuit," *News Media and the Law* 24 (2000), http://proquest.umi.com/pqdweb (accessed April 20, 2001).

7. Skip Hollandsworth and Pamela Colloff, "How the West Was Won Over," *Texas Monthly,* March 1998, https://web.lexis-nexis.com/universe (accessed April 20, 2001).

8. "The Beef Industry v. Oprah: Will the Queen of Talk Have the Last Word on Beef?" *CNN Burden of Proof,* January 20, 1998 (CNN transcript), https://web.lexis-nexis.com/universe (accessed April 20, 2001).

9. Sheldon Rampton and John Stauber, "One Hundred Percent All Beef Baloney: Lessons from the Oprah Trial," *PR Watch* 5, no. 1 (1998), http://www.prwatch.org/prwissues/1998Q1/oprah.html (accessed April 20, 2001).

10. *Texas Beef Group v. Oprah Winfrey,* U.S. Dist. Court, N.D. Texas, 2:96–

CV-208-J, 11 F. Supp. 2d 858, decided February 26, 1998, LEXIS 3559, https://web.lexis-nexis.com/universe (accessed April 20, 2001).

11. Kay Ledbetter, "Paul Engler," *Amarillo Globe-News,* May 19, 2000, http://www.amarillonet.com/stories/051900/his_engler.html (accessed February 5, 2003).

12. Alan Guebert, "Who's Paul Engler? And Why Is He Still Suing Oprah?" *Pantagraph,* May 10, 1998, https://web.lexis-nexis.com/universe (accessed October 11, 2002).

13. Center for Science in the Public Interest, "Food-Disparagement Laws: State Civil and Criminal Statutes," *Coalition for Free Speech: Foodspeak,* http://www.cspinet.org/foodspeak/laws/existlaw.htm (accessed November 25, 2002). These states enacted the statute in the following order: Louisiana, Idaho, Mississippi, Georgia, Colorado (the only state in which the statute is criminal, not civil), South Dakota, Texas, Florida, Arizona, Alabama, Oklahoma, Ohio, and North Dakota.

14. Epstein, "Where's the Beef?"

15. Quoted in Kenneth Smith, "'Let Me Warn You . . .': Oprah, the Law, and Bad-Mouthing Foods," *Priorities for Health* 10, no. 1 (1998), http://www.acsh.org/publications/priorities/1001/oprah.html (accessed October 10, 2002).

16. Thomas Goetz, "After the Oprah Crash," *Village Voice,* April 29, 1997, 39–41, http://proquest.umi.com/pqdweb (accessed April 20, 2001).

17. Michele Simon, "Veggie Libelous: Free Speech at Stake in Oprah Winfrey Trial," *Informed Eating Newsletter,* January 1998, http://www.informedeating.org/docs/veggie_libelous.html (accessed October 12, 2002).

18. "Jury Rejects Oprah Winfrey Beef Suit," *Legal Intelligencer,* February 27, 1998, 4, https://web.lexis-nexis.com/universe (accessed April 20, 2001).

19. Oprah Winfrey, "A Matter of Principle," interview with Diane Sawyer, *20/20 Monday,* March 2, 1998 (ABC transcript), 10.

20. "Jury Rejects Oprah Winfrey Beef Suit."

21. Quoted in Hollandsworth and Colloff, "How the West Was Won Over."

22. "Oprah's Cattle-Country Trial Finally Ready to Get Underway," *Corpus Christie Caller Times Interactive,* January 21, 1998, http://www.caller2.com/texas/tex2274.html (accessed October 11, 2002).

23. "Appeals Court Upholds Win in 'Mad Cow' Lawsuit."

24. Lawrence Baines, "The Medium Is the Master," *Secondary English* 2000, http://www.secondaryenglish.com/mediumismaster.htm (accessed August 2, 2004).

25. Dwight Woodward, "Tuning In," *Perspectives: Research, Scholarship, and Creative Activity at Ohio University* (Spring–Summer 1997), http:www.ohiou.edu/perspectives/9701/prospec11.htm (accessed October 27, 2002).

26. American Civil Liberties Union, "Freedom of Expression," 23, http://www.aclu.org/FreeSpeech/FreeSpeech.cfm?ID=9461&c=42 (accessed February 20, 2003).

27. Rodney Smolla, "Speech—Overview," *First Amendment Center,* http://www.firstamendmentcenter.org/Speech/overview.aspx (accessed February 20, 2003).

28. *State of the First Amendment 2002, First Amendment Center,* http://www.firstamendmentcenter.org/about.aspx?id=2185 (accessed February 20, 2003).

29. Kenneth A. Paulson, "Foreword: We Lose Sight of Our Rights When Freedom and Fear Collide," *State of the First Amendment 2002,* 2, http://www.firstamendmentcenter.org/PDF/sofa2002report.PDF (accessed February 20, 2003).

30. Gina Holland, "Free-Speech Cases Await Supreme Court after Summer Break," Associated Press, August 19, 2002, https://web.lexis-nexis.com/universe (accessed October 10, 2002).

31. "Cattle Rancher to Sue Oprah Winfrey for Libel Because of Her Comments Regarding Beef Safety," *NBC Nightly News,* June 5, 1997 (NBC transcript), https://web.lexis-nexis.com/universe (accessed October 11, 2002).

32. "Texas Cattlemen Filed Lawsuit against Oprah," *CNN Crossfire,* January 5, 1998 (CNN transcript), https://web.lexis-nexis.com/universe (accessed October 11, 2002).

33. Chip Chandler, "Media Put Amarillo in the Spotlight," *Amarillo Globe-News,* January 21, 1998, http://www.amarillonet.com/stories/012198/put.shtml (accessed October 8, 2002).

34. Aristotle, *On Rhetoric: A Theory of Civic Discourse,* trans. George A. Kennedy (New York: Oxford University Press, 1991), 37.

35. Ibid., 121.

36. George A. Kennedy, introduction, notes, and appendices for *On Rhetoric: A Theory of Civic Discourse* (New York: Oxford University Press, 1991), 163.

37. Ibid.

38. Ann Oldenburg, "Trial Starts Today: Did TV Talk Show Queen Turn Fans off Beef? Supporters Contend They're Oprah's Fans, Not Followers," *USA Today,* January 20, 1998, https://web.lexis-nexis.com/universe (accessed October 10, 2002).

39. Irv Kupcinet, "Kup's Column," *Chicago Sun-Times,* February 1, 1998, 14, https://web.lexis-nexis.com/universe (accessed October 8, 2002).

40. There is also current scholarship regarding *The Oprah Winfrey Show* in relation to television, the talk-show genre, and discourse theory. See Laurie L. Haag, "Oprah Winfrey: The Construction of Intimacy in the Talk Show Setting," *Journal of Popular Culture* 26, no. 4 (1993): 115–21; Gloria-Jean Masciarotte, "'C'mon Girl': Oprah Winfrey and the Discourse of Feminine Talk,"

Genders 11 (1991): 81–110; and Corinne Squire, "Empowering Women: *The Oprah Winfrey Show,*" *Feminism and Psychology* 4, no. 1 (1994): 63–79.

41. Joshua Gamson, *Claims to Fame: Celebrity in Contemporary America* (Berkeley: University of California Press, 1994), 170.

42. P. David Marshall, *Celebrity and Power: Fame in Contemporary Culture* (Minneapolis: University of Minnesota Press, 1997), 131.

43. Jim Kirk and Tim Jones, "Texas Beef Trial Puts Power of Oprah on Display," *Chicago Tribune,* January 21, 1998, http://pqasb.pqarchiver.com/ chicagotribune/doc/25512364.html (accessed October 15, 2002); Richard Roeper, "Oprah's Sheep Ready to Follow Every Whim," *Chicago Sun-Times,* January 22, 1998, https://web.lexis-nexis.com/universe (accessed October 8, 2002).

44. "Drama Outside Courtroom on Day One of Oprah vs. Cattlemen," *CNN The World Today,* January 20, 1998 (CNN transcript), https://web.lexis-nexis.com/universe (accessed October 11, 2002).

45. Cliff Edwards, "Talk Show to Move to Texas during Defamation Trial," Associated Press, January 7, 1998, https://web.lexis-nexis.com/universe (accessed October 10, 2002).

46. Mark Babineck, "Oprah Brings More Star Power to Texas Panhandle," Associated Press, January 23, 1998, https://web.lexis-nexis.com/universe (accessed October 10, 2002).

47. "Winfrey Testimony," *ABC Good Morning America,* February 4, 1998 (ABC transcript), https://web.lexis-nexis.com/universe (accessed October 11, 2002).

48. Robert Feder, "Roe & Garry Will Meet 'Harry & Sally' on Ch. 7," *Chicago Sun-Times,* February 19, 1998, https://web.lexis-nexis.com/universe (accessed October 8, 2002).

49. Marshall, *Celebrity and Power,* 119.

50. Mike Cochran, "Oprah Beef Trial Stampedes Amarillo," Associated Press, February 1, 1998, https://web.lexis-nexis.com/universe (accessed October 10, 2002).

51. Tom Gliatto et al., "Where's the Beef?" *People Weekly,* February 16, 1998, 170, http://proquest.umi.com/pqdweb (accessed April 20, 2001).

52. Drew Jubera, "Oprah the Queen of Talk Comes to Texas to Face Her Critics, But Finds a Lot of Friends," *Atlanta Journal-Constitution,* January 25, 1998, B01, http://proquest.umi.com/pqdweb (accessed October 12, 2002).

53. "Eye on Oprah: Winfrey Fans Distribute Fliers," *Amarillo Globe-News,* January 21, 1998, http://www.amarillonet.com/stories/012198/014–4679.005.shtml (accessed October 11, 2002).

54. Shanna Foust-Peeples, "Eye on Oprah: Oprah-Watchers Might Want to Try Jogging," *Amarillo Globe-News,* January 23, 1998, http://www.amarillonet.com/stories/012398/011–8875.001.shtml (accessed October 11, 2002).

55. "Oprah Winfrey vs. the Texas Cattle Industry," *Rivera Live,* February 3, 1998 (CNBC transcript), https://web.lexis-nexis.com/universe (accessed October 11, 2002).

56. "Oprah Winfrey to Take the Stand Again in Her Beef Defamation Trial in Amarillo, Texas," *CBS This Morning,* February 4, 1998 (CBS transcript), https://web.lexis-nexis.com/universe (accessed October 11, 2002).

57. "Oprah Winfrey Takes Stand in Defamation Suit Filed against Her by Texas Cattlemen," *Today,* February 4, 1998 (NBC transcript), https://web.lexis-nexis.com/universe (accessed October 11, 2002).

58. "Oprah Winfrey to Take Stand . . . in Amarillo, Texas."

69. Chip Brown, "'It's Not the Evening News'—Defiant Oprah Defends Opinions on Show," Associated Press, February 5, 1998, https://web.lexis-nexis.com/universe (accessed October 10, 2002).

60. "Oprah Winfrey Takes Command on the Stand," *CNN Today,* February 4, 1998 (CNN transcript), https://web.lexis-nexis.com/universe (accessed October 11, 2002).

61. "Oprah Winfrey Takes the Witness Stand for Third Straight Day in Amarillo," *CBS This Morning,* February 5, 1998 (CBS transcript), https://web.lexis-nexis.com/universe (accessed October 11, 2002).

62. Chip Brown, "Winfrey Tries to Charm the Jury at Beef-Defamation Trial," Associated Press, February 6, 1998, https://web.lexis-nexis.com/universe (accessed October 15, 2002).

63. Chip Brown, "Oprah Says Talk Show Merely Forum for Debate," Associated Press, February 4, 1998, https://web.lexis-nexis.com/universe (accessed October 15, 2002).

64. "Oprah Winfrey's Second Day on the Witness Stand," *ABC World News This Morning,* February 5, 1998 (ABC transcript), https://web.lexis-nexis.com/universe (accessed October 11, 2002).

65. "Oprah Winfrey Concludes Three Days of Testimony in Her Trial with Cattlemen," *CBS This Morning,* February 6, 1998 (CBS transcript), https://web.lexis-nexis.com/universe (accessed October 11, 2002).

66. "Oprah Winfrey Expected to Take Stand in Cattle Industry Defamation Lawsuit," *NBC Nightly News,* February 1, 1998 (NBC transcript), https://web.lexis-nexis.com/universe (accessed October 11, 2002).

67. "Oprah Winfrey Takes Stand in Defamation Suit Filed against Her by Texas Cattlemen."

68. Sam Howe Verhovek, "Talk of the Town: Burgers v. Oprah," *New York Times,* January 21, 1988, https://web.lexis-nexis.com/universe (accessed October 15, 2002).

69. Ibid.

70. "Drama Outside Courtroom on Day One of Oprah vs. Cattlemen."

71. Jubera, "Oprah the Queen of Talk Comes to Texas to Face Her Critics."

72. "Oprah Libel Trial," *Morning Edition,* National Public Radio, February 18, 1998, (transcript), https://web.lexis-nexis.com/universe (accessed October 11, 2002).

73. Cochran, "Oprah Beef Trial Stampedes Amarillo."

74. Ibid.

75. Quoted in Tim Jones, "Whopper of a Media Circus Kicks Off," *Chicago Tribune,* January 20, 1998, http://pqasb.pqarchiver.com/chicagotribune/doc/25485426.html (accessed October 15, 2002).

76. "Amarillo Residents Trying to Resume Life as Usual in Wake of Oprah Winfrey Trial," *NBC Nightly News,* February 28, 1998, https://web.lexis-nexis.com/universe (accessed October 11, 2002).

77. National Council against Health Fraud, *NCAHF News* 20, no. 4 (July–August 1997), http://www.ncahf.org/nl/1997/7–8.html (accessed February 20, 2003).

78. Kevin M. Williams, "Networks to Fall Silent Friday," *Chicago Sun-Times,* April 18, 1996, https://web.lexis-nexis.com/universe (accessed October 11, 2002).

79. EarthSave International, "EarthSave Backs Oprah, Lyman, and Free Speech," press release, February 1998, http://www.earthsave.org/news/press1.htm (accessed February 20, 2003).

80. "Oprah Winfrey Not Liable: 'Free Speech Not Only Lives It Rocks,'" *CNN Breaking News,* February 26, 1998 (CNN transcript), https://web.lexis-nexis.com/universe (accessed April 20, 2001).

Part III

Oprah Winfrey on the Page

Oprah's Book Club
and the American Dream

Malin Pereira

In their essay "America Dreamin': Discoursing Liberally on *The Oprah Winfrey Show*" Debbie Epstein and Deborah Lynn Steinberg assert that although the show identifies the failures and limitations of the American Dream for women and African Americans and, to a lesser extent, for the lower classes, in the end, it recuperates this classic mythology by affirming that self-actualization is indeed the key to social and economic success. They argue that this belief that the American Dream is accessible to everyone, regardless of the social forces governing their lives, dominates the narrative of the show. Not surprisingly, Epstein and Steinberg are critical of *The Oprah Winfrey Show*'s promotion of such middle-class liberal values and its related failure to offer meaningful critiques of the ways sexism, racism, classism, and heterocentrism shape the lives of many Americans.[1] However, the original Oprah's Book Club—an aspect of the show they do not discuss—offers an implicit critique of this narrative of accessibility, even if it is a critique the show itself might attempt to repress. The novels of Toni Morrison, *She's Come Undone* by Wally Lamb, *We Were the Mulvaneys* by Joyce Carol Oates, *House of Sand and Fog* by Andre Dubus III, *Cane River* by Lalita Tademy, and *The Corrections* by Jonathan Franzen, all selections for the original book club, do in fact expose the difficulties that many Americans have accessing the middle-class security that constitutes the realization of the American Dream.

Further, the episodes in which these books are discussed do not uniformly comply with the recuperation of the American Dream that

191

Epstein and Steinberg identify as the dominant discourse in *The Oprah Winfrey Show*. Instead, a nascent awareness that the dream is illusory erupts in book club discussions, an awareness that the show nevertheless attempts to evacuate or suppress. Whether or not the show's narrative is deliberately framed to assert the primacy of individual agency in achieving the American Dream, the literature—and audience members' and authors' discussion of it—plays a subversive role in that discourse, the effects of which are expressed symptomatically.[2] Notably, as the books selected for study become more self-consciously literary, the criticisms they pose become more difficult to contain, exemplified by the eruptions of audience members, book club participants, and the authors themselves. The narrative of possessive individualism that sustains the idea of the American Dream as accessible is increasingly challenged.

As Cecilia Konchar Farr notes in her book *Reading Oprah,* the "American Dream comes true again and again on *Oprah!*" through Winfrey herself and the books she selects. Farr's endnote discussing Epstein and Steinberg's article, though acknowledging a concern about the show's emphasis on individualism and the power of capitalism to maintain inequities, ultimately does not affirm their argument. Instead, Farr claims that the book club's "talking readers" are the voices of the dispossessed who, through the book club, have punched a hole in the status quo.[3] Likewise, Kathleen Rooney points out the "doctrine of mindless American optimism" controlling *The Oprah Winfrey Show,* as demonstrated by the show's "master narrative" imposed on the novels through competing narratives.[4] Both authors position themselves as primarily in favor of the book club. As Rooney sums it up, her book is "a largely positive appraisal of the club as an important and influential cultural institution, one which . . . has made substantial progress toward effacing and eradicating decrepit, frequently racist and misogynistic cultural hierarchies."[5] Although Rooney's and Farr's arguments do not specifically disallow the one I pursue here, neither seems particularly interested, as both espouse a mostly positive understanding of the book club phenomenon.

The dismissal and then reclamation of the American Dream is evident in several of the earliest selections for the original book club, such as *She's Come Undone* by Wally Lamb, announced January 22, 1997. *She's Come Undone* follows Dolores as she experiences abandonment by her father, the death of her mother, obesity, rape, a destructive relationship, and, finally, healing and a new relationship. The novel initially critiques the sexism, classism, and racism of American society, demonstrating how social and economic security is predominantly unavailable to women who lack money, beauty, or access to other resources. By the end, though, the plot reaffirms the idea that individuals are primarily self-actualized, self-made men and women. Dolores, motivated by therapy, has lost weight, started college, found a life partner who loves her, and achieved economic stability. She may still be working class and outside of the "ideal," but she has nevertheless recuperated a modified form of the American Dream. When I taught this novel in my "Oprah's Books" course in 2003, several female students loved the novel for this very reason. One student said in a class discussion, "It means that even if you don't fit the myth, you can still have your own American Dream, and it's OK."

Other early Oprah's Book Club choices, however, refuse to endorse the American Dream in any version. Toni Morrison's *Song of Solomon,* Winfrey's second selection (announced October 18, 1996), is, as many literary critics have noted, a scathing critique of the disfiguring effects of American materialism on three generations of an African American family. Milkman Dead's hunt for his grandfather's gold, his father Macon Dead's fatal middle-class acquisitive worldview, and Pilate's granddaughter's self-destruction in the department-store world of material beauty relay to readers in no uncertain terms that the materialism implicit in the American Dream can be deadly when enacted by African Americans. As evidenced by *Song of Solomon,* from the beginning of the book club endeavor, the works selected by Winfrey proffer the possibility for meaningful critiques, rather than affirmations, of the parallels drawn between financial capital and personal capital. The tension between the meanings of *She's Come Undone* and *Song of Solomon* is palpable.

The original Oprah's Book Club forms a text of forty-seven selections and the episodes in which they are discussed, a text whose prevailing theme is the supremacy of American mythologies of individual action as the primary means to success. Notably, a significant number of selections depict the dream failing, only to be reconstituted in a new version, along the lines of Epstein and Steinberg's thesis. Generally this is true of the book club's more "popular" literature selections, including *The Pilot's Wife* by Anita Shreve, the story of a woman who believes that she has a solid marriage and a stable middle-class life until she is wronged by her husband. This betrayal forces her to progress beyond the facile version of the American Dream she has been inhabiting, surviving to reinvent her life anew. But the recuperation of the dream as manifest in Shreve's work is also true of more "literary" selections, as demonstrated by *We Were the Mulvaneys* by Joyce Carol Oates. In Oates's novel, the seemingly "perfect" American family disintegrates because it cannot constructively deal with the date rape of the daughter. Although the plot and themes of this novel are far more complex than those of *The Pilot's Wife,* the end is similar in its affirmation of individual success. The final, triumphant scene is a family reunion in which all the surviving members reunite on the Fourth of July, the definitive American holiday. They are drastically changed, much less perfect and far more "authentic" than their earlier preformed roles as popular cheerleader, class brain, football hero, and mom, but each of them, the novel emphasizes, has found his or her own version of the dream.

Yet under this plot of affirmation lies a repressed narrative that demonstrates the political unconscious of the text. Here I am referencing Frederic Jameson's classic concept that the literary text, or any cultural artifact, "far from being completely realized on any one of its levels tilts powerfully into the . . . political unconscious, of the text, such that the latter's dispersed *semes* . . . insistently direct us to the informing power of forces or contradictions which the text seeks in vain wholly to control or master (or manage, to use Norman Holland's suggestive term)."[6] The political unconscious of Oprah's Book Club is a critique of the American Dream and consumer capitalism, a repressed plot that builds over the six years of the club's existence and ultimately leads to its demise in 2002 and later reconstruction in 2004. In several episodes, one can see the symptomatic disruptions of "managing" the book club through silences, disagreements, broken snatches of arguments, crying, and even public carping between the show's host and the featured author; in the case of Jonathan Franzen, his episode was canceled.

A key element fueling the repressed plot is Winfrey's increasing selection of more "literary" works, thus introducing more ambiguity and complexity. Also notable is the repeated selection of Toni Morrison (four times, accounting for one-quarter of the African American selections, which made up one-quarter of the total original book club selections), whose books refuse white American materialism and reject the sentimentality of the myth of an equitable American Dream as unsuitable for black Americans, while at the same time detailing how it has been denied to blacks. Although it is difficult to ascribe sole agency for the book selections to Winfrey herself, there are some compelling reasons to consider this repressed plot as symptomatic of Winfrey's own ambivalence about the American Dream and consumer capitalism. First, it seems plausible that the selections are made principally by Winfrey and that they reflect, to a large extent, her personal views and reading tastes. Throughout *The Oprah Winfrey Show*, she has consistently presented herself as a reader. Furthermore, despite a large circle of employees, Winfrey has exercised principal control of her show over the years, most evidenced in 1994 by her split with longtime producer Debra DiMaio, who resigned rather than turn the show in the more thoughtful direction Winfrey desired.[7] Last, Winfrey's roots in the civil rights and feminist movements provide an activist foundation informing her stated goals for *The Oprah Winfrey Show*, which include empowering women and children and fighting racism,[8] however she might manage those goals to accommodate market forces. Together, these factors suggest that the repressed plot in the texts of the original Oprah's Book Club can be viewed at least partially as expressive of the contradictions within Winfrey herself.

That the original version of Oprah's Book Club moved from emphasizing popular fiction to privileging literary works is evident in the chronological list of selections. In 1996 to 1999, the majority of novels selected were by writers considered "popular" rather than those considered "literary." In using these terms I do not intend to diminish the former or elevate the latter. First, these popular writers, as Susan Wise Bauer notes, are often writing in the tradition of the nineteenth-century sentimental novel, a previously devalued genre that has only relatively recently been given the serious attention it deserves.[9] Second, R. Mark Hall's astute identification of Winfrey as a "literacy sponsor," using popular fiction to lure audience members into reading less familiar works, validates something we all can respect: Winfrey has gotten people to read in an age when it seems to be in danger of obsolescence.[10] Last, by "literary," I mean that the text pays particular attention to participating in a literary conversation about aesthetics—"how" the story is told rather than just "what" is being told—which usually leads to some degree of aesthetic experimentation in the text. (Obviously, this can also lead to literary works being less popular, as the intended reader is someone steeped in that aesthetic conversation and interested in parsing through innovative aesthetic effects.) In the first three years of the club, very few self-consciously literary selections were made. Exceptions included Edwidge Danticat's *Breath, Eyes, Memory;* Toni Morrison's *Song of Solomon* and *Paradise;* and Ernest Gaines's *A Lesson before Dying.* Interestingly, all these literary selections are by African American writers. One might consider Jane Hamilton's *The Book of Ruth* or Kaye Gibbons's *Ellen Foster* to be more literary (rather than popular) selections, but according to conventional definitions, on a continuum between the literary and the popular, Danticat and Morrison are surely the most literary. In total, out of thirty selections, approximately six are literary from 1996 to 1999.

Beginning in 2000, however, the balance shifts dramatically toward the literary and away from the popular. By my count, at least one-half the texts are by writers with established literary pedigrees. To the works of Morrison Winfrey adds novels by Isabel Allende, Joyce Carol Oates, Sue Miller, Jonathan Franzen, Barbara Kingsolver, and Andre Dubus III—all writers whose place in conversations about literary aesthetics is established or up-and-coming. (Dubus is the son of the late and highly regarded short-story writer Andre Dubus.) To be sure, Winfrey selected some texts that are more interested in what is being told than the method used to tell it, such as *Cane River* by Lalita Tademy, a former executive who quit her job to write the story of her female ancestors who struggled with enslavement and color privilege. Although the novel tells a compelling story, all the characters' voices sound alike. Still, at least ten of the eighteen selections between 2000 and 2002 could be classified as literary novels.[11]

The shift toward the literary in 2000 introduced eruptions into the show discourse. One possible reason is that the attention in literary texts to how the story is told emphasizes language that allows and even demands connotation, which is inherently ambiguous. Connotation and ambiguity are textual "soft spots" in an overt show discourse that supports the American Dream, allowing multiple interpretations and uncertainties rather than firm closure and easy answers. Texts such as *The Poisonwood Bible* by Barbara Kingsolver (a selection in 2000) offer complex, diverse, and even contradictory views on their subject, as compared with a novel such as *She's Come Undone,* which clearly delineates who is good, who is bad, what is wrong, and how to fix it. *The Poisonwood Bible*'s multiple narrators refuse any one point of view as definitive and thus contribute to a literary text with a highly complex and very unidealistic understanding of the American Dream. The high ratio of literary novels in the last two years of the original club helps undermine any overt book club recuperation of the American Dream, creating a complex text that is much more difficult to "manage."

Several episodes of Oprah's Book Club from 2000 to 2002 demonstrate an increasing disruption of the club's overt plot of affirming the possibility of individual triumph independent of social forces. The *We Were the Mulvaneys* episode (March 8, 2001), for instance, reveals how eruptions of complex truths can occur even when they have been "managed" in the show discourse by the author's support of an overt plot of recuperation. This episode opens with author Joyce Carol Oates explicitly stating that this novel is about forgiveness. Yet one of the participants, BJ, refuses that theme both directly and indirectly. BJ differs markedly from the other audience members invited to the staged discussion of the novel: she is the only one who is clearly working class, as evidenced by her neglected dental work, inexpensive clothes, basic haircut, little makeup, and general look of wear. The other women are distinctly comfortable looking in comparison and present themselves as middle class: Jane is a realtor; Celeste, a sales rep; Lori, an English teacher; and Kathy, a stay-at-home mom. BJ's profession, in contrast, is not stated. Instead, she is presented as an example of an individual who has been banished from her family because she was raped—the same situation experienced by the daughter in *We Were the Mulvaneys*. BJ's working-class presence on the show brings the economic costs of such banishment to the foreground, a price the character Marianne also pays but that Oates represses by having her marry a successful veterinarian by the end of the novel. BJ receives much empathy from the group and becomes its instructor in an underside of American society that they clearly cannot imagine. She describes a time when she was destitute and called her family, asking if she could return: they offered to take in her baby, but not her. The other women are horror-struck and express sympathy but seem unable to imagine the realities of her failure to achieve the American Dream. No one asks how she survived, what jobs she had to take to subsist.

Finally, BJ resists being scripted into a narrative where, by virtue of her surviving, she is expected to demonstrate personal largesse to those who impeded her. This happens for Marianne in the novel, yet at the end of the show, BJ corrects author Oates and the others on the book's stated theme of forgiveness. When asked to go see her dying father, BJ agrees, but not for him—for herself. BJ tells the group, it is a moment of surrendering to what has happened to you, *not* forgiving the person who did it. She has not forgiven her father for her banishment, and she makes what it has cost her palpable. The group members visually exhibit mixed responses to her stance; Oates purses her lips, and Winfrey changes the subject.

The episode prior to *We Were the Mulvaneys* also demonstrates symptoms of awareness that the pursuit of capital as the way to achieve success can be destructive as a way of life. *House of Sand and Fog,* unlike *We Were the Mulvaneys,* does not attempt to recuperate the American Dream anew; instead, Dubus depicts his characters as so prideful and selfish in their pursuit of economic and social success that, as one of my students put it, they are willing to kill each other to get it. The tragedy Dubus creates is the tragedy of our American Dream. The novel works like Brechtian theater; the episodic plot structure, the increasingly outlandish behavior of the characters, and their clearly flawed points of view (which prevent full audience sympathy) work together to jar the audience out of any complacent acceptance of modern capitalist society as a natural way of life. Dubus's intent is not to direct his readers toward the catharsis of emotions instigated by the novel's tragedy; rather, he wishes them to adopt an attitude critical of capitalism's shortcomings and perhaps even a desire to work toward political and economic change.

What is interesting is the effect this overtly political novel has on the episode's discourse. Winfrey introduces the show with, "Never read a book like this. What began as a book I couldn't put down became a discussion where people could not shut up. It was an all-out book club battle." Once the political unconscious of Oprah's Book Club becomes transparent, the floodgates are let loose. The transcript shows a discussion that even Winfrey could not manage. The participants say things like, "I could not disagree more"; "Then you don't have compassion in you"; "That won't make it on the air"; "Would you give us a break, here?"; "I gave the book away"; and "I feel naked." The author even remarks at one point, "I'm about to cry." It is by far the most contentious and emotionally diverse of the book club episodes. And, in the midst of the discussion, the painful truth that Dubus wants the audience to see emerges: Winfrey points out the racism and classism the novel exposes and asserts, "I think a lot of what people call racism in the country is really classism," to which Dubus responds, "Yeah, Hallelujah. Hallelujah." A panelist states, "and we deny it," acknowledging the repressive mechanisms at work. Dubus sums up, "It goes against the American Dream to talk about being classist."[12]

In editing this taped discussion for television, there is an attempt to reframe the arguing as another story that is classic to American mythology—namely, the son who follows in the footsteps of his father. The show opens and closes with extended scenes in which Dubus, alone, talks about his life and how he wrote the novel, and then about his father, who died just days after the novel was published. This narrative emphasizes the standard themes of the American Dream, such as finding one's path in life and the importance of inheritance. After the all-out battle of the taped discussion, the episode's closing vignette, with Dubus telling how he and his brother Jeb built their father's coffin and dug his grave themselves, seems to symbolically enact the reburial necessitated by the show's insistent plot of a triumphant American Dream. The truths that emerged—about how corrupted and untenable our national mythologies of success are, and how we know this but deny it—are symbolically reburied, as required by Harpo management.

Just a few months after these two episodes aired, the ultimate symptom erupted in the form of the show that never happened—Jonathan Franzen's appearance for his book *The Corrections*. After Franzen's book was chosen in September 2001, he made remarks expressing some degree of ambivalence about its being an Oprah's Book Club selection. Much has been written about his comments—that he is "the snob who dissed Oprah,"[13] that he does not want female readers,[14] and that he wants his work to be seen as literary rather than popular.[15] In terms of my thesis—that the original Oprah's Book Club embodies an increasing awareness of the untenable realities of the American Dream—the debacle over *The Corrections* is the culminating eruption critiquing American mythologies and late market capitalism. As Chris Lehmann points out, one of Franzen's concerns was that his book's selection meant that it would bear Winfrey's corporate logo, which is precisely the main concern of his novel: that market forces and "corrections" have become the existential metaphor of the American self. Every character's very being, the novel attests, is enmeshed in its capitalist expression. There is no other identity space. As Lehmann notes, Oprah's Book Club is "the most powerful market force in American publishing."[16] Franzen's concern, then, pulls the curtain back on the Wizard of Oz, revealing the real machinations behind the public discourse that Winfrey creates about the book club. That she revoked his invitation to appear on her show enacts a repression of that eruption. Lehmann asks, "Why not have Franzen appear on the show and air his views about the book club with its members?" The answer is, of course, that such an episode would turn into an overt acknowledgement of the political unconscious of the club.

Franzen's essay on *The Oprah Winfrey Show* mess, "Meet Me in St. Louis," reenacts this pulling aside of the curtain by relating his experience during the taping of the show.[17] According to Franzen, the film crew had already begun working with him on the segment and may, in fact, have precipitated some of his ambivalent feelings about his book's being selected. The crew insisted on filming him in St. Louis, where he was raised, instead of in New York, where he has lived most of his adult life. He found himself being packaged in the role of midwestern prodigal son, returning home to a family that no longer lives there or even exists (his parents are deceased). He and the head of the crew disagreed about filming him at his parents' old house; Franzen refused, and the crew chief sulked. In his account, Franzen reveals his deep feelings of emotional invasion and exploitation at being packaged as a story of the American Dream fulfilled, a story that glorifies his suburban midwestern upbringing in contrast to the artistic accomplishments of the novel. According to Franzen, he was made to feel that by refusing the American Dream plot, he was failing as an Oprah's Book Club author—which he promptly began to do that evening at a book signing, where he made some ambivalent remarks. It is apparent from his essay that Harpo Productions was trying to manage the subversive dimensions of the novel by appropriating both Franzen's identity and his novel's main theme into a safe American Dream narrative. And why should he resist? Isn't it every author's dream to write an Oprah's Book Club selection?

Not surprisingly, Winfrey ended her original book club just six months after the Franzen upheaval, in April 2002. Faced with ongoing criticism of both the selections and the participants' tendency to relate to the books rather than analyze them, along with an increasingly unmanageable critique of the American Dream and consumer capitalism, it had become clear that Oprah's Book Club needed to go on a hiatus for restructuring. Rooney's essay on the episode in which Winfrey ended the book club suggests that Winfrey already knew what the new Oprah's Book Club would be. During one of the final commercial breaks, Winfrey says that "she wants to take time to return to the classics ... that she spent the previous weekend rereading *The Great Gatsby*, a title to which the audience responds appreciatively."[18]

In 2004 Winfrey's re-created book club turned its focus on the classics, thereby adjusting the dynamics of the club to manage several of the disruptive elements of the emerging critique of the American Dream.[19] First, in selecting classics, one can usually bypass authors, because most of them are dead by the time their books have been deemed classics. Authors such as Franzen are thus circumvented, containing one possible source of eruption. Second, instead of focusing primarily on American literature, this incarnation of the club is avowedly international in scope, thus eliminating any steady focus on the United States or its economic system. Third, although the classics club still includes audience members, their role has been substantially diminished, and the promotional package has been expanded to include celebrities and travel to the exciting locale of the novel. Such a move offers more control over the participants, as well-chosen celebrities can be counted on to comply with the script, and the emphasis on travel keeps the focus off the home front. Fourth, the reenvisioned club is pointedly and actively educational, with academics obviously involved in the production of the Web site background information, study questions, and e-mail reading assistance. This presents any subversive ideas as intellectual and as part of educating readers at the theoretical level rather than at a practical, real-world level.

The Oprah's Book Club episode on John Steinbeck's *East of Eden* provides an example of how effectively the classics club manages literature's subversive potential and instead emphasizes ideas supportive of the American Dream and consumer capitalism. Overall, the show presents this classic novel as furthering the "embourgeoisement" (to borrow Sharon O'Dair's term) of Winfrey's audience members—that is, as a tool for acquiring a bourgeois identity as part of achieving the

American Dream. The episode opens with a focus on touristic travel, featuring gorgeous views of Steinbeck country in Monterey, California. After two surprised audience members are selected to join the road trip for the show (making their dream come true), the footage shows planes flying to California. Once in California, Winfrey tours landmarks and scenery from the security of a van, at one point greeting the trees, "hello, hello, hello!" In another scene, supposedly the next day, Winfrey waves to cars from her van. When I showed this episode to my 2004 class, the students remarked that Winfrey seemed almost manic and quite false compared with the original book club episodes we had watched. One said that she seemed egotistical and self-absorbed in her fame and the status of the book club; another pointed out that she was clearly selling the new Oprah's Book Club. A third noted how marginalized the audience members were, relegated to a distant set of chairs on the lawn of Steinbeck's home (in a carefully orchestrated array of colorful Oprah's Book Club T-shirts) and allowed only two token representatives in the taped discussion with Steinbeck's son, a celebrity, an academic, and Winfrey.

Authority in the episode is focused on Steinbeck's son, Thom, who provides substantial biographical information linking the novel to Steinbeck's family; on two celebrities, Kelsey Grammer and Jane Seymour (her taped comments precede the discussion on the lawn); and, of course, on Winfrey herself. Seymour's authority comes from playing the character Cathy in the movie version of the novel; she calls it "the best role of my career." She is the first to emphasize the main theme of the novel, "thou mayest," on which Winfrey rests the entire episode. Grammer's authority is stated by Winfrey at the beginning of the lawn discussion: "He knows everything about this book." But ultimately, it is not at all clear why he is there, except that he is a celebrity and can be very funny. Winfrey maintains the center, relaying the main idea of "timshel"—free will—through herself. Both Winfrey and Grammer read selections from the novel. A literary critic, Margo Jefferson, speaks briefly and suffers from an inadequate introduction and minimal discussion time. She and the two female audience members speak the least, and their comments garner little in the way of response.

As the episode peaks, the audience member Kathy speaks the lesson that the audience is to learn: that timshel "gives the power to me, rather than the circumstance." As Thom intones that you should "never

Chicago Public Library
Lozano
10/14/2011   10:22:12 AM
-Patron Receipt-

ITEMS BORROWED:

1:
Title: Jesus and money : a guide for times
Item #: R0430400828
Due Date: 11/4/2011

2:
Title: The Oprah phenomenon /
Item #: R0424628743
Due Date: 11/4/2011

-Please retain for your records-

ERODRIGU

avoid the choices you've made," the American flag waves brightly on the Steinbeck house in the background. The lesson turns to the benefits of education, with Thom revealing that his dad taught him to love education and that teachers are his "favorite people." Grammer and Thom agree that, with this novel, you get to participate in its meaning by "filling in parts." Because "you do the work," they say, "books are better than film," allowing readers to use their own ideas and imagination. The episode concludes with the new charity component of Oprah's Book Club: Oprah's Angel Network will give $50,000 worth of books to Monterey County children from proceeds from the sale of Oprah's Book Club products on the Web site.

From this example, it is apparent that Winfrey has effectively implemented a set script that has two themes: (1) you are responsible for your own choices, and (2) educating yourself in literature is part of achieving the American Dream. The timshel idea—that even though you cannot control what you have been given, you can control what you do about it—dovetails neatly with the prevailing discourse in *The Oprah Winfrey Show* critiqued by Epstein and Steinberg. As they point out, "a dominant assumption of Oprah, her guests and studio audience, and of the ways in which the show is structured, seems to be that choices are freely made and can be altered at will and by 'working on oneself.'" As they show, the "notion that choice is free, rather than contingent, clearly undermines an audience's willingness to consider" how outside factors "might reduce the parameters of the possible."[20] Winfrey's management of her first classic literary selection, then, perfectly coincides with the dominant discourse of her show, supporting the idea that the American Dream is available to everyone in modified versions and that no systemic forces prevent one's achievement of that dream. Further, the educational mission of this version of Oprah's Book Club envelops literary classics into consumer capitalism by making them a pathway toward the American Dream: reading the classics with the help of the experts on the Oprah Web site is to choose travel, celebrities, and charity work, all of which are accoutrements of having "made it," in that they represent disposable time and income. This Oprah's Book Club helps you acquire the classics the way you might acquire the diamond pinkie ring Winfrey was sporting a few years back.

Although the overt plot of Winfrey's classics book club seems clear, we might expect and even hope that inherent contradictions will create symptoms that eventually erupt into show discourse. One possible "soft spot" for future eruptions is the international emphasis, which may allow concerns about globalization to come to the forefront or may become increasingly problematic to maintain while the United States pursues aggressive antiterrorist policies, such as the war in Iraq. Protesters could effectively target the traveling book club, and although the created show would not contain that footage, the nightly news could. The costs of travel and security could get expensive. Another potential source of eruption lies in the audience of fans, who, like my students, may find the controlling discourse too patronizing and narrow. Confined to a small space in the revamped book discussions, they may choose to drop Oprah's Book Club altogether.[21]

Notes

1. Debbie Epstein and Deborah Lynn Steinberg, "American Dreamin': Discoursing Liberally on *The Oprah Winfrey Show*," *Women's Studies International Forum* 21, no. 1 (1998): 77–94.

2. All my information on Oprah's Book Club episodes comes from either transcripts supplied by Burrelle's transcripts or videotapes of the episodes. I owe a deep debt to Dinah Peterson, who supplied me with all her personal tapes of Oprah's Book Club episodes.

3. Cecilia Konchar Farr, *Reading Oprah: How Oprah's Book Club Changed the Way America Reads* (Albany, N.Y.: SUNY Press, 2005), 65, 139.

4. Kathleen Rooney, *Reading with Oprah: The Book Club that Changed America* (Fayetteville: University of Arkansas Press, 2005), 42.

5. Ibid., xii.

6. Frederic Jameson, *The Political Unconscious* (Ithaca, N.Y.: Cornell University Press, 1982), 49.

7. George Mair, *Oprah Winfrey: The Real Story* (Secaucus, N.J.: Citadel Stars Book, 1996), 352–55.

8. Epstein and Steinberg, "American Dreamin'," 78.

9. Susan Wise Bauer, "Oprah's Misery Index," *Christianity Today* 42, no. 14 (1998): 71.

10. R. Mark Hall, "The 'Oprahfication' of Literacy: Reading 'Oprah's Book Club,'" *College English* 65, no. 6 (July 2003): 648.

11. Rooney, *Reading with Oprah*, ch. 3, attempts to divide the book club selections by making some similar critical and aesthetic judgments, although it differs considerably from my effort here by labeling the books as good or bad.

12. "Oprah's Book Club," January 24, 2001 (transcript), 1, 5, 23, 11, 16.

13. Charles Paul Freund, "Franzen's Folly: The Novelist vs. High Art's Dark Other," *Reason* 33, no. 8 (January 2002): 59.

14. Francine Fialkoff, "Franzen: Too Highbrow for Oprah?" *Library Journal* 126, no. 19 (November 15, 2001): 52.

15. See ibid.; Freund, "Franzen's Folly"; and Kathy Rooney, "Oprah Learns Her Lesson," *Nation* 274, no. 19 (May 20, 2002): 56–60.

16. Chris Lehmann, "The Oprah Wars," *American Prospect,* December 2, 2002, 40.

17. Jonathan Franzen, *How to Be Alone: Essays* (New York: Picador, 2003).

18. Rooney, "Oprah Learns Her Lesson," 57.

19. Rooney, *Reading with Oprah,* takes a decidedly different view of the classics version of the book club, seeing it as a "marked improvement" (191). Her reading of each of the elements I discuss is entirely positive (185–212).

20. Epstein and Steinberg, "American Dreamin'," 83.

21. As this collection goes to press, Winfrey has already abandoned the classics version of the book club, following a summer of three Faulkner novels. The third version of the book club will focus on memoirs. In terms of my thesis, this change offers enough material for another essay.

Some Lessons before Dying

*Gender, Morality, and the Missing Critical Discourse
in Oprah's Book Club*

Roberta F. Hammett and Audrey Dentith

As educators, feminists, cultural critics, and lovers of reading for pleasure, we are fascinated by Oprah's Book Club. Oprah Winfrey's ability
to call attention to the work of otherwise marginalized authors and to
promote a widened readership of their novels among a largely conventional fiction-reading public—as she did in the original incarnation of
the book club—is remarkable. It is doubtful that writers of color such as
Ernest Gaines, Maya Angelou, and Toni Morrison would have become
household names and best-selling authors without the status and publicity that flowed from Winfrey's endorsement of their writing. With
professional as well as personal excitement, we awaited the announcement of each selection, anticipating the possibility of dynamic public
conversations about the significant social issues of race, class, gender,
and sexuality that were central to the works chosen. We hoped for improved literacy practices and serious, erudite conversations occurring
in the public sphere of daytime television. Clearly, we presumed that
Winfrey's selections, which highlighted significant social and cultural
issues, would evoke the interest of individuals who might not otherwise
engage in such discussions. Their interest, in turn, would demand and
thus facilitate new reading practices.

Unfortunately, we were disappointed: Winfrey did not facilitate
these critical discussions as we envisioned them. Her treatment of the
works seemed superficial and purposeless, barely addressing the significant themes and issues of power and marginality with which the

books' authors engaged. Overall, Winfrey did not take advantage of opportunities to encourage critical discourse that might have promoted a
greater understanding of the nature of race, culture, identity, and class
in our society. By foregrounding facile readings of the works, Winfrey ultimately foreclosed any possibility for an actual deconstruction of
the dynamics of power that alternative readings might have opened up.
That such conversations never materialized may be key to the original
book club's eventual demise—perhaps we were not the only disappointed consumers.[1] Criticisms of the social politics were not the only
ones mounted. Some observers criticized Winfrey's lack of literary or
cultural sophistication in her book club activities, while others made
disparaging remarks about the soap opera–like quality of the show itself
and the host's indignant responses to criticisms of her choices, both
literary and interpretive.

Yet, despite this barrage of criticism, we still believe that the original Oprah's Book Club possesses an enormous amount of value as a
cultural artifact and institution. Attending to the operations of the club
allows us to deconstruct Winfrey's pedagogical strategies as a means of
illuminating the tacit ideologies she favors. We argue that it was these
ideologies, manifest as particular pedagogical practices, that curtailed
the book club's potential and worked to surreptitiously (and successfully) thwart the achievement of a critical discourse and an emergent
critical literacy among participants.

Oprah's Book Club

Beginning in 1996 (and ending in 2002), Winfrey promoted books
that she selected for her audience to read, and she did so in various
ways. First, she named the selection with great fanfare at the end of
a book club show and repeated the announcement on several subsequent occasions. After this on-air announcement, however, electronic
media assumed the primary role as disseminator of book club information. Reading guides appeared on Oprah.com, accompanied by other
background information and resources; a newsletter was distributed to
e-mail subscribers; and an electronic discussion board was established.
Through these various forums, *The Oprah Winfrey Show* solicited guests
for the televised book club discussion.

Oprah's Book Club, designed to get "America reading again,"[2] certainly appeared to produce new readers among the American public. On the discussion boards in particular, participants described how Oprah's Book Club had transformed them from nonreaders to avid readers. For example, one person wrote:

> I didn't like to read. I can't remember reading a book since high school. That is until *The Reader.* I loved that book and have not stopped reading from Oprah's choices. I even went back to the beginning and have read most of her selections. I have recently joined a Barnes and Noble book club where we discuss Oprah's books. Thanks Oprah.[3]

Another reader, Shirley, offers a similar experience:

> I read very seldom. . . . I decided to "catch the wave." I bought the current book, loved it, listened to the book club, and I was hooked. Since then, I have read every book which Oprah was reviewing, and thoroughly enjoyed the book reviews. It's so much fun to see the review after reading the books. . . . I have truly fallen in love with reading.[4]

During the *White Oleander* show, one anonymous audience member confessed:

> I have not read a book since high school. I hated reading. I even faked my way through all my reading courses in high school and college. I read this whole thing cover to cover and just couldn't stop. It was wonderful.[5]

Winfrey found such testaments rewarding. After all, such proclamations not only affirmed that the book club was functioning as intended—to "get America reading"—but also illustrated that readers were being transformed by this experience. Perhaps most rewarding for Winfrey was their appreciation for something she valued. As she stated in one book club episode:

> I am overjoyed that so many of you shared in my passion for reading. Some of you who didn't have a passion now have a

passion. It's been one of the many gratifying things that you all have allowed me to do on this show, so thanks to everybody who has been reading for reading and watching.[6]

If such personal accounts by previous nonreaders were not enough, book sales further demonstrated that Winfrey was successful in encouraging adult reading.

Independent of any critique of Winfrey's interpretive practices, getting adults to read is an important accomplishment in and of itself. Studies have demonstrated that literacy activities practiced in the home strongly influence children's learning and their later school success. Similarly, the literacy practices of adults promote their ongoing learning and enhance their skills and confidence.[7] Further, we maintain that reading produces particular kinds of knowledge and has great potential to shape social values and cultural understanding. However, it is our contention that the pedagogies of the original Oprah's Book Club and the way these books were selected, discussed, and celebrated favored particular forms of knowledge and social practices. This proclivity on the part of Winfrey ultimately limited the potential for developing a more sophisticated critical literacy among readers. Her strategies and activities, in fact, served to reify particular constructions of gender among women and to promote unrestricted individualism—values that are highly privileged and often work to thwart social critique and a more critical citizenry.

Winfrey's Pedagogies

From the beginning, Oprah's Book Club sanctioned particular reading practices. For example, *The Oprah Winfrey Show* provided reading guides on a weekly basis that focused on direct textual meanings—that is, on authorial intention. Discussions tended to center around what given scenes or events signified, what metaphors and symbols were used by the author and what they denoted, what the various characters in the work represented, and what the themes were and how various textual elements contributed to their development. Scholars of reading often refer to such interpretive practices as "close readings," and they point out that such strategies tend to favor transparency and directness over evasiveness and ambiguity. In close reading, there is generally only one meaning—or, to be more direct, one moral—to be drawn from a creative work. This was the pedagogical approach most often deployed in high school literature classes of the 1960s, so it is appropriate that Winfrey, educated during this period, should choose it as her approach to literary study.

This emphasis on themes, plotline and structure, narrative style of the author (including voice), characters and their actions, and the meaning or significance of quotations, objects, or events was also evident in the other book club forums. Questions about these aspects of the books were common in the electronic discussion boards, and during the book club shows, Winfrey often focused the conversation on these elements. For example, in one humorous exchange during *The Poisonwood Bible* show, when members of the Page Turners Book Club told Winfrey that they voted on the best sex scene in the novels they had read, Winfrey mocked, "Forget plot lines, themes, antagonists,"[8] as though such items were the only true indicators of one's ability to read and understand texts.

Likewise, Winfrey encouraged her audience to focus on the descriptive power of the language and its metaphorical meanings. During the episode featuring *White Oleander,* she commented, "And did most of you all know that that's the metaphor for Ingrid, that she's beautiful but toxic? I love it when you figure that out."[9] "Getting it," or intuiting the preferred or authorized understanding of a book or passage, was a common concern. For example, Winfrey commented about *Cane River,* "It's a book about the author's own ancestors and how they triumph over extreme hardship. We received thousands of letters from so many of you who found strength in the struggles of the four women in *Cane River.* Thank you all for writing. And even more than that, thank you all for getting it, because so many of you hit upon points that were exactly what the author had set out to do."[10]

Complementing this traditional text-centered reading practice was Winfrey's experiential-based response to works. In reading-response practices and pedagogies, the focus is on the meanings that readers create when their reading is shaped by their experiences, predispositions, and knowledge.[11] It is appropriate, then, that Winfrey, who frequently uses her own experience to form a sympathetic bond with others or to interpret their experiences, took this approach during television broadcasts and in electronic book discussions. For example, she invited readers to "testify," that is, to describe how the book affected them and changed their own life perspectives.[12] In the *White Oleander* discussion, Winfrey remarked, "I love it when a book can change the way you look at things."[13] One reader admitted on the discussion board:

> I am so fortunate to have experienced this book. It taught me that my problems for that one day or one month, could never be as bad as what Astrid went through and at such a young age. It taught me to never take for granted anything I receive and to make sure that for every person I meet in my life, to learn something from that person.[14]

Another reader expressed a similar connection with the book:

> As a mother of 3 little girls who left an abusive marriage, no car, no home, I could not help but relate to the mother of this book. I keep making comparisons between the daughters and my own girls.[15]

Others described how they were inspired to change their lives as a result of reading Winfrey's book club selections:

> I never read fiction until August of 2000. I looked towards each new Oprah bookclub book as an assignment with a book report due at the end. I didn't know I had it in me to finish a book due to my busy life being a mother, but I did and now I'm in college. I wouldn't be here today with out learning I had it in me to finish five bookclub books in a row. Thanks Oprah.[16]

Clearly, the act of sympathetically identifying with fictional characters led these readers to reassess their own lives, even if it did not necessarily force a more critical engagement with hegemonic forces or discourses. The act of drawing comparisons with these characters vis-à-vis reader response has the potential to inspire and even motivate.

Obviously, textual interpretation and reader response are sound pedagogical tools that serve a particular purpose in opening up a text, whether it be cultural or personal education. Certainly, it seems obvi-

ous that Oprah's Book Club was consciously and deliberately pedagogical, in that it intended readers to engage critically with a work and
provided the guidance and methods to do so. In fact, readers attested
to new competencies, pleasures, and literary insights as a result of their
participation in the book club. However, Winfrey's prioritizing of these
particular pedagogies limited the scope of interpretation in significant
ways. In particular, we note three areas of limitation that served to reify
popular but injurious social beliefs and values, as well as detract from
readers' abilities to deconstruct existing power relations and challenge
existing structures. They are (1) the practice of gendered readings of the
selections and Winfrey's approaches to interpretation; (2) the overreliance
on morality and individual self-improvement; and (3) the glaring absence
of a discourse of critical literacy regarding the nature of power relations
with respect to race, class, gender, ethnicity, and sexual orientation.

Gendered Reading

Like the audience of *The Oprah Winfrey Show* and the heroines of the
book club selections, the original book club participants were usually
women. Female authors outnumbered males by approximately three
to one, and almost all the novels' protagonists were female. Men occasionally attended Oprah Book Club shows, where they were in the
minority. During *The Poisonwood Bible* episode, Winfrey called first on
Steve, "the only man in the room." When Steve claimed that he "loved
it," Winfrey was pleased to conclude, "And it's also a guy book."[17] Yet
participating in Oprah's Book Club is clearly not understood as a "masculine" activity. In an online discussion, Sean said the following:

> I am a man and i love watching Oprah show. . . . Oprah does
> not touch many mens hearts around here but like it does me
> and my friend Daniel . . . people at school think we are like gay
> but were not we just think oprah is like better than anything
> else . . . and we want to become part of the Oprah book club.
> . . . I know it is a book review but i just had to get it out and
> let it out for the coolest idol me and dan have.[18]

In effect, an ideological supposition that reading is one of "women's
pleasures" is understood and reified. Moreover, Winfrey herself does not

problematize this notion when she categorizes a work as "a guy book." Instead, her comments help solidify conventional notions of women as natural readers of sentimental and emotionally laden works.

That few men participate—or admit to participating—in Oprah's Book Club may not be due solely to the emotional tenor of the novels; another factor may be the female-centered narrative. The heroine may be white, black, or Asian; she may be mixed race; but she is generally always young, intelligent, resourceful, and artistic. Frequently she is thwarted or meets unreasonable opposition; the narrative trajectory documents her attempts to overcome these limitations, and readers inevitably sympathize and thus identify with her. In this way, the selections of Oprah's Book Club invoke the nineteenth-century tradition of sentimental novels written for an audience of women. Notably, in the sentimental novel, the heroine's adventure or trouble is rarely external, resulting from travel or an experience in the wider world; instead, it is usually internal or domestic, often under her own roof. For the contemporary television viewer, home has the potential to be such a site, one that might equally reproduce the elements of danger, trauma, and cruelty. These elements are apparent in such selections as *White Oleander* and *Black and Blue*.

As in the nineteenth-century novel, the contemporary protagonist of Oprah's Book Club selections exhibits similar resources in overcoming her situation. That is, the central female character must be morally sound and necessarily capable if she is to overcome the inequalities and hardship she faces. Key to such triumph is, of course, learning to recognize her own talents and resourcefulness and using her individual capabilities to seize opportunities within herself. In this way, Oprah's Book Club selections imply a naturalized construction of female or male identities and, in particular, a specific feminine ideal.

Of significant interest, however, is the fact that in the majority of the novels discussed, or in the discussions of the novels themselves, this recognition of one's own abilities, talents, or resourcefulness is usually not contingent on or influenced by social politics or cultural identities. Gender, race, and social class are not significant indicators of oppression or privilege but, rather, benign descriptors that are not related to or determined by the dynamics of the social power relations inherent in the everyday lives of the characters. It is more often a matter of individual aptitude and stamina, a simple case of using one's own will and dexterity to meet and master obstacles—not unlike the narrative of Winfrey's own rise. In effect, such stories and the ways they are discussed within the many venues of Oprah's Book Club all work to minimize the social implications of cultural identities, including gender, race, and social class, and thwart any deeper understanding of social politics in the contemporary world. Ultimately, these notions reify a culture of individualism while subverting the importance of gender, race, or class identities. As a result, gender (as well as other aspects of identity) is considered to embody natural, biological, undisputable, and insignificant qualities. Although this may not be problematic for those who read for pleasure, these situations may tacitly convey the belief that central flaws are manifest among women and must be overcome individually. Women must then celebrate their own achievement of success and happiness without any challenge to or question of society's gendered notions and the limitations that emanate from these beliefs. Women, thus, are urged to adapt and succumb to society's demands or expectations rather than develop the tools and skills to both challenge and subvert dominant ideologies that limit women's (and men's) roles in society.

Morality and Self-Improvement

Janet Fitch, author of the novel *White Oleander*, commented:

> I think that Oprah's on a mission to improve the lives of the average American in various ways. And one of them is to bring literature to people who would normally not be quite as demanding in their reading tastes, to show them that writing can be more than just entertainment. That it can change people, it can make us more human.[19]

Although Winfrey's pedagogies might seem predictable and somewhat superficial, a significant intent is apparent in her book club selections. Nearly all the books conform to a particular pattern, which is largely characterized by the main character's oppressive childhood, terror as an adult or prolonged exposure to abuse and mistreatment, or unfortunate possession of some appreciably misunderstood trait. That all the central characters are able to overcome their fate is moving and inspirational for readers.

One of the prompts on the electronic discussion board asked readers: "Has an Oprah's Book Club book changed your life in any way?
Do you have a different outlook because of something a Book Club
discussion guest or author said on the show? Tell us your story." As
requested, respondents took advantage of the opportunity to describe
not only their transformation into avid readers but also their journeys
toward self-improvement and self-empowerment. As a woman identifying herself as "nelly arrigan" wrote:

> its because of u oprah that I have the courage to get up every
> morning. you helped me beat my drug addiction and survive
> the trauma of teenage pregnancy. i watched one of your pro-
> grammes and learned that i can lead a better life and i have
> the courage within to face the challenges that each day will
> bring. Thanks to your programme i have learned that life is to
> be enjoyed rather than endured.[20]

Another respondent, ANGI JOY, wrote (using all uppercase letters):

> I was given the book *She's Come Undone,* and I related to many
> of the experiences and tragedies that happened. My divorce is
> not done yet, but the abuse is no longer there and my 4 year
> old and I are starting a new life in a new state and are very
> happy. The whale episode I related to in a very personal way,
> but with the dolphins and now we can go down to the pier
> 20 min. from our home and watch them play and it gives me
> a sense of accomplishment that I was in a very bad place, and
> I made the change, and the difference for a better life. I smile
> again, and my daughter is finally happy. Thank you so much
> for helping me know that I can do it with a little courage and
> a lot of determination."[21]

These messages attest to the success of Oprah's Book Club as a means
to actually improve the lives of readers and help them overcome adversity. As Winfrey told *Publishers Weekly,* "It's another thing for somebody
who hasn't picked up a book since they were forced to in high school
to read [Morrison's] *Song of Solomon* and start thinking differently about
their own life as a result."[22]

Winfrey's early book selections exemplified a literary tradition that has become the American standard. It is most firmly centered in the moral tradition that began with books such as *The New England Primer* (1686–1690)[23] and continues in the present with the explicit didacticism of William J. Bennett's *The Book of Virtues*. In early America, as today, popular fiction and inexpensive street literature competed for women's reading time with more morally uplifting books intent on teaching them how to improve their lives.[24] Winfrey has commented frequently on the power of books to teach and inspire. She explains, "I learned to read at age three and soon discovered there was a whole world to conquer that went beyond our farm in Mississippi."[25] Elsewhere she claims, "Books showed me there were possibilities in life, that there were actually people like me living in a world I could not only aspire to but attain. Reading gave me hope. For me, it was an open door."[26] Each novel in the original incarnation of the book club coincided with this tradition of American moral intent. Each one was read and discussed in order to teach the audience how to overcome hardship and make their lives better through their own volition. This style of didactic education overemphasizes a model of individualistic self-improvement that fits only too well with American ideological traditions. A moral approach to life's hardships, rugged individualism, and a "pull yourself up by the bootstraps" mentality all underline commonly understood American values and standards.

Of course, such stories aptly describe the trajectory of Winfrey's own life journey and, as such, offer the illusion that such success must surely be the reward of all who truly believe and persist. Oprah's Book Club selections tell a story—her own story—over and over again in different ways with different characters and different situations, all of which are presented as a means of inspiring and encouraging a supposedly downtrodden American reader. This story of the self-made individual is an all-too-familiar American refrain that presumes equal access to opportunity for all, regardless of identity or social status. Thus, race, class, and gender become nonexistent or insignificant identities within an overemphasized individualistic ideal of one's own abilities, aptitude, and potential for success. Oprah's Book Club selections and her pedagogies work to affirm and repeat such ideologies in a wide and very public arena.

Winfrey's ideologies acquiesce to a liberal, dominant American ideology that urges us to pull ourselves up by our own bootstraps. Winfrey, it seems, has decided that her readers can be similarly motivated, as she was, and are just as likely to encounter the much-deserved rewards that she did. Janet Lowe describes Winfrey as "black, southern, born out of wedlock and into poverty," adding, "nevertheless, at an early age she decided—she chose—to take charge of her destiny and become a woman of influence."[27] And Winfrey herself says:

> I was raised with an outhouse, no plumbing. Nobody had any clue that my life could be anything but working in some factory or cotton field in Mississippi. Nobody—nobody. I feel so strongly that my life is to be used as an example to show people what can be done.[28]

Like the previously quoted respondents on the electronic bulletin board, characters in Oprah's Book Club selections often construct new identities, literally and figuratively. Frannie, the abused wife of a police officer in *Black and Blue,* by Anna Quindlen, leaves him and assumes a new life. Dolores's psychotherapist in Wally Lamb's *She's Come Undone* advises her, "If you will only visualize your own beauty you can make it real. . . . On a symbolic level, we could say you are midwifing yourself, . . . couldn't we?"[29] Ninah, in *The Rapture of Canaan,* reinvents her own story: "I weave in lies, and I weave in love, and in the end, it's hard to know if one keeps me warmer than the other. . . . It's imperfect, but I could walk on it."[30]

This is not to say that the Oprah's Book Club selections uniformly end with the characters embracing isolation and disengagement; this is not so. In each case, the self, in the process of being remade by the self, turns outward to society at large. Turning outward and embracing community is presented as a means of affirming the self, the ultimate affirmation. In *The Book of Ruth,* the title character decides, "Each man's struggle is mine." Dominick adopts his ex-girlfriend's baby, goes to lunch with his hated stepfather, volunteers at the children's cancer ward, reunites with his wife, and embraces his newfound Native community.[31] It is unfortunate that Oprah's Book Club does not incorporate such an outward turn and encourage readers to act together to bring about systemic change.

The Missing Critical Discourse

Ultimately, although it inspired many to read and some to act, this first version of Oprah's Book Club failed to provide a forum for the development of cultural and critical literacies among its participants. Rather, the pedagogical approaches taken by Winfrey resulted in a reinscription of conventional American beliefs and ideologies. The televised episodes and Internet discussions did not consent to any deepened discussion of marginalization as represented by many of the books' central characters. The discussions on television and on the Internet failed to consider aspects of discrimination experienced by certain social groups and the power relations that support marginalization and exclusion, a necessary foundation for the development of expanded forms of literacy, such as cultural and critical literacies.[32]

Cultural and critical pedagogies work to promote an understanding of culture and power as evidenced by the social relations depicted in stories and events in our society. Cultural literacy promotes an awareness of the social attributes of race, class, gender, nationality, and ethnicity. Critical and cultural literacies involve the uncovering of practices and representations that are arranged and prescribed to create particular meanings. Cultural literacy practices, which operate from a perspective that attends to social relations and social constructions, include discussions of language, images, and written representations that help us understand others and ourselves in particular ways. It is the revelation and articulation of taken-for-granted meanings that can "help us locate ourselves and others in the economic, social, and political relations of our times."[33] Discussion of the cultural symbols and practices manifest in the stories told by these authors might pave the way for the acquisition of critical literacy and deeper understanding. Such critical literacy helps us make meaning of our interactions and experiences by illuminating the scripts that determine how people view themselves and their relationships to others from different social situations and statuses.[34]

In our analysis of the transcripts of several *Oprah* shows, presented later, we point out specific opportunities to illuminate the cultural relevance of particular events, language, and themes that might have led readers to develop a more critical perspective. Instead, Winfrey "missed" or avoided such conversations and instead substituted her own sentimental or liberal interpretations, as discussed earlier. At significant junctures, Winfrey failed to take cues provided by her audience participants and guests, resulting in unrealized potential for discourse about and engagement with controversial issues and missed opportunities to further the literacy of her viewing audience. On many occasions, she even distorted the spoken words of others in ways that avoided or circumvented forms of social and cultural critique, a maneuver that indicates her ultimate attention to popularity polls and television ratings.

As noted previously, reader response privileges "feeling" as the most the significant aspect of a reading. This practice was evident in the *Cane River* book discussion when one unidentified woman remarked, "My own parents were brought together with the idea that they would produce light-skinned children." Another replied, "the color-struck issue is still prevalent today. I feel sad about that for our people. We're still judging people on color instead of character." The idea of identity as a purely individual construction as opposed to a partially socially constituted one fits with the liberal notions of racism facilitated by Winfrey and characterized in this discussion. The suggestion is that racism can be eradicated by sympathetic identification, leading to regret and a desire to judge people more fairly. Later in the *Cane River* discussion, an audience member commented, "The Sunday gatherings in the book inspired me to start a tradition of my own with my family." Another shared, "I truly loved *Cane River* because it connected me with my history and the women in my family." Another speaker said, "It touched my soul."[35] But, we add, it did not propel any of the viewers to examine the inequities of race, class, and so forth, or at least not according to the script of the show.

Culturally, we accept the notion that readers should connect personally and emotionally to the texts they read; however, this form of interpretive identification can also result in a superficial form of reading, and it does not help writers such as Lalita Tademy realize their objectives. During her episode, Tademy commented, "In going back and doing a lot of research, what I found was that—that the field slaves and house slaves were treated differently and some people played into that. And it lasted—it's one of the repercussions, I believe, of slavery that we are still living with, in part, today."[36] Winfrey failed to engage and expand on this key point of the text, one that might have taken the readers into a more critical discussion of intra- as well as interracial relations. Instead, Winfrey selected one Ms. Gilliam to participate in the dinner-party discussion, and her interpretation of the book was summed up in her comment, "I realized when I read this book that we are all one family."[37] Such comments allude to a color-blind philosophy, so prevalent in the United States, that diminishes the social structures that privilege whites and marginalize people of color.

A more critical approach on Winfrey's part would encourage readers to reflect deeply on their identities, the political ramifications of their multiple subject positions, the social structures that limit those on the margins, and the possibilities for engaging in a process of identity (re)construction that might unsettle their contentment with the worldview.[38] Such identities and views are sources of power and privilege—or not. Reflecting on multiple subject positions means understanding how marginalization within one category (for example, race) may be offset by privileges in another (for example, sexuality or class). Questioning and destabilizing the privileges associated with these identities is a social project that all can participate in and that provides an opportunity to move from talk to action.

Winfrey too often closed down chances for a more critical, ideological discussion of the books she chose because they explored issues with political and social significance. For example, during *The Poisonwood Bible* show, an anonymous audience member observed. "I noticed in reading *The Poisonwood Bible* that we often assume that we know better than other cultures. How presumptuous of us to think that we can change cultures that have been in place for thousands of years." Rather than using this opportunity to discuss American imperialism, past and present, Winfrey joked, "Go on, testify." This response conveyed a sense of the personal guilt Americans might feel, but unfortunately, it lightened the tone of the conversation, which then moved on to a discussion of how good the book was. Nonetheless, Winfrey's announcement script had her characterize the book as an examination of a "shameful chapter in U.S. history that shattered the Congo dream for independence." Author Barbara Kingsolver then gave a detailed explanation of the political context of the book and her background research and concluded:

And at this moment in history [1959–1960], the United States stepped in and usurped the independence of the Belgian Congo. This is a book about taking responsibility, really, and finding redemption. We have to live with this. We didn't make that decision. You didn't, I didn't, but we inherited that decision. We have to live with it.

The book ends with the words "Walk forward into the light." Don't forget that this was done in our names, but take it, use it, make the future something different, something better on account of it.[39]

Winfrey, dumbstruck, said, "Wow." And then she asked, "Can you imagine spending twenty years writing a book?" There was no discussion in this episode of what form acts of redemption might take, nor was there an opportunity to explore how to take responsibility or make the future different. In fact, the ensuing conversation moved on to writing, personal connections with characters and plotlines, and, inevitably, the previously taped dinner-party book discussion. As the audience prepared to view the segment in which four lucky readers joined Winfrey and Kingsolver amid white linen, crystal, china, and shiny flatware, an audience member observed how meaningless the contents of the hope chest became. Winfrey commented, "Yeah, you look at your own life differently, did you not, too?"[40] No one seemed to notice that the materialistic splendor of the set provided a sharp contrast to the context of the book and the insights just expressed by the audience.

Later in the show, Winfrey again missed the point when Kingsolver commented on a pivotal paragraph in the book:

I really wanted to do two things, two big things for my readers. One is that I wanted to lay open this secret part of our history that we don't even want to know about, this awful thing that our government did to the Congo. But that's only half—that was only half the task of this book. I also wanted to ask, "Now what?" for every person who has ever asked themselves, "How do I live in a world where men do such abominable things to their own kind? How do I live? How do I raise my kids in the presence of evil?"[41]

Winfrey's next words (to the readers at the table) were, "Tell me how the book changed you, or moved you, opened you?" This question failed to elicit a conversation in response to Kingsolver's query but allowed guest Wright to raise the issue of the missionary family's useless possessions, prompting Winfrey to comment, "reading it made me think of all the just—amenities of my life that you [I] absolutely take for granted"[42]

Winfrey's responsibility is, primarily, to entertain American daytime television viewers, and we are fully cognizant of the fact that serious, critical exploration cannot dominate every show and book discussion. However, as the facilitator of these discussions, Winfrey failed to take up some of the issues that were clearly intended by the authors. She failed to make even the slightest connection between the social issues raised in these books and some of the concerns she has discussed on other shows and promoted in her philanthropic activities such as the Children's Miracle Network—an indication of the popular television hostess's resolve not to stir the waters of controversy. As long as she kept things light and focused on individual experiences and interpretations, the implicit ideologies of mainstream America were left untouched and unchallenged.

In the discussion of *White Oleander*, a book that presents an indictment of the foster care system, Winfrey diverted attention too quickly from a guest's comment on institutionalized social work ("It should be mandatory reading for anybody who's working in foster care") to her own enjoyment of the book. Author Janet Fitch commented on her role as an artist: "I think rather than trying to fix ourselves into some sort of physical perfection or, you know, psychological perfection, I think we—we'd be better off putting that energy into being more human, trying to deepen ourselves, trying to care about other people more and accepting." But again, Winfrey deflected the point, offering a toast instead: "Well, here's to you, Janet Fitch, and one of—certainly one of the best books I've ever read."[43] There was no opportunity to explore Fitch's question of how we can be more human, how we can improve our world in a day-to-day, here-and-now way, and in a way that Winfrey actually accomplishes on some of her shows.

One might have expected this pattern of evasion to change when Winfrey broached a work that explicitly addresses one of the most complex issues in American life: race.[44] In particular, *Cane River* attempts to initiate a discussion about the construction of race and white privilege. As author Lalita Tademy said in her introduction at the beginning of the show, "One of the things that I didn't want to sidestep when I wrote this book was my own discomfort with my great-grandmother Emily's color-struck attitudes, and that is her having a sort of a—liking people better that were light skinned as opposed to darker skinned." Winfrey later noted, "I knew that you would start some stuff in the country with everybody," but she did not proceed beyond that observation.[45] Comments on race remained superficial, failing to make explicit and problematic the multiple differences within African American life and their relation to whiteness and its continuing privileges. Even talk of slavery was silenced because it makes white people feel guilty.

Obviously, the book club selections raised imperative social issues of race, poverty, and oppression, and just as obviously, Winfrey chose them in part for their foregrounding of such issues. During conversations with the authors and audience members, important questions were raised that might have led to a critical examination of power structures in the United States and how they are maintained. However, as we have demonstrated, despite the possibilities for critical discourse, Winfrey missed those opportunities. Although we feel some sense of loss over the celebrated (original) Oprah's Book Club enterprise, we believe that a more thoughtful format might have shaped this endeavor in significant ways that might have prompted important conversations among Americans. We mourn the many possibilities not realized, for Oprah's Book Club might have named and described a critical project, an emergent critical literacy among a wider American public and a social justice political agenda—a new American Dream.

Notes

1. David Teather, "Chat Queen Shelves Her Book Club," *Guardian,* April 8, 2002.

2. Ibid.

3. aimeeswede, message boards, www.Oprah.com, 07:53 P.M., April 27, 2001, message 4 of 118, "Oprah's Book Club Discussion: Has Oprah's Book Club Changed your Life?" http://boards.oprah.com/WebX?13@66.gN5BbIf0Fua.2@. eed99d7.

4. "*White Oleander*/Oprah's Book Club," *The Oprah Winfrey Show,* June 15, 1999 (Burrelle's transcript), 5.

5. Ibid.

6. "*Cane River*/Oprah's Book Club," *The Oprah Winfrey Show,* September 24, 2001 (Burrelle's transcript), 1.

7. Lesley Mandel Morrow, *Literacy Development in the Early Years* (Boston:

Allyn and Bacon, 1997); Denny Taylor, *Family Literacy: Young Children Learning to Read and Write* (Portsmouth, N.H.: Heinemann, 1987).

8. "*The Poisonwood Bible*/Oprah's Book Club," *The Oprah Winfrey Show*, August 23, 2000 (Burrelle's transcript), 3.

9. "*White Oleander*/Oprah's Book Club," 1.

10. "*Cane River*/Oprah's Book Club," 4.

11. Wolfgang Iser, *The Act of Reading* (Baltimore: Johns Hopkins Press, 1978); Judith A. Langer, "Literacy and Schooling: A Sociocognitive Perspective," in *Literacy for a Diverse Society,* ed. Elfrieda Hiebert (New York: Teachers College Press, 1991); Louise M. Rosenblatt, *The Reader, the Text, the Poem: The Transactional Theory of the Literary Work* (Carbondale: Southern Illinois University Press, 1978); Jane Tompkins, ed., *Reader Response Criticism: From Formalism to Poststructuralism* (Baltimore: Johns Hopkins Press, 1981).

12. "*The Poisonwood Bible*/Oprah's Book Club," 5.

13. "*White Oleander*/Oprah's Book Club," 6.

14. Sun Moon Stars, message boards, www.Oprah.com, 03:13 P.M., May 10, 2001, message 37 of 118.

15. Francine, message boards, www.Oprah.com, 12:52 A.M., May 11, 2001, message 40 of 118.

16. Kathy23061, message boards, www.Oprah.com, 8:49 P.M., April 30, 2001, message 7 of 118.

17. "*The Poisonwood Bible*/Oprah's Book Club," 1–2.

18. Sean, message boards, www.Oprah.com, 11:51 P.M., July 19, 2001, message 70 of 118.

19. Laura Miller, "On Writing *White Oleander,*" in *White Oleander* by Janet Fitch (Boston: Little, Brown, 1999), end pages.

20. nelly arrigan, message boards, www.Oprah.com, 04:12 P.M., May 20, 2001, message 14 of 118.

21. ANGI JOY, message boards, www.Oprah.com, 01:32 P.M., September 3, 2001, message 94 of 118.

22. "Oprah's Book Club Enters a New Chapter by Cutting Back," CNN International.com, April 2, 2002, http://edition.cnn.com/2002/SHOWBIZ/books/04/05/oprah.book.club/index.html.

23. Cited in Harvey J. Graff, *The Legacies of Literacy: Continuities and Contradictions in Western Culture and Society* (Bloomington: Indiana University Press, 1987).

24. Ibid.

25. Bill Adler, *The Uncommon Wisdom of Oprah Winfrey* (Secaucus, N.J.: Birch Lane Press, 1997), 52.

26. Alan Ebert, "Oprah Winfrey Talks Openly about Oprah," *Good Housekeeping,* September 1991, 62, cited in Janet Lowe, *Oprah Winfrey Speaks: Insight from the World's Most Influential Voice* (New York: John Wiley and Sons, 1998), 21.

27. Lowe, *Oprah Winfrey Speaks,* xiii.

28. Kinny Littlefield, "Oprah Still Enjoying Her Power," *St. Louis Post-Dispatch,* May 28, 1997, cited in Lowe, *Oprah Winfrey Speaks,* 8.

29. Wally Lamb, *She's Come Undone* (New York: Random House, 1994), cited in Susan Wise Bauer, "Oprah's Misery Index," *Christianity Today* 42, no. 14 (1998): 73.

30. Sheri Reynolds, *The Rapture of Canaan* (New York: Putnam Publishing Group, 1996), cited in Bauer, "Oprah's Misery Index," 74.

31. Jane Hamilton, *The Book of Ruth* (New York: Anchor Books/Doubleday, 1990), cited in Bauer, "Oprah's Misery Index," 74.

32. Colin Lankshear and Peter McLaren, eds., *Critical Literacy: Politics, Praxis, and the Postmodern* (Albany, N.Y.: SUNY Press, 1993); Donaldo Macdeo, *Literacies of Power: What Americans Are Not Allowed to Know* (San Francisco: Westview Press, 1994); Claudia Mitchell and Kathleen Weiler, eds., *Rewriting Literacy: Culture and the Discourse of the Other* (New York: Bergin and Garvey, 1991); Patrick Shannon, *Reading Poverty* (Portsmouth, N.H.: Heinemann, 1998).

33. Shannon, *Reading Poverty,* 10.

34. Marie M. Clay, *Becoming Literate: The Construction of Inner Control* (Portsmouth, N.H.: Heinemann, 1991); Mitchell and Weiler, *Rewriting Literacy.*

35. "*Cane River*/Oprah's Book Club," 4, 5.

36. Ibid., 3.

37. Ibid., 6.

38. Shafali Lal, "Dangerous Silences: Lessons in Daring," *Radical Teacher* 58 (2000): 12–15.

39. "*The Poisonwood Bible*/Oprah's Book Club," 6, 7–8.

40. Ibid., 9.

41. Ibid., 10.

42. Ibid., 11.

43. "*White Oleander*/Oprah's Book Club," 6, 13.

44. Julie Kailin, *Antiracist Education: From Theory to Practice* (New York: Rowman and Little, 2002); Beverly Daniel Tatum, *"Why Are the Black Kids Sitting Together in the Cafeteria" and Other Conversations about Race* (New York: Basic Books, 1997); Cornel West, *Keeping Faith: Philosophy and Race in America* (New York: Routledge, 1993).

45. "*Cane River*/Oprah's Book Club," 3, 10.

Making Corrections to Oprah's Book Club

Reclaiming Literary Power for
Gendered Literacy Management

Sarah Robbins

In the fall of 2001, the juggernaut of Oprah Winfrey's original book club hit a roadblock. Up until that time, Winfrey's television-based reading community had been humming steadily along, generating un-precedented sales for every book she selected while garnering zealous participation from fans, as well as praise from organizations such as the American Library Association. Oprah's Book Club had been big news on the American cultural scene from the moment of its inception. As *Time* magazine reported in December 1996, the novels Winfrey chose for her show were catapulted into the upper echelons of best-seller sta-tus.[1] As analyses such as R. Mark Hall's would later observe, Winfrey's original book club also merited serious attention from scholars: she was generating a dramatic shift in Americans' reading habits both by creat-ing new readers and by successfully drawing them into active social spaces for collaborative literacy, such as the Web site that complemented the discussions staged on her television show.[2]

When Winfrey selected Jonathan Franzen's novel *The Corrections* in 2001, however, she set in motion a series of arguments about the content and method of her book club phenomenon. This conflict high-lighted American culture's persistent tension between highbrow and lowbrow texts, between institutions associated with high-culture literary aesthetics and those linked to popular consumption. These developments underscored perennial conflicts between masculine and feminine models for "good reading"—disparities that may have led to the book club's hiatus and its subsequent reconstitution in a different form. In revamping her book club to focus on classic novels that are also studied regularly in high schools and colleges, Winfrey eventually managed to mediate the gender-based conflict over reading that had erupted during the Franzen episode—a conflict that temporarily threatened her position as a social arbiter with cultural as well as sales-figure influence. The strategies she used to reclaim authority over American reading cast her work as literacy manager in a guise that, significantly, also allowed her to accrue new brands of influence. Winfrey's management of nation-wide reading patterns expanded from a focus on sharing sympathetic personal responses to the teaching of culturally significant lessons. As a marker of her widespread social power, the *ways of reading* promoted by Oprah's Book Club shifted from decisively sentimentalized, feminized approaches—emphasizing a highly personal consumption of text—to include a serious study of books more in line with high school and university curricula. Winfrey reformulated her own role, accordingly, from what some critics had cast as *sob sister* to that of *teacher* with a social conscience and productive intellectual connections. In making "correc-tions" in the focus of her book club, Winfrey ensured that her position as a major arbiter of America's literary culture would be restored and strengthened—even as she recast the phenomenon of the television book club into a new shape.

Oprah's First Book Club in Race-Based Historical Context

To understand both the notable influence exerted by the original club and the strategies Winfrey used to remake it, we need to situate this sub-field of her vast domain of social influence within several interlocking contexts, including the history of book clubs in the United States and their relationship to debates about gendered and race-oriented reading of American literature.

As Elizabeth McHenry points out in the epilogue to her study of nineteenth-century African American literary societies, Winfrey's first book club developed in part out of a tradition through which black leaders created alternative sites of literacy to acquire shared social power. Like the black-led literary societies McHenry researched, Winfrey's early book club self-consciously positioned itself outside the institutional framework of formal educational institutions, which have too often failed to recognize the significant contributions of African American readers and writers to U.S. literary culture. In that vein, McHenry's groundbreaking study helps us see connections between the community-building literacy practices in Winfrey's original book club (such as holding some "meetings" on a set designed like a living room and others around a dinner table) and organizations such as the Saturday Nighters, an African American literary society launched in the 1920s in Washington, D.C. Like Georgia Douglas Johnson hosting readers and writers in her home on Saturday evenings, Winfrey organized her first book club in ways that built a supportive environment for club members to learn and grow together. Indeed, as McHenry suggests, "One reason for the great success of Oprah's [original] Book Club is that it provide[d] its 'members' with a collective experience similar to that found in earlier literary societies as well as contemporary book clubs and reading groups" organized by and for African Americans.[3] Like the Go on Girl! Book Club founded in 1991, Winfrey's original book club aimed to provide more than just an occasion for discussing reading in intellectual terms. Echoing member Monique Greenwood's characterization of the Go on Girl! group that preceded Winfrey's mass-audience version, Oprah's Book Club promoted personal conversations linked more to relationships and aspirations than to analyses of texts' literary features.[4]

Another important link between Winfrey's first club and African American literacy practices has to do with its push to build readership numbers. Along those lines, as McHenry's work suggests, we can better appreciate the savvy choices behind Winfrey's management of her original book club when we connect it to forerunner entrepreneurial enterprises from the African American community, such as Terry McMillan's broad-based (and highly successful) marketing of her early novels, which bypassed the traditional literary establishment and instead reached directly into the social spaces frequented by middle-class blacks in the United States (e.g., community centers, sororities, churches). As McHenry notes, Winfrey's original book club sometimes drew fire from critics because of its then-unusual move to bring together two media typically viewed as enemies—television and books. But this linkage was actually quite consistent with parallel efforts by other African Americans to carve out alternative sites of reading—outside the academy—as accessible venues for black participation in culture formation.[5] In this regard, Winfrey's first book club was also carrying on a tradition of African American–led, institutionalized literacy building going back to schools, seminaries, and colleges developed by and for blacks beginning during Reconstruction; black forays into the national publishing industry, such as the creation of national periodicals like the *Women's Era*;[6] and the self-conscious construction of female leaders such as Frances E. W. Harper, Josephine Ruffin, Ida B. Wells-Barnett, and Anna Julia Cooper as social literacy promoters.[7] Thus, although Winfrey's initial book club—like the other elements in her media empire—was clearly intended to reach an interracial mass market, we can better understand the subtle, strategic elements of its resistance against high-culture institutions if we note its indebtedness to race-related alternative literacy practices.

Perhaps even more than race, however, a key feature shaping the literacy practices of Winfrey's original book club was gender. Winfrey cast the club as a shared experience for all women—particularly those women interested in personal growth. As a number of scholars have observed, the original book club took a highly gendered and populist approach to the act of reading, emphasizing affect over intellect, pleasure over highbrow study, and shared, life-related meaning making over decontextualized aesthetic analysis. Citing a number of Winfrey's early book club presentations, Elizabeth Long emphasizes how "Winfrey made, both visually and through the voices of real readers," a case for reading as "experiential rather than analytic. Books offered moral instruction, the potential for seeing oneself anew or for exploring faraway worlds imaginatively, and the possibility of becoming part of an Oprah-centered community of readers." As Long notes, such a vision of reading "stands independent of the contemporary academy" and "tends to linger at a reading level characterized mainly by identification," stressing "a direct dialogue between the book and readers' emotional concerns."[8]

During a July 6, 2001, show celebrating the book club's success up to that time, Winfrey reinforced this highly personalized approach to literacy, citing "the struggles, the accidents, the injustices, the love affairs and the unknown places we discover inside ourselves" through reading.[9] In this characterization, strategically positioned just after an impressive survey of the geographically diverse places her club members had traveled by way of the books they had read, Winfrey affiliated her club with a far more important terrain: an interior space of women's feelings and experiences.

Throughout its first years, Winfrey's fans clearly appreciated the club's commitment to building a feminized reading community separated from academic-style analysis—and from day-to-day family responsibilities. Like the women readers studied by Janice Radway in her pathbreaking *Reading the Romance,* members of Winfrey's first book club considered their time with these fictional texts a form of escape, as well as, ironically, a social experience holding great relevance for their interpersonal relationships.[10] Along those lines, Winfrey described typical book club aficionados as "moms" who had "to steal their time to read while watching their kids play in the park" or even, in a practice she discouraged, "while driving" children to activities.[11] To illustrate this pattern, on a show celebrating the club's activities, Winfrey presented examples of club members clamoring for just thirty minutes of reading time and even hiding from their families to claim it. But such private reading gained its greatest meaning and strength, she suggested, through the book club's shared discussions, which included layers of feminized sociability ranging from taped scenes of a select group who had earned the right (by writing in to the show about the selection) to converse directly with the author, to the live studio audience on the day of the book club broadcasts, to the viewers at home. Highly aware of and reinforcing these interactions across various social layers of literacy, Winfrey repeatedly invited viewers into these discussions by way of direct addresses to the audience at home both in her television episodes and on her Web site.

In a July 2001 broadcast, Mary, a dedicated club participant, explained her enthusiasm in just such social terms: "I look forward to it because I don't have a houseful of readers at home. So I want these discussions." Elaborating in reply to a query from Winfrey, Mary pointed out how helpful it was "to hear what other people have to say." Another enthusiast, Linda Robertson, described her club-based reading of *River, Cross My Heart,* and especially her participation as one of the featured discussants on the show, as crucial to recovering from the death of her sister. Rereading the novel through the lens of the show's group conversations, and supported by a personal inscription from author Breena Clarke, Robertson found peace.[12]

Social critic Sabrina Gosling offered a related characterization of the book club in a 2001 essay describing its history up to that point. Gosling suggested that Winfrey had "really found the perfect format and presentation for her audience" by placing an "emphasis . . . on one's emotional response to the book."[13] In reviewing the show's presentation of books such as *While I Was Gone* and *The Poisonwood Bible*, Long noted that Winfrey "involved" her audience experientially by reading letters from viewers about the recommended books, referencing details from online discussion boards, and engaging the audience in conversation—all of which helped strengthen "an identification between Oprah and the audience's emotional lives and opinions." In this way, the book being read collaboratively "was constructed entirely in terms" of a central "emotional issue."[14]

Descriptions like Long's positioned the first book club outside the domain of academic literary study, to emphasize its populist bent. Though clearly valid on one level, this characterization of the original club obscured another important aspect of its heritage—one that carried over into its second-phase identity. Thus, despite shifts in emphasis after the book club's rebirth in the summer of 2003, there were some consistencies in the brand of literacy being promoted in both versions. In particular, examining how Winfrey's project promoting women's reading was affiliated with academic feminists' positions on literature's social role, especially as adapted by her mentor Toni Morrison, can help us better appreciate the sophisticated management strategies behind Winfrey's powerful cultural work as a literacy manager.

Reading Like a Woman

The approaches to reading that Winfrey nourished through the first club represented a successful call for women to take control over American literary consumption. These approaches are traceable to the pioneering work by feminist critic Judith Fetterley in the 1970s. In her now-classic manifesto *The Resisting Reader: A Feminist Approach to American Fiction,* Fetterley dubbed literature "political" and asserted that American literature in particular was troublingly "male," consistently cast in "designs" that "encouraged, legitimized, and transmitted" a male vision of social reality. "To read the canon" of American literature was, Fetterley declared, "perforce to identify as male," a situation that was particularly disempowering to women, since so much of American literature claimed to be "defining what is peculiarly American about experience and identity."[15] Fetterley backed up her claim through a series of feminist readings of classic American literature, including narratives by such giants in the field as William Faulkner, Nathaniel Hawthorne, Ernest Hemingway, F. Scott Fitzgerald, and Henry James. She argued that, in their school-based readings, American females were being force-fed a diet of male experiences as the only true avenue to being American, so it was small wonder that they wound up on the margins of social power: "To be excluded from a literature that claims to define one's identity is to experience a peculiar form of powerlessness—not simply the powerlessness which derives from not seeing one's experience articulated, clarified, and legitimized in art, but more significantly the powerlessness which results from the endless division of self against self, the consequence of the invocation to identify as male while being reminded that to be male—to be universal, to be American—is to be *not female*." Fetterley made her point on one level simply by marshaling a male array of literary luminaries as the primary claimants to canonical status. But she also pushed her analysis beyond a basic critique of *what* was included in the canon to a detailed assault on *how* women in the United States were being trained to read the national literature. Characterizing the processes of literary study being foisted on female students as "*immasculation* of women by men," Fetterley affiliated with criticism by Elaine Showalter, who had dubbed the effects of the literary curriculum on women as an "'apprenticeship in negative capability,'" which resulted in American women's becoming "'timid, cautious, and insecure.'"[16]

Appearing as it did during the 1970s academic feminist movement, Fetterley's book announced itself as "more than a chapter in cultural history"—it was "an act of survival" based on the idea that what and how we read "drenches us . . . in its assumptions." Accordingly, she presented her book not just as a text for scholarly study but also as a lesson in rereading, "a self-defense survival manual for the woman reader lost in 'the masculine wilderness of the American novel.'"[17] Implicit (and sometimes quite explicit) in this work, of course, was a call for further action—a call to reread the male-dominated classics in "resisting" ways, but also to identify new texts for women to read, along with specific new approaches to reading that would counter the "immasculation" tendency promoted by male authors' push for the (purported) universal. By extension, the next major step in the battle begun by Fetterley would be to read women's texts like women.

In several significant ways, Winfrey's first book club represented a generation-later response to the call first articulated in Fetterley's scholarship and further explored in feminist classrooms during the years between these two activist interventions into American literary culture. However productive feminist scholars' efforts to re-form the canon of American literature had been by 1996, the relationship between gender and American literature was still highly vexed. Many school and university literature courses had made room for women authors (as evidenced, for instance, by content changes in the dominant survey anthologies, such as Norton's and Heath's; publishing projects such as the Feminist Press's recovery of suppressed women's texts from the past; and the development of new course syllabi).[18] Nonetheless, the processes of analysis (such as a historical, depersonalized close reading) still being promoted in many classrooms tended to discourage women from finding what they sought, *as* women readers, in literary texts. And the male giants had hardly been dislodged from their dominance over the canon. Against this backdrop of continuing feminist calls for new models of gendered reading, Winfrey's first book club was inaugurated.

As commentators have frequently stressed, *The Oprah Winfrey Show* audience is primarily female, so it was hardly surprising that Winfrey almost always selected books with a female protagonist and with a plot focused on women-centered issues. What has garnered less attention from scholars is the way Winfrey's advocacy for novels by African American women writers enabled her to avoid the problem that critics such as bell hooks have identified in many early feminists' interventions into American cultural life—that is, the tendency to overgeneralize white women's experiences as standing in for those of all women. Winfrey's reading list mixed such "white" novels as Joyce Carol Oates's *We Were the Mulvaneys* (January 2001), Barbara Kingsolver's *The Poisonwood Bible* (June 2000), Anita Shreve's *The Pilot's Wife* (March 1999), Janet Fitch's *White Oleander* (May 1999), and Ursula Hegi's *Stones from the River* (February 1997) with books by African American writers such as Pearl Cleage's *What Looks Like Crazy on an Ordinary Day* (September 1998), Edwidge Danticat's *Breath, Eyes, Memory* (May 1998), and Maya Angelou's *The*

Heart of a Woman (May 1997). In doing so, Winfrey worked to build a cross-racial community of readers, approximating the kind of antiracist solidarity that hooks had called on feminists to promote but had not yet materialized in the 1980s. Indeed, hooks's plea for "black and white women" to "come together"—to seek "unity" through "common connections"—was, on a number of levels, addressed through Winfrey's use of shared reading to forge cross-racial unity grounded in both gendered social issues and women's collaborative responses to them.[19]

Winfrey's move to use literary texts as a way of building solidarity among black and white women was supported on several occasions by the cultural capital of Nobel Prize–winner Toni Morrison. With *Sula* (April 2002), *The Bluest Eye* (April 2000), *Paradise* (January 1998), and *Song of Solomon* (October 1996), Morrison's novels dominated the selections for the first Oprah's Book Club.[20] And Winfrey's presentations to the television audience certainly celebrated Morrison's literary stature, such as when Winfrey described her "favorite living author of novels" as having "received nearly every writing award possible, culminating when the Nobel Prize was bestowed in 1993."[21]

In the case of Winfrey's ongoing cultural work, though, the main source of social currency being touted in Morrison's works was their intense and productive connection to the lived experience of women—a power that Winfrey constructed as potentially transcending issues of race. Significantly, in this regard, when celebrating the history of the first book club on the May 2002 show, which marked the end of the club's original version, Winfrey chose this striking comment from Morrison to highlight themes in *The Bluest Eye:* "Race—when you know somebody's race, that's the least information you have. You don't know anything. The real information is elsewhere." Reinforcing a focus on gendered life experiences, Winfrey praised the role that a "great book" could play, to make "us look closer in the mirror," and then prompted the author to compare creating such writing to a mother's giving the gift of pure affection to her children. Later, on the same show, Winfrey explained her love of the novel *Sula* in part by noting that the title character "says she knows about other *colored* women" and "knows how they're living." But then Winfrey and Morrison discussed the writing of *Sula* in terms directly reminiscent of hooks's call for women's cross-racial harmony building. Morrison declared: "The feminist movement was just beginning and women were saying, 'We have got to stop competing with each other. We should love one another. We should be friends with one another,' and I thought, 'That's odd.' In my community, black women have always been other black women's best friends, so that when my mother said 'sister' about a neighbor, she really meant it in this very, very profound way."[22]

Throughout the small-group discussion of Morrison's oeuvre, Winfrey steered the conversation to suggest how her book club had worked to extend this race-based tradition of African American female friendship, transforming it into a cross-racial social practice. For instance, referencing *Sula*'s depiction of "two girls, opposite in every way, who develop a relationship that goes beyond friendship," Winfrey described the book's potential impact in this way: "To be a woman living in the world and not to have read the book, then you've missed out on so much of what women have to share with each other, what women have to give to each other." Then, to illustrate her point, she presented some of the club members' responses to the novel in gendered terms. Significantly, the first reader highlighted on the show described her initial uncertainty about the novel's value and meaning, then reframed that response in terms of the influence of the club's gendered role: "I read it only because you [Winfrey] suggested it. Otherwise, I would never even have picked it up, but I read it . . . and I said, 'OK. This is a nice book. I'm glad I read it.' And I just put it down. And I'm going, 'This can't be one of your top choices of books without me—without me feeling that way.' So I said . . . 'there's got to be something else.' . . . I knew that you were trying to teach us about women and friendship and motherhood."[23]

Morrison herself then picked up on another reader's comment that Winfrey "made us think" by affirming Winfrey's framework for reading the novel for life guidance rather than aesthetic analysis. "It's about living your life," including "how you negotiate your life with other people," Morrison declared, leading the club member to agree that the book and the social reading process were "real life." Continuing their discussion of the novel with several other club members who had been selected to appear based on their letters of application, Winfrey and Morrison repeatedly positioned the club's reading process in a gendered context focused on feelings and life experiences. For instance, Morrison explained that "your friend may not always be nice," but if she provides "a kind of love," then "you have to hang on to it." Similarly, while interpreting a conversation between Hannah and Eva in the novel, Winfrey characterized a point of dialogue as what "every . . . woman, mother ever wanted to say." These comments led one reader in the discussion group to observe, "I saw my mother in that," and "I love my mother. Sometimes I don't tell her enough." Later in the conversation, this same reader expressed her gratitude to Morrison and, indirectly, to Oprah's Book Club: "I love you for allowing me to be able to read something that helps me identify who I am and identify relationships. Thank you for always writing things that you feel and that I feel and that other women feel."[24]

This highly gendered construction of shared reading in the last show featuring the original book club both echoed and reinforced the brand of literacy Winfrey had been promoting. For example, in the November 16, 2000, show on *Drowning Ruth,* club members participating in the small-group discussion repeatedly equated the characters in the book with real people, comparing their actions with experiences in the readers' own lives. A club member named Ellen Marie characterized her reaction to one scene in personal terms, citing her aversion to "weak men" as guiding her reading. Another, describing her response to the novel's main character, noted, "when I started to dislike her was when she didn't tell" a family secret. Such comments led Winfrey to celebrate: "I love this. It's like these people are real." After a commercial break, Winfrey set the tone for the succeeding discussion by casting the book club's ideal reading process as a highly affective practice, an enhanced form of therapy that readers at home could achieve through life choices based on their responses to this literature: "It is just remarkable to me . . . how a work of fiction can touch and, really, begin to help heal the lives of readers in ways that a lot of self-help books and therapy and conversations cannot. Our lesson from 'Drowning Ruth,' for a lot of people, is this; that if you are harboring any kind of family secret, y'all need to let it out; let it go. Maybe this Thanksgiving is a good time. Just everybody around the table talk about their feelings. See how that dinner goes."[25]

Resetting the Dining Room Table:
The Battle over *The Corrections*

When Winfrey imagined this "table talk about . . . feelings," the kind of feminized social management of a family dinner conversation that she was recommending seemed readily available to her and her viewers as a site of shared power, given the success of her book club so far. But in October 2001, with such holiday dinners just over the horizon, Winfrey's choice of a new text for the club prompted a battle that reverberated for months. Jonathan Franzen's *The Corrections* boasted a front-cover illustration strikingly in line with Winfrey's description of a holiday dinner as an ideal time for middle-class American families' emotional sharing: place settings carefully arranged, dishes full of hearty food, and neatly dressed kids watching motherly arms lowering a turkey to the spot of honor. But, as Don DeLillo, David Wallace, Pat Conroy, and Michael Cunningham (all, we might note, male authors themselves) suggested in promotional blurbs for the novel, Franzen's primary audience consisted of readers very different from those Winfrey had been celebrating on her book club shows. In this case, the terms used to describe Franzen's novel—"merciless" (Wallace), "edgy" (DeLillo), "utterly unsentimental" (Cunningham), and "going to hunt with the big cats" (Conroy)—stand out in retrospect as signals of the conflict to come, since they highlight connections between Franzen's book and a literary tradition very different from the feminized sentimentalism Winfrey had been promoting.

Franzen's novel becoming an Oprah's Book Club selection brought to the forefront of public consciousness a cluster of issues already associated with the book club as a phenomenon by then. To recapture a sense of how the conflict over *The Corrections* played out at the time, I will revisit two articles from the *Chicago Tribune* in the fall of 2001.[26] The *Tribune* is an apt venue for this analysis, since it is Winfrey's hometown newspaper and, as a major Second City newspaper, offers an instructive venue for tracking the American heartland's engagement with major social questions. In particular, coverage of the flap by Julia Keller, a cultural critic for the paper, highlighted how the Franzen-Winfrey controversy represented a gendered battle of the books with ramifications beyond this specific episode.

The *Tribune*'s October 29, 2001, article on the conflict laid the groundwork for this gendered reading. Presented as a dialogue between Keller and a male reporter, Mark Caro, the story situated Franzen's negative reaction to *The Corrections* being selected for the club within a larger framework of debate over literary taste and men's versus women's rightful positions as arbiters of American culture. Perhaps unsurprisingly, Keller and Caro began their report with contrasting comments about the *Oprah* logo and its meaning on the cover of books. Caro defended Franzen's "reservations" about placing the symbol on his novel. Describing himself as preferring a "book cover to serve the book alone," Caro compared the *Oprah* logo to the technique of placing the image of a movie star on the cover of a book once it has been optioned to Hollywood. Thus, Caro noted, "I don't want to have to think about Oprah any time I look at the book." Brushing aside Caro's effort to damn the book club through a linkage with movies, Keller responded by proposing that Franzen's purported discomfort with the *Oprah* logo was merely "a red herring." Instead, she suggested, Franzen was "embarrassed . . . to be associated with a daytime TV talk show," since, to the "'literary' author" Franzen "fancie[d] himself to be, that would be slumming." Although it was also linked implicitly to issues of social class, as the Caro-Keller exchange continued, their he said–she said, back-and-forth pattern clearly underscored the gendered nature of the Franzen-Winfrey battle. And, in that sense, Keller pointed out that her colleague's lumping of Winfrey's choices with low-culture status, based mainly on the corporate logo boosting book sales, was inconsistent with such high-culture affiliations as having Nobel Prize–winner Toni Morrison as a designated author. Caro declared that "Oprah does have a value, one that may be complimentary to Toni Morrison" yet at the same time "out of synch to Franzen, like it would be to, say, James Ellroy or Orson Scott Card." Thus, the male reporter cast his own discomfort with the club in markedly gendered terms—taking a stance he underscored by complaining that his wife (of all people!) had chosen to read Franzen's novel after Winfrey selected it. In the end, then, although they closed their shared column in a playful tone, these two reporters reiterated both the content and the overtly gendered viewpoints linked to the controversy itself.[27]

In a follow-up feature published on November 12, Keller continued to cover the story as a conflict over gendered literary values. Describing a public reading that Franzen had given at the Newberry Library, Keller characterized the event as having been hijacked by the Winfrey-Franzen melee. The event was pulled into the flap despite efforts by Franzen and his copresenter, Pulitzer Prize–winning author Michael Chabon, to head off any controversy by specifying that all questions from audience members must apply to both of them. Attendees would have none of this transparent maneuvering, Keller reported, and one of the first questioners deftly framed a query to force the issue: "'How . . . has the receipt of prizes—one from the Pulitzer committee, one from a talk-show host—affected both authors?'" According to Keller, such a question was predictable, given that "the controversy [wouldn't] die" and "publications from *The Washington Post* and *The Boston Globe* to *The Onion* and *Entertainment Weekly*" had been "tak[ing] their whacks at Franzen." Hence, as Keller noted, the otherwise literary occasion at the Newberry had become "a hot ticket," and the event itself (Keller seemed to chuckle) had "seemed livelier . . . than is typical for author readings." Admitting that Franzen's novel had already been selling well before Winfrey's selection of it, Keller nonetheless went on to reiterate and extend her earlier reading of the ongoing uproar as a sign of the "highbrow-lowbrow split in American culture."

In the final section of her story on the reading at the Newberry Library, Keller pulled back somewhat from her previous characterization of Franzen as a male aggressor roughly dismissing the feminized cultural work of Winfrey and her milieu of daytime television. Describing the professorial novelist as "in many ways an unlikely figure to have stumbled into a ruckus with a TV star," Keller quoted Franzen's explanation that some of his "'few expressions of discomfort'" were "'now being read as my scathing criticism of the book club,'" and she included his comments repositioning Winfrey herself within a broad category to which he humbly pledged loyal allegiance—"'readers'"—as well as his avowal that "'the distinction between high audiences and low audiences is false.'"[28]

But Franzen's repeated attempts to retreat from his earlier portrayal of Oprah's Book Club as promoting a debased, feminized literacy could hardly be accepted at face value, since his initial, unfiltered remarks had tapped so forcefully into long-standing debates within the larger culture. Thus, even a self-identified friend of Franzen's, Laura Miller, had called the episode a "book lovers' quarrel" and situated the controversy in a broader framework of cultural authority issues linked to gender. Quoting Franzen's comments soon after his book was selected, Miller joined other commentators in highlighting his dismissal of the feminized social context for reading in which book club inclusion would place his otherwise high-art novel: "'[Winfrey's] picked some good books, . . . but she's picked enough schmaltzy, one-dimensional ones that I cringe,'" Franzen had sniffed. Despite her friendship with the novelist, for Miller, such comments exacerbated an already intense, sustained war between "two resentful camps" in "America's book culture," one viewing itself "as scorned by a snooty self-styled elite and the other see[ing] itself as keepers of the literary flame." Further, from Miller's perspective, "the fact that one is often characterized as female and the other as male resonates with the edgy relations between the sexes of late." And, she suggested, Franzen had helped situate this particular flap with Winfrey squarely within this gendered battleground by describing male readers as "'put off'" by what he termed "'Oprah books,'" to the extent that his book's selection for her show might actually drive away readers rather than generate them.[29]

Especially with the use of rhetorical flourishes such as "schmaltzy," Franzen was tapping into deeply held prejudices against sentimentalism, the literary mode that a number of critics, from journalism as well as the academy, had been using as a shorthand for gendering Oprah's Book Club. (Michael Cunningham's back-cover characterization of Franzen's *The Corrections* as "utterly unsentimental" is noteworthy in this regard.) In short, in setting up such a dichotomy between book club selections as "schmaltzy" and high-art texts as "unsentimental," Franzen and others were actually reasserting a long-standing strategy of displacing women's writing and reading from legitimate literary culture by virtue of pigeonholing its content and preferred methods for appealing to readers. However, as June Howard observed in a thoughtful interdisciplinary treatment of sentimentalism, although the practice of linking such binary divisions (high-low, male-female, unsentimental-sentimental) has a long history in American literary circles, many of these efforts to stigmatize women's texts ignore important elements in the history of sentimentalism that tie it to male traditions and influence. These include its roots in eighteenth-century British writing by male authors such as Henry Mackenzie (*The Man of Feeling*), Samuel Richardson (*Clarissa*), and Laurence Sterne (*Tristram Shandy*); its links to philosophers such as Lord Shaftesbury; and its continued effective use through the nineteenth century by Charles Dickens.[30] Similarly, we can point to the complex deployment of sentimentality by a range of American male authors, ranging from Mark Twain's complex blend of sentiment and antisentimental satire to strategically romantic texts such as Nicholas Sparks's big-selling novels today.

Winfrey did not cite the gender trouble implicit in the Franzen controversy as a major factor in sending her book club shows into hiatus soon after *The Corrections* episode. Nonetheless, several signs pointed to a connection between the extended conflict and her decision. Intriguingly, although Winfrey stated that the problem was finding enough books she liked well enough to recommend highly, several posters to her Web site's book club discussion board pointed to the Franzen episode as being at the heart of the shutdown. Although authors and their publishers loved the boost in sales that accompanied being chosen by Winfrey, coverage of *The Corrections* controversy had highlighted others' active resentment of Winfrey's intervention into literary culture. At the same time, some of Winfrey's own book club members had been critiquing her choices for different reasons, such as her ongoing predilection for Toni Morrison's novels, which some of the show's fans found overly demanding.[31]

In any case, Winfrey's announcement in the spring of 2002 that *Sula* would be the last book club selection prompted yet another burst of news coverage and a gaggle of would-be substitutes. Judging from the message board responses, many of her fans viewed any prospective replacements with suspicion, and some club members described themselves as being in mourning over a stunning, at times even debilitating, loss in their personal lives. After the last show, the online chat spaces filled with poignant (sometimes "schmaltzy") tributes to the club, with members' strong sense of gratitude to Winfrey for making them readers mingling with grief over their lost literacy guide. Antisentimental pundits tracked this development too, of course, poking fun at the sentimental language of such contributors and caricaturing the seeming inability of America's "moms" to choose books for themselves.

In withdrawing from the cultural work of middle-class literacy management, Winfrey seemed at first to be ceding social authority to the masculine tradition of American literature and literature reading. But, as it turned out, she had deserted the field of battle only temporarily. In the summer of 2003 she roared back with a vengeance and with a newly crafted approach to serving as a key arbiter of American reading habits.

Oprah Winfrey's Second Book Club: Institutionalizing Domesticated Literacy

In the final chapter of *Managing Literacy, Mothering America,* a cultural history of maternally guided reading practices in U.S. middle-class society, I offered a tentative analysis of the demise of Oprah Winfrey's first book club. I speculated that the suspension of the club offered a telling example of the faded power of a genre I call the domestic literacy narrative. In tracing the early development of the American domestic literacy narrative back to the early Republic, *Managing Literacy, Mothering America* argued that middle-class women were already using their home-based management of children's reading to claim a significant form of public work. I also showed that the recognition of that role and its depictions in many literary texts through the nineteenth century should counter our sometimes oversimplified view of domestic work, especially child rearing, as separate from the civic sphere. In that vein, narratives depicting mothers teaching children to read—particularly those that portrayed the future influence on such children as adult citizens—played an important part in framing a home-based, female, middle-class social role with culture-making power far beyond the home. Following the development of the flexible domestic literacy narrative genre through the nineteenth century and into the twentieth, I showed that it was continually being adapted to the expanded social opportunities becoming available to middle-class women. For example, stories about schoolteachers shaping society through motherly literacy management in their classrooms expanded the genre's reach and influence, as did adaptations with benevolent maternal reformers managing the literacy of childlike immigrants or missionaries exporting Americanized literacy and social values to religious schools overseas. Over the course of the nineteenth century, roughly speaking, I found two different strands of this genre extension operating, sometimes together in the same texts. One was created by, for, and about women whose management of others' literacy could lead to new agency for themselves and their students (often disenfranchised groups such as freed slaves, the urban poor, or Native Americans in reservation schools). The other was a pseudo-benevolent narrative that wound up reinforcing the dominant social structure while purporting to provide uplift. The most complex adaptations of the genre came from women writers such as Frances Harper and Anzia Yezierska, who learned to appropriate its tools to promote the social advancement of marginalized groups with whom they identified, including women. By the middle of the twentieth century, however, the domestic literacy narrative had faded away from the literary scene, as more scientific approaches to schoolteaching replaced motherly moral suasion in classrooms, and as women's suffrage made the indirect exercise of political power through work such as child rearing and classroom teaching a less significant means of achieving social influence.[32]

In contrast to this trend, the first version of Oprah's Book Club seemed to be a clear case of the domestic literacy narrative's making a comeback in its original, most home-based form. Winfrey's living-room sets and her highly affective approaches to teaching moral life lessons echoed the maternal strategies for managing middle-class literacy that had been central to early forms of the genre. Framing her book discussions in highly sentimental terms, and asking her club members to construct stories about their own reading experiences as life guiding, Winfrey's original club affiliated itself with the gendered tradition of social literacy that had been central to the domestic literacy narrative from the early nineteenth century onward. Thus, in the book club's content and methods, I saw a revitalization of the feminized literacy that had been so appealing to earlier generations of women. Perhaps that is why, when Winfrey appeared to abdicate her role as a motherly literacy manager, I felt a sense of loss somewhat akin to that of the club members who posted mournful messages on her Web site.

Now, with the benefit of time to analyze the shape and direction of Winfrey's second and third versions of her book club, I realize that I underestimated the resilience of the domestic literacy narrative genre in general and of Winfrey as motherly teacher of American women in particular. After studying the ways Winfrey presented her second-stage book choices, I see that the revised club drew on multilayered elements from domestic literacy narratives, including at a new "meta" level of institutionalization. By enlarging the techniques of the genre, Winfrey's revamped book club used a re-formed brand of feminized literacy guidance to claim broader and deeper cultural power. Indeed, when we retrace the full history of Winfrey's book club from its early form through its current one, we can see how her own narrative of gendered American literacy management—claimed, threatened, and then reclaimed—represents a recapitulation and extension, in miniature, of the larger history of the domestic literacy narrative.

Winfrey's first book club was grounded in and continually referenced her own personal narrative of uplift through literacy. Placing herself at the center of the show's book club discussions (sometimes, in fact, dominating the conversations), Winfrey also drew strategically from her life experiences as a reader to validate literacy as a tool to empower and to accrue authority to herself as a sponsor of others' literacy.[33] As Hall has noted, Winfrey used personal stories of finding solace and models for uplift through reading as a springboard to influence others. "In promoting herself," Hall observed, "Winfrey promote[d] books, and, in promoting books, she promote[d] herself. This is a simple formula that she suggest[ed would] work for others." Accordingly, through her performances as an empowered reader in her first book club, Winfrey modeled "the theme of transformation through literacy."[34] She also embodied a maternal guide like those home-based teachers of early domestic literacy narratives.

A crucial problem with this strategy emerged, however, during the ruckus over Winfrey's selection of *The Corrections*. Having centered the cultural capital of the first book club within the figure of herself as a motherly reader, teaching her viewers how to acquire and use feminized, sentimental literacy, Winfrey found that her own as well as the club's social authority was jeopardized during the Franzen episode by critiques of her book choices and the club's ways of reading in gendered terms. That is, attacks on the club, given its organization around Winfrey's personal, maternal literacy, evolved into attacks on Winfrey herself and on her brand of domesticated instruction. In resurrecting the club in the summer of 2003, however, Winfrey reframed its use of domesticated literacy management and, in doing so, expanded the model itself, thereby acquiring enhanced influence for herself and the genre.

First, in terms of content, she shifted her individual book choices from contemporary texts that she found worthy on a personal level to recognized classics whose literary value was unassailable. Beginning with John Steinbeck (*East of Eden*, June 2003) and including novels by Alan Paton (*Cry, the Beloved Country*, September 2003), Gabriel Garcia Márquez (*One Hundred Years of Solitude*, January 2004), and Leo Tolstoy (*Anna Karenina*, June 2004), Winfrey's choices from 2003 through summer 2005 were safe from the "chick book" critique that had erupted during the Franzen flap. Significantly, though, Winfrey continued to weave in books by women writers, with Carson McCullers's *The Heart Is a Lonely Hunter* and Pearl Buck's *The Good Earth* claiming spots in the spring and fall of 2004, respectively. Perhaps even more important, the male-authored texts that Winfrey selected were often in line with the sentimental mode of literature she had championed in the first club. In tapping *Anna Karenina* over *War and Peace,* for instance, Winfrey chose a classic with great romantic appeal for women readers. (The description of *Anna Karenina* on the Oprah's Book Club Web site was telling in this regard, hailing the novel as "one of the most enthralling love affairs in the history of literature—it truly was the 'Harlequin Romance' of its day."[35]) Along those lines, when she announced *East of Eden* as the first reading for her reconfigured club, Winfrey contrasted it with *The Grapes of Wrath,* which she had earlier identified on her Web site as one of her favorite books. Pitching to her female audience's tastes, she explained that "Steinbeck is famous for *Grapes of Wrath,*" but *East of Eden* "may actually be better," since the latter novel "has it all: love and betrayal and greed and murder and sex. It is layered. It is the riveting saga of two families set in Salinas Valley, California."[36]

While affirming a continued commitment to emotion-oriented plots that would be compelling for her female audience, Winfrey's characterization of *East of Eden* also signaled her new club's strategic emphasis on books' settings. Although her choices for the original club had sometimes highlighted intriguing, far-away places (such as the Congo of Barbara Kingsolver's *The Poisonwood Bible*), and although the shows had typically included video scenes shot in locales linked to the novels (such as Louisiana for Ernest Gaines's *A Lesson before Dying*), in the second version of her book club, Winfrey placed an increased emphasis on readers *connecting* to setting. For example, the Web site now tended to identify books based on particular locations—such as an extensive "Visit Colombia" section for *One Hundred Years of Solitude*—thereby casting the reading experience as taking book clubbers outside of their personal lives and interior emotions and into the larger world. Along those lines, the Web site overview announcing Winfrey's book selection for fall 2004 pictured members of the book club traveling from Russia (the setting for the summer reading of *Anna Karenina*) to China (the setting for the new choice, *The Good Earth*). By underscoring reading as grounded in virtual visits to distant settings, Winfrey took the reading process more self-consciously outside of the domestic setting that had been the central site of experience and interpretation in the first version of the club.

Accordingly, Winfrey's new book club repeatedly positioned readers themselves outside the intimate settings of the living room and dining room that had been favored in the first version of the club. On the June 2003 show celebrating the "return" of the club, Winfrey pumped up viewers' enthusiasm—and emphasized how far-flung club members were—in a series of segments with local women television celebrities and book club aficionados in New York, Los Angeles, and Atlanta excitedly opening the packages containing their new books. Winfrey actually began the show that day with video vignettes of herself making surprise visits to various settings for reading *outside* the studio, and she promised at the end of the show that her new "Book Club mobile" would be taking the club reading process out on the road.

In all these moves to reposition the work of the club beyond the pseudo–living room of her television studio, Winfrey signaled an extension of feminized reading beyond the purely emotional and domestic locations of interpretation and influence emphasized earlier. Now, in an echo of the historical expansion of the domestic literacy narrative over the nineteenth century, Winfrey's frameworks for reading increasingly indicated that book clubbers would be both bringing the world into their lives through reading and carrying their influence out into the world. Further, the types of personal learning and social influence women could achieve through their shared reading were being reconfigured to focus explicitly on broad social issues rather than personal fulfillment. For example, when presenting *The Heart Is a Lonely Hunter,* Winfrey invited actress Marlee Matlin and former Miss America Heather Whitestone McCallum to describe their experiences dealing with deafness and their advocacy for others facing that challenge, thereby modeling ways of moving from personal, emotional reflection to social action.

In perhaps her most strategically sophisticated move to accrue enhanced authority for the club (as well as deflect accusations of its being "schmaltzy"), Winfrey appropriated the forces of feminist and multicultural academia. For each book selected, Winfrey also chose a well-regarded scholar to serve as a "literary guide" on her Web site. For instance, Virginia Spencer Carr presented material on *The Heart Is a Lonely Hunter* and answered e-mail queries from club members; Liza Knapp provided similar academic expertise for *Anna Karenina;* Harley Oberhelman served as scholarly commentator for *One Hundred Years of Solitude;* and in the summer of 2005 African American scholar Thadious Davis contributed her views on William Faulkner's novels. While skillfully subsuming these scholarly perspectives within her literacy network,

Winfrey also adjusted her own commentaries on the novels to place more emphasis on critical reading. For instance, her weekly e-mails to readers of *Anna Karenina* were just as likely to interpret shifts in character development, quote particular passages, and sum up thematic developments as they were to describe her personal emotional response to the text. Similarly, on the Web site Winfrey invited book clubbers to read the novels through a variety of lenses simultaneously or to choose from an array of possibilities, thereby allowing for both personal response and intellectual analysis. For instance, in calling on readers to consider Tolstoy's novel, the Web site stated:

> One of the most fascinating things about Tolstoy's *Anna Karenina* is how many different ways you can read it. It is a quintessential Russian novel. It's an example of Russian Realism. It ponders feminism and the 19th-Century question of a woman's role within her society. It's a family novel. It's a novel of adultery. It fits into the high Victorian tradition made up of large novels that focus on small lives.
>
> Discover three of the most popular and lasting of *Anna's* "faces," as explained by some of the world's most approachable Tolstoy scholars. Plus, if you like a certain take on *Anna,* the experts suggest what should be next on your reading list.[37]

In selecting the "experts" to help her book clubbers explore these various genres, Winfrey purposefully identified the most "approachable" Tolstoy scholars. Inviting them to write for her reading audience, Winfrey established a bridge between academic reading and mass culture—a bridge that she reinforced by presenting scholars' work on Tolstoy and *Anna Karenina* in highly accessible prose organized around topics of interest to book club members. For example, in writing about Tolstoy and the British Victorian novel, Amy Mandelker explained, "When Anna Karenina wanted a good book to read to take her mind off of her problems as she rode the night train from Moscow to St. Petersburg, she reached for an English novel." Mandelker then described the influence that English writers of his day, such as Charles Dickens and George Eliot, were having on Tolstoy. Similarly, Judith Armstrong considered *Anna Karenina* as a novel of adultery, pointing to its unique position, in that regard, in Russian literature. Anne Hruska (whose biography for the Web site combined information about her academic work with the domestic detail that she "lives with her son in Princeton, New Jersey") discussed "The Family Novel" to situate *Anna Karenina* in a tradition of domestic novels and recommended further reading ranging from Charlotte Brontë's *Jane Eyre* to Toni Morrison's *Beloved* and Dave Eggers's *A Heartbreaking Work of Staggering Genius*.[38] In all these cases, Web pages for Winfrey's reorganized book club countered the usual divide between academic and extracurricular literacy in ways that affirmed simultaneously the reading abilities of her broad female fan base and the implicit commitment to democratizing literary reading represented by the contributions of her "experts." Thus, as a complement to "The Finish Line" portion of the Web site, which celebrated the success of "Moms who hadn't read a book since high school" to "book clubbers who had never tackled Tolstoy,"[39] Winfrey's reshaping of academic expertise into an easily accessible form asserted her ability to build an "Everywoman" community through literacy.

By reaching into the institutional culture of academia to create new infrastructures for her book club, Winfrey repeated the pattern that the genre of the domestic literacy narrative had developed over the nineteenth century, moving from maternally managed reading instruction situated in the home (such as the living room sets of the first Oprah's Book Club) to an expanded feminization of literacy in the larger culture as women gained access to more professional venues in society. In Winfrey's case, when her role as an arbiter of literature and reading was threatened by gender-based attacks, she was able to call on the resources of her communications empire to reassert her authority—and in gendered terms. Thus, even as she expanded the techniques of reading available to her club members, she continued to affirm its foundation in sentimental, domesticated work.

As a sign of this complex blending of feminized literacy approaches and expanded institutional force, we need look no further than Winfrey's description of the particular edition of *Anna Karenina* she wanted club members to buy in 2004:

> First of all, get this edition. You see the one with the little flowers on the cover and it'll have the little banner? Look for the Oprah's Book Club little sticker there because there's lots of different editions. This is an award-winning translation, so

you're really going to get scared if it's not translated well, OK? This is the official Oprah's Book Club edition with the little flowers. And I'm going to be reading along with you. And you'll see the sticker. So if you don't see the sticker, then that's not the one to get because this is the translation that we're going to be talking about online. And we're going to help you online, I'm going to tell you, because I'm going to—I've hired the people to help myself I—because there are some people who aren't scared, who—who've read it and—and understand what's going on.[40]

In its rich interplay of imagery, Winfrey's insistence that 'book club members find the right edition of *Anna Karenina* interwove elements from the personal, feminized, and sentimental tradition of reading she was continuing to honor and the new resources she was bringing to bear on her literacy project. Combining "little flowers" with an "award-winning translation," the cover of the book signaled to readers—and to potential adversaries of the club—that Winfrey's Everywoman readers were now joining forces with academic expertise. So, as she reassured book clubbers that she would be "reading along with you" and that "we're going to help you online," Winfrey conveyed her confidence in the expanded support structure she had designed for her club, one that even allowed her to choose a book she had not yet read herself.

Overall, Winfrey's second version of the book club attempted a remarkable balancing act. Continuing to address the needs and interests of her loyal female audience, she simultaneously expanded the content and methods for reading she encouraged them to use. Taking on strategies for studying texts that brought enhanced authority to her cultural work, she orchestrated complex interplays among the intellectual, social analysis, and personal response. In carrying out this complicated maneuver of extending her literacy management beyond its domesticated purview into broader cultural realms, and with enhanced professional resources, Winfrey reconfigured her management of American literacy to take advantage of multiple social support networks. Meanwhile, by combining the wide array of tools represented by the Web site, e-mail, television, and more, Winfrey institutionalized the model for domestic literacy management while still maintaining, at the core of the reading enterprise, a focus on feminized content and response.

Coda: The Club Remade Again

On September 23, 2005, the front page of the *New York Times* heralded the return of living authors to Winfrey's reading enterprise by announcing her latest selection, *A Million Little Pieces,* James Frey's wrenching 2003 tale of addiction and cure that, at the time, was believed to be an authentic memoir. Journalist Edward Wyatt explained the change in part by quoting Winfrey herself: "'what I like to do most . . . is sit and talk to authors about their work. It's kind of hard to do that when they're dead.'"[41] Others reporting on this shift of the reading list back to its roots echoed Wyatt, pointing out that even though sales of Faulkner's novels had reached new heights during the summer 2005 three-book promotion project, the numbers never reached the levels typical of selections from the first version of the club. Margo Hammon and Ellen Heitzel declared that Vintage had printed 600,000 copies of a boxed set of Faulkner's novels in anticipation of Winfrey's summer endorsement but had sold only about half (still an impressive number for "a notoriously difficult writer to parse"); further, they noted, "there were no programs devoted to the Bard of the South" to complement the admittedly "abundant teaching aids on Oprah's Website."[42] As Cecilia Konchar Farr explained in an online essay, in the first version of the book club, "readers encircled Oprah and the writer. They shared the discussion and the stage. Without a writer sitting next to her, without readers surrounding her, Oprah just couldn't seem to summon up the talk for the classics." Although "we're disappointed that Oprah's commanding presence couldn't resurrect the lively dead writers our culture has turned to stone monuments," Farr stated, Winfrey's return to contemporary authors would undoubtedly be welcomed by most of her reading fan base, and certainly by writers and publishers.[43] Similarly, David Usborne, analyzing the development for an audience of British followers of American popular culture, quipped that "it is hard to bring dead writers on to the set to chat about their works" and declared that Winfrey's "quest for the classics was only moderately successful," since participation in the club had "begun to dwindle."[44]

But Usborne and others suggested that the ongoing evolution of Winfrey's work as manager of American literacy needed to be read in a historical context as well—specifically, with some attention to the gender politics of her earlier conflict with Franzen. Usborne playfully quoted Winfrey as insisting that "Jonathan Franzen was not even a blip on the radar screen of my life," but he simultaneously speculated that "her decision to scale back the club [in 2002] was a reaction to [her] public spat" with Franzen. Karen Long offered a more detailed recounting of the Franzen controversy as an essential context for understanding the cultural relevance of Winfrey's latest move. And Long clearly relished contrasting Franzen's response to his novel's being named an Oprah's Book Club selection with Frey's reaction, as it had been reported earlier in the *Washington Post:* "'Once you're an Oprah writer, . . . you're an Oprah writer for life." Indeed, Frey described himself as "thrilled" to be selected, according to Steven Barrie-Anthony of the *Los Angeles Times,* who pointedly juxtaposed this response of "unabashed enthusiasm" from Frey "with the qualms [of] Jonathan Franzen."[45] Rather than having his invitation to join the club withdrawn for bad manners, Frey happily appeared on the show where his book was announced as both the newest selection and the harbinger of more contemporary publications to come. He even brought along his mother, who had been an avid member of the club for years. However much he had suffered from the addictions described in his memoir, it seemed that Frey understood the gendered power of Winfrey's book club.

As a marker of Winfrey's resurgent authority, Frey's happiness goes beyond both his expressed personal disdain for "literati" and his assertion that "it's amazing so many people are going to read my book."[46] Frey's response—like the burst of gender-oriented reporting on this zigzag in the book club's content and method—indicates that Winfrey's influence on American culture is as alive as the contemporary authors to whom she has again hitched her star. And in the interim between the jolt of the Franzen episode and her reassertion of more overtly sentimental, feminized, Oprah-branded literary power, we can marvel at her co-opting of numerous tools with patriarchal underpinnings—including the classics, the academy, and the business of publishing—to manage that very reclamation.

Notes

1. David E. Thigpen, "Winfrey's Winners," *Time,* December 2, 1996, 84. Thigpen describes sales of Jacquelyn Mitchard's *The Deep End of the Ocean* as hovering around 100,000 copies before Winfrey tapped the novel, and leaping

to over 850,000 afterward. He documents similar patterns for Toni Morrison's *Song of Solomon* (from 374,000 to 895,000) and Jane Hamilton's *The Book of Ruth* (from 85,000 to 600,000), Winfrey's second and third picks for the original club.

2. R. Mark Hall, "The 'Oprahfication' of Literacy: Reading 'Oprah's Book Club,'" *College English* 65, no. 6 (July 2003): 647–48.

3. Elizabeth McHenry, *Forgotten Readers: Recovering the Lost History of African American Literary Societies* (Durham, N.C.: Duke University Press, 2002), 310. On the Saturday Nighters in particular, see 251–95.

4. McHenry notes that African American reading clubs enjoyed a resurgence beginning in the 1980s and that many of the clubs placed a premium on social interaction. In many cases, she explains, "Although reading literature provides the catalyst for their coming together, the impact of black women's association with a reading group is usually felt on both an intellectual and an emotional or spiritual level" (*Forgotten Readers*, 303).

5. McHenry connects Winfrey's first book club with such culturally oriented activities as "the black press in the nineteenth century" working as "a vehicle through which early African Americans implicitly took part in debates about the formation of American literature and the voices it would include" (*Forgotten Readers*, 314). She points to Terry McMillan's tremendous book sales as awakening the publishing establishment to black readers as a viable and, indeed, large market. McMillan "knew that a black book-buying public and a black readership existed," so she carried out her own marketing plan, resulting in such blockbuster sales as she achieved for *Waiting to Exhale*, her third novel, which quickly sold almost 400,000 copies and snagged a paperback deal for $2.64 million" (ibid., 298).

6. Anne Ruggles Gere and Sarah Robbins, "Gendered Literacy in Black and White: Turn-of-the-Century African-American and European-American Club Women's Printed Texts," *Signs* 21, no. 3 (Spring 1996): 643–78.

7. For one insightful treatment of African American women's activist role in social literacy in the late nineteenth and early twentieth centuries, see Jacqueline Jones Royster, *Traces of a Stream: Literacy and Social Change among African American Women* (Pittsburgh: University of Pittsburgh Press, 2000). For a helpful treatment of the model career of Frances E. W. Harper as a literacy organizer for her race, see Frances Smith Foster's introduction to *A Brighter Coming Day: A Frances Ellen Watkins Harper Reader* (New York: Feminist Press, 1990), 3–40.

8. Elizabeth Long, *Book Clubs: Women and the Uses of Reading in Everyday Life* (Chicago: University of Chicago Press, 2003), 205–6. Long's interpretation is echoed by Rona Kaufman, "'That, My Dear, Is Called Reading': Oprah's Book Club and the Construction of a Readership," in *Reading Sites: Social*

Difference and Reader Response, ed. Patrocino P. Schweickart and Elizabeth A. Flynn (New York: Modern Language Association, 2004), 221–55. See especially Kaufman's argument that Winfrey's original club "offered an alternative literacy to the academy's dominant literacy," in part "because the purpose of the club was to reunite literature (or literary fiction and nonfiction) with those who can read it but have chosen not to," and in part because the club promoted "a kind of experiential reading that gives agency to the reader" (225).

9. *The Oprah Winfrey Show,* July 6, 2001 (Harpo Productions transcript), 15.

10. Janice A. Radway, *Reading the Romance: Women, Patriarchy, and Popular Literature,* with a new introduction by the author (Chapel Hill: University of North Carolina Press, 1991).

11. *The Oprah Winfrey Show,* July 6, 2001, 11. Winfrey expressed concern over clubbers' practice of reading while driving. To counter it, she suggested strategies for negotiating potential reading time, such as scheduling whole-family reading activities and asking for time instead of other types of gifts.

12. Mary and Linda were both model members used to illustrate the club's influence in the July 6, 2001, episode referenced earlier. Winfrey opened the show that day by saluting the book club for having "touched so many lives," and she offered a wide range of illustrations to support her point.

13. Sabrina Gosling, "Boek Wereld," *Cape Librarian Magazine,* May–June 2001, 22–24.

14. Long, *Book Clubs,* 203.

15. Judith Fetterley, *The Resisting Reader: A Feminist Approach to American Fiction* (Bloomington: Indiana University Press, 1978), xi–xii.

16. Ibid., xiii, xx, xxi, xxii. Overall, Fetterley declared, American women who read literature as they were being taught in school actually lost all sense of identity: "Intellectually male, sexually female, one is in effect no one, nowhere, immasculated" (ibid., xxii).

17. Ibid., viii.

18. See Paul Lauter, *Canons and Contexts* (New York: Oxford University Press, 1991). See also *Heath Anthology of American Literature,* 4th ed., ed. Paul Lauter and Richard Yarborough (New York: Houghton Mifflin, 2001); *The Norton Anthology of American Literature, Shorter Version,* 6th ed., ed. Nina Baym (New York: W. W. Norton, 2002).

19. bell hooks, *Ain't I a Woman: Black Women and Feminism* (Boston: South End Press, 1981), 156–57. Hooks had bemoaned the fact that, "in regards to race, the women's movement has become simply another arena in which white and black women compete to be the chosen female group. This power struggle has not been resolved by the formation of opposing interest groups" (156). I am arguing that, by forming a cross-racial, nationwide "interest group" bound by shared literacy, Winfrey strategically countered the problem hooks had described.

20. *Sula* was the last book chosen for the original club. On that broadcast, Winfrey declared to Morrison: "There would never have been a Book Club had there not been you as an author." *The Oprah Winfrey Show,* May 2, 2002 (Harpo Productions transcript), 9.

21. Ibid., 12. Significantly, as Barbara Sicherman has pointed out, "Oprah's Book Club did more for Toni Morrison's sales than the Nobel Prize in Literature." See "Connecting Lives: Women and Reading, Then and Now," in *Women in Print: Essays on the Print Culture of American Women from the Nineteenth and Twentieth Centuries,* ed. James P. Danky and Wayne A. Wiegand (Madison: University of Wisconsin Press, 2006), 5.

22. *The Oprah Winfrey Show,* May 2, 2002 (transcript), 5, 10–11, 13 (emphasis added), 13.

23. Ibid., 12, 14.

24. Ibid., 14, 16, 18.

25. *The Oprah Winfrey Show,* November 16, 2000 (Harpo Productions transcript), 12, 15.

26. For parallel coverage in the *New York Times* and other sources, see Sicherman, "Connecting Lives," 19, n. 10.

27. Julia Keller and Mark Caro, "O, No! O, Yes! Is Oprah's Logo a Plus or a Minus? He Loathes It. She Smells a Red Herring," *Chicago Tribune,* October 29, 2001, North Sports Final Edition, 5.1. The parallel he-versus-she structure of the article's subtitle lays out the gendered battle lines for the story's content.

28. Julia Keller, "Franzen vs. the Oprah Factor: The 'Dissing' of Winfrey Hovers over Authors' Talk," *Chicago Tribune,* November 12, 2001, North Sports Final Edition, 5.3.

29. Laura Miller, "Book Lovers' Quarrel," Salon.com, http://www.salon.com/books/feature/2001/10/26/franzen_winfrey/index.html (accessed March 8, 2002).

30. June Howard, "What Is Sentimentality?" *American Literary History* 11, no. 1 (Spring 1999): 70–77. Besides reconstructing a history of literary sentimentalism that recognizes the place of men in its tradition, Howard also draws on disciplines from outside the humanities, such as biology and anthropology, to illustrate that much of the work on sentimentalism among scholars of literature has oversimplified this complicated social phenomenon.

31. Significantly, online club members' criticism of Morrison's being virtually a regular on the list was not mounted directly as a need for more lowbrow literature or as a race-related issue. Rather, readers wanted greater variety, and one correspondent wondered why Winfrey had neglected young black male authors such as E. Lynn Harris and Eric Jerome Dickey.

32. Sarah Robbins, *Managing Literacy, Mothering America: Narratives on Women's*

Reading and Writing in the Nineteenth Century (Pittsburgh: University of Pittsburgh Press, 2004).

33. See Deborah Brandt, "Sponsors of Literacy," *CCC: College Composition and Communication* 49 (May 1998): 165–85. Brandt's concept of literacy sponsors focuses more on social class than gender, but it is quite compatible with my own framework of maternal literacy managers using domestic literacy narratives to exercise social influence.

34. Hall, "The 'Oprahfication' of Literacy," 651–52.

35. "*Anna Karenina:* Leo Tolstoy," Oprah's Book Club Web site, http://www.oprah.com/obc_classic/featbook/anna/novel/anna_novel_main.jhtml (accessed October 1, 2004).

36. "Oprah's Book Club Returns," *The Oprah Winfrey Show,* June 18, 2003 (Harpo Productions transcript), 10.

37. "Genre: The Many Faces of *Anna Karenina,*" Oprah's Book Club Web site, http://www.oprah.com/obc_classic/featbook/anna/genre/anna_genre_main.jhtml (accessed October 1, 2004).

38. Amy Mandelker, "Tolstoy and the Victorians: What Book Was Anna Reading on the Train?"; Judith Armstrong, "The Novel of Adultery: The True Shock of *Anna Karenina*"; and Anne Hruska, "The Family Novel: Calling the Family into Question," all on Oprah's Book Club Web site, http://www.oprah.com/obc_classic/featbook/anna/genre/anna_genre_a.jhtml (accessed October 1, 2004).

39. "The Finish Line," Oprah's Book Club Web site, http://www.oprah.com/obc_classic/featbook/anna/20040915/20040915_slide_main.jhtml (accessed October 1, 2004).

40. "Brad Pitt, Cameron Diaz, Olsen Twins: After the Show," *The Oprah Winfrey Show,* May 31, 2004 (Harpo Productions transcript), 18.

41. Edward Wyatt, "Oprah's Book Club Reopening to Writers Who'll Sit and Chat," *New York Times,* September 23, 2005, A1, C13.

42. See Margo Hammond and Ellen Heitzel, "The Book Babes Reflect on the Return of the Queen," *Book Standard,* September 28, 2005, http://www.thebookstandard.com/bookstandard/community/commentary_display.jsp?vnu_content_id=1001218435 (accessed October 14, 2005).

43. Cecilia Konchar Farr, "Oprah's Return to 'New' Books Gives Writers Reason to Cheer," *TwinCities.com: Pioneer Press,* September 27, 2005, http://www.twincities.com/mld/twincities/news/editorial/12747957.htm (accessed October 14, 2005). Farr is also the author of a helpful overview of Winfrey's initial book club: *Reading Oprah: How Oprah's Book Club Changed the Way America Reads* (Albany, N.Y.: SUNY Press, 2005).

44. David Usborne, "Authors of the World Rejoice as Oprah's Book Club Embraces Modern Literature," *Independent: Online Edition,* October 13, 2005,

http://enjoyment.independent.co.uk/books/news/article314743.ece (accessed October 14, 2005).

45. Ibid.; Karen R. Long, "In Oprah's Club, Anyone Can Belong," *Plain Dealer*, October 2, 2005, http://www.cleveland.com/entertainment/plaindealer/index.ssf?/base/entertainment/1128159587325940.xml&coll=2&thispage=1 (accessed October 14, 2005); Steven Barrie-Anthony, "Gritty Memoir Gets a Boost from Oprah," *Los Angeles Times,* October 6, 2005, http://www.mercurynews.com/mld/mercurynews/living/12831296.htm (accessed October 14, 2005).

46. Barrie-Anthony, "Gritty Memoir."

Knowing for Sure

Epistemologies of the Autonomous Self in O, the Oprah Magazine

Marjorie Jolles

A common popular narrative of female empowerment is the story of the woman who goes looking for personal satisfaction and "completion" in others and, after much disappointment, only truly finds it in herself. This narrative suggests a vague link to American popular conceptions of feminism, which for some includes the political, ethical, and cultural ideologies that argue for women's self-determination.[1] Some of these ideologies associated with the popular cultural version of American feminism are drawn from modern liberal theory, which, in celebrating self-determination as the superior path to selfhood, conflates personal authenticity with personal autonomy. According to the logic of this conflation, the authentic woman is one who is willing to define herself against the social grain, who is willing to defy expectations, who is willing to belong to no one but herself in the pursuit of self-knowledge. Others are perceived as threats to authenticity, as unambiguously outside the borders of the self. Detachment from community, in this brand of American popular feminism, therefore appears to be required for self-knowledge.

A persistent spokeswoman for this equation is Oprah Winfrey as she appears in her personal column, "What I Know for Sure," in each issue of *O, the Oprah Magazine.* In the Winfreyan discourse, the highest virtue is attached to being "true to oneself"—which is to say authentic and autonomous to the point of nonconformity, if necessary. Not surprisingly, living too much for others is constructed as a moral failure.

Feminist commitment, though, need not entail or require detachment from others, even if popular narratives suggest otherwise. In fact, notable feminist theorists have been trenchant critics of the modern liberal conflation of autonomy with personal authenticity. These theorists provide a way out of these problematic formulations of feminine selfhood, and so I bring them into a dialogue with this Winfreyan discourse precisely to highlight how dissimilar they are, despite some popular linkages.

In this essay I trace the development and articulation of Winfrey's mandate to her readers that they "live their best life," which for Winfrey entails espousing a vision of total, radical autonomy in the spheres of love, work, and family.[2] I argue that this specific understanding of authentic selfhood rehearses classic American rhetoric of self-reliance that historically left little room for the feminine. In so doing, I highlight inherent contradictions, ambivalences, and paradoxes in Winfrey's characteristically American message to her readers concerning their full emotional, spiritual, and physical flourishing. Winfrey's prescriptions to readers for finding the pathways to true selfhood and personal fulfillment are, at their foundation, paradoxical because she does not acknowledge that one's self is deeply, inextricably mediated by one's social and material world. Winfrey's notions of self in its relationship to others position her against various feminist critics, including feminist philosophers such as Iris Young and Eva Feder Kittay, who theorize the self's attachment to others in ways that undermine the self-other dichotomy, and feminist theorists of color, such as Patricia Hill Collins, Gloria Anzaldúa, and Maria Lugones, who have argued against individualism in favor of community as the primary grounding of identity. In particular, I highlight the limits of Winfrey's repeated conflation of autonomy with moral superiority and its failure to address features of everyday life for women in material terms and in the social networks and communities in which they are embedded.

Echoes of Emerson

"Nothing can bring you peace but yourself."[3] In the February 2004 issue of O, Winfrey quotes this Ralph Waldo Emerson edict in her "What I Know for Sure" column. In doing so, Winfrey explicitly attaches herself to a thinker whose ideas are frequently echoed, albeit implicitly, in much of what she knows for sure. In her meditations on love, family, and personal fulfillment, Winfrey echoes Emerson's defiant rhetoric of self-determination and nonconformity, which includes a characterization of society as repressive, limiting, and a threat to the purity of the self. For Emerson, prior to socialization the self exists as a source of unlimited passion and creativity, and its task is thus to preserve its natural virtue upon (reluctantly) entering into social life. Society and the world—or, more specifically, other people—are constructed as oppositional to the self, threatening to extinguish its inner fire.[4]

In "Self-Reliance," Emerson asserts that man and society occupy oppositional positions, with man described as naturally authentic, and society as a force of assimilation and restraint. For him, the voices of heroic individualism are "the voices which we hear in solitude, but they grow faint and inaudible as we enter into the world."[5] In this dualistic formulation, Emerson conjures a presocial self, a self that exists prior to "enter[ing] into the world." Moreover, Emerson attaches natural—which is to say, superior—virtue to the presocial self, describing the entrance into the social world as an experience of significant loss. Such a description suggests that social and political isolation is essential for the full flourishing of the self. As I will show, these same assumptions about the self and society are at the heart of "What I Know for Sure."

In "The Over-Soul," Emerson calls man "a stream whose source is hidden," suggesting the mystery of creation and the distance between the self and its core authentic essence.[6] In emphasizing this notion of the self as an interior essence, Emerson describes the self as fundamentally alienated and yearning for resolution through a return to its life force, located deep within. Naturalistic themes permeate Emerson's rhetoric of the self, likening its essence to a stream and, elsewhere, a "light"[7] and a "fire."[8] Emerson blames "society" for sending the source of this stream into hiding and frequently describes it as a drain on the self, robbing it of its primal, essential source.

Emerson includes one's own sense of self-knowledge among the many losses the self endures upon entering the sphere of the social. In "Self-Reliance," he elaborates the epistemic risk involved in sharing a world with others, demanding that we "live no longer to the expectation of these deceived and deceiving people. Say to them, 'O father, O mother, O wife, O brother, O friend, I have lived with you after appearances hitherto. Henceforth I am the truth's. . . . I appeal from your customs. I must be myself.'"[9] This oppositional construction does not merely divide the self from others; it pits other people exclusively against the self's personal truth, suggesting that others present not only an affective, moral, or material threat to the self but an epistemic threat as well. The close proximity of "I am the truth's" to "I must be myself" gestures toward a powerful rhetorical slippage in which truth and the autonomous self are collapsed into one; by extension, the false self is the self of relationship and attachment. This vision of the self—as non-conformist, as an inner stream, as fire, as the truth—are all uncannily, repeatedly rehearsed in Winfrey's particular "What I Know for Sure" discourse at the textual, rhetorical, and ideological levels.

The Rhetoric of Epistemology

"What I know for sure": what is one to make of Winfrey's cadenced refrain? What rhetorical ends are served through the rhythmic repetition of "what I know for sure," repeated not only from month to month with each successive issue but also as the authoritative echo within the column itself? Surely this repeated phrase helps establish Winfrey's ethos as someone who has the authority to speak derived from a lifetime of learning. But even more than establishing this authoritative ethos, "what I know for sure" highlights Winfrey's status as an epistemic agent. Winfrey presents herself as an authentic woman in full possession of self-knowledge and thus in full possession of self, as if they are one and the same. By offering up these pieces of prescriptive wisdom to her readers, Winfrey is in effect saying, "I know this for sure, and you should too." Asserting "what I know for sure" is significantly different from offering up "what I have learned for sure." Winfrey's chosen locution represents a privileging of solitary epistemological practices over those grounded in collective process. The declaration of "what I know for sure" sits ambiguously alongside her detailed personal accounts, within the text of the column, of when, where, and with whom she learned what she knows. Winfrey *does* acknowledge *learning* this wisdom. But her choice to return the locus of that knowledge to the self, as the column's title suggests, reflects her own belief that *knowing* for sure is more autonomous and thus stronger—not merely rhetorically but also epistemologically, morally, and politically—than *learning* for sure.

Although her epistemology may be solitary, Winfrey is nevertheless aware that what she knows for sure will be shared with others. In each monthly column, she invokes a loving community, constituted by her readers. Through the deft rhetorical device of the intimate first person, Winfrey both singles herself out and establishes a bond. Each column takes as its point of departure bits of charming autobiographical information—"sometimes I spend the whole day in my pajamas"[10] or "there I am sitting in Mr. Hooper's fifth-period algebra class"[11]—and builds to articulate the more abstract lessons that Winfrey knows for sure. The autobiographical information helps Winfrey establish legitimacy and specificity while also connecting with readers, many of whom can understand the column's lessons through the experiences of their own days spent in pajamas or their own memories of their algebra teachers. It is at once a self-reflexive move and a mirroring. In grounding what she knows for sure in the personal, and in conveying it with empathy and expressiveness, Winfrey is employing features of what Patricia Hill Collins has described as Afrocentric feminist epistemology, a practice wedded to an ethic of care in which "all views expressed and actions taken are thought to derive from a central set of core beliefs that cannot be other than personal."[12] In privileging the personal as the exclusive source of her knowledge, Winfrey appears to be engaged in a sort of consciousness-raising method, yet in content, she rejects one of the key tenets of such a practice: community.

Winfrey's epistemological authority—she does not just know, after all; she knows *for sure*—is further legitimated by her rhetorical skill in soliciting agreement. At the rhetorical level, she effectively merges with her reader.[13] She moves seamlessly from "I" to "you," suggesting that her truth will resonate with the reader's. This sort of gesturing to a shared world is, of course, ironic, given her insistence that her reader listen to nobody but herself.

The direct, intimate tone of "What I Know for Sure" rarely changes. There are, however, variations in how self-knowledge is characterized or how the device of self-knowledge appears. There are at least three intertwined registers of self-knowledge that Winfrey deploys to maximal effect: the narrative, the autonomous, and the temporal. These registers of self-knowledge are not discrete frames or axes but rather rhetorical stances or devices that, when engaged simultaneously, produce seductive visions of full, personal thriving. Self-knowledge appears in the narrative register when Winfrey asserts that others have expectations of the self that go against the self's own sense of self; they have a story of the self that differs from the self's own story. The autonomous register of self-knowledge is apparent in suggestions that others may think they know what is true about the self, but as Winfrey reassures her reader, only she, the reader, truly knows herself. Both the narrative and autonomous devices repeat the familiar Emersonian rhetoric that casts "these deceived and deceiving people" as pulling the self away from her truth, away from herself. Messages rendered in the temporal register of self-knowledge suggest a self unfolding over time toward ever-greater autonomy, authenticity, and truth. The self is described as in a constant state of spiritual and self-searching, invoking the Emersonian theme of a self alienated from its essence, seeking to return. The temporal aspect of this self's unfolding dovetails nicely with the monthly publication of O, as if each issue's "What I Know for Sure" column offers a benchmark for the forward-directed unfolding of the self, facilitated by the steady revelation of greater self-knowledge, which, it seems, reliably occurs in monthly increments.

In March 2004 Winfrey proclaimed, "The way to choose happiness is to follow what is right and real and the truth for you. You can never be happy living someone else's dream. Live your own. And you will for sure know the meaning of happiness."[14] Here Winfrey offers a dualistic interpretation of affective life, neatly assigning self and other to oppositional positions. Like Emerson, Winfrey is sure that we each have a truth—"what is right and real and the truth for you"—and that we can gain access to it if only other people will get out of our way. Winfrey summons an image of a self who loses her transparency upon entering into a relationship, a self whose epistemic vision is clouded by the expectations of others, whose alienation from her personal truth is the result of competing narratives, and who acts as proof that "you can never be happy living someone else's dream." Additionally, Winfrey writes in the autonomous and temporal registers of self-knowledge by encouraging the self to forget what her loved ones know about her and to seek her truth from her own inner source.

In September 2003 Winfrey asked, "Does what you're doing now feel right? Does it fill you up or leave you drained? Forget what everyone else wants for you. This is not your mother's or your best friend's journey. Your role is not just as your husband's wife, your boss's employee, or your children's mother. . . . We were all born with this fire, but beginning in childhood, we let others snuff it out."[15] Likening the self's inner energy to "this fire," Winfrey is directly summoning Emersonian notions of the passionate, presocial self. Likewise, by pointing to those primary others in her reader's world—mother, best friend, husband, boss, children—she deploys another Emersonian trope, depicting these relationships as drains on her soul. Knowing for sure in this instance engages the narrative, autonomous, and temporal registers. For Winfrey, the roles that others offer the reader—daughter, best friend, wife, employee, mother—do not match the self's own truth, her own self-narrative. This construction also demands that the reader know autonomously what "feels right" for her, and to back up this claim, Winfrey invokes an originally authentic self "born with this fire" but snuffed out over time by others.

Although the authentic self may be a "fire" at times, it is also repeatedly described as a deep reservoir that can be full or empty, abundant or drained. Others drain us; we alone fill ourselves up. The self is not made or even sustained by others; instead, it is self-generated, something to be protected against the encroaching forces of assimilation that other people represent. In April 2004 Winfrey claimed, "I know for sure that you cannot give and give and give to everybody else and not give back to yourself. You will end up empty. . . . Replenish the well of yourself, *for* yourself first."[16] She sounds this note again only three months later, this time integrating an analysis of the gendered division of affective labor:

> That's because as women we've been programmed to sacrifice everything in the name of what is good and right for everyone else. Then if there's an inch left over, maybe we can have a piece of that. We need to deprogram ourselves. I know for sure that you can't give what you don't have. If you allow yourself to be depleted to the point where your emotional and spiritual tank is empty and you're running on fumes of habit, everybody loses. Especially you.[17]

The "need to deprogram ourselves" suggests a faith that a self exists outside of the social, a need to retreat from the influences of others, and a palpable frustration with the fact of other people. Winfrey is, in effect, arguing that for women to be strong, they must return to a presocial,

Archimedean point of purity. The moral prescription that the self find happiness not in others but in herself also participates in the Emersonian fantasy of a presocial existence in which, free from constraint, the self can finally shine.

Relational Subjectivity

The failure of "What I Know for Sure" to adequately reflect the fact of women's relational embeddedness is not a minor flaw. Because separating from others is at the core of Winfrey's conception of her reader's full thriving, the entire "What I Know for Sure" project fails in any real, material sense to provide a vision of a feminine subjectivity as both authentic and autonomous. Individuals simply cannot detach from *all* their commitments, nor would many of them wish to. These impractical, unappealing, and impossible prescriptions only highlight the privilege that separating actually requires. For Winfrey to go all the way with this message, she must acknowledge the ambiguous positions where life actually takes place, where we belong to others as well as to ourselves, where identity accrues as a result of, not despite, attachment. Instead, Winfrey leaves her committed reader in a dissonant place, unable to translate this rhetoric into a practical formula for greater fulfillment in life. What Winfrey is selling may work at the rhetorical level, but it lacks enough of a progressive critique to represent any kind of breakthrough in popular discourses of women's empowerment.

There are, though, feminist critics working in the area of relational subjectivity who suggest alternative methods for women to rethink personal flourishing. Winfrey's self-as-reservoir metaphor lends itself particularly well to addressing questions of feminine subjective autonomy and attachment in the cases of pregnancy and motherhood, situations in which women experience attachment to others in profound corporeal, affective, and political ways that exceed the self-as-wellspring–others-as-drain dichotomy. Despite her repeated expressions of respect for mothers, Winfrey's fantasy of the self who achieves secure detachment from others does not appear able to accommodate them.[18] Accounts of pregnancy and motherhood as oppressive are not uncommon in some discourses of feminine self-determination that cling to an ideology of anxious individualism. However, work in the areas of relational identity, lesbian feminism, and multicultural feminism has contributed innovative accounts of the self as productively enhanced by relationships, rather than swallowed up by them.

A wide range of feminist thinkers in the 1970s and 1980s began reconsidering the negative conflation of women with nature, reclaiming and reevaluating experiences such as pregnancy and dependence as positive and thereby rejecting the notion that these feminine practices or modes of bodily being were *inherently* inferior or damaging to women outside of their cultural degradation as such. Challenging the woman-as-nature discourses and moving to creatively open up the meanings of pregnancy and motherhood helped initiate a movement to rethink embodiment as not merely the nagging, accidental material grounding of the self but as an essential part of the subject-formation process that is mediated as much by ideology as by "nature." As part of the breakdown of the modern notion of the self as an isolated consciousness, the self and its body began to be construed as cultural products created by immediate relations, as well as through social structures and processes of cultural entrainment. As part of this turn, feminist philosophers began advancing the notion of the relational self—that is, the self that achieves selfhood not through transcendence of the social but through relationship; the self for whom relationships and others are not drains on individuality. Instead, personal authenticity for the relational self is created through engagement with others within an already culturally mediated field.

Iris Young presents a rather literal commentary on attachment with her phenomenological account of the relational, corporeal, interdependent self in the essay "Pregnant Embodiment." There, she offers an account of pregnant subjectivity that not only exceeds the traditional categories of self and other but also proposes to redistribute the meanings of those categories entirely. Although she is indebted to Merleau-Ponty's work on embodiment, Young argues that his phenomenological-existentialist conception of the body as the locus of consciousness requires conceiving of the subject as singular in both selfhood and body, assuming "the subject as a unity." Young claims that pregnancy is a concrete experience of the self as literally constituted by otherness to the degree that both division and unity are impossible; it is an experience in which the self is definitely not one but not entirely two either, where the boundaries between self and other are unclear, "a body subjectivity that is decentered, myself in the mode of not being myself."[19]

During the early stages of pregnancy, Young feels the movement of the fetus and describes it as follows: "It is *my* feeling, *my* insides, and it feels somewhat like a gas bubble, but it is not; it is different, in another place, belonging to *another*, another that is nevertheless my body." Suddenly the categories of mine–not mine, inner-outer, you–me are problematic: "Pregnancy challenges the integration of my body experience by rendering fluid the boundary between what is within, myself, and what is outside, separate. I experience my insides as the space of another, yet my own body."[20]

Agency for the pregnant woman in Young's account is always partial, always impure. She occupies an ambiguous position: simultaneously willful consciousness—able to make decisions and choices—and unruly bodily being(s)—unsure of where "me" ends and "you" begins. The pregnant woman is self and other at once, yet because she is neither one purely, these dichotomous categories break down. This self is neither single nor double but somewhere in between, and living in such ambiguity and dynamism makes her an unlikely candidate for taking up Winfrey's project, which requires allegiance to the dualistic logic of modern discourses of identity.

Pregnant women and mothers are bonded to others affectively as well. Eva Feder Kittay discusses the relational self who sustains her identity through affective, political, and material relations, thereby challenging the dualistic discourses of modern autonomy to account for the self on whom another life is entirely dependent. To have one's identity entail caring for another poses a problem for the Emersonian-Winfreyan model of autonomy, which takes for granted the autonomy (and equality) of all subjects. For Kittay, dependency workers—those "upon whom the dependent persons depend"—are faced with the problems of speaking for (at least) two people at once and inhabiting the public and private spheres simultaneously.[21] And, significantly, it is women who have historically fallen into the category of dependency workers.

The intersubjectivity of the dependency worker is a problem, however, only if autonomy is construed as a given or a goal that cannot allow interdependencies. Feminist philosophers developed the notion of the relational self precisely as a critique of the individualism that "creates a conceptual illusion that dependencies do not exist—or at least are not a political matter."[22] The relational self in Kittay's work on dependency emerges as a self whose values, beliefs, and demands necessarily include those of others. One is epistemologically, morally, physically, and politically informed by another to the degree that the other is implied in the very subject herself. Autonomy, defined as thinking for oneself, appears unavailable to the subject who cares for others, since "the voice of the dependency worker is not the independent voice of the equal autonomous agent of liberal political theory; it is a voice sometimes blending the interests of the caregiver and care-recipient, sometimes torn between conflicting interests."[23] Moreover, dependency challenges the public-private distinction; caring for others, historically considered a private act that takes place within the private sphere of the family, influences the voice of the dependency worker as citizen to the extent that her dependents' needs and rights blend or conflict with her own. Her public and private worlds become, like her voice, blurred, and the purity of those positions compromised.

Caregivers are not a small minority for whom special rules apply; for Kittay, attachment—in terms of care, but certainly not limited to it—grounds all human experience. Kittay and other critical feminist theorists do not demand that women can or should inhabit the illusory position of radical autonomy; instead, they argue that in its failure to accommodate the "interdependencies" that "create the central bonds of human life," the fantasy of autonomy is grossly inadequate.[24]

These feminist critiques against individualism suggest that the retention of dualisms such as self-other and free-constrained only reproduce the harsh conditions under which women find no room to, in Winfrey's rhetoric, "live their best lives." A woman's "liberation" does not entail simply becoming a self unencumbered by relationship; it amounts to rethinking the discourses that uphold these dualistic constructions. For a progressive, critical feminism, the construction of women's lives that relies on these dichotomies fails to engage the question of how, when identity is fundamentally relational, one can ever speak or think purely for oneself or, in Winfrey's case, know oneself for sure.

Young's and Kittay's essays approach the problem of the autonomous subject from different philosophical perspectives. Both are important not only for their diverse contributions to the notion of the relational self but also because they point out the considerable discursive, practical, and political exclusions required to maintain the integrity of the concept of the autonomous subject. Such a subject can have neither dependents nor corporeal attachments. If authenticity is defined as becoming one's own woman, then it seems that women with integral attachments to others forfeit access to authenticity.

Community, Family, Impurity

At the level of the private individual, pregnancy, motherhood, and dependency care are all rich examples of conditions and practices that undermine the project of conceiving the self and its needs in opposition to others and their demands. Feminist analyses of the self in community also help challenge the oppositional model at the structural, public level. Specifically, feminist theorists of color have shown ways to think about the self in community that eschew ideologies of radical individualism and self-interest, or what Patricia Hill Collins calls "public, market-driven, exchange-based community models." Such a market model dominates contemporary culture in which community is understood "as arbitrary and fragile, structured fundamentally by competition and domination." Echoes of this model persist in "What I Know for Sure," whereas, according to Collins, "Afrocentric models of community stress connections, caring, and personal accountability." African American culture gives us the locutions "brother" and "sister" as shorthand for men and women united in struggle. Assigning family signifiers to nonblood relations indicates not a retreat from connection and community but a strong, vital pull toward it. Collins also points to the African American tradition of "othermothers—women who assist bloodmothers by sharing mothering responsibilities" to describe the rich networks in which black American women and families thrive.[25]

These notions of the self as constituted by community can actually destabilize heteronormativeness more than Winfreyan compulsory individuality can. Judging from her repeated, vaguely hostile characterization of others as drains on the self, it seems that Winfrey is—however ambivalently—inclined toward opening up a space for her readers to envision a full life that does not necessarily entail marriage and parenting.[26] Models of self, community, and family found in African American culture and as outlined by Collins allow for a more concrete way out of normative expectations regarding partnership, monogamy, and family, while still leaving room for self-definition. "Self," Collins writes, "is not defined as the increased autonomy gained by separating oneself from others. Instead, the self is found in the context of family and community," but only if we rethink community as life-giving rather than draining.[27]

Likewise, Gloria Anzaldúa's work on *mestizaje* reveals that visions of the self as pure, and purely her own, are fantasies supported by the refusal to acknowledge our own hybridity and interconnectedness. The *mestiza,* Anzaldúa's figure of an especially fluid, antidualist, postcolonial feminist consciousness, understands that identity comes from the fact that women must "continually walk out of one culture and into another." Rather than longing for tight borders under the sign of anxious individualism, Anzaldúa advocates an embrace of ambiguity, rejecting the rigidity of dualistic paradigms and of the borders of the self, arguing that "rigidity means death."[28]

Just as Winfrey puts epistemic concerns at the center of her Emersonian individualism, achieving self-knowledge is of equal concern to feminist theorists who favor relational subjectivity. Maria Lugones argues that "we are fully dependent on each other for the possibility of being understood and without this understanding we are not intelligible, we do not make sense, we are not solid, visible, integrated; we are lacking."[29] Thus, for Lugones, one cannot live outside of community, for it provides the basic foundation for identity, for visibility, for making sense. The self of Winfreyan individualism, in its constant, self-conscious separation from others and defense of its borders, appears to be more fragile than solid. Connection to others need not pull the self away from itself but can, instead, be cause for greater integration and visibility, both features that Winfrey would ascribe to a fully thriving woman.

Like Anzaldúa, Lugones has elsewhere used the trope of purity-impurity to connote the dichotomy of autonomy-attachment. She links it to the question of self-knowledge when she claims, "The subject who can occupy such a [pure] vantage point . . . must himself be pure . . . so as to occupy the vantage point and perceive unity amid multiplicity. He must not himself be pulled in all or several perceptual directions; he must not perceive richly."[30] Winfrey's fetish with the purity of her epistemological position does not allow the richness of perception that Lugones associates with multiplicity and the impure. Instead, Winfrey's purity protects—or prevents—her from being pulled in too many directions.

In her groundbreaking text *Lesbian Ethics,* Sarah Hoagland introduced the notion of "autokoenony," or "the self in community," to the feminist revision of the self as grounded in relationship.[31] The autokoenonous self experiences her selfhood in close relation to otherness and sees otherness not as a threat but as a necessary, constituting force. The autonomous self, for Hoagland, is defined in opposition to others, who are defined as threats or limits to an otherwise unlimited self, much like the self of "What I Know for Sure." Under the autonomy model, both the self and others are things to be controlled. Community, that space where others lurk, is thus also a force of constraint. Construing community as a threat to happy selfhood is to suggest that social and political isolation is essential for the full flourishing of the self. The construction of society as an alienating force also reinforces the sense of the self as presocial, as the keeper of an essential fire, or life force, deep within that gets buried when the self is exposed to others. The autokoenonous self, in contrast, "is one who is aware of her self as one among others within a community that forms her ground of being, one who makes her decisions in consideration of her limitations as well as in consideration of the agendas and perceptions of others. She does not merge with others, nor does she estrange herself; she *interacts* with others in situations."[32] Month after month, Winfrey vehemently cautions her readers against precisely this kind of consideration.

The truth is that we live our lives in what Simone de Beauvoir called "situation," an embedded, living, breathing context that is supported on multiple axes through multiple relations, commitments, and attachments.[33] Life in "situation" is a life of ambiguity and entanglement, where one is simultaneously one's own subject and others' object, a self for itself and for others. Women's lives most of all reflect this kind of rich engagement. To sell women authenticity on a platform of defiance and rejection of others is, in effect, to forever deny us that authenticity.

Conclusion: The Question of Love

Winfrey clearly argues in "What I Know for Sure" that the authentic feminine self is necessarily the autonomous self. She also, oddly, valorizes what she considers one reward of such autonomy: romantic love. Winfrey acknowledges that strong, authentic women might have a healthy distance from the influence of others, but they often have fulfilling love and romance in their lives. Thus Winfrey repeatedly engages two competing impulses: on the one hand, that the presocial self is the true self, and only the pursuit of autonomy can restore the self to this truth; on the other hand, we all crave and deserve love and regard having it—in the form of a healthy primary romantic relationship—as a salient index of full personal flourishing. In fact, at various points throughout the many installments of "What I Know for Sure," Winfrey seems to suggest that one is in a position to experience such healthy love, romance, sex, and affective connection only *after* one has successfully separated from the webs of relationship, enabling one to find truth.[34]

One need not endorse these paradoxical messages in order to claim the value of self-respect and a loving relationship. Communitarian, relational models of selfhood enable both. To resolve some of these fundamental paradoxes, Winfrey has powerful resources in feminist thinkers who effectively challenge the value, virtue, and sustainability of an autonomous self and who offer powerful accounts of love that support the relational view.

In 2002 Winfrey held both impulses at once when she implored her readers to let go of the fantasy that others can fill them up and tend to that task themselves. Through a subtle logic of mutual exclusivity, in which connection to others magically does not require abdicating some personal power, she claimed:

> What we're striving for is authenticity. . . . Married or single, if you're looking for a sense of completion, I encourage you to look inward. . . . What I know for sure is that if you're looking for your happily-ever-after in the arms and eyes of another person, you will always be disappointed. In the end, you're the only person who can satisfy the deepest craving that every one of us shares—the need to feel significant. If you don't already know you have significance, the process of discovering that is the very work you were put on this earth to do. . . . The irony of relationships is that you're usually not ready for one until you can say from the deepest part of yourself, "I will never again give up my power to another person." Only then will you be a woman who's ready for the strongest kind of connection.[35]

That is the "irony of relationships," indeed. Winfrey deserves credit for rejecting the notion that another person can ever be the *sole* source of one's identity. Notice, however, the defiant tone and hostile, individualistic characterization of what occurs in a relationship: we "give up power to another person." What Winfrey does not acknowledge is the power we derive from others. Rather than redefining attachment as a constitutive, positive force, Winfrey's prescription for achieving fullness seems to require casting off the draining effects of others, as if achieving strength and agency and living one's best life are incompatible with having deep bonds to others. Until we rethink how we understand personal "power" vis-à-vis relations with others—until we accept that others are just as responsible for giving us power as they are for taking it away—this problematic dualism will appear reasonable.

If we accept that selves are not merely sharing space with others but are necessarily and substantively constituted, transformed, and sustained by them, then we lose some of that epistemological anxiety concerning the knowability of the self's boundaries that causes us to long to "know for sure." Especially in explorations into love and politics, where subjective opening and closing are of primary importance, it seems that Winfrey cannot deviate from a notion of a fixed, oppositional, presocial self. Embracing our reliance on relationship does not render us powerless to choose which relationships will fortify us best, and *that*—the power to choose with whom we will "live our best lives"—is among the worthiest promises of feminism. Following philosopher Kelly Oliver, if we were to rethink loving subjectivity against the hostile individualistic model as it circulates in "What I Know for Sure," we could embrace relationships as that which fill us up, rather than drain us, and embrace love as "an ethics of differences that thrives on the adventure of openness."[36]

Notes

1. By referring to this sensibility as "American popular feminism," I do not mean to suggest a necessary, firm separation between academic feminism and feminist theory, on the one hand, and nonacademic feminist ideologies that circulate in American popular culture, on the other. Surely the two inform and overlap with each other, and surely there are numerous sites of feminist activity and thinking located in neither the academy nor mainstream popular culture. Nevertheless, part of this essay's larger argument is that a good deal of feminist rhetoric found in American popular culture seems doomed to fail women when put into practice and that academic (for

lack of a better word) feminist theories of relational subjectivity can address those failures.

2. Always implicit and frequently explicit in Winfrey's logic is the idea that in order to "live one's best life" (a paraphrasing of a frequent Winfrey theme and the name of a regular *O* feature), one must "know" certain things "for sure."

3. Ralph Waldo Emerson (from the essay "Self-Reliance") in Oprah Winfrey, "What I Know for Sure," *O, the Oprah Magazine,* February 2004, 206.

4. See Ralph Waldo Emerson, *The Portable Emerson,* ed. Carl Bode (New York: Viking Penguin, 1981), specifically the essays "Self-Reliance," "Experience," "The Transcendentalist," "The Poet," and "The Over-Soul."

5. Emerson "Self-Reliance," 141.

6. Emerson "The Over-Soul," 210.

7. Emerson "Self-Reliance," 151.

8. Emerson "The Transcendentalist," 108.

9. Emerson "Self-Reliance," 155.

10. Oprah Winfrey, "What I Know for Sure," *O, the Oprah Magazine,* April 2004, 254.

11. Oprah Winfrey, "What I Know for Sure," *O, the Oprah Magazine,* December 2003, 260.

12. Patricia Hill Collins, *Black Feminist Thought: Knowledge, Consciousness, and the Politics of Empowerment* (New York: Routledge, 1990), 218.

13. Winfrey has been described as a master at this sort of empathic merge in the context of her television talk show. See Laurie L. Haag, "Oprah Winfrey: The Construction of Intimacy in the Talk Show Setting," *Journal of Popular Culture* 26 (1993): 115–21.

14. Oprah Winfrey, "What I Know for Sure," *O, the Oprah Magazine,* March 2004, 246.

15. Oprah Winfrey, "What I Know for Sure," *O, the Oprah Magazine,* September 2003, 286.

16. Oprah Winfrey, "What I Know for Sure," *O, the Oprah Magazine,* April 2004, 254.

17. Oprah Winfrey, "What I Know for Sure," *O, the Oprah Magazine,* July 2004, 190.

18. The May 2003 issue of *O* celebrated motherhood, but not without obvious ambivalence. For all the articles extolling the virtues of motherhood, there were also articles with titles such as "How Not to Turn into Your Mother," "12 Things a Stepmother Should *Never* Say," "The Well-Trained Mother," and "Make Your Own Mother." In that month's "What I Know For Sure" column, however, Winfrey claimed, "I know for sure that few callings are more honorable," and she referred to mothers as "great spiritual teachers." Taken

together, the message in this issue about motherhood was more anxious than comfortable. See *O, the Oprah Magazine,* May 2003, 290.

19. Iris Marion Young, "Pregnant Embodiment: Subjectivity and Alienation," in *Throwing Like a Girl and Other Essays in Feminist Philosophy and Social Theory* (Bloomington: Indiana University Press, 1990), 141–59, 162.

20. Ibid., 162–63 (emphasis added).

21. Eva Feder Kittay, "Human Dependency and Rawlsian Equality," in *Feminists Rethink the Self,* ed. Diana Tietjens Meyers (Boulder, Colo.: Westview Press, 1997), 219.

22. Ibid., 222.

23. Ibid.

24. Ibid.

25. Collins, *Black Feminist Thought,* 53, 223, 119.

26. This is not to say that Winfrey envisions a full life as a life without love, however. I address the question of how Winfrey broadcasts competing mandates—to separate and to love—in the final section of this essay.

27. Collins, *Black Feminist Thought,* 105.

28. Gloria Anzaldúa, "La Conciencia de la Mestiza: Towards a New Consciousness," in *Writing on the Body: Female Embodiment and Feminist Theory,* ed. Kate Conboy, Nadia Medina, and Sarah Stanbury (New York: Columbia University Press, 1997), 233–47, 234, 235.

29. Maria Lugones, "Playfulness, 'World'-Travel, and Loving Perception," in *Women, Knowledge, and Reality: Explorations in Feminist Philosophy,* 2d ed., ed. Ann Garry and Marilyn Pearsall (New York: Routledge, 1997), 424.

30. Maria Lugones, "Purity, Impurity, and Separation," in *The Second Signs Reader,* ed. Ruth-Ellen B. Joeres and Barbara Laslett (Chicago: University of Chicago Press, 1996), 282.

31. Sarah Lucia Hoagland, *Lesbian Ethics: Toward New Value* (Palo Alto, Calif.: Institute of Lesbian Studies, 1988), 145.

32. Ibid.

33. Simone de Beauvoir, *The Second Sex,* trans. and ed. H. M. Parshley (New York: Vintage, 1989), 728–32.

34. A perhaps more cynical, yet nevertheless plausible, interpretation of the coexistence of these dual impulses in the "What I Know for Sure" discourse would argue that normative coupling is presented not merely as a by-product of self-determination but as its *reward*—the implicit promise being that following one's own heart will land one a man.

35. Oprah Winfrey, "What I Know for Sure," *O, the Oprah Magazine,* March 2002, 216.

36. Kelly Oliver, *Witnessing: Beyond Recognition* (Minneapolis: University of Minnesota Press, 2001), 20.

Oprah Winfrey's Branding of Personal Empowerment

Damiana Gibbons

Fresh from the successful launch of Oprah's Book Club and the continued success of *The Oprah Winfrey Show,* Winfrey launched *O, the Oprah Magazine* in May–June 2000. In that premier issue, Oprah Winfrey proclaimed her desire to guide her readers toward personal empowerment while linking their success to her own self-empowerment: "This is the defining question of my life: How do you use your life to best serve yourself and extend that to the world? One answer is this magazine. To be able to share all the things I have learned and have access to other people's wisdom, and then put that into words that can benefit you, is a challenge and thrill for me."[1] Ideally, both parties gain some benefits from the magazine. Winfrey gets "a challenge and thrill," and readers get "all the things [she has] learned" and "access to other people's wisdom." Winfrey takes the wisdom of experts, combines it with her own, and presents it to the public, thus fashioning herself as an icon for self-empowerment. The readers, in turn, become recipients of Winfrey's knowledge. This interaction between Winfrey and her readers may seem like a win–win situation, but there is a subtle manipulation of message occurring here.

Lynette Clemetson, in a *Newsweek* article that declared Winfrey one of the "Women of the Century," summarized *O, the Oprah Magazine* beautifully:

Without a single guide to thin thighs or a saucier sex life, *O*
is a glossy rendering of Winfrey's on-air motivational crusade,

encouraging readers to revamp their souls the way Martha Stewart helps them revamp their kitchens. With articles on topics like women who rush too much, soul-searching interviews with celebrities like Sidney Poitier and flourishes like pull-out quotes from the likes of Winston Churchill and Deepak Chopra, O is reeling in a whole new breed of Oprah devotees: professionals with little time to watch her show. And with 150 ad pages per issue (stellar for even the hottest mags), it has Madison Avenue types paying new attention to the woman who used to cry with dysfunctional families on TV.[2]

The idea that the magazine symbolizes Winfrey's "motivational crusade, encouraging readers to revamp their souls," holds much truth. The diversity of self-help gurus and content, such as the "soul-searching interviews" and "pull-out quotes," speaks to the tightly controlled user-friendliness of O. The claim that Winfrey is attempting to gain a new demographic of "professionals with little time to watch her show" is close to the mark in terms of the intended audience for this magazine, which is clearly indicated by the success stories included. Last, the notion that Winfrey has become a financial powerhouse in another medium with extensive advertising shows that Winfrey's goal blends seemingly "selfless" self-help messages with a sharp eye for the financial bottom line.

More than self-help or spiritual guidance, then, O is a forum for Oprah Winfrey to "brand" self-empowerment in general. In this process of branding, any product or idea that appears in the magazine is labeled "Oprah." Essentially, Winfrey tells female consumers that if they strive to be as much like her as possible, they can create for themselves personal empowerment or fulfillment, just as she has. They need only buy the products or consume the ideas she advertises. More important, Winfrey, as the "Oprah" icon, also appropriates intellectual property, such as aesthetic appeal or interviewee responses, as an indirect method of branding those ideas as "Oprah's." The irony in the self-help messages in O is substantial: the readers' "self-help" must be overseen by a powerful icon if it is to succeed. Winfrey's branding of the goods and ideas in O form the foundation for how she controls not only her message of generalized self-help but also her readers' self-empowerment. She sells the idea that she will provide a clear path to self-empowerment, thus branding the path and the audience's self-empowerment. Readers participate in consuming the self-help by creating an identity that is similar to "Oprah." All they need to do is assemble the various parts of the "Oprah" program—advice from her gurus, her favorite things, her favorite books, and so forth—to gain their new, improved identity. The gathering of all these elements, disseminated in multiple media, in a single text serves to reinforce their primacy. Although the television show may anchor Winfrey's empire, this text is always available as a reminder of the "Oprah" program. In this way, Winfrey's branding of self-help is an intriguing example of Michel Foucault's modern Panopticon. Exploring his theories on how power is structured in society demonstrates how Winfrey's version of the Panopticon is created and maintained in *O* and how readers employ "technologies of the self," using their own desire to believe in themselves combined with the techniques outlined by Winfrey's Panopticon.

Panopticism

According to Foucault in *Discipline and Punish: The Birth of the Prison,* Panopticism is a technology that arose in the eighteenth century, similar to other technologies, such as industrialization and agronomy. Panopticism is based on Jeremy Bentham's Panopticon, an architectural plan for an ideal prison (it could also be applied to mental hospitals or schools). In this structure, the architecture itself sets up the control system for the prisoners. The prison cells surround the guards' rooms, forming a hexagon. The guards' rooms are always kept dark, while the prisoners' cells are made of glass and are kept lit at all times. The prisoners assume that they will be monitored and punished if they violate the rules supposedly established by the guards (the form such punishment will take is not discussed). The prisoners assume that they are under constant surveillance because it is always possible for them to be viewed, but they cannot see the guards in the center of the hexagon. This assumption of constant scrutiny leads the prisoners to fear punishment at all times, which leads them to control their own behavior. As Foucault writes, "The Panopticon is a machine for dissociating the see/being seen dyad: in the peripheric ring, one is totally seen, without ever seeing; in the central tower, one sees everything without ever being seen."[3] This dynamic is constitutive of the Panoptic gaze, whereby those being controlled do not see or understand who or what controls them.

This Panoptic gaze is crucial to the foundation of control, as those who are subjected to the gaze learn to control their own behavior, with or without the presence of an actual guard. In this way, "a real subjection is born mechanically from a fictitious relation. . . . He who is subjected to a field of visibility, and who knows it, assumes responsibility for the constraints of power; he makes them play spontaneously upon himself; he inscribes in himself the power relation in which he simultaneously plays both roles; he becomes the principle of his own subjection."[4] After a time, there is no need for an actual guard in the architectural structure, as long as the prisoners believe that they are being watched, even if they are not; as a result, they begin to self-police.

According to Foucault, the power structures fundamental to the Panopticon also work in a similar manner in larger society. At its simplest level, it is the way that power functions in society. He argues that members of this society control themselves based on invisible means of coercion called disciplines. In the larger society, as in the prison, the structure and the gaze inherent in the structure are no longer necessary. The person or message controlling and the people controlled no longer need to be physically proximate. Instead, disciplinary mechanisms form the foundation of control, and people self-police in response to these mechanisms. Foucault summarizes the goal of the Panopticon when he states:

> The celebrated, transparent, circular cage, with its high tower, powerful and knowing, may have been for Bentham a project of a perfect disciplinary institution; but he also set out to show how one may "unlock" the disciplines and get them to function in a diffused, multiple, polyvalent way throughout the whole social body. . . . Bentham dreamt of transforming into a network of mechanisms that would be everywhere and always alert, running through society without interruption in space or in time. The panoptic arrangement provides the formula for this generalization. It programmes, at the level of an elementary and easily transferable mechanism, the basic functioning of a society penetrated through and through with disciplinary mechanisms.[5]

In this theory, then, power structures have moved from the actual physical structure of the Panopticon to the more nebulous and more pervasive "disciplines." These disciplinary mechanisms have spread to every part of society, and they function in a way that is "polyvalent," which means, in this case, that the disciplines interact with and react to one another. These disciplines form the foundation for how people in a basic society function within it. A simplified example is the way disciplinary mechanisms are inherent in driving a car. In the United States, drivers do not need to be reminded to drive on the right side of the road each time they drive; most do so without self-reflection. Also, American car manufacturers place the steering wheel on the left side of the car. Both these actions enforce a system set up by the Department of Transportation, but drivers do not require constant reminders to follow the rules.

These disciplinary mechanisms, then, are techniques of being or ways of controlling. People act in line with these techniques. In this way, members of society act on their own bodies in ways that maintain the control of the power structures. The focus is on changing oneself, whether the perceived threat of punishment exists or not. Foucault expands his discussion of power relations to include individuals' place within them in *Technologies of the Self: A Seminar with Michel Foucault*. Using the "technology of the self," individuals "effect by their own means or with the help of others a certain number of operations on their own bodies and souls, thoughts, conduct, and way of being, so as to transform themselves in order to attain a certain state of happiness, purity, wisdom, perfection or immortality."[6] Given this idea, the readers of O magazine help themselves to "effect their own means" with the help of the magazine to "transform themselves."

Extending Foucault's analysis, I next examine how Winfrey's presence in O sets up visible and invisible techniques of controlling readers' intended responses, forming what I call Winfrey's Panopticon. The irony of her Panopticon is that Winfrey is the one who is constantly seen by both viewers of *The Oprah Winfrey Show* and readers of O magazine. In a twist on Foucault's Panopticon, it is the way in which Winfrey structures this visibility that forms the disciplinary mechanisms of her Panopticon. Winfrey is visible in ways that brand not only her media enterprises, such as her talk show and book club, but also the ideas of others, which she adopts. In the case of O, Winfrey provides the disciplinary mechanisms for readers through her consumable self-help concepts. The articles, advertisements, and interviews maintain a focus on Winfrey's supposed purpose of helping women to better themselves.

In some ways, the techniques of control are obvious, but more often, they are obscured. One can identify Winfrey's Panoptic gaze most readily when she is most visible, such as on the cover of each issue or in the editorials she writes. This gaze embodies the disciplinary mechanisms, which become less visible when Winfrey brands concepts as "Oprah." The control is created and maintained by Winfrey and the editors as they consistently brand different parts of the magazine and its contributors as "Oprah."

Selling Winfrey and Her Enterprises: The Panoptic Gaze at Work

On one level, O magazine is straightforward in terms of promoting and selling actual goods and services. The first level of marketing sells the magazine by emphasizing the connection between it and Oprah Winfrey. It is the most visible level of the branding of goods as "Oprah." In addition to being named after Winfrey, every issue of O has Winfrey, and Winfrey alone, on the cover. This collapsing of Winfrey and the magazine is a key selling point. For example, each issue has individual subscription cards similar to those found in all magazines that encourage readers to subscribe. The cards in O, though ostensibly serving the same purpose, function differently. In *Cosmopolitan,* for example, the subscription card has a small image of an issue of the magazine on one side with the slogan "Act Now! Save up to 57%."[7] The subscription cards promote and sell only the magazine. The cards in O, however, advertise Winfrey as much as the magazine. For instance, one card has the words "Oprah Anytime" scrolled across the top, with a picture of Winfrey occupying approximately one-third of the remaining space. A smaller picture of the magazine occupies less space, but Winfrey's picture is on the cover. Rather than relying on a typical slogan in isolation to advertise the magazine, such as "O Anytime," the visual images convey the impression that if readers subscribe to the magazine, they will gain unlimited access to Winfrey beyond her scheduled program. Of course, subscribers will *not* gain unlimited access to Winfrey, or even access that is linked in any way to the authentic individual, but the message is that the magazine will be a close second to the "real" Oprah Winfrey.

Oprah's Personal Growth Summits, a series of lectures that Winfrey offered in three cities during the summer of 2000, further illustrate how she bridges the branding of products and the branding of concepts. Although advertisements for the summits lasted only through the first few issues of *O*, because the summits ran for such a short time, they formed an interesting connection between Winfrey's activities outside of the magazine and the articles contained within it. The line between Oprah Winfrey the icon and the articles began to blur. Readers were asked to connect the summits with their own empowerment, but above all, they were asked to connect these summits with Winfrey herself. The subscription cards ask readers to make the same connection, but the summits made this connection even clearer. In these advertisements, Winfrey's picture was displayed prominently in the center of the page (the sponsors' logos were much smaller and located at the bottom of the page). The text read, "Come hear Oprah's inspirational advice for mapping out your own personal growth plan in this special seminar series." As with the other Winfrey enterprises, the self-help message was linked with Winfrey herself. Her "inspirational advice" would form the "map" for "personal growth." To emphasize this connection, the next few lines quoted Winfrey: "You only have to believe that you can succeed, that you can be whatever your heart desires, be willing to work for it, and you can have it."[8] Success was linked with knowing one's "heart['s] desires" and a "willing[ness] to work for it"; however, this referred not to the participants' knowledge but to Winfrey's. The participants must "know" and be "willing," but they need not perform any actual "work" to achieve this success, other than purchasing a ticket and attending the seminar. Winfrey presented this "know[ledge]" and "willing[ness]" as actual labor she would perform on behalf of her audience. After the summits concluded, the editors included an article on the events, replete with clichéd advice to readers, instructing them to "discover [their] true calling," "compose a mission statement," and "develop a sense of authentic power."[9] The article was more a recitation of the demographics of the audience at the summits than the promised self-help guide. The combination of self-help advice and demographics bridged the gap between selling a service and selling ideas. The "service" provided by Winfrey was in fact an encounter with a canon of branded advice, and Oprah Winfrey was the author. Already, the ideas were becoming more marketable than the short-lived "service" itself. Certainly the people who attended the summits had additional access to Winfrey's message by being physically located in the same space, and the Panopticon was made visible to those participants by that proximity. When the summits were discussed in *O,* readers might not have the same proximity, but the message remained. The Panopticon was becoming disciplinary mechanisms.

The personal growth summits have been changed into an online format called the "Live Your Best Life Workshop" on Oprah.com.[10] In the May 2004 issue of *O* magazine, this new interactive workshop was introduced as being more convenient, giving readers access to the workshop and Winfrey's ideas at any time. The advertisement for the online version included a quotation from Winfrey displayed on the first half of the page: "Let your light shine. Shine within you so that it can shine on someone else. Let your light shine." Next to a picture of Winfrey, on the bottom half of the page, readers were encouraged to log on to Oprah.com to find fulfillment. The copy read, "Experience an interactive version of Oprah's Live Your Best Life workshop, customized for you, on Oprah.com! Oprah's life stories and life lessons, along with the complete Oprah-guided Live Your Best Life workbook. Your chance to explore *you,* at your own pace."[11] Ironically, readers who subscribe to this site will not be exploring themselves; they will be exploring "Oprah's life stories and life lessons" and an "Oprah-guided" workbook. The service provided here is crafted to appeal to the self-improvement goals of the readers, but it is also carefully controlled. The disciplinary mechanisms created by the summits in their original form become more illusive and more powerful in this new medium.

Branding Concepts:
Making Self-Help into Disciplinary Mechanisms

The structure of the magazine further enhances a Winfrey-centered Panopticon. *O*'s "uplift" is carefully blended and user-friendly. First, each issue has one main goal identified as "This Month's Mission," such as "Generosity," "Stress Relief," "Balance," and "Confidence."[12] These missions help readers focus on one self-help goal rather than asking them to solve all their problems at once. More important, *O* makes each mission manageable by breaking it down into smaller components represented in the editorials and articles and in the magazine itself. These components ensure that readers can understand what steps they should follow to gain the full benefits of the Winfrey self-help program.

One example of these components is the calendar included in each issue. This calendar offers self-help questions and quotations that are intended to help readers focus on achieving a prescribed goal every day. For example, the mission in the March 2001 issue is "Self-Esteem: The 'O' Guide to Getting It." The introduction to the calendar states: "We live in an age of self-affirmation, but having self-esteem is about more than repeating certain mantras to yourself each morning. Developing real self-worth means working to accord yourself the same respect, generosity, and gentleness that you would give anyone you love deeply. It's about making a journey to know and appreciate yourself better. Even more, it's about trusting what your own heart is telling you."[13] First, this introduction asserts that other self-help models—such as repeating mantras—do not work. The next three vague sentences break down the concept of self-esteem into "bite-size" pieces. The first sentence tells women that they can gain self-esteem through loving and respecting themselves. The second sentence promises self-esteem to women who make "a journey" (no doubt led by the calendar). The third sentence focuses on "trusting what your own heart is telling you." Each of these imprecise goals can be fulfilled by reading and responding to the calendar on a daily basis. The advice and quotations promote the mission by keeping it present in readers' lives through their daily interaction with the calendar. The calendar's vague language cloaks the readers' dependence in the trappings of independence.

These diffused self-help messages are a prime example of Foucault's disciplinary mechanisms. Disciplines generalize power: "Discipline may be identified neither with an institution nor with an apparatus; it is a type of power, a modality for its exercise, comprising a whole set of instruments, techniques, procedures, levels of application, targets; it is a 'physics' or an 'anatomy' of power, a technology."[14] According to Foucault, the disciplinary mechanisms work only after the disciplines have moved into individuals' lives. As he posits, "In appearance, the disciplines constitute nothing more than an infra-law. They seem to extend the general forms defined by law to the infinitesimal level of individual lives; or they appear as methods of training that enable individuals to become integrated into these general demands."[15] In the case of O, readers become part of the disciplinary mechanism by following the guidelines set out by the calendar and by incorporating Winfrey's message into the "infinitesimal level of [their] individual lives." Yet they are made to think that they are autonomous because they are answering questions and exploring their own identities. The "training" for the readers is learning to know themselves, or becoming self-realized. Those who succeed by becoming self-realized can become "integrated into [the] general demands" of Winfrey's message. They use their "technologies of the self"—in this case, their everyday lives. But the selling point—that these women are helping themselves *by* themselves—is a fiction. They have become part of and subject to the disciplinary mechanism.

When Winfrey creates consumable goods out of ideas—in the process, generating the means of control—the structure of the disciplinary mechanisms becomes obscured. The first step in making ideas consumable and obscuring these mechanisms is to appropriate the names and ideas of a certain group of recognizable people. Aside from the fact that Winfrey positioned her best friend, Gayle King, as editor-at-large, many of the regular contributors to the magazine are what we might consider anointed Winfrey "gurus," people who appear on her show on a regular basis or who got their start in some sort of Winfrey enterprise, such as Oprah's Book Club. Although Dr. Phil McGraw is the most famous of these individuals, contributions from experts who first appeared on her talk show—including Gary Zukav, Bob Greene, and Art Smith—dominate the bulk of advice columns on food, fitness, and the like in O, especially in the initial issues, thus creating a continuity between the discourse of the show and that of the magazine. The columns of some gurus, such as McGraw and Suze Orman, have become a mainstay of the magazine. Winfrey appropriates these people's ideas and brands them "Oprah"; in the process, the people themselves become minibrands that circulate throughout her various media. Readers know that if they need relationship advice, they should consult the representative of the "relationship brand," Dr. Phil. If they require fitness advice, they need to consult the "fitness brand," Bob Greene. Filtering her influence through this stable of gurus makes it appear that Winfrey is not controlling all parts of the magazine or the self-help messages; instead, readers begin to associate the different gurus with O, the enterprise that unites the different brands. This is particularly notable because these people would never appear onstage simultaneously.

Even interview subjects are not immune from becoming reconfigured as "Oprah" brands. The only interviewee responses published are those that support O's messages. In her introductions to the interviews, Winfrey often mentions the lengthy amount of time she spends with the interviewees but that much of the actual discussion is omitted. Granted, all magazines edit for length, but *O*'s editing clearly serves the purpose of enforcing the articulated mission of the month. For example, in the October 2000 issue, the mission was "Trust Yourself." In Winfrey's interview with Sidney Poitier, she muses, "All of the work I do is about helping people realize who they are. The whole quest for each of us is to become more of who we are meant to be. So how does someone get to that?" He responds, "We all have different selves: There is a public self, a private self and a core self." Poitier does not seem to agree that one can pinpoint one coherent and stable "self." Yet Winfrey's point is that finding one coherent self is possible (even desirable), especially with *O*'s guidance. Poitier is not following the script; therefore, Winfrey follows with the directed question, "How do you learn to trust that core self?"[16] She has missed Poitier's point deliberately: he does not advocate that there is one core self, but rather that many different selves emerge in different contexts. But that concept does not conform with the issue's mission, so Winfrey skips over the possibility of other selves to reiterate the primacy of the core self. In short, Winfrey selects the information she wants to convey to her readers and weeds out anything that she sees as unacceptable to her purpose. In this way, she demonstrates Foucault's idea that in order for the Panopticon to work, the controlling force must include certain people, ideas, and products, while necessarily excluding others:

> That is why discipline fixes; it arrests or regulates movements; it clears up confusion; it dissipates compact groupings of individuals wandering about the country in unpredictable ways; it establishes calculated distributions. It must also master all the forces that are formed from the very constitution of an organized multiplicity; it must neutralize the effects of counter-power that spring from them and which form a resistance to the power that wishes to dominate it: agitations, revolts, spontaneous organizations, coalitions—anything that may establish horizontal conjunctions.[17]

In this case, the "counter-power" is Poitier's definition of selves, but Winfrey must "fix" a definition to "clear up confusion" about her "mission." The concepts that she includes fit into the brand she is creating, thus cementing her control.

The Gaze Returned: Audience Self-Policing

Not only does *O* set up visible and invisible means of controlling the messages and the readers' intended responses; the magazine also extends these categories of inclusion and exclusion to manage how readers are supposed to control their own responses to the disciplinary mechanisms, their own "technologies of the self." Such inclusion and exclusion encourage readers to self-police. For example, in an article entitled "I Get Fit (with Help from My Friends)," the different parts of the Panopticon are represented as united. In this article, Winfrey outlines a workout support group that she started with some of her "friends." This article falls under the umbrella of a larger self-help campaign championed in the magazine called "Healthy 4 2000" and spearheaded by Bob Greene, Winfrey's "fitness brand." This article begins with Winfrey's observations about the unhealthy weight gain by one of her employees/ friends, *Oprah Winfrey Show* producer Lisa Erspamer. In an effort to help her friend, Winfrey invited a group of women (other employees from Harpo and Gayle King) to a "spa week" at one of her farms. Other Winfrey gurus, such as Phil McGraw and Art Smith, were on hand to offer advice and healthy eating. Of course, Winfrey codes this message as fostering the empowerment of Erspamer, the other spa participants, and readers, but it amounts to Winfrey taking charge of this self-help campaign.[18]

After explaining how the "Spa Girls" started, Winfrey highlights Erspamer's success story to show readers that this campaign can work for them. Then she includes the oaths the women took, taking their words—or at least the words created for the Spa Girls—to validate the entire group experience and spur others to action. She cements the readers' expected response with a short how-to guide for creating their own "Spa Girls weekend."[19] Interspersed throughout the "Spa Girls" article are references to Oprah.com, pictures of Winfrey, and examples of other articles in the magazine intended to provide motivation. Winfrey tells readers how to navigate through the different "Oprah" enterprises and through the magazine itself in order to adopt her recommended goals. The magazine is successful because the readers agree to try the self-help ideas or at least to buy the magazine and subject themselves to the field of visibility creation by Winfrey. Readers thus self-police when they buy the magazine and the products suggested.

O's follow-up Spa Girls article in the next issue provides a compelling model for readers. In this article, titled "Running on—and on—with Oprah," the focus is the success story of the entire group, which trained and finished a half-marathon. The interesting part of this article is how Winfrey "motivated" the group to do the marathon. First, without the group's consent, she announced on *The Rosie O'Donnell Show* that the group would run the half-marathon. Sheri Salata, a Spa Girl member and the author of the article, describes the group's reaction: "To this very day, she doesn't think it was her idea, but nobody else in our little workout club made that claim on national television. This is what that one conversation [between Winfrey and O'Donnell] has meant for us."[20] Winfrey decides what her group will aspire to and accomplish. She is in control, and the other members follow, but she attempts to obscure that control with the supposition that they are simply a group of friends trying to get physically fit together. Winfrey claims that it was not "her idea," but Salata questions that claim and asserts Winfrey's dominance by outlining how the group worked to complete the task of running the half-marathon. Although they took a vote, the tone of the article indicates that the Spa Girls had little free choice. When two members voice dissent, they are quickly, if mildly, mocked as a means of maintaining discipline. Notably, even Gayle King dissents. Salata states, "Early on, Gayle expressed concern about bone loss from all this running. . . . Oprah howled."[21] It is unclear what form this "howl" took, but the end result was that Winfrey got her way. The details of how they convinced King to toe the line are not mentioned, but the author follows this anecdote with a consideration of how difficult it must be for King to work out by herself in Connecticut while the rest of the Spa Girls work out in Chicago. King is represented as a weak link because she is too far away to be controlled by the group and—more importantly—by Winfrey. Essentially, anyone who does not follow the program set out by Winfrey and her gurus is a weak link. In this second article, the Spa Girls are presented as less of a success story and more of a cautionary tale about how dissenting employees in Winfrey's corporation will be perceived. One must keep in mind that Winfrey maintains strict control over her employees, including the requirement that all employees at Harpo sign lifetime confidentiality agreements.[22] There-fore, the fact that the Spa Girls completed the half-marathon is more a testament to the success of the system Winfrey created than to the suc-cess of the individual members. However, the implication for readers is more intriguing, because this article also functions as a subtle warning: if they refuse to participate in the consumption of the "Oprah" brands, they will become the weak link in the group of Oprah Winfrey fans, and they might be excluded from the group.

Why would readers buy into this control? For Winfrey's Panopti-con to be effective, the readers must agree to participate in it. Judging from the popularity of the magazine (O had the most successful maga-zine launch in history), the message of participation is getting through to many readers. At a basic level, this "technology of the self" is possible for these readers because they have already accepted the "Oprah" brand in its various enterprises; they believe in the social realm of "Oprah" and are willing to accept the magazine as part of the larger enterprise. Because most readers were viewers first, they were already implicated. Thus, by examining Winfrey's other enterprises, we can gain a sense of the social realm under which Winfrey's readers operate. Using Sartre's dialectic of signification, Janice Peck analyzes Oprah's Book Club and Oprah.com specifically and discovers that "to read 'Oprah's books,' watch her program, post to her web site, or peruse her magazine is to enter a field of relations within which the reader/viewer strives to real-ize practical objectives. The meaning of her activity, however, cannot be understood independently from the imperatives of the worked matter she encounters or the relations with others it sets into motion."[23] Win-frey's television show and Web site gain meaning from the interactions of viewers and users while they make meaning. This interaction only momentarily traps meaning. The "Oprah" enterprises and the viewers and users are locked into a dynamic that makes and remakes meaning by the very nature of the dynamic. Winfrey's audience members benefit from this interaction simply by the act of meaning making.

Readers want to believe in Winfrey's Panopticon. They want to believe that the successful self-empowerment that her multiple me-dia enterprises promote is possible. Winfrey's ever-present visibility re-minds them of the prime example of this success. She has earned the right to be their guide because she has (at least as presented through various media) triumphed over her demons. No matter how successful the messages, however, readers seem to want some semblance of control. On the surface, readers agree to this self-help regimen because they believe they will gain self-empowerment. What appears to be a straightforward belief in the external force of Winfrey's Panopticon is, in actuality, complicated by the more important belief (or desire for belief) that the readers have in themselves, in their own ability to enact change in themselves. It is this change that is at the heart of "technologies of the self." People are willing to accept certain forms of control if they will be able to effect some sort of change—in this case, a positive change of self-empowerment. *O* sets up techniques that help readers improve themselves. Readers believe in themselves; therefore, they use these techniques or agree to the techniques and use their own bodies to transform themselves. In some ways, the ease and accessibility of the Panopticon's structures demonstrate that the readers have some control over the techniques, if only because they use their bodies in time- and energy-efficient ways. To that end, the magazine's monthly missions provide a coherent focus, while the streamlining of the message in the articles, interviews, and advertisements makes self-empowerment undemanding.

Although the readers appear to have some control over this Panopticon, in reality, the focus of *O* is on creating a self-help cycle to keep Winfrey's Panopticon functioning. Winfrey encourages her readers to strive for self-actualization continually: "Regardless of how good you feel—and I'm feeling pretty good myself—you can live more intensely, more vibrantly, more purposefully. You always have the potential to get better. That, as I see it, is one of the purposes of your life: not to be good but to continuously get better, to constantly move forward, creating the highest, grandest vision and to be led by that vision every day."[24] Winfrey gives her readers "one of the purposes of [their lives]." The more they strive for "the highest, grandest vision," the more they will consume Winfrey's vision, ensuring the life of her Panopticon.

Notes

1. Oprah Winfrey, "What I Know for Sure," *O, the Oprah Magazine,* May–June 2000, 57.

2. Lynette Clemetson, "Women of the New Century: Oprah on Oprah," *Newsweek,* January 8, 2001, 40–41.

3. Michel Foucault, *Discipline and Punish: The Birth of the Prison,* trans. Alan Sheridan (New York: Vintage Books, 1995), 202.

4. Ibid., 203.

5. Ibid., 209.

6. Michel Foucault, "Technologies of the Self," in *Technologies of the Self: A Seminar with Michel Foucault,* ed. Luther H. Martin, Huck Gutman, and Patrick H. Hutton (Amherst: University of Massachusetts Press, 1988), 18.

7. *Cosmopolitan,* July 2004.

8. *O, the Oprah Magazine,* May–June 2000.

9. *O, the Oprah Magazine,* September 2000, 106–8.

10. The Personal Growth Summits have gone through many changes, from the "Live Your Best Life Tour" in 2001, to no tour in 2002, to the "Live Your Best Life Tour" at Oprah.com in 2003 and 2004. Currently, the picture and slogans in the advertisements in *O* match those on the "Live Your Best Life" home page. For only $24.95, one can gain access to empowerment.

11. *O, the Oprah Magazine,* May 2004, 30 (emphasis added).

12. These "missions" were the focus of the following months: December 2000, October 2002, April 2003, and May 2004, respectively.

13. *O, the Oprah Magazine,* March 2001, 41.

14. Foucault, *Discipline and Punish,* 215.

15. Ibid., 223.

16. *O, the Oprah Magazine,* October 2000, 311.

17. Foucault, *Discipline and Punish,* 219.

18. *O, the Oprah Magazine,* July–August 2000, 139–44.

19. Ibid., 142.

20. Ibid.; *O, the Oprah Magazine,* September 2000, 185.

21. Ibid., September 2000, 188.

22. Juliet Walker discusses a February 2000 court case involving Elizabeth Coady, a former Harpo employee who attempted to sue Harpo to break the confidentiality agreement. The Illinois Court of Appeals upheld the agreement. Walker uses this case to consider what it is that determines Winfrey's business decisions—"ethics or profits." She ultimately suggests that it is ethics, but her argument is founded on little substantive proof, especially in comparison to the extensive evidence she provides of how Winfrey built her financial empire. Juliet Walker, "Oprah Winfrey, the Tycoon: Contextualizing the Economics of Race, Class, and Gender in Black Business History in Post–Civil Rights America," in *Black Business and Economic Power,* ed. Alusine Jalloh and Toyin Falola (Rochester, N.Y.: University of Rochester Press, 2002), 509–13.

23. Janice Peck, "The Oprah Effect: Texts, Readers, and the Dialectic of Signification," *Communication Review* 5 (2002): 172.

24. Winfrey, "What I Know for Sure," 57.

"What Is Africa to Me?"

The Oprah Winfrey Leadership Academy

Jennifer Harris

On New Year's Day 2007, a select coterie of African American celebrities found themselves in Henley-on-Klip, south of Johannesburg, South Africa. The event was the opening of the Oprah Winfrey Leadership Academy, devoted to the education of impoverished South African girls. The mood was ebullient as guests such as Tina Turner, Mariah Carey, Spike Lee, Quincy Jones, and Sidney Poitier toured the fifty-two-acre facilities. While the entering class was composed of 152 students, the school is meant to eventually house 450 girls at a time. As Nelson Mandela observed, "This school will provide opportunities to some of our young people they could never imagine, had it not been for Oprah. The key to any country's future is in educating its youth. Oprah is therefore not only investing in a few young individuals but in the future of our country. We are indebted to her for her selfless efforts."[1] Winfrey's academy is the fulfillment of a promise made to Mandela to build a school to educate the next generation of South African leaders.[2] Yet her efforts no doubt surpassed Mandela's expectations: at an estimated cost of $40 million, the boarding school features impressive classrooms and dormitories, as well as a ten-thousand-volume library, dining hall, theater, yoga studio, and beauty salon. Announced Winfrey, "It doesn't stop here. When the girls graduate, they will go to the university of their choice anywhere in the world."[3]

Back home in the United States, the response to the publicity surrounding the school's opening was mixed. On the one hand, Winfrey was lauded for her philanthropy. On the other, critics dissected

293

what they saw as the school's excesses, including china settings and 200-thread-count sheets handpicked by Winfrey, a library with a fireplace, tennis courts, and spacious closets.[4] Criticisms of the Leadership Academy fall into two camps. The first claims that Winfrey could have built more schools to educate a greater number of children for the same amount of money: "Shame on you Oprah. $40 million dollars for a school in South Africa for 152 children when the rest of the poor black children in that country have a substandard education if any."[5] The school is "embarrassingly overdone" and an example of "ludicrous extravagance" according to one blogger, who finds the embroidered bedding particularly infuriating.[6] Winfrey's response to such comments is to challenge the lack of value accorded to African girls. Noting that African architects first submitted designs for school buildings that resembled chicken coops, Winfrey asserts, "These girls deserve to be surrounded by beauty, and beauty does inspire. . . . I wanted this to be a place of honor for them because these girls have never been treated with kindness."[7] While some see any improvement on the poverty of the girls' previous lives as satisfactory, Winfrey's logic is that the girls will learn best in an environment that doesn't simply sustain them, but rather fully nurtures them.

Even as some question how Winfrey exercises her philanthropy abroad, others question her decision to contribute so much money to a non-American cause. Fox News ran a story titled "Why Didn't Oprah Help Poor Children in U.S.?" While most online commentators defend her right to do what she wishes with her money, others ask, "How many schools in the USA could be built with $40 million?" claiming "she could have helped alot of american kids with schools here." Even those who acknowledge the value of the cause still take umbrage: "While I am ALL FOR helping our sisters in Africa, where does that leave our African brothers and the future of their education?! Better yet . . . can we start at home?!" The anger in such critiques is palatable: "How in the hell does she go to Africa to help black girls and walk past her own right there in the city where she does her show?"[8]

In this instance, Winfrey's defense of her actions incited more controversy than the original subject of the South African school. In a candid moment Winfrey spoke of her frustrations with American society: "Say what you will about the American educational system—it does work. . . . If you are a child in the United States, you can get an education." She continues, "I became so frustrated with visiting inner-city schools that I just stopped going. The sense that you need to learn just isn't there. . . . If you ask the kids what they want or need, they will say an iPod or some sneakers. In South Africa, they don't ask for money or toys. They ask for uniforms so they can go to school."[9] Characterizing impoverished U.S. schoolchildren as greedy and superficial, Winfrey perhaps unintentionally aligns herself with some members of the black middle and upper class who, having themselves survived the residual segregation and racism of post–civil rights U.S. life, see their successors as unappreciative of the sacrifices and struggles of previous generations. By contrast, reports of students from the Leadership Academy paint them as overwhelmingly grateful to their benefactress.[10]

Ultimately, Winfrey's funding of the school, in combination with her comments about U.S. inner-city students, led to a small faction deriding her as un-American.[11] A particularly potent charge in recent times, it is even more loaded when leveled against a black woman, invoking the forms of conditional belonging historically extended to African Americans. While such views have waned, they are resurrected when African Americans, or select immigrant groups, are perceived as privileging diasporic ties over national ones. Clearly, donating money to charities that extend basic necessities to countries designated as third world is considered a humanitarian gesture. However, funding facilities that substantially exceed minimum U.S. standards is perceived as excessive. The irony is that Winfrey, often invoked as an example of the American Dream fulfilled, is deemed un-American for spending her capital as she wishes—something generally recognized as a fundamentally American right. Moreover, such charges ignore that the bulk of Winfrey's donations—an estimated $263 million between 2003 and 2007—goes to U.S. charities and causes.[12]

If a small group saw Winfrey as betraying America by diverting her resources elsewhere, another group was more angered by Winfrey's voiced frustration with inner-city children and the implied criticism of the values conveyed to them by their parents. Her comments have been interpreted as a betrayal of African American codes of racial loyalty.[13] These assert that to "criticize or challenge other members of the community in public" is to undermine the community overall, especially if such criticisms can be deployed to support anti-black stereotypes.[14] African American celebrities, in particular, must carefully navigate this minefield, for, as Randall Kennedy observes, "the black who succeeds in a multiracial setting must constantly contend with suspicions harbored by other blacks that his or her success derives, at least in part, from 'selling out.'"[15] Part and parcel of selling out is the disavowal of African American value systems that have historically privileged black solidarity as a survival strategy. In this instance, Winfrey was seen as downplaying the effect of systemic oppression on the lives of impoverished African American youth. According to this logic, it is not the fault of the students that they value sneakers over books: they are trapped in an underfunded system that is failing them, and they have no hope that any education they do receive will assist them in breaking out of a cycle of poverty. That Winfrey refused this narrative should not be surprising: on her show, in her magazine, and in her public appearances, Winfrey actively encourages individuals to take control of and responsibility for their own lives. In this ethos, to not acknowledge individual agency is to undermine the individual. However, in moving from aspirational messages to explicit critiques, Winfrey was deemed by some to have broken ranks.

Ultimately, most commentators refuted criticisms that Winfrey is un-American or violated racial etiquette. However, the fact that a disproportionate amount of energy was expended doing so speaks to the potency and currency of the charges. Whole articles were devoted to dissecting and dismissing the criticism, and online commentators filled comment box after comment box defending Winfrey's right as an American to speak her mind and spend her money as she wished.[16] Yet noticeably absent from such defenses is the acknowledgement that Winfrey's Leadership Academy is fundamentally rooted in not only American belief systems but African American ones. Namely, Winfrey's choice to focus on education in South Africa—rather than health and farming initiatives, as the Bill and Melinda Gates Foundation has done—invokes the ideology of racial uplift. That she relates her venture in South Africa to her African American identity signals an engagement with the sensibilities of pan-Africanism as practiced in the United States. Thus it is that the Oprah Winfrey Leadership Academy signals less Winfrey's international ties than her national ones.

As a discourse, racial uplift emerged in the late nineteenth century. With the failure of Reconstruction, it became clear to black leaders that if negative perceptions of African Americans were to change, the responsibility fell—however unfairly—on their shoulders. Accordingly, African American leaders encouraged their brethren to embrace bourgeois American values as a means of proving their equality. Thus, as Kevin K. Gaines observes, "For many black elites, uplift came to mean an emphasis on self-help, racial solidarity, temperance, thrift, chastity, social purity, patriarchal authority, and the accumulation of wealth."[17] But part and parcel of racial uplift is the idea that those who have already achieved material success are responsible for fostering the moral progress of the black underclass—lifting as they climb, according to the maxim—with moral progress understood as a precondition for material progress and stability. The idea that one must "lift" others is not merely a matter of noblesse oblige; it is rooted in a belief that the lives of all African Americans are in some way intertwined. For some of racial uplift's progenitors, this sense of obligation stemmed from racial solidarity or a sense of shared history; for others it reflected the reality of white racism, whereby any African Americans might be judged by the conduct of the least desirable of the race.

Regardless of its practitioners' motivations, the discourse of racial uplift retained its currency well into the mid-twentieth century, influencing the U.S. civil rights movement. Even as the movement demanded equal rights for African Americans, it did so on terms that reified the values of racial uplift, in particular bourgeois respectability.[18] Thus access to equal education, seen as the gateway to financial opportunity, was one of the crucial pillars of the movement.

For Winfrey, the values privileged by racial uplift, as preached by her father, have come to define her life. Vernon Winfrey stressed the same values of self-help, moral rectitude, and material progress that were current almost a hundred years earlier. But above all he underscored the import of education to his daughter, who was born the same year as the landmark *Brown v. Board of Education* ruling, which declared segregated schools unconstitutional. Unable to complete high school himself until he was twenty-five, the elder Winfrey experienced firsthand the link between education and financial stability: "I missed a couple of better paying jobs after I was in Nashville because I didn't read as fast as I should have. . . . And so I emphasized to Oprah the need for getting something that no one can take from you. She complained sometimes about other children dressing better than she did. . . . And I said to her, 'You get something in here'—pointing to his head—'and you can dress like you want to in days to come.' She can dress pretty good now if she wants to."[19]

Clothing replaces sneakers and iPods in his story, but the message is clear: parents have a responsibility to inculcate their children with values that will help them succeed; following that, the children are responsible for using what they have been given to advance themselves materially. This pattern of transmission replicates the logic of racial uplift. The difference is, however, that while education is an important tenet of racial uplift and civil rights, it is the crucial pillar of Oprah Winfrey's philosophy of self-help and social responsibility. In this light, her focus on education, not only in funding the Leadership Academy but also in her donations to numerous U.S. schools, is logical. Notably, the three institutions of higher education that have benefited most from Winfrey's largesse—Spelman College, Morehouse College, and her alma mater, Tennessee State University—are all historically black. In giving to historically black colleges and universities, Winfrey fulfills the central responsibility of racial uplift, while also acknowledging the crucial role such institutions played in providing opportunities for African American advancement in a pre–civil rights South.

In contrast to racial uplift, which is predominantly intranational in focus, pan-Africanism imagines African Americans in a diasporic context. As a concept it emerged in the early twentieth century, a rebuttal to negative representations of the African continent and its inhabitants as uncivilized—a belief Winfrey recalls holding as a child:

> I was ashamed . . . if anybody asked "You from Africa?" in the school. I didn't want anybody to talk about it. And if it was ever discussed in any classroom I was in, it was always about the Pygmies and the, you know, primitive and barbaric behavior of Africans. And so if I was in a classroom with other kids—I remember like wanting to get over that period really quickly. The bare-breasted *National Geographic* pictures? I was embarrassed by all of it. I was one of those people who felt, "I'm not African, I'm American." They were primitive. Primitive and barbaric is the way I thought Africa was.[20]

In addition to refuting such popular representations of the continent and its peoples, pan-Africanism also aims to overcome the kind of disassociations and disavowals that Winfrey recounts feeling as a child. Notably, pan-Africanism proposes that "all Black people are Africans, and that as Africans, [Black people] are bound together Racially, Historically, Culturally, Politically, and Emotionally."[21] However, whereas racial uplift attracted the educated middle classes and elites, early disciples of pan-Africanism were less likely to fit into those categories. Followers of Marcus Garvey's powerful pan-Africanist movement of the late 1910s and early 1920s, for instance, were not generally considered of the "respectable" classes.[22] This idea that pan-Africanism was a philosophy for the masses persisted into the 1960s with the versions forwarded by figures like Maulana Ron Karenga and the organization US, which invented Kwanzaa, a "pseudo-African 'traditional' festival."[23]

As the example of Kwanzaa suggests, pan-Africanism as generally practiced in the United States is concerned less with the lived reality of various peoples in the African continent and more with finding a usable past that will empower contemporary African Americans. In this way it is less a movement of revolutionary black nationalism than of cultural black nationalism that aims to overthrow European customs and worldviews in favor of ones deemed African.[24] To this end, pan-Africanism draws on spiritual concepts from a variety of traditions. Key among these are the centrality of community to one's own well-being and the honoring of one's ancestors.

It is these aspects of pan-Africanist thought that are most present in Winfrey's own discourse. She remarks: "Whenever I find myself in a difficult situation, I'm reminded of a line from a Maya Angelou poem called 'Our Grandmothers': *I go forth / alone, and stand as ten thousand. I think of all who've come before me.*"[25] Winfrey frequently cites Angelou and her poetry, with its emphasis upon ancestry and continuity as a means of endurance, as an inspiration. However, it is not merely a matter of remembering one's ancestors, it is also about communing with them. Winfrey posits a very real spiritual and even utilitarian connection to her antecedents, one that sustains her: "Before I have a big meeting or decision to make, I go and sit with my ancestors. Literally, I go and sit in my closet and I say their names. I just say their names so that when I walk into the space, I don't walk alone."[26]

Winfrey's imaginings of her ancestral line does not begin with North America. She recounts feeling connected to Africa's Zulu people, asserting: "When I'm in Africa, I always feel that I look Zulu. I feel connected to the Zulu tribe." In a 2006 documentary that traced her family tree, Winfrey warns the narrator, Henry Louis Gates Jr., "If you tell me I'm not Zulu, I am going to be very upset." Faced with historical and DNA evidence that demonstrates the unlikelihood of her connection, Winfrey does not back down, claiming "she still feels that, spiritually, she is fundamentally related to the Zulu people."[27]

Winfrey's identification with the Zulu is not incidental. Due to their nineteenth-century exploits, the Zulu people developed a reputation as fierce warriors who forcefully opposed colonization. The image of the "Zulu Warrior" has come to pervade popular culture, including music and cinema. As a character in an influential 1964 film on the Anglo-Zulu War of 1879 remarked, "A Zulu regiment can run—*RUN*—fifty miles, and fight a battle at the end of it!"[28] For Winfrey, a model of determination, to claim a relation to the continent's best-known warrior figure seems fitting, however anachronistic it might be. But choosing one's African ancestry is also in keeping with the U.S. practice of pan-Africanism, where a spiritual tie is just as important as an actual geographic connection, if not more so.

The difference is that rather than simply articulating a pan-Africanist sense of a spiritual connection and/or racial solidarity or drawing on an ancestral past to bolster a North American present, Winfrey is in a position to dispense substantial resources to those in Africa in need. Given her beliefs, it is not surprising that she has focused her efforts not on the Kpelle people in Liberia, to whom DNA tests linked her matrilineal line, but rather on residents of South Africa, where Zulus form the largest ethnic group. While no ethnic breakdown is available for the Leadership Academy students—who come from nine different South African provinces—it is clear girls from Zulu homes are represented.[29] Such a breakdown is not necessary to identify the direct beneficiaries of her second South African educational endeavor, the Seven Fountains School, located in a remote town in eastern KwaZulu-Natal. Though funded in part by the Angel Network charity, which Winfrey founded, it is clear that the choice of location is hers.[30]

While Winfrey's decision to fund educational institutions in South Africa invokes both racial uplift and pan-Africanist discourses, it also reworks them. As it has been historically practiced in the United States, racial uplift is primarily intranational in focus. While the accomplishments of individuals from other parts of the African diaspora may be invoked, they serve primarily to attest to the capabilities of blacks more generally. Likewise, pan-Africanism most often focuses on incorporating elements of African culture, religion, and philosophy in North American life, as a means of supplanting Eurocentric ways of thinking and being that have historically devalued African Americans. In choosing to actively fund schools in South Africa on an ongoing basis, Winfrey demonstrates an expanded sense of racial solidarity, one rooted in a lived connection.

Just as Winfrey expands the scope of racial uplift beyond the nation, and pan-Africanism beyond the cultural, she also defies late-twentieth-century models of celebrity charitable projects in Africa. In the 1980s such projects came to the fore with the singles "Feed the World" (1984) and "We are the World" (1985), which raised significant money to combat famine in Ethiopia. Both songs, which feature choirs of contemporary pop stars, are notable for their lack of specific references to Ethiopia as well as their lyric expression of potentially condescending sentiments. In the 1990s and 2000s, the most common form of celebrity involvement in Africa has been as a spokesperson for a cause of some kind, whether through a charitable organization (such as UNICEF) or a humanitarian one (like the United Nations). In this way celebrities such as Bono, Angelina Jolie, George Clooney, and others have drawn on their cachet to bring the general public's attention to an issue.

While some celebrity ambassadors demonstrate significant knowledge of and investment in issues, they are ultimately working through organizations. The model Oprah Winfrey adopts is different: in the case of education in South Africa, she does not attempt to draw attention to a cause; instead she directly intervenes to rectify a problem. (Admittedly, her very attempt to rectify it is enough to draw further attention to it.) Likewise, in the case of education in South Africa, she favors direct action and involvement, rather than letting others determine how to disperse her resources. This control over how her charitable donations are distributed is important to Winfrey, who retains control of Oprah's Angel Network as both president and chairperson. That said, this project was initiated, as noted earlier, at the request of Nelson Mandela. It appears to be a meeting of minds: in a statement about her longstanding desire to build a school that would help disadvantaged girls, Winfrey wrote: "I wanted it to be in South Africa because of my African roots and my love and respect for Nelson Mandela."[31] Mandela is of significant consequence to Winfrey, who claims, "His grace and wisdom make me want to be a better human being."[32] Imprisoned for twenty-seven years by an apartheid regime he had resisted, Mandela emerged unbroken in 1990, becoming president in 1994 in the country's first democratic election.

In the United States, Nelson Mandela is frequently linked to Martin Luther King Jr. Too young to contribute to the fights of the U.S. civil rights movement, Winfrey nonetheless has "vivid memories" of hearing Martin Luther King Jr.'s "I Have a Dream Speech," delivered during the 1963 March on Washington. She recalls: "I thought . . . I want to do that. I want to lead a march. I wasn't thinking I like wanted to go to that march, I was thinking: Oh! I want to do that one day."[33] Thus, South Africa and Mandela represent an opportunity not simply to participate vicariously in the civil rights movement, but to lead as well. It is therefore not incidental that she sees the children of the Leadership Academy as her daughters: just as her father gave her an opportunity, she in turn is facilitating them.

At the same time that Winfrey expands and reworks the discourses of racial uplift and U.S. pan-Africanism to include direct action in contemporary Africa, the project of the Leadership Academy has also been criticized for less positive aspects we might also recognize as stemming from those discourses. U.S. pan-Africanism has been critiqued for not sufficiently differentiating between African nations and peoples; Winfrey has been taken to task for not understanding the ways the lives of underprivileged South African girls and women might not conform to her understanding of racial and sexual oppression and resistance.[34] If pan-Africanism is criticized for drawing selectively from African culture and history to benefit African Americans, without acknowledging contemporary Africans, Winfrey's academy faces similar charges that it does not meet local needs. According to John Donnelly: "Some leaders of grass-roots organizations said that they are helping thousands of orphans with budgets of only tens or hundreds of thousands of dollars and that Winfrey's school was a prominent example of a project that fulfills an outsider's vision and not a community's."[35] Amid claims of extravagance, akin to those voiced in the United States, but for different reasons, the South African government withdrew from the project.[36]

Even as artwork specially commissioned from African artists is featured prominently throughout the academy, there are rumors that the school is culturally insensitive to its South African pupils, forbidding them from returning home for funerals of extended family members, and limiting contact with parents and guardians.[37] If true, such actions are contrary to the school's proclaimed philosophy: according to Jean Countryman, who helped establish the school, "The core values of the Oprah Winfrey Leadership Academy are rooted in ubuntu," one of the ideological cornerstones of post-apartheid South Africa. While no direct translation exists, it is premised upon a philosophy of mutual interdependence and support, or "I am because you are. I am because we are."[38] Certainly, efforts have been made to instruct the Leadership Academy staff in applying the principle, with seminars conducted by Mbule-lo Vizikhungo Mzamane, a professor at the University of Kwazulu-Natal.[39] And yet, criticisms persist from parents and locals, who say that they are excluded from the academy and its community. Chicago, not Cape Town or Pretoria, determines what is said and done within the academy's walls.[40]

If U.S. pan-Africanism is sometimes perceived as inadequately engaged with the lived reality of various African peoples, the application of North American racial uplift, with its emphasis on a particular kind of respectability, might be seen as another form of colonialism. Winfrey's school is modeled on the exclusive Miss Porter's Boarding School, whose alumni include members of the Kennedy and Vanderbilt families.[41] This sensibility is reflected in the aesthetic of the academy, which is decorated in a tasteful neutral palette of beiges and browns with dark natural wood accents, and the occasional colorful local basket or painting, and seems less "child friendly" than it does an example of bourgeois taste. If Winfrey's academy is intended to inculcate her girls with appropriate values to enable their advancement, they are values reinforced by an aesthetic that preaches gentility and decorum.

It is therefore fitting that at the Leadership Academy iPods and sneakers have been replaced with other items—like china place settings—which likewise signal financial resources, but in a very different way. If wearing the latest sneakers testify that an individual is conversant with current trends, 200-thread-count sheets indicate that one is discerning and has taste.[42] In each instance, the item speaks for the individual, but the message is very different: one signals money, the other signals class. It is thus not that the Oprah Winfrey Leadership Academy disavows materialism in the pursuit of education. Rather, it promotes a very specific kind of materialism, one familiar to viewers of *Oprah* and readers of *O, the Oprah Magazine:* it is not a matter of who has the most stuff, it is a matter of whose stuff best conveys their gentility. Note that those critics who found the quality of the student bedding excessive did not question the value of good bedding generally—they just questioned whether these girls should have it. However, there is no doubt that had Winfrey given out sneakers deemed overpriced, the response would have been very different, questioning the intrinsic value of the shoes—as Winfrey's own earlier critique did. What Winfrey sets out to inculcate in her students is a sense of quality, their own, primarily, which is reflected in that of the items which surround them. The question deserves to be asked: is this also fostering a sense of middle-class materialism incommensurate with the priorities the academy has set for its students? But other questions also deserve consideration, such as: how can a library with a fireplace, or matched china place settings, ruin a girl for life? Are young women not empowered when they are able to function with ease in privileged situations, as opposed to being overwhelmed or intimidated? Those who claim that the luxurious surroundings will leave the students unprepared to return to village life are missing the point: these girls are not being trained for the lives their mothers led.

Given the reality of life for those living in poverty in South Africa, the very real problems many of the students have faced, and the problems with staff the school has survived, the U.S. criticism of Oprah Winfrey's Leadership Academy seems, for the most part, specious. The tenor of much of the criticism voiced on blogs and in online communities appears petty, a resentment both of Winfrey's ability to give and not being included in the giving. As a celebrity, she is conceived of as public property with a concomitant obligation to those who consume her. Thus, online commentators who have taken issue with the Leadership Academy most often have voiced an implicit sense of entitlement to Winfrey's resources, not simply financial, but also emotional. According to this logic, in allocating money to South African projects, Winfrey not only denies direct U.S. beneficiaries, she also denies her U.S. viewers the vicarious emotional satisfaction tied to national pride they might feel at seeing a U.S. family or community benefit. This is the kind of vicarious pleasure that keeps the ratings of *Extreme Makeover: Home Edition* high, even as homes built for deserving families far exceed their actual needs, surpassing the kinds of excesses of which Winfrey's academy has been accused.[43] Beyond the nationality of the beneficiaries, the other crucial difference might be that *Extreme Makeover: Home Edition* shops at Sears; Winfrey does not.

Ultimately, as pointed out elsewhere in this volume, for many Americans, Oprah Winfrey represents a deracinated fulfillment of the American Dream: she survived poverty and abuse to become one of the most powerful individuals in the nation. Racial uplift and the civil rights movement do not figure in this narrative—as they might, given the history of Tennessee State University—nor does pan-Africanism. Importantly, the narrative of Winfrey is fiercely national, and when Winfrey's race is invoked, it is often as one more "handicap"—as a source of prejudice or racial oppression—to be overcome. But as Winfrey's own statements and affiliations attest, and the example of her academy demonstrates, this is not the narrative she has adopted for herself. As she posits it, her rise is the result of hard work, certainly, but also of ancestral strength and fortitude—"I feel like I have not even the right to be tired, because I know I come from this" she states.[44] In other words, her heritage is not an obstacle but a rich resource. Building a school in Africa, then, is not only an act of international charity, racial uplift, or even of diasporic connection, but also a means of repaying a personal debt. That said, the $40 million Oprah Winfrey Leadership Academy is an act of repayment that could only have been imagined by an American.

Notes

1. Sapa, "Mandela Cheers Oprah's New School," January 2, 2007, *Independent Online,* http://www.iol.co.za/index.php?set_id=1&click_id=105&art_id=iol1167724874160B243 (accessed August 15, 2008).

2. "Oprah's Promise," *Anderson Cooper 360,* CNN, January 2, 2007.

3. Shanthini Naidoo, "A Dream Come True for 152 Lucky Schoolgirls," *Johannesburg Times,* January 2007, http://www.thetimes.co.za/SpecialReports/Education/Article.aspx?id=353505 (accessed August 15, 2008).

4. Allison Samuels, "Oprah Goes to School," *Newsweek,* January 8, 2007, http://www.newsweek.com/id/56724/output/print (accessed August 30, 2008).

5. Editors of DiversityInc, "Why Are People Picking on Oprah? It's a Diversity Issue," January 4, 2007, http://diversityinc.com/public/1107.cfm (accessed August 30, 2008).

6. Steve Temkin, "Oprah-fy my world.—Part II," May 23, 2007, http://www.thatpissesmeoff.com/ (accessed August 30, 2008).

7. Samuels, "Oprah Goes to School."

8. John Gibson, "Why Didn't Oprah Help Poor Children in U.S.," *The Big Story with Gibson and Nauert,* January 3, 2007, http://www.foxnews.com/story/0,2933,241265,00.html (accessed August 30, 2008); Anonymous question: "Since Oprah has opened a $40 million dollar school in Africa that has ONLY 150 students I have been wondering—How many schools in the USA could be built with $40 million? And who thinks Oprah is rediculous for what she has done?" June 18, 2008, http://www.answerbag.com/q_view/811732 (accessed August 30, 2008); Comment by "Terri," on January 5, 2007, in response to Capri, "Controversy as to Why Oprah Winfrey Built the $40 Million Dollar School in Africa and Not Here in the United States," January 3, 2007, http://nosysnoop.wordpress.com/2007/01/03/controversy-as-to-why-oprah-winfrey-built-the-40-million-dollar-school-in-africa-and-not-here-in-the-united-states/ (accessed August 30, 2008); http://www.stuffebplike.com/?p=128 (accessed August 30, 2008; site discontinued).

9. Samuels, "Oprah Goes to School."

10. The families of students have been quite clear that they do not hold Winfrey responsible for the abusive actions of a former school employee. The seriousness with which she treated the incident has also been lauded by South African commentators. Kashiefa Ajam, "Oprah Lights Up Her School with Party," *Johannesburg Star,* December 01, 2007, 3.

11. Paul Huebl, "Oprah Opens $40 Million School in South Africa," *Crime, Guns, and Videotape,* January 2, 2007, http://www.crimefilenews.com/2007/01/oprah-opens-40-million-school-in-south.html (accessed August 30, 2008).

12. "The 50 Most Generous Philanthropists," *Business Week,* November 26, 2007, http://bwnt.businessweek.com/interactive%5Freports/philanthropy%5Findividual/ (accessed October 12, 2008); "Oprah Winfrey's Charities Worth More Than $200 Million," January 2, 2008, http://www.weblo.com/asset_news/25633/Harpo_Inc./Oprah_Winfrey_s_Charities_Worth_More_Than_200_Million/ (accessed October 12, 2008).

13. Eugene Robinson. "It's Not All About the iPods, Oprah," *Washington Post,* January 9, 2007, A15.

14. Keith Boykin, "Condoleezza's Vice," January 10, 2006, http://www.keithboykin.com (accessed October 12, 2008).

15. Randall Kennedy, *Sellout: The Politics of Racial Betrayal* (New York: Pantheon, 2008), 67.

16. See, for instance: Carol Lloyd, "Piling on Oprah," January 5, 2007, http://www.salon.com/mwt/broadsheet/2007/01/05/oprah/ (accessed Au-

gust 30, 2008); Editors of DiversityInc, "Oprah Bashing: Why Is Her S. Africa School Under Fire?" January 3, 2007, and "Why Are People Picking on Oprah? It's a Diversity Issue," January 5, 2007, http://diversityinc.com/public/1107.cfm (accessed August 30, 2008).

17. Kevin K. Gaines, *Uplifting the Race: Black Leadership, Politics, and Culture in the Twentieth Century* (Chapel Hill: University of North Carolina Press, 1996), 2.

18. Gaines, *Uplifting the Race,* 259.

19. Henry Louis Gates Jr., *Finding Oprah's Roots, Finding Your Own* (New York: Crown, 2007), 44.

20. Gates, *Finding Oprah's Roots,* 150.

21. Algernon Austin, *Achieving Blackness: Race, Black Nationalism, and Afrocentrism in the Twentieth Century* (New York: New York University Press, 2006), 85.

22. David Levering Lewis, *When Harlem Was in Vogue* (New York: Alfred Knopf, 1981), 37.

23. Stephen Howe, *Afrocentrism: Mythical Pasts and Imagined Homes* (New York: Verso, 1998), 216.

24. Austin, *Achieving Blackness,* 112, 70–76.

25. Oprah Winfrey, "This Month's Mission," *O, the Oprah Magazine,* May 2004, http://www.oprah.com/article/spirit/inspiration/pkgcelebrateyou/omag_200405_mission/1 (accessed October 12, 2008).

26. Gates, *Finding Oprah's Roots,* 90.

27. Gates, *Finding Oprah's Roots,* 151, 155.

28. Cy Endfield, director, *Zulu* (Embassy Pictures, 1964), 139 minutes.

29. "KZN Girls Head for Oprah's School," *Durban (South Africa) Daily News,* November 20, 2006, 9.

30. "Singing and Dancing Heralds Oprah's School," *Pretoria News,* March 17, 2007, 3.

31. Oprah Winfrey, "Statement from Oprah Winfrey," *Boston Globe,* January 20, 2007, http://www.boston.com/news/world/africa/articles/2007/01/20/statement_from_oprah_winfrey/ (accessed October 12, 2008).

32. Oprah Winfrey, "Men We Love," *O, the Oprah Magazine,* June 2006, http://www.oprah.com/slideshow/omagazine/slideshow1_ss_omag_200306_men/6, (accessed October 12, 2008).

33. Gates, *Finding Oprah's Roots,* 78.

34. Rita Barnard, "Oprah's Paton, or South Africa and the Globalization of Suffering," *English Studies in Africa* 47, no. 1 (2004): 85–109.

35. John Donnelly, "Outside Oprah's School, a Growing Frustration," *Boston Globe,* January 20, 2007, http://www.boston.com/news/world/africa/articles/2007/01/20/outside_oprahs_school_a_growing_frustration/ (accessed October 12, 2008).

36. "Oprah's Promise," *Anderson Cooper 360,* CNN, January 9, 2007.

37. Lumka Oliphant, "Rumblings of Discontent at Oprah School," *Johannesburg Star,* March 3, 2007, 3; Kashiefa Ajam, "Controversy Shadows Oprah's Academy," *Cape Town Cape Argus,* October 27, 2007, 15; Celean Jacobson, "Oprah Opens South African School She Helped Fund," *Cape Town Mail and Guardian,* March 16, 2007, http://www.mg.co.za/article/2007–03–16-oprah-opens-south-african-school-she-helped-fund (accessed August 15, 2008).

38. Jennifer D. Jordan, "Educator Finds Inspiration in S. Africa," *Providence Journal,* May 2, 2007, http://www.projo.com/news/content/countryman_2_05–02–07_IG5FLEN.3559840.html (accessed October 12, 2008).

39. Mbulelo Vizikhungo Mzamane, "Constructing a Teaching and Learning Community Using Ubuntu/Botho," paper presented at Oprah Winfrey Leadership Academy for Girls, Henley-on-Klip, Gauteng, January 24, 2007.

40. Admittedly, some of the complaints seem spurious: local police are upset they are not allowed to patrol the heavily fortified school. The fortifications themselves have been criticized, but are not unusual for schools of this kind, and seem practical given the problems with property crime in South Africa. Helen Grange, "Squabbles Plague Oprah's School," *Johannesburg Star,* August 3, 2007, 11.

41. Cara Bouwer, "Oprah Gives SA's Needy Girls the Generous Gift of Opportunity," *Rosebank (South Africa) Business Day,* January 3, 2007, http://www.businessday.co.za/articles/economy.aspx?ID=BD4A351231 (accessed August 15, 2008).

42. Given that one can now purchase 1000-thread-count sheets, the whole emphasis upon 200-thread-count seems somewhat funny. Moreover, thread count is not the ultimate indicator of bedding quality; however, what is important is that commentators believed to be so, in the process revealing their own ignorance. See "The Truth about Thread Count," http://www.linenplace.com/product_guide/truth_about_thread_count.html (accessed November 3, 2008).

43. See, for example, giving "6-bedroom, 7-bath, 7-television house to a family of 4." "This New House," *Mother Jones,* March-April 2005, http://www.motherjones.com/news/exhibit/2005/03/exhibit.html (accessed November 3, 2008).

44. Gates, *Finding Oprah's Roots,* 122.

Contributors

AUDREY M. DENTITH is assistant professor, Department of Administrative Leadership, University of Wisconsin–Milwaukee. Her essays have appeared in *Gender and Education, Democracy and Education,* and the *Journal of Vocational Education Research.* She is currently working on a book on feminist leadership in education.

DAMIANA GIBBONS is a doctoral student in curriculum and instruction at the University of Wisconsin–Madison with a major in literacy studies and a minor in composition and rhetoric. Her research focuses on media production, identity, and literacy.

ROBERTA F. HAMMETT is professor in the Faculty of Education at Memorial University of Newfoundland. She teaches undergraduate courses in secondary English education and educational uses of computer technologies and graduate courses in multiliteracies, critical media literacy, research, and curriculum studies. She previously served as associate dean for graduate programs.

JENNIFER HARRIS is associate professor of English at Mount Allison University, Sackville, New Brunswick. Her essays have appeared in *African American Review, Canadian Review of American Studies, English Language Notes, Journal of American Culture,* and elsewhere. She is managing editor of the Alphabet City book series, published by MIT Press.

ELLA HOWARD is assistant professor of English at Armstrong Atlantic State University. She has written on second-wave feminism and the history of design. Her current research projects focus on the history of advertising, women's media, and urban poverty.

EVA ILLOUZ is a professor in the Department of Sociology at the University of Jerusalem. She has served as a visiting professor at a number of universities, including Princeton University, and is the author of three books, among them *Oprah Winfrey and the Glamour of Misery: An Essay on Popular Culture* (Columbia University Press, 2003).

NICHOLAS JOHN is a research fellow at the Interdisciplinary Center for Technology Analysis and Forecasting by Tel Aviv University. His research interests include the globalization of culture and the role of technology in such processes. He has conducted the first large socio-historical study of the diffusion of the Internet to Israel.

MARJORIE JOLLES is assistant professor of women's studies, California State University, Fullerton. Her work includes publications in *Critical Matrix: The Princeton Journal of Women, Gender and Culture, American Philosophical Association's Newsletter on Feminism and Philosophy*, and *Feminist Teacher*. Her current research is on the female body as a medium for the rhetoric of empowerment.

The first woman sportswriter at the *Chicago Tribune*, LINDA KAY is associate professor of journalism at Concordia University in Montreal, Quebec. Kay's main research interest is pioneering female journalists in Canada and their oral histories. Last year, a division of Rowman & Littlefield published her memoir, *The Reading List*, which details the fateful meeting of a young journalist, a famous author, and a convicted murderer.

DENISE MARTIN is assistant professor in the Departments of Pan-African Studies and Humanities at the University of Louisville. She teaches courses on African and African American religion and culture. Her research interests include traditional cosmology, culture, symbolism, and beliefs in societies of Africa and the diaspora.

MARIA MCGRATH is assistant professor of history and humanities at Bucks County Community College. She has published in *Eating in Eden: Food and American Utopias* (University of Nebraska Press, 2006) and *Business and Economic History On-Line*.

VALERIE PALMER-MEHTA is assistant professor in the Department of Communication and Journalism at Oakland University in Rochester, Michigan. Her research examines how power, influence, and ideas circulate in society through the media and public discourse. Some of her publications may be found in *Text and Performance Quarterly, Women's Studies in Communication, Communication Teacher, Journal of American Culture,* and *Black Women's Intellectual Traditions: Speaking Their Minds.*

MALIN PEREIRA is chair of the Department of English at the University of North Carolina at Charlotte. She has published in *African American Review, Contemporary Literature, Tulsa Studies in Women's Literature,* and *Modern Fiction Studies.* Her most recent book is *Rita Dove's Cosmopolitanism* (University of Illinois Press, 2003).

JENNIFER RICHARDSON is assistant professor in the Department of English and Communication at SUNY Potsdam. She teaches undergraduate and graduate courses in rhetoric and composition. She has presented papers about composition studies and rhetorical and cultural theory at the Western States Composition Conference, the National Conference of the Popular Culture Association and American Culture Association, and the Conference on College Composition and Communication.

SARAH ROBBINS is coordinator of the American Studies Program and the Gender and Women's Studies Program at Kennesaw State University. She is the author of *Managing Literacy, Mothering America* (University of Pittsburgh Press, 2004, 2006), winner of a *Choice* book award from the American Library Association, and *The Cambridge Introduction to Harriet Beecher Stowe* (Cambridge University Press, 2007).

TARSHIA L. STANLEY is professor of English at Spelman College. She teaches courses in film studies and visual imagery, particularly as each pertains to images of women. She has authored several articles critiquing black women in African American, African, and Caribbean cinema as well as black female iconography in popular culture.

ELWOOD WATSON is professor of history at East Tennessee State University. His work has appeared in the *Journal of Religious Thought*, the *Journal of Black Studies*, the *Journal of African American History*, and elsewhere. He is the author of *Outsiders Within: Black Women in the Legal Academy after Brown v. Board* (Rowman & Littlefield, 2008).

Index